THE

DOCTOR AND STUDENT

OR

DIALOGUES

BETWEEN A

DOCTOR OF DIVINITY AND A STUDENT IN THE
LAWS OF ENGLAND

CONTAINING THE

GROUNDS OF THOSE LAWS

TOGETHER WITH

QUESTIONS AND CASES CONCERNING THE EQUITY THEREOF

REVISED AND CORRECTED

By WILLIAM MUCHALL, GENT

TO WHICH ARE ADDED TWO PIECES CONCERNING

SUITS IN CHANCERY BY SUBPŒNA

I. A Replication of a Serjeant at the Laws of England, to certain Points alledged by a
Student of the said Laws of England, in a Dialogue in English between
a Doctor of Divinity and the said Student.

II. A little Treatise concerning Writs of Subpœna.

THE LAWBOOK EXCHANGE, LTD.
Clark, New Jersey

ISBN 978-1-886363-49-6

Lawbook Exchange edition 1998, 2014

The quality of this reprint is equivalent to the quality of the original work.
The irregular pagination is reproduced as it was found in the original work.

THE LAWBOOK EXCHANGE, LTD.

33 Terminal Avenue
Clark, New Jersey 07066-1321

Please see our website for a selection of our other publications
and fine facsimile reprints of classic works of legal history:
www.lawbookexchange.com

Library of Congress Cataloging-in-Publication Data

Saint German, Christopher, 1460?-1540.
    [Dyaloge in Englysshe bytwyxt a doctoure of dyvynte and a student
in the lawes of Englande]
    The doctor and student, or, Dialogues between a doctor of divinity
and a student in the laws of England, containing the grounds of
those laws together with questions and cases concerning the equity
thereof / revised and corrected by William Muchall.
      p.   cm.
    Originally published: Cincinnati : R. Clarke & Co., 1874.
    Includes index.
    ISBN 1-886363-49-8 (cloth : alk. paper)
    1. Law—Great Britain. I. Muchall, William. II. Title.
KD662.S25 1998
349.42—dc21   98-11338
                                            CIP

Printed in the United States of America on acid-free paper

THE

DOCTOR AND STUDENT

OR

DIALOGUES

BETWEEN A

DOCTOR OF DIVINITY AND A STUDENT IN THE LAWS OF ENGLAND

CONTAINING THE

GROUNDS OF THOSE LAWS

TOGETHER WITH

QUESTIONS AND CASES CONCERNING THE EQUITY THEREOF

REVISED AND CORRECTED

By WILLIAM MUCHALL, GENT

TO WHICH ARE ADDED TWO PIECES CONCERNING

SUITS IN CHANCERY BY SUBPŒNA

I. A Replication of a Serjeant at the Laws of England, to certain Points alledged by a
Student of the said Laws of England, in a Dialogue in English between
a Doctor of Divinity and the said Student.

II. A little Treatise concerning Writs of Subpœna.

CINCINNATI

ROBERT CLARKE & CO

1874

PREFACE.

It is presumed that no particular apology is necessary to be made for introducing to the notice of the profession a new edition of the *Doctor and Student;** a book which has been considered ,of the first authority, not only by the best and most admired of our legal writers,† but by the courts of *Westminster-hall.*

The species of composition in which it is written must likewise add to its value, and intitle it to approbation.‡ Dialogue is universally allowed to be an agreeable method of writing, which never fails to instruct more than any other, by its peculiar tendency to make a more favorable and lasting impression upon the mind.

Perhaps the language is not so pure as might be expected from a modern author, nor so correct as altogether to adapt itself to the taste of the curious. But this is a defect (if a defect it can be called) which should be overlooked for the intrinsic merits of the book itself. *Coke upon Littleton*, and the ancient Reports, which contain such a variety of matter, and such a fund .of legal information, are not perhaps superior in point of style to the

---

* The original author was *Christopher Saint Germain*, of the *Inner Temple*, a barrister of such extensive knowledge in the laws of his country, that he was supposed to be equal to most men of his time. Soon after his book was published, (which was in the year 1518,) he was engaged in a smart controversy with a serjeant at law relative to a point of doctrine advanced by him in the twelfth chapter of the first dialogue, the particulars of which may be seen in the first volume of Mr. *Hargrave's* Collection of Tracts. He was moreover excellently skilled in the civil and canon laws, and well acquainted with most of the liberal sciences. After spending a long life of much piety, usefulness, and integrity, he died at the age of eighty, and was buried in the parish church of *St. Alphage, London,* near *Cripplegate.*

† See Mr. *Reeve's* History of the *English* law, 4th vol., p 416; Sir *William Jones's* essay on the Law of Bailments, and *Blackstone's* Commentaries, in which the *Doctor and Student* is quoted or mentioned with peculiar marks of respect.

‡ Vide the introduction to a work of the late Mr. *Jacob*, intitled the Student's Companion, p. 4.

Doctor and Student, and yet no one who is disposed to make a *steady* progress in his profession will object with any degree of seriousness to the quaintness of expression which he will find in those valuable repositories of ancient learning. On the contrary, he will perceive it to be his business to attend more to *things* than words, and that he is not to quarrel with his author, because his grammar may be false, or his diction unpolished.

For these reasons, and others that might be named, the Editor did not judge it prudent in him to alter the language, as some might expect, but has left it just in the same state in which it appeared in the last edition. He thinks nothing could have justified such an alteration. Were not the editors of *Swinburne* on Wills and Testaments justly censured for presuming to correct the style of that learned performance ?*

All that has been done therefore in the present edition of the *Doctor and Student* is merely an addition of some notes and references which have been inserted with a view to illustrate the subject matter, and to shew how the law has been altered by acts of parliament and judicial decisions. In the execution of his plan it will be seen that the Editor has had much labour, and taken considerable pains. But these are circumstances which will be considered of no great moment with him, if his endeavours may in any measure contribute to ease the difficulties, to lessen the embarrassments, and to improve the mind of a young beginner in the study of our *English* jurisprudence.

---

* See 4 Burn's Eccl. Law, 371, 372.

THE

TABLE

OF THE

FIRST DIALOGUE.

The Introduction 1
Chap. 1. Of the law eternal 2
II. Of the law of reason, the which by doctors is called the law of na-
  ture of reasonable creatures 5
III. Of the law of God 7
IV. Of the law of man 9
V. Of the first ground of the law of England 12
VI. Of the second ground of the law of England 15
VII. Of the third ground of the law of England 17
VIII. Of the fourth ground of the law of England 25
IX. Divers cases wherein the student doubteth whether they be only
  maxims of the law, or that they be grounded upon the law of
  reason 31
X. Of the fifth ground of the law of England 34
XI. Of the sixth ground of the law of England 35
XII. The first question of the doctor, of the law of England and con-
  science 37
XIII. What sinderesis is 39
XIV. Of reason 40
XV. Of conscience 41
XVI. What is equity 44
XVII. In what manner a man shall be holpen by equity in the laws
  of England 47
XVIII. Whether the statute hereafter rehearsed by the doctor be
  against conscience, or not 50
XIX. Of what law this question is to be understood; that is to say,
  where conscience shall be ruled after the law 52
XX. Divers cases where conscience is to be ordered after the law 56
XXI. The first question of the student. If any infant that is of the
  age of twenty years, and hath reason and wisdom to govern himself, selleth his land, and with the money thereof buyeth other

land of greater value than the first was, and taketh the profits thereof; whether may the infant ask his first land again in conscience, as he may by the law?............................... 60

XXII. The second question of the student. If a man that hath lands for term of life be impanelled upon an inquest, and thereupon leeseth issues, and dieth; whether may those issues be levied upon him in the reversion in conscience, as they may be by the law?.. 62

XXIII. The third question of the student. If a tenant for term of life, or years, do waste, whereby they be bound by the laws to yield to him in the reversion treble damages, and so shall forfeit the place wasted; whether he is also bound in conscience to pay those damages, and to restore that place wasted immediately after the waste done, as he is in the single damages, or that he is not bound thereto till the treble damages and place wasted be recovered in the king's court....................................... 64

XXIV. The fourth question of the student. If a man enfeoff other in certain land upon condition that if he enfeoff any other, that it may be lawful for the feoffor and his heirs to re-enter, etc., whether is this condition good in conscience, though it be void in the law?.. 64

XXV. The fifth question of the student. If a fine with proclamation be levied according to the statute, and no claim made within five years, etc., whether is the right of a stranger extincted thereby in conscience, as it is in the law?...................... 66

XXVI. A question made by the doctor, how certain recoveries that be used in the king's courts to defeat tailed land may stand with conscience... 68

XXVII. The first question of the student concerning tailed lands.... 81

XXVIII. The second question of the student concerning tailed lands.. 82

XXIX. The third question of the student concerning tailed lands.... 84

XXX. The fourth question of the student concerning recoveries of inheritances intailed... 87

XXXI. The fifth question of the student concerning tailed lands..... 88

XXXII. The sixth question of the student concerning tailed lands.... 91

THE

TABLE

OF THE

SECOND DIALOGUE.

The Prologue.. 97
The Introduction... 98
Chap. 1. The first question of the student. Whether the tenant in tail
after possibility of issue extinct may with conscience do waste.... 101
II. What is meant by this term, when it is said, *Thus it was at the
common law*... 105
III. The second question of the student. Whether the goods of men
outlawed be forfeit in conscience, as they be by the law.......... 107
IV. The third question of the student, of waste done by a stranger in
the lands that be in the hands of particular tenants, etc.......... 111
V. The fourth question of the student. Whether a man may with
conscience be of counsel against him that he knoweth is the heir
of right, but he is certified bastard by the ordinary. 115
VI. The fifth question of the student. Whether a man may with conscience be of counsel with a man at the common law, knowing that
the defendant hath sufficient matter to be discharged in the
chancery, that he may not plead at the common law............ 118
VII. The sixth question of the student. Whether a man may with
conscience be of counsel against the feoffee of trust in an action
of trespass that he bringeth against his feoffor of trust for taking
the profits.. 120
VIII. The seventh question of the student. If a man by way of distress cometh to his debt, but he ought not to have distrained for it,
what restitution is he bound to make.......................... 122
IX. For what thing a man may lawfully distrain.................. 125
X. The eighth question of the student. Whether executors be bound
in conscience to make restitution for a trespass done by a testator;
and whether they be bound to pay debts upon a contract first, or
make the said restitution..................................... 128
XI. The ninth question of the student. Whether he that hath goods
delivered him by force of a legacy is bound in conscience to pay
(ix)

the debt upon a contract that the testator ought, if the executors
have no other goods in their hands........................ 133
XII. The tenth question of the student. If a man have issue two sons,
and die seised of certain lands in fee, the eldest dieth without
issue, the youngest recovereth by assise of *Mort d'ancestor* the land,
with damages from the death of the father, whether there he be
bound in conscience to pay the profits to the executors of the
eldest brother for the time he lived........ 136
XIII. The eleventh question of the student. What damages the tenant
in dower shall recover in conscience where her husband died not
seised, but she demanded her dower, and was denied........... 138
XIV. The twelfth question of the student. If a man knowing another
to have right to his land, causeth a fine with proclamation to be
levied, according to the statute, and he that hath right maketh no
claim within five years, whether he be barred in conscience, as he
is in the law............................ 142
XV. The thirteenth question of the student. If a man that hath a
child by his wife, do that in him is, to have had possession of his
wife's land, and she dieth before he can have it, whether in conscience he shall be tenant by the courtesy...................... 143
XVI. The fourteenth question of the student. If the grantor of a rent
enfeoffeth the grantee of the rent of part of the lands, etc.,
whether the whole rent be extinct in conscience, as it is in the
law.......... 146
XVII. The fifteenth question of the student. If he that hath a rent out
of two acres be named in a recovery of the one acre, he not
knowing thereof, etc., whether his whole rent be extinct in conscience, etc.................................... 151
XVIII. The sixteenth question of the student. If a man have a villein
for term of life, and the villein purchaseth lands in fee, and he
that hath the villein entereth, whether he may with conscience
keep the lands to him and to his heirs, as he may by the law..... 153
XIX. The seventeenth question of the student. If a man in the case
next before inform him that is in the reversion of the villein, that
after the death of the villein he hath right to land, and counselleth
him to enter, whereupon great suit and charges follow, what
danger is this to him that gave the counsel..................... 156
XX. The eighteenth question of the student, upon a feoffment made
upon condition, that the feoffee shall pay a rent to a stranger,
how the feoffment shall weigh in law and conscience........... 159
XXI. The nineteenth question of the student, upon a feoffment in fee,
and it is agreed that the feoffee shall pay a rent to a stranger, how
feoffment shall weigh in law and conscience.................... 162
XXII. How uses of land first began, and by what law, and the cause
why so much land is put in use................................ 165
XXIII. The diversity between two cases, whereof one is put in the
twentieth chapter, and the other in the twenty-first chapter of this
present book... 170

XXIV. What is a nude contract, or naked promise, after the laws of England, and whether any action may lie thereon............... 176

XXV. The twentieth question of the student. If a man that hath two sons, one before espousals, and the other after espousals, by his will bequeatheth to his son and heir all his goods, which of the sons shall have his goods in conscience....................... 181

XXVI. Whether an abbot may with conscience present to an advowson of a church that belongeth to the house, without assent of the covent... 187

XXVII. If a man find beasts in his ground doing hurt, whether he may by his own authority take them, and keep them, till he be satisfied of the hurt... 191

XXVIII. Whether a gift made by one under the age of twenty-five years be good... 193

XXIX. If a man be convict of heresy before the ordinary, whether his goods be forfeited.. 195

XXX. Where divers patrons of an advowson, and the church voideth, the patrons vary in their presentments, whether the bishop shall have liberty to present which of the incumbents that he will or not... 196

XXXI. How long time the patron shall have to present to a benefice. 199

XXXII. If a man be excommenged, whether he may in any case be assoiled without making satisfaction....................... 202

XXXIII. Whether a prelate may refuse a legacy.. 203

XXXIV. Whether a gift made under a condition be void, if the sovereign only break the condition................................ 207

XXXV. Whether a covenant made upon a gift to the church, that it shall not be aliened, be good 209

XXXVI. If the patron present not within six months, who shall present.. 212

XXXVII. Whether the presentment and collation of all benefices and dignities, voiding at Rome, belongeth only to the pope........... 217

XXXVIII. If a house by chance fall upon a horse that is borrowed, who shall bear the loss.................................... 219

XXXIX. If a priest have won much goods by saying of mass, whether he may give those goods, or make a will of them.............. 221

XL. Who shall succeed a clerk that dieth intestate................ 224

XLI. If a man be outlawed of felony, or be attainted of murder or felony, or that is an Ascismus, may be slain by every stranger.... 226

XLII. Whether a man shall be bounden by the act or offence of his servant or officer.. 228

XLIII. Whether a villein or a bondman may give away his goods.... 236

XLIV. If a clerk be promoted to the title of his patrimony, and after selleth his patrimony, and after falleth to poverty, whether shall he have his title therein.. 240

XLV. Divers questions taken by the student out of the sums called *Summa Rosella* and *Summa Angelica*, which he thinketh are

necessary to be seen how they stand and agree with the laws of
the realm 243

XLVI. Where ignorance of the law excuseth in the laws of England,
and where not 248

XLVII. Certain cases and grounds where ignorance of the deed excuseth in the laws of England, and where not 253

XLVIII. The first question of the doctor, how the law of England may
be said reasonable, that prohibiteth them that be arraigned upon
an indictment of felony or murder, to have counsel 256

XLIX. The second question of the doctor, whether the warranty of
the younger brother that is taken as heir, because it is not known
but that the eldest brother is dead, be in conscience a bar unto the
eldest brother as it is in the law 259

L. The third question of the doctor, whether if a man prosecute a
collateral warranty, to extinct a right that he knoweth another man
hath to land, it be a bar in conscience, as it is in law 262

LI. The fourth question of the doctor, of the wreck of the sea 265

LII. The fifth question of the doctor, whether it stand with conscience
to prohibit a jury of meat and drink till they be agreed of their
verdict 268

LIII. The sixth question of the doctor, whether the colours that be
given at the common law in assises, actions of trespass, etc., stand
with conscience, because they be most commonly feigned 269

LIV. The seventh question of the doctor, concerning the pleadings in
assise, whereby the tenants use sometime to plead in such manner
that they shall confess no ouster 274

LV. The eighth question of the doctor, whether the statute of forty-
five Edward the Third, of *Sylva cædua*, stand with conscience. 278

TABLE

TO THE

ADDITIONS.

Chap. I. What power the parliament hath over such things as be brought with dead bodies to their burials, and that be claimed by some curates to pertain to their church 303

II. Whether the parliament may enact, that no lands shall come hereafter into mortmain by licence nor without licence 308

III. Whether the parliament may break all appropriations that be made against any statute, or against the good order of the people 309

IV. That all sanctuaries, and also who shall have his clergy, be under the power of the parliament, to order as they shall think convenient 311

V. What power the parliament hath in the trees and grass in churchyards 312

VI. What the parliament may do touching suits for dilapidations taken in the spiritual court 314

VII. Whether the parliament may enact that no priest shall wear any cloth made out of the realm, and whether it may order the salary of chaplains 316

VIII. If there were a schism in the papacy, what the parliament might do therein 319

IX. If it were enacted, that if one call another thief or murderer, that the suit should be taken thereupon in the king's court, and not in the spiritual court, I think the statute were good 324

X. Whether the parliament may enact, that no religious person, under a certain pain, shall receive into the habit of their religion any child under a certain age to be appointed by the parliament 325

XI. Whether the parliament may prohibit, that no ordinary, under a certain pain, shall admit none to the order of priesthood, except they be sufficiently learned 328

XII. Who shall have the tithes of the waste grounds that be within no parish, and what power the parliament hath therein 331

XIII. What authority the parliament hath concerning visitations 336

(xiii)

DOCTOR AND STUDENT.

INTRODUCTION.

A DOCTOR of divinity, that was of great acquaintance and
familiarity with a student in the laws of England, said thus
unto him : I have had a great desire of long time to know
whereupon the law of England is grounded ; but because
the most part of the law of England is written in the French
tongue, therefore I cannot, through mine own study, attain
to the knowledge thereof; for in that tongue I am nothing
expert.   And because I have found thee a faithful friend
to me in all my business, therefore I am bold to come to
thee before any other, to know thy mind, what be the very
grounds of the law of England, as thou thinkest.

Stud. That would ask a great leisure, and it is also above
my cunning to do it : nevertheless, that thou shalt not think
that I would wilfully refuse to fulfil thy desire, I shall with
good will do that in me is to satisfy thy mind.   But I pray
thee that thou wilt first shew me somewhat of other laws
that pertain most to this matter, and that doctors treat of,
how laws have been begun ; and then I will gladly shew
thee, as methinketh, what be the grounds of the law of
England.

Doct. I will with good will do as thou sayest.   Wherefore thou shalt understand that doctors treat of four laws,

the which (as me seemeth) pertain most to this matter. The first is the *law eternal*. The second is the *law of nature* of reasonable creatures, the which, as I have heard say, is called by them that be learned in the law of England, the *law of reason*. The third is the *law of God*. The fourth is the *law of man*. And therefore I will first treat of the *law eternal*.

DIALOGUE I.

CHAPTER I.—*Of the law eternal.*

LIKE as there is in every artificer a reason of such like things as are to be made by his craft: so likewise it behoveth that in every governor there be reason and a foresight in the governing of such things as shall be ordered and done by him to them that he hath the governance of. And forasmuch as Almighty God is the creator and maker of all creatures, to which he is compared as a workman to his works, and is also the governor of all deeds and movings that be found in any creature : therefore as the reason of the wisdom of God (inasmuch as creatures be created by him) is the reason and foresight of all crafts and works that have been or shall be ; so the reason of the wisdom of God, moving all things by wisdom made to a good end, obtaineth the name and reason of a law, and that is called the law eternal.

And this law eternal is called the first law : and it is well called the first, for it was before all other laws, and all other laws be derived of it. Whereupon St. Augustine saith, in his first book of *free arbitrement,* that in *temporal laws nothing is righteous ne lawful, but that the people have derived to them out of the law eternal.* Wherefore every man hath right and title to have that he hath righteously, and of right wise judgment of the first reason, which is the law eternal.

Stud. But how may this law eternal be known? For, as the apostle writeth in the second chapter of his first epistle to the Corinthians, *quæ sunt Dei nemo scit, nisi Spiritus Dei;* that is to say, no man knoweth what is in God but the Spirit of God; wherefore it seemeth that he openeth his mouth against heaven, that attempteth to know it.

Doct. This law eternal no man may know, as it is in itself, but only blessed souls that see God face to face. But Almighty God of his goodness sheweth of it as much to his creatures as is necessary for them, for else God should bind his creatures to a thing impossible; which may in no wise be thought in him. Therefore it is to be understood that three manner of ways Almighty God maketh this law eternal known to his creatures reasonable. *First*, by the light of natural reason; *secondly*, by heavenly revelation; *thirdly*, by the order of a prince, or any other secondary governor that hath power to bind his subjects to a law.

And when the law eternal or the will of God is known to his creatures reasonable by the light of natural understanding, or by the light of natural reason, that is called the *law of reason:* and when it is shewed by heavenly revelation in such manner as hereafter shall appear, then it is called the *law of God:* and when it is shewed unto him by the order of a prince, or of any other secondary governor that hath a power to set a law upon his subjects, then it is called the *law of man*, though originally it be made of God. For laws made by man that hath received thereto power of God, be made by God. Therefore the said three laws, that is to say the law of reason, the law of God, and the law of man, the which hath several names after the manner as they be shewed to man, be called in God one law eternal.

And this is the law of which it is written *proverbiorum octavo*, where it is said, *per me reges regnant and legum conditores justa discernunt;* that is to say, by me kings reign, and makers of law discern the truth. And this sufficeth for this time for the law eternal.

·CHAP. II.—*Of the law of reason, the which by doctors is called the law of nature of reasonable creatures.*

First it is to be understood, tħat the *law of nature* may be considered in two manners, that is to say, generally and specially. When it is considered generally, then it is referred to all creatures, as well reasonable as unreasonable : for all unreasonable creatures live under a certain rule to them given by nature, necessary to them for the conservation of their being. But of this law it is not our intent to treat at this time. The law of nature specially considered, which is also called the *law of reason*, pertaineth only to ·creatures reasonable, that is, man, which is created to the image of God.

And this law ought to be kept as well among Jews and Gentiles, as among christian men : and this law is alway good and righteous, stirring and inclining a man to good, and abhorring evil. And as to the ordering of the deeds of man, it is preferred before the law of God, and it is written in the heart of every man, teaching him what is to be done, and what is to be fled ; and because it is written in the heart, therefore it may not be put away, ne it is never ·changeable by no diversity of place, ne time : and there-fore against this law, prescription, statute nor custom may not prevail : and if any be brought in against it, they be not prescriptions, statutes nor customs, but things void and against justice.* And all other laws, as well the laws of God as to the acts of men, as other, be grounded there-upon.

Stud. Sith the law of reason is written in the heart of every man, as thou hast said before, teaching him what is to be done, and what is to be fled, and the which thou sayest may never be put out of the heart, what needeth it then to have any other law brought in to order the acts and deeds ·of the people? †

---

* Hob. 148; Consideration on the law of forfeitures, 20, 21.
† 7 Rep. 12.

Doct. Though the law of reason may not be changed, nor wholly put away; nevertheless, before the law written, it was greatly lett and blinded by evil customs, and by many sins of the people, beside our original sin; insomuch that it might hardly be discerned what was righteous, and what was unrighteous, and what was good, and what evil. Wherefore it was necessary, for the good order of the people, to have many things added to the law of reason, as well by the church as by secular princes, according to the manners of the country and of the people where such additions should be exercised. And this law of reason differeth from the law of God in two manners. For the law of God is given by the revelation of God; and this law is given by a natural light of understanding. And also the law of God ordereth a man of itself, by a nigh way, to the felicity that ever shall endure; and the law of reason ordereth a man to the felicity of this life.

Stud. But what be the things that the law of reason teaches to be done, and what to be fled? I pray thee shew me.

Doct. The law of reason teacheth, that good is to be loved, and evil is to be fled: also that thou shalt do to another, that thou wouldest another should do unto thee; and that we may do nothing against truth; and that a man must live peacefully with others; that justice is to be done to every man; and also that wrong is not to be done to any man; and that also a trespasser is worthy to be punished; and such other. Of the which follow divers other secondary commandments, the which be as necessary conclusions derived of the first. As of that commandment, that good is to be beloved; it followeth, that a man should love his benefactor: for a benefactor, in that he is a benefactor, includeth in him a reason of goodness, for else he ought not to be called a benefactor; that is to say, a good doer, but an evil doer: and so in that he is a benefactor, he is to be beloved in all times and in all places.* And this law also

* Cic. 1, 2, de legibus.

suffereth many things to be done : as that it is lawful to put
away force with force; and that it is lawful for every man
to defend himself and his goods against an unlawful power.
And this law runneth with every man's law, and also with
the law of God, as to the deeds of man, and must be always kept and observed, and shall always declare what
ought to follow upon the general rules of the law of man,
and shall restrain them if they be any thing contrary unto it.

And here it is to be understood, that after some men,
the law whereby all things were in common, was never of
the law of reason, but only in the time of extreme necessity. For they say, that the law of reason may not be
changed; but they say, it is evident, that the law whereby
all things should be in common, is changed : wherefore
they conclude, that was never the law of reason.

CHAP. III.—*Of the law of God.*

The *law of God* is a certain law given by revelation to a
reasonable creature, shewing him the will of God, willing
that creatures reasonable be bound to do a thing, or not to
do it, for obtaining of the felicity eternal. And it is said,
for the obtaining of the felicity eternal, to exclude the
laws shewed by revelation of God for the political rule of
the people, and which be called *judicials*. For a law is not
properly called the law of God, because it was shewed by
revelation of God, but also because it directed a man by the
nearest way to the felicity eternal; as been the laws of the
Old Testament, that been called *morals*, and the laws of the
evangelists, the which were shewed in much more excellent
manner than the law of the Old Testament was : for that
was shewed by the mediation of an angel; but the law of
the evangelists was shewed by the mediation of our Lord
Jesus Christ, God and man. And the law of God is always
righteous and just, for it is made and given after the will
of God. And therefore all acts and deeds of man be called
righteous and just, when they be done according to the law
of God, and be conformable to it. Also sometime a law

made by man, is called the law of God. As when a law taketh his principal ground upon the law of God, and is made for the declaration or conservation of the faith, and to put away heresies, as divers laws canon, and also divers laws made by the common people, sometime do; the which therefore are rather to be called the law of God, than the law of man. Yet nevertheless all the laws canon be not the laws of God: for many of them be made only for the political rule and conservation of the people.* Whereupon John Gerson, in the treatise of the *spiritual life of the soul*, the second lesson, and the third corollary, saith thus: All the canons of bishops nor their decrees be not the law of God: for many of them be made only for the political conservation of the people. And if any man will say, Be not all the goods of the church spiritual, for they belong unto the spiritualty, and leading to the spiritualty? We answer, that in the whole political conservation of the people, there be some specially deputed and dedicated to the service of God, the which most specially (as by an excellency) are called *spiritual men*, as religious men are. And other, though they walk in the way of God, yet nevertheless, because their office is most specially to be occupied about such things as pertain to the commonwealth, and to the good order of the people, they be therefore called *secular men or lay men*. Nevertheless, the goods of the first may no more be called spiritual than the goods of the other, for they be things more temporal, and keeping the body, as they do in the other. And by like reason, laws made for the political order of the church be called many times spiritual, or the laws of God; nevertheless it is but improperly: and other be called civil, or the laws of man. And in this point many be oft times deceived, and also deceive other, the which judge the things to be spiritual, the which all men know be things temporal and carnal. These be the words of John Gerson, in the place alleged before. Farthermore, beside the law of rea-

---

* Preface to Burn's Ecc. Law, 1 B. C. 82.

son and the law of man, it was necessary to have the law of God, for four reasons.

The *first*, Because man is ordained to the end of the eternal felicity, the which exceedeth the proportion and faculty of man's power. Therefore it was necessary that, beside the law of reason and the law of man, he should be directed to his end by the law of God.

Secondly, Forasmuch as for the uncertainty of man's judgment, specially of things peculiar and seldom falling, it happeneth oft times to follow divers judgments of divers men, and diversities of laws; therefore, to the intent that a man without any doubt may know what he should do, and what he should not do, it was necessary that he should be directed in all his deeds by a law heavenly, given by God, the which is so apparent that no man may swerve from it, as is the law of God.

Thirdly, Man may only make a law of such things as he may judge upon, and the judgment of man may not be of inward things, but only of outward things; and nevertheless it belongeth to perfection that a man be well ordered in both, that is to say, as well inward as outward. Therefore it was necessary to have the law of God, the which should order a man as well of inward things as of outward things.

The *fourth* is, Because, as St. Augustine saith in his first book of *free arbitrement*, the law of man may not punish all offences: for, if all offences should be punished, the commonwealth should be hurt, as is of contracts; for it cannot be avoided, but that as long as contracts be suffered, many offences shall follow thereby, and yet they be suffered for the commonwealth. And therefore that no evil should be unpunished, it was necessary to have the law of God that should leave no evil unpunished.

CHAP. IV.—*Of the law of man.*

The *law of man* (the which sometime is called the *law positive*) is derived by reason, as a thing which is neces-

sary, and probably following of the law of reason and of
the law of God. And that is called *probable*, in that it
appeareth to many, and especially to wise men to be true.
And therefore in every law positive well made, is somew at
of the law of reason, and of the law of God; and to discern the law of God and the law of reason from the law
positive is very hard. And though it be hard, yet it is
much necessary in every moral doctrine, and in all laws
made for the commonwealth. And that the law of man be
just and rightwise, two things be necessary, and that is to
say, wisdom and authority. Wisdom that he may judge
after reason what is to be done for the commonalty, and
what is expedient for a peaceable conservation and necessary sustentation of them; authority, that he have authority
to make laws. For the law is derived of *ligare*, that is to
say, to bind. But the sentence of a wise man doth not bind
the commonalty, if he have no rule over them. Also to
every good law be required these properties : that is to say,
that it be honest, rightwise, possible in itself, and after the
custom of the country, convenient for the place and time,
necessary, profitable, and also manifest, that it be not cap-
tious by any dark sentences, ne mixt with any private
wealth, but all made for the commonwealth. And after St.
Bridget, in the fourth book, in the hundred and twenty-
ninth chapter, every good law is ordained to the health of
the Soul, and to the fulfilling of the laws of God, and to
induce the people to fly evil desires, and to do good works.
Also the cardinal of Camerer writeth, Whatsoever is
righteous in the law of man, is righteous in the law of God.
For every man's law must be consonant to the law of God.
And therefore the laws of princes, the commandments of
prelates, the statutes of commonalties, ne yet the ordinance
of the church, is not righteous nor obligatory, but it be
consonant to the law of God.*

And of such a law of man that is consonant to the law
of God, it appeareth who hath right to lands and goods and

---

* 2 Shep. Abr. 356.

who not : for whatsoever a man hath by such laws of man,
he hath righteously ; and whatsoever he hath against such
laws, is unrighteously had.

For laws of man not contrary to the law of God, nor to
the law of reason, must be observed in the law of the soul :
and he that despiseth them, despiseth God, and .resisteth
God.   And furthermore, as Gratian saith, because evil men
fear to offend, for fear of pain ; therefore it was necessary
that divers pains should be ordained for divers offences, as
physicians ordained divers remedies for several diseases.
And such pains be ordained by the makers of laws, after
the necessity of the time, and after the disposition of the
people.   And though that law that ordained such pains
hath thereby a conformity to the law of God, (for the law
òf God commandeth that the people shall take away evil
from among themselves ;) yet they belong not so much to
the law of God, but that other pains (standing the first
principles) might be ordained and appointed therefore.
That is the law that is called most properly the *law positive*, and the *law of man*.

And the philosopher said in the third book of his *ethicks*,
that *the intent of a maker of a law is to make the people
good, and to bring them to virtue.*   And although I have
somewhat in general shewed thee whereupon the law of
England is grounded (for of necessity it must be grounded
of the said laws, that is to say, of the law eternal, of the
law of reason, and of the law of God :) nevertheless I pray
thee shew me more specially whereupon it is grounded, as
thou thinkest, as thou before hast promised to do.

Stud. I will with good-will do therein that lieth in me,
for thou hast shewed me a right, plain, and straight way
thereto.   Therefore thou shalt understand that the law of
England is grounded upon six principal grounds. *First,*
It is grounded on the *law of reason. Secondly,* On the
law of God.   Thirdly, On divers general *cstoums of the
realm. Fourthly,* On divers *principles* that be called *maxims.   Fifthly,* On divers *particular customs.   Sixthly,*
On divers *statutes* made in parliaments by the king, and

by the common council of the realm. On which grounds
I shall speak in order as they be rehearsed before. And
first of the *law of reason.*

CHAP. V.—*Of the first ground of the law of England.*

The first ground of the law of England is the *law of
reason,* whereof thou hast treated before in the second
chapter, the which is kept in this realm, as it is in all other
realms, and as of necessity it must needs be, (as thou hast
said before.)

Doct. But I would know what is called the *law of nature* after the laws of England.

Stud. It is not used among them that be learned in the
laws of England to reason what thing is commanded or
prohibited by the law of nature, and what not, but all the
reasoning in that behalf is under this manner. As when any
thing is grounded upon the law of nature, they say, that
reason will that such a thing be done; and if it be prohibited by the law of nature, they say it is against reason, or
that reason will not suffer that to be done.

Doct. Then I pray thee shew me what they that be
learned in the laws of the realm hold to be commanded or
prohibited by the law of nature, under such terms, and after
such manner, as is used among them that be learned in the
said laws.

Stud. There be put by them that be learned in the laws
of England two degrees of the law of reason, that is to say,
the law of reason *primary*, and the law of reason *secondary*. By the law of reason *primary* be prohibited in the
laws of England murder (that is, the death of him that is
innocent), perjury, deceit, breaking of the peace, and many
other like. And by the same law also it is lawful for a man
to defend himself against an unjust power, so he keep due
circumstance. And also if any promise be made by menace
to the body, it is by the law of reason void in the laws of
England. The other is called the law of *secondary* reason,
the which is divided into two branches, that is to say, into

a law of secondary reason *general*, and into a law of secondary reason *particular*. The law of a secondary reason *general* is grounded and derived of the general law, or general custom of property, whereby goods moveable and immoveable be brought into a certain property, so that every man may know his own thing. And by this branch be prohibited in the laws of England disseisins, trespass in lands and goods, rescuss, theft, unlawful with-holding of another man's goods, and such other. And by the same law it is a ground in the law of England that satisfaction must be made for a trespass, and that restitution must be made of such goods as one man hath that belong to another man; the debts must be paid, covenants fulfilled, and such other. And because disseisins, trespass in lands and goods, theft, and other had not been known, if the law of property had not been ordained; therefore all things that be derived by reason out of the said law of property, be called *the law of reason secondary general*, for the law of property is generally kept in all countries.

The law of reason *secondary particular* is the law that is derived of divers customs general and particular, and of divers maxims and statutes ordained in this realm. And it is called *the law of reason secondary particular*, because the reason in that case is derived of such a law that is only holden for law in this realm, and in none other realm.

Doct. I pray thee shew me some special case of such a law of reason secondary particular, for an example.

Stud. There is a law in England, which is a law of custom, that if a man take a distress lawfully, that he shall put it in pound overt, there to remain till he be satisfied of that he distrained for.* And then thereupon may be asked this question, that if the beasts die in pound for lack of meat, at whose peril die they? whether die they at the peril of him that distrained, or of him that oweth the beasts?†

* Co. Litt. 47.
† 2 Inst. 106.

Doct. If the law be as thou sayest, and that a man for a just cause taketh a distress, and putteth it in the pound overt,* and no law compelleth him that distrained to give them meat,† then it seemeth of reason that if the distress die in pound for lack of meat, that it died at the peril of him that oweth the beasts, and not of him that distrained; for in him that distrained there can be assigned no default, · but in the other may be assigned a default, because the rent was unpaid.

Stud. Thou hast given a true judgment, and who hath taught thee to do so but reason derived of the said general custom? And the law is so full of such secondary reasons derived out of the general customs and maxims of the realm, that some men have affirmed that all the law of the realm is the law of reason. But that cannot be proved, as me seemeth, as I have partly shewed before, and more fully will shew after. And it is not much used in the laws of England, to reason what law is grounded upon the law of the first reason primary, or on the law of reason secondary, for they be most commonly openly known of themselves; but for the knowledge of the law of reason secondary is greater difficulty, and therefore therein dependeth much the manner and form of arguments in the laws of England.

And it is to be noted, that all the deriving of reason in the law of England proceedeth of the first principles of the law, or of something that is derived of them: and therefore no man may right wisely judge, no groundly reason in the laws of England, if he be ignorant in the first principles. Also all birds, fowls, wild beast of forest and warren, and such other, be excepted by the laws of England out of the said general law and custom of property :‡ for by

---

* In the case of a distress for rent, it is not necessary for the person distraining to take the cattle or beasts to a pinfold, as by statute 11 G. 2, c. 19, s. 10, he may impound them on any convenient part of the land chargeable with the rent.

† Finch. Law, 137; 6 Mod. 105.

‡ See Statutes 9 Geo. 1, c. 22; 13 Car. 2, c. 10; 10 Geo. c. 32; 5 Geo. 3, c. 14; 22 and 23 Car. 2, c. 25, respecting the stealing and killing of deer, robbing of warrens, and stealing of fish.

the laws of the realm no property may be of them in any
person, unless they be tame.* Nevertheless the eggs of
hawk, herons, or such other as build in the ground of any
person, be adjudged by the said laws to belong to him that
oweth the ground.†

CHAP. VI.—*Of the second ground of the law of England.*

The second ground of the law of England is the *law of
God:* and therefore for punishment of them that offend
against the law of God, it is enquired of many courts in
this realm, if any hold any opinion secretly, or in any other
manner against the true catholick faith; and also if any
general custom were directly against the law of God, or if
any statute were made directly against it: as if it were or-
,dained that no *alms* should be given for no necessity, the
custom and statute were void. Nevertheless the statute
made in the thirty-fourth year of king Edward III.,‡
whereby it is ordained, that no man, under pain of imprisonment, shall give any alms to any valiant beggars that
may well labour, that they may so be compelled to labour
for their living, is a good statute, for it observeth the intent
of the law of God. And also by authority of this law
there is a ground in the laws of England, that he that is
accursed shall maintain no action in the king's court, except it be in very few cases;§ so that the same excommunication be certified before the king's justices in such manner as the law of the realm hath appointed.‖ And by the
authority also of this ground the law of England admitteth
the spiritual jurisdiction of *dismes* and *offerings*, and of all
other things that of right belong unto it;¶ and receiveth

---

* 1 H. P. C. 511; Fost. 366; Finch. Law, 176; 2 Inst. 199; 2 B. C. 391,
392.
† 2 B. C. 394.
‡ Repealed by 1 Ed. 6, c. 3, and 21 Jac., c. 28.
§ Excommunication is no plea in a qui tam. 12 Co. 61; Gilb. Hist. of
C. B. 164.
‖ 1 Roll. Abr. 883; Co. Litt. 133, 134.
¶ Wood's Inst. 4; 2 Inst. 625.

also all laws of the church duly made, and that exceed not the power of them that made them.   Insomuch that in many cases it behoveth the king's justices to judge after the laws of the church.

Doct. How may that be, that the king's justices should judge in the king's courts after the law of the church? for it seemeth that the church should rather give judgment in such things as it may make laws of, than the king's justices.

Stud. That may be done in many cases, whereof I shall for an example put this case : If a writ of *right of ward* be brought of the body, etc.   And the tenant confessing the tenure, and the nonage of the infant, saith, that the infant was married in his ancestor's days, etc., whereupon twelve men be sworn, which give this verdict that the infant was married in the life of his ancestor, and that the woman in the life of his ancestor sued a divorce, whereupon sentence was given that they should be divorced, and that the heir appealed, which hangeth yet undiscussed, praying the aid of the justice to know whether the infant in this case shall be said married or no : in this case, if the law of the church be that the said sentence of divorce standeth in his strength and virtue until it be annulled upon the said appeal, that the infant at the death of his ancestor was unmarried, because the first marriage was annulled by that divorce, and if the law of the church be, that the sentence of the divorce standeth not in effect till it be affirmed upon the said appeal ; then is the infant yet married, so that the value of his marriage cannot belong unto the lord : and therefore in this case judgment conditional shall be given, etc.   And in likewise the king's justices in many other cases shall judge after the law of the church,* like as the spiritual judges

* Thus if administration is granted to B. of the goods of A. *durante minore ætate* of C. and it comes out in pleading that C. is of the age of seventeen years, the court ought to take notice of the ecclesiastical law, and that the administration is determined.   Cro. Car. 516; Cro. Eliz. 602. So if an infant at the age of fourteen makes a will of his personal estate, the temporal courts will not controul it, but take notice, that by the spirit-

must in many cases form their judgment after the king's laws.*

Doct. How may that be, that the spiritual judges should judge after the king's laws? I pray thee shew me some certain case thereof.

Stud. Though it be somewhat a digression from our first purpose, yet I will not withsay thy desire, but will with good-will put thee a case or two thereof, that thou mayest the better perceive what I mean. If A. and B. have goods jointly, and A. by his last will bequeathe his portion therein to C. and maketh the said B. his executor, and dieth, and C. asketh the execution of this will in the spiritual court: in this case the judges there be bound to judge that will to be void,† because it is void by the laws of this realm. And likewise if a man be outlawed, and after, by his will, bequeath certain goods to John at Stile, and make his executors, and die, the king seiseth his goods, and after giveth them again to the executors, and after John at Stile sueth a citation out of the spiritual court against the executors, to have execution of the will: in this case the judges of the spiritual court must judge the will to be void, as the law of the realm is that it is; and yet there is no such law of forfeiture of goods by outlawry in the spiritual law.‡

CHAP. VII.—*Of the third ground of the law of England.*

The third ground of the law of England standeth upon divers general *customs* of old time used through all the realm, which have been accepted and approved by our

---

ual law a will at that age, of personal estate, is good. 2 Mod. 315; Godolphin, 276; Lord Raym. 262.

* Wood's Inst. 4.

† See the reason of this, postea, 186. But a joint merchant, or a man that has a joint stock in a farm, may devise his share by his will, and it will be good. 2 B. C. 399; Co. Litt. 182.

‡ 4 Burn's Ecc. Law, 56; Swin., part 11, sec. 21.

sovereign lord the king, and his progenitors, and all his subjects.* And because the said customs be neither against the law of God, nor the law of reason, and have been alway taken to be good and necessary for the commonwealth of all the realm ;† therefore they have obtained the strength of a law, insomuch that he that doth against them, doth against justice : and these be the customs that properly be called the *common law*. And it shall alway be determined by the justices whether there be any such general custom or not, and not by twelve men.‡ And of these general customs, and of certain principles that be called *maxims*, which also take effect by the old custom of the realm (as shall appear in the chapter next following), dependeth most part of the law of this realm. And therefore our sovereign lord the king, at his coronation, among other things, taketh a solemn oath that he shall cause all the customs of his realm faithfully to be observed.§

Doct. I pray thee shew me some of these general *customs*.

Stud. I will with good-will ; and first, I shall shew thee how the custom of the realm is the very ground of divers courts in the realm, that is to say, of the *chancery*, of the *king's bench*, of the *common pleas*, and the *exchequer*, the which be courts of record ;‖ because none may sit as judges in these courts, but by the king's letters patents.¶ And these courts have divers authorities, whereof it is not to treat at this time. Other courts there be also only grounded by the custom of the realm, that be of much less authority than the courts before rehearsed. As in every shire within the realm there is a court that is called the *county*, and

---

* Wood's Inst. 4.
† 2 Inst. 179.
‡ Noy's Max. 18; Co. Litt. 344; post. 25.
§ 1 B. C. 234; 3 Burn's Ecc. Law, 352.
‖ 3 B. C. 40, 41, 43.
¶ The reason here given for the courts of Westminster being courts of record does not seem quite satisfactory. I apprehend they are accounted courts of record because their acts and judicial proceedings are recorded. 3 B. C. 24. Besides, it is not true that all the judges derive their authority from the king's letters patent, for the chief justice of the king's bench is

another that is called the *sheriff's torne;** and in every manor is a court that is called a *court-baron*, and to every fair and market is incident a court that is called a court of *piepowders*. And though in some statutes is made mention sometime of the said courts; yet nevertheless, of the first institution of the said courts, and that such courts should be, there is no statute nor law written in the laws of England. And so all the ground and beginning of the said courts depend upon the custom of the realm; the which custom is of so high authority, that the said courts ne their authorities, may not be altered, ne their names changed, without parliament.

Also by the old custom of the realm, no man shall be taken, imprisoned, disseised, nor otherwise destroyed, but he be put to answer by the law of the land : and this custom is confirmed by the statute of *magna charta, cap.* 26.

Also by the old custom of the realm, all men great and small shall do and receive justice in the king's courts : and this custom is confirmed by the statute of *Marlb., cap.* 1.

Also by the old custom of the realm, the eldest son is only heir to his ancestor; and if there be no sons, bu daughters, then all the daughters shall be heirs.† And so it is of sisters and other kinswomen. And·if there be neither son, daughter, brother, nor sister, then shall the inheritance ascend to the next kinsman or kinswoman of the whole blood to him that had the inheritance, of how many degrees soever they be from him.‡ And if there be no heir general nor special, then the land shall escheat to the lord of whom the land is holden.

Also by the old custom of the realm, lands shall never ascend or descend from the son to the father or mother, nor

made by writ, and the chancellor by delivering the great seal to him, and taking an oath to serve the king and his people faithfully in his office. Wood's Inst. 459.

* 3 B. C. 35; Ib. 32, 33.
† Co. Litt. 14; 2 B. C. 214.
‡ 2 B. C. 224; Ib. 246.

to any other ancestor on the right line, but it shall rather
escheat to the lord of the fee.*

Also if an alien have a son that is an alien, and after is
made denizen, and hath another son, and after purchaseth,
lands, and dieth; the youngest son shall inherit as heir,
and not the eldest.†

Also if there be three brethren, and the middest brother
purchase lands, and dieth without heir of his body; the
eldest brother shall inherit as heir to him, and not the
younger brother.

And if land in fee-simple descend to a man by the part
of his father, and he dieth without heir of his body; then
the inheritance shall descend to the next heir of the part of
his father.‡   And if there be no such heir of the part of his
father, then if the father purchaseth the lands, it shall go
to the next heir of the father's mother, and not to the next
heir of the son's mother, but it shall rather escheat to the
lord of the fee.   But if a man purchase lands to him and
to his heirs, and die without heir of his body, as is said before; then the land shall descend to the next heir of the
part of his father, if there be any; and if not, then to the
next heir of the part of his mother.§

Also if the son purchaseth lands in fee, and dieth without
heir of his body;‖ the land shall descend to his uncle,
and shall not ascend to his father: but if the father have
a son, though it be many years after the death of the elder
brother, yet that son shall put out his uncle, and shall enjoy the lands as heir to the elder brother for ever.

Also by the custom of the realm, the child that is born
before espousals is bastard, and shall not inherit.¶

Also the custom of the realm is, that no manner of goods

---

* Litt., sec. 3.
† 2 B. C. 249; Cro. Jac. 539.
‡ 2 B. C. 222.
§ Wood's Inst. 218.
‖ Litt., sec. 3.
¶ 3 New Abr., title Bastardy, 310, 315.

nor chattels, real nor personal, shall ever go to the heir, but
to the executors, or to the ordinary, or administrators.*

Also the husband shall have all the chattels personals
that his wife had at the time of the espousals or after,†
and also chattels real, if he overlive his wife, but if he sell
or give away the chattels real, and die, by that sale or gift the
interest of the wife is determined, or else they shall remain
to the wife, if she overlive her husband.‡   Also the husband shall have all the inheritance of his wife, whereof he
was seised in deed in the right of his wife during the espousals, in fee, or in fee-tail general,§ for term of life, if
he have any child by her, to hold as tenant by the curtesy
of England; and the wife shall have the third part of the
inheritance of her husband, whereof he was seised in deed
or in law after the espousals, etc.   But in that case the wife
at the death of her husband must be of the age of nine
years, or above, or else she shall have no dowry.‖

Doct. What if the husband at his death be within the
age of nine years?

Stud. I suppose she shall yet have her dower.   Also the
old law and custom of the realm is, that after the death of
every tenant that holdeth his land by knights service, the
lord shall have the ward and marriage of the heir, till the
heir come to the age of twenty-one years;¶ and if the heir
in that case be of full age at the death of his ancestor, then
he shall pay to his lord his relief, which at the common
law was not certain, but by the statute of *magna charta* it
is put in certain;** that is to say, for every whole knight's
fee to pay *C. s.* and for a whole barony to pay a hundred
marks for relief, and for a whole earldom to pay *C. l.* and

---

* Off. of Executor, 53, 57, 58, 59; post. 130.
†Co. Litt. 351.
‡Roll's Abr. 342.
§ Likewise it seems that the husband shall be tenant by the curtesy, if he
is seised in right of his wife of the special tail.   Co. Litt. 29.
‖ Litt., sec. 36; Co. Litt. 33; 2 Inst. 234.
¶ Litt., sec. 103.
**2 B. C. 66; Litt., sec. 112.

after that rate.   And if the heir of such a tenant be a woman, and she, at the death of her ancestor, be within the
age of fourteen years, then by the common law she should
have been in ward only till fourteen years, but by the stat.
of W. 1, in such case she shall be in ward till sixteen years.*
And if at the death of her ancestor she be of the age of
fourteen years, or above, she shall be out of ward, though
the land be holden of the king, and then she shall pay relief as an heir male shall.†

Also of lands holden in socage, if the ancestor die, his
heir being within the age of fourteen years, the next friend
to the heir, to whom the inheritance may not descend, shall
have the ward of his body and lands till he shall come to
the age of fourteen years, and then he may enter.   And
when the heir cometh to the age of twenty-one years, then
the guardian shall yield him an account for the profits
thereof by him received.‡

Also such an heir in socage, for his relief, shall double
his rent to the lord the year following the death of his ancestor : as if his ancestor held by 12d. rent, the heir in the
year following shall pay the 12d. for his rent and other 12d.
for his relief; and the relief he must pay, though he be
within age at the death of his ancestor.§

Also there is an old law and custom in this realm,‖ that
a freehold by way of feoffment, gift, or lease, passeth not
without livery of seisin be made upon the land according,¶
though a deed of feoffment be thereof made and delivered :

* Litt., sec. 103; 2 B. C. 67.
† Kitchen on Courts, 110; 2 B. C. 67.
‡ Litt., sec. 123; Kitchen on Courts, 111; Hargrave's Ed. of Co. Litt. 89.
§ Litt., sec. 127.
‖ Finch. Law, 132; Noy's Max. 59.
¶ It is not absolutely necessary, though perhaps it is the better way to
make livery and seisin upon the land; for if it is made in sight of it only
by the words, "I give you yonder land, enter and take possession." This is
sufficient in law to pass the freehold, if the feoffee enters during the life
of the feoffor. 2 B. C. 316. This method of alienating property by feoffment with livery and seisin, though the usual conveyance of land for a
long series of years, is now almost superseded by the modern conveyance of lease and release, which, in fact, amounts to a feoffment.

but by way of surrender, partition and exchange, a freehold may pass without livery.*

Also if a man make a will of land whereof he is seised in his demesne as of fee, that will is void :† but if it had stood in feoffee's hands, it had been good. And also in London such a will is good by the custom of the city, if it be enrolled.‡

Also a lease for term of years is but a chattel by the law, and therefore it may pass without any livery of seisin : but otherwise it is of a state for term of life, for that it is a freehold in the law, and therefore livery must be made, or else the freehold passeth not.§

Also by the old custom of the realm a man may distrain for rent-service of common right; and also for a rent reserved upon a gift in tail, a lease for term of life, of years, and at will :‖ and in such case the lord may distrain the beasts of tenants, as soon as they come upon the ground; but the beasts of strangers that come in but by manner of an escape he may not distrain, till they have been levant and couchant upon the ground.¶ But for debt upon an obligation, nor upon a contract, nor for account, ne yet for arrearages of account, nor for no manner of trespass,** reparations, nor such other, no man may distrain.††

And, by the old custom of the realm, all issues that shall be joined between party and party in any court of record within the realm, except a few whereof it needeth not to treat at this time, must be tried by twelve free and lawful men of the visne,‡‡ that be not of affinity to none of the

---

* Likewise by confirmation, devise, fine, or recovery, and since the statute of uses, by bargain and sale enrolled, lease, and release, etc.

† Post. 58.

‡ 1 Roll. Abr. 556; post. 35.

§ 2 B. C. 314.

‖ Litt., sec. 213, 214; Co. Litt. 142.

¶ 2 Lutw. 1573, 1577.

** This cannot be true, for a man may distrain for trespass damage-feasant.

†† Post. 123.

‡‡ It was formerly the custom for jurors to come from the vicinity or hun-

parties; and, in other courts that be not of record, as in the county, court-baron, hundred, and such other like, they shall be tried by the oath of the parties, and not otherwise, unless the parties assent that it shall be tried by the homage.* And it is to be noted that lords, barons, and all peers of the realm be excepted out of such trials, if they will,† but if they will wilfully be sworn therein, some say it is no error : and they may, if they will have a writ out of the chancery directed to the sheriff, commanding him that he shall not impanel them upon no inquest.‡

And of this that is said before it appeareth, that the customs aforesaid, or other like unto them, whereof be very many in the laws of England, cannot be proved to have the strength of law only by reason. For how may it be proved by reason that the eldest son shall only inherit his father, and the younger to have no part; or that the husband shall have the whole land for term of his life as tenant by the curtesy, in such manner as before appeareth, and that the wife shall have only the third part in the name of her dower; and that her husband shall have all the goods of his wife as his own, and that if he die, the wife living, that his executors shall have the goods, and not the wife? All these and such other cannot be proved only by reason, that it should be so, and no otherwise, although they be reasonable ; and that, with the custom therein used, sufficeth

---

dred where the matter in dispute arose, pursuant to the maxim, *vicini vicinorum facto præsumuntur scire,* but now by stat. 4 and 5 Ann., c. 16, the jury are to come, *e corpore comitatus,* from the body of the county, in which the action is triable. 3 B. C. 360. But this statute does not extend to indictments or other criminal suits, and it is conceived that no act has been made to include any such, except the stat. 24 G. 2, 2 c. 28, which relates to actions on penal statutes. However, notwithstanding the law stands thus as to criminal prosecutions, yet it is the practice of every day for the sheriff to summon juries from the county without the least regard to the visne of each indiotment, though it gives the prisoner an opportunity, if he pleases, of challenging for default of hundredors. 2 H. H. P. C. 272, 273.

   * Co. Litt. 158.
   † Trials per pais, 1st part, 105.
   ‡3 B. C. 361; Vin. Abr., title Trial, 208.

in the law, and a statute made against such general customs
ought to be observed, because they be not merely the law
of reason.

Also the law of property is not the law of reason, but the
law of custom, howbeit that it is kept, and is also most
necessary to be kept, in all realms, and among all people;
and so it may be numbered among the general customs of
the realm. And it is to understand that there is no statute
that treateth of the beginning of the said customs, ne why
they should be holden for law; and therefore after them
that be learned in the laws of the realm, the old custom of
the realm is the only and sufficient authority to them in
that behalf. And I pray thee shew me what doctors hold
therein, that is to say, whether a custom only be a sufficient
authority of any law.

Doct. Doctors hold that a law grounded upon a custom
is the most surest law; but this thou must always understand therewith, that such a custom is neither contrary to
the law of reason, nor the law of God.* And now I pray
thee shew me somewhat of the *maxims* of the laws of England, whereof thou hast made mention before in the 4th
chapter.†

Stud. I will with good-will.

CHAP. VIII.—*Of the fourth ground of the law of England.*

The fourth ground of the law of England standeth in
divers principles that be called in the law *maxims*, the
which have been always taken for law in this realm;‡ so
that it is not lawful for any that is learned to deny them;
for every one of those maxims is sufficient authority to
himself. And which is a maxim, and which not, shall
alway be determined by the judges, and not by twelve

* Co. Litt. 141.
† Kitchen on Courts, title Customs.
‡ Co. Litt. 10, 67.

men.* And it needeth not to assign any reason why they were first received for maxims, for it sufficeth that they be not against the law of reason, nor the law of God, and that they have always been taken for a law. And such maxims be not only holden for law, but also other cases like unto them, and all things that necessarily follow upon the same are to be reduced to the like law ; and therefore most commonly there be assigned some reasons or considerations why such maxims be reasonable, to the intent that other cases like may the more conveniently be applied to them. And they be of the same strength and effect in the law as statutes be. And though the general customs of the realm be the strength and warrant of the said maxims, as they be of the general customs of the realm ; yet because the said general customs be in a manner known through the realm, as well to them that be unlearned as learned, and may lightly be had and known, and that with little study, and the maxims be only known in the king's courts, or among them that take great study in the law of the realm, and among few other persons ; therefore they be set in this writing, for several grounds, and he that listeth may so account them, or if he will, he may take them for no ground, after his pleasure. Of which maxims I shall hereafter shew thee part.

First, There is a maxim† that escuage uncertain maketh knight's service.‡

---

* Noy's Max. 18; ante, 18.

† Litt., sec. 120.

‡ By the statute 12 Car. 2, c. 24, " for taking away the court of wards, and liveries and tenures in knight's service, and purveyance, and for settling a revenue upon his majesty," it is enacted, that all wardships, primer seisins, and ousterlemains, values and forfeitures of marriage, and all tenures by homage, fines for alienation, knight's service, and escuage, and also acts for marrying the daughter or knighting the son, and all tenures of the king in capite, shall be taken away. And by the same statute, all sorts of tenure held of the king, or others, are turned into free and common socage, except tenures in frankalmoign copyholds, and the honorary services of grand serjeantry.

Also there is another maxim,* that escuage certain makes socage.

Also, that he that holdeth by castle-guard, holdeth by knight's service,† but he holdeth not by escuage : and that he that holdeth by xxs. to the guard of a castle, holdeth by socage.

Also there is a maxim,‡ that a discent taketh away an entry.

Also, that no prescription in lands maketh a right.§

Also, that a prescription of rent and profits apprender out of land maketh a right.||

Also, that the limitation of a prescription generally taken is from the time that no man's mind runneth to the contrary.¶

Also, that assigns may be made upon lands given in fee, for term of life, or for term of years, though no mention be made of assigns ; and the same law is of a rent that is granted ; but otherwise it is of a warranty, and of a covenant.

Also, that a condition to avoid a freehold cannot be pleaded without deed ; but to avoid a gift of chattel, it may be pleaded without deed.**

Also, that a release or confirmation made by him, that at the time of the release or confirmation made had no right, is void in the law, though a right come to him after ;†† except it be with warranty, and then it shall bar him to all right that he shall have after the warranty made.

Also, that a right or title of action that only dependeth in action, cannot be given or granted to none other but only

---

* Co. Litt. 87.
† Ib.
‡ Litt., sec. 385.
§ Finch. 132.
|| 2 B. C. 264.
¶ Post. 308; Co. Litt. 114.
** Vin. Abr., title Facts, 67.
†† Vin. Abr., title Release, 299.

to the tenant of the ground, or to him that hath the rever-
.sion or remainder of the same land.*

Also, that in an action of debt upon a contract, the defendant may wage his law :† but otherwise it is upon a lease of lands for term of years, or at will.‡

Also, that if an exigent, in case of felony, be awarded against a man, he hath thereby forthwith forfeited his goods to the king.§

Also, if the son be attainted in the life of the father, and after he purchaseth his charter of pardon of the king, and after the father dieth ;‖ in this case the land shall escheat to the lord of the fee, insomuch that though he have a younger brother, yet the land shall not descend to him : for by the attainder of the elder brother the blood is corrupt, and the father-in-law died without heir.

Also, if an abbot or prior alien the lands of his house, and dieth ;¶ in this case, though his successor have right to the lands, yet he may not enter, but he must take his action that is appointed him by law.

Also, there is a maxim in the law, that if a villein pur-
-chase lands, and the lord enter, he shall enjoy the land as

---

* 10 Rep. 48; Shep. Touch. 229.

† Wager of law is where defendant swears before compurgators that he owes the plaintiff nothing. Formerly this practice was much in use, as appears by its making a conspicuous part of our English jurisprudence. But it is now only in actions of debt upon simple contract, or for amercements in actions of detinue or account, where the debt may have been paid, and the accounts balanced, without any evidence of either, that defendant can wage his law, and not where there is any specialty by bond or deed; and as defendant is allowed to wage his law in an action of debt, it is but seldom brought upon a simple contract, being supplied by an action of trespass on the case, for the breach of a promise or assumpsit; and this being an action of trespass, no law can be waged therein; so that wager of law is now quite out of use, but still it is not out of force. Black. Com. 3 V. 341.

‡ 12 Mod. 679; 2 Salk. 684; Co. Litt. 295.

§ This is not law, for in this case he forfeits both real and personal es-
:tate to the lord.

‖ 2 B. C. 253; Co. Litt. 13.

¶ Post. 32.

his own :* but if the villein alien before the lord enter, the alienation is good. And the same law is of goods.†

Also, if a man steal goods to the value of twelve pence, or above, it is *felony*, and·he shall die for it.‡ And if it be under the value of twelve pence, then it is but *petit larceny*, and he shall not die for it,§ but shall be otherwise punished after the discretion of the judges, except it be taken from the person; for if a man take any thing, how little soever it be, from a man's person, feloniously, it is called *robbery*, and he shall die for it.‖

Also, he that is arraigned upon an indictment of felony, shall be admitted, in favor of life, to challenge thirty-six jurors peremptorily;¶ but if he challenge any above that number, the law taketh him as one that hath refused the law, because he hath refused three whole inquests, and therefore he shall die : but with cause he may challenge as many as he hath cause of challenge to. And farther, it is to be understood, that such peremptory challenge shall not be admitted in appeal,** because it is at the suit of the party.††

Also, the land of every man is in the law inclosed from

---

* Litt., sec. 177; Finch. 159.

† But the law was widely different in the case of the king, who had a villein, for notwithstanding the alienation, he might enter.   Perk., sec. 29.

‡ 1 H. P. C. 503.

§ Ib. 504.

‖ Ib. 532, 536.

¶ The author or his printer is not here quite correct as to the number of jurors, which it was allowed the prisoners to challenge in cases of felony; as the boundary fixed by the common law, and which was thought to be reasonable was only thirty-five, that is, one under three full juries, and therefore if the prisoner challenged thirty-six, he was sentenced to the *peine forte et dure*, as one that had no intention to be tried at all. The number thirty-five may now be challenged by the prisoner in cases of high and petit treason, but in cases of murder, or felony, by stat. 22 H. 8, c. 14, he can make no more than twenty peremptory challenges. 2 H. P. C. 269; 2 Hawk. 414; Co. Litt. 156.

** Kitchen on Courts, 52.

†† But in Viner's abridgments, title Trial, 252, it is laid down, that a peremptory challenge may be taken in an appeal, and with as good reason· as in a prosecution at the suit of the king.

other, though it lie in the open field: and therefore if a
man do a trespass therein, the writ shall be, *Quare clausum
fregit.*

Also, the rents, commons of 'pasture, of turbary, reversions, remainders, nor such other things which lie not in
manual occupation, may not be given nor granted to none
other without writing.*

Also, that he that recovereth debt or damages in the
king's courts, by such an action wherein a *capias* lay in the
. process, may within a year after the recovery have a *capias
ad satisfaciendum,* to take the body of the defendant, and
to commit him to prison till he have paid the debt and damages: but if there lay no *capias* in the first action, then the
plaintiff shall have no *capias ad satisfaciendum,* but must
take a *fieri facias,* or an *elegit* within the year, or a *scire
facias* after the year, or within the year, if he will.

Also, if a release or confirmation be made to him that, at
the time of the release made, had nothing in the land, etc.,
the release or confirmation is void, except in certain cases,
as to vouch, and certain other which need not here to be remembered.†

Also, there is a maxim in the law of England, that the
king may disseise no man, nor that no man may disseise
the king, ne pull any reversion or remainder out of him.‡

. Also, the king's excellency is so high in the law, that no
freehold may be given to the king, nor be derived from him,
but by matter of record.§

Also, there was sometime a maxim and a law of England,
that no man should have a writ of right but by special suit
to the king, and for a fine to be made in the *chancery* for
it.   But these maxims be changed by the statute of *magna
charta, cap.* 16, where it is said thus, *nulli negabimus, nulli
vendemus rectum vel justitiam.*‖   And by the words, *Nulli*

* Co. Litt. 48; 121 Stat.; 29 Car. 2, c. 3; 2 Cro. 217; Finch. Law, 108.
† Co. Litt. 265, 270.
‡ 3 B. C. 257.
§ 2 B. C. 346; Noy's Max. 4.
‖ 2 Inst. 55; 1 B. C. 141.

negabimus, a man shall have a writ of right of course in the *chancery* without suing to the king for it: and by the words, *Nulli vendemus*, he shall have it without fine. And so many times the old maxims of the law be changed by statutes. Also, though it be reasonable, that for the manifold diversities of actions that be in the laws of England, there should be diversities of process, as in the real actions after one manner, and in personal actions after another manner; yet it cannot be proved merely by reason, that the same process ought to be had, and none other : for by statute it might be altered. And so the ground of the said process is to be referred only to the maxims and customs of the realm.

And I have shewed thee these maxims before rehearsed, not to the intent to shew thee specially what is the cause of the law in them, for that would ask a great respite : but I have shewed them only to the intent that thou mayest perceive that the said maxims, and other like, may be conveniently set for one of the grounds of the laws of England. Moreover there be divers cases whereof I am in doubt whether they be only maxims of the law, or that they be grounded upon the law of reason; wherein I pray thee let me hear thine opinion.

Doct. I pray thee shew those cases that thou meanest; and I shall make thee answer therein as I shall see cause.

CHAP. IX.—*Hereafter follow divers cases wherein the student doubteth whether they be only maxims of the law, or that they be grounded upon the law of reason.*

The law of England is, that if a man command another to do a trespass, and he doth it, that the commander is a trespasser.* And I am in doubt, whether that it be only by a maxim of the law, or that it be by the law of reason.

Also, I am in doubt upon what law it is grounded, that

---

* Br. Trespass, pl. 148.

the accessary shall not be put to answer before the principal, etc.*

Also, the law is, that if an abbot† buy a thing that cometh to the use of the house, and dieth, that his successor shall be charged.‡ And I am somewhat in doubt upon what ground that law dependeth.

Also, that he that hath possession of land, tho' it be by, disseisin, hath right against all men but against him that hath right.§

Also, that if an action real be sued against any man that hath nothing in the thing demanded, the writ shall abate at the common law.

Also, that by the alienation of the tenant, hanging the writ, or his entry into religion, or if he be made a knight, or if she be a woman, and take an husband hanging the writ, that the writ shall not abate.||

Also, if land and rent that is going out of the same land, come into one man's hand of like estate, and like surety of title, the rent is extinct.¶

Also, if land descend to him that hath right to the same land before, he shall be remitted to his better title, if he will.**

Also, if two titles be concurrent together, that the eldest title shall be preferred.††

---

*By the common law the accessary shall not be compelled to answer to the indictment till the principal is tried; but if he will waive that privilege, he may, and put himself upon his trial before the principal. 1 H. H. P. C. 623. The law, however, is now so much altered by statute, that receivers of stolen goods, knowing them to be stolen, may be compelled to answer for the misdemeanor, although the principal can not be taken. 1 Ann., c. 9, s. 2; 5 Ann., c. 31, s. 5; 4 Geo. 1, c. 11, and see 4 B. C. 318, and Foster's Crown Law, 373.

†By the statutes 27 H. 8, c. 28; 31 H. 8, c. 13; 32 H. 8, c. 14, s. 1, and 37 H. 8, c. 4, all monasteries and religious houses are dissolved, and the whole body of abbots and priors totally eradicated.

‡ B. Abbe, pl. 9; 22 H. 6, 56.

§ 3 New Abr. 97.

|| Viner's Abr., title Abatement.

¶ Wood's Inst. 195.

** Ib. 528.

†† Noy's Max. 15.

Also, that every man is bound to make recompence for
such hurt as his beasts shall do in the corn or grass of his
neighbour, though he know not that they were there.
Also, if the demandant or plaintiff, hanging his writ, will
enter into the thing demanded, his writ shall abate.* And
it is many times very hard and of great difficulty to know
what cases of the law of England be grounded upon the
law of reason, and what upon custom of the realm; and
though it be hard to discuss it, it is very necessary to be
known, for the knowledge of the perfect reason of the law.
And if any man think that these cases before rehearsed be
grounded upon the law of reason, then he may refer them
to the first ground of the law of England, which is the law of
reason, whereof is made mention in the fifth chapter.†
And if any man think that they be grounded upon the law
of custom, then he may refer them to the maxims of the
law, which be assigned for the fourth ground of the law of
England, whereof mention is made in the eighth chapter,
as before appeareth.‡

Doct. But I pray thee shew me by what authority it is
proved in the laws of England that the cases which thou
hast put before in the eighth chapter, and such other which
thou callest maxims, ought not to be denied, but ought to
be taken as maxims. For sith they cannot be proved by
reason, as thou agreest thyself they cannot, they may as
lightly be denied as affirmed, unless there be some sufficient
authority to approve them.

Stud. Many of the customs and maxims of the laws of
England be known by the use and the custom of the realm
so apparently that it needeth not to have any law written
thereof.§ For what needeth it to have any law written that
the eldest son shall inherit his father,‖ or that all the daugh-

---

* Doct. Pl. 5.
† Ante, 13.
‡ Ante, 25.
§ 1 B. C. 64.
‖ Ante, 19.

3

ters shall inherit together as one heir, if there be no son ;*
or that the husband shall have the goods and chattels of his
wife that she hath at the time of the espousals, or after :†
or that a bastard shall not inherit as heir; or the executors
shall have the disposition of all the goods of their testator ;‡
and if there be no executors, that the ordinary shall have
it, and the heir shall not meddle with the goods of his ancestor, but if any particular customs help him?

   The other maxims and customs of the law that be not so
openly known among the people may be known partly by
the law of reason, and partly by the books of the laws of
England, called *Years and Terms*, and partly by divers
records remaining in the king's courts, and in the treasury,
and specially by a book called the *Register*,§ and also by
divers statutes, wherein many of the said cus oms and maxims be oft recited, as to a diligent searchei will evidently
appear.

CHAP. X.—*Of the fifth ground of the law of England.*

   The fifth ground of the law of England standeth in divers
particular customs, used in divers counties, towns, cities,
and lordships in this realm : the which particular customs,
because they be not against the law of reason, nor the law
of God, though they be against the said general customs or
maxims of the law, yet nevertheless they stand in effect,
and be taken for law : but if it rise in question in the king's
courts, whether there be any such particular custom or not,
it shall be tried by twelve men, and not by the judges, except the same particular custom be of record in the same .
court. ‖   Of which particular customs I have hereafter noted
some for an example.

   First, there is a custom in Kent that is called *Gavelkind*,

---

* Litt., sec. 241
† Co. Litt. 351.
‡ Ante, 21; post. 224; post. 225.
§ Preface to Doug. Rep. 10; 1 B. C. 71.
‖ Noy's Max. 18.

that all the brethren shall inherit together, as sisters at the common law.*

Also, there is another particular custom that is called *Burgh-english*, where the younger son shall inherit before the eldest; and that custom is in Nottingham.†

Also, there is a custom in the city of London, that freemen there may, by their testament inrolled, bequeath their lands that they be seised of to whom they will, except to mortmain : and if they be citizens and freemen, that they may also bequeath their lands to mortmain.‡

Also, in *Gavelkind*, though the father be hanged the son shall inherit.§ For their custom is, *The father to the bough, the son to the plough.*

Also, in some countries the wife shall have the half of the husband's land in the name of her dowry, as long as she liveth sole.‖

And in some country the husband shall have the half of the inheritance of his wife, though he have no issue by her.¶

Also, in some country an infant when he is of the age of fifteen years may make a feoffment, and the feoffment good :** and in some country, when he can mete an ell of cloth.

CHAP. XI.—*Of the sixth ground of the law of England.*

The sixth ground of the law of England standeth in divers statutes made by our sovereign lord the king and his progenitors, and by the lords spiritual and temporal, and the commons in divers parliaments, in such cases where

---

* Post. 56; Stat. 31 H. 8, c. 3.

† Litt., sec. 165; post. 56.

‡ 1 Roll. Abr. 556; 3 Cro. 347.

§ That is, if the father is hanged for felony; for if he is attainted of treason, and hanged, the lands are forfeited to the king. Consideration on Law of Forfeitures, 62.

‖ 1 Cro. 121.

¶ Co. Litt. 30.

** 1 B. C. 78; 2 Bac. Abr. 638.

the law of reason, the law of God, customs, maxims, ne
other grounds of the law seemed not to be sufficient to
punish evil men and to reward good men.* And I remember not that I have seen any other grounds of the law
of England, but only these that I have before remembered.
Furthermore it appeareth of that I have said before, that
ofttimes two or three grounds of the law of England must
be joined together, or that the plaintiff can open and declare his right, as it may appear by this example. If a
man enter into another man's land by force, and after make
feoffment for maintenance to defraud the plaintiff from his
action; in this case it appeareth that the said unlawful entry
is prohibited by the law of reason: but the plaintiff shall
recover treble damages,† that is by reason of the statute
made in the eighth year of king Henry VI, cap. 9.‡ And
that the damages shall be cessed by twelve men,§ that is
by the custom of the realm. And so in this case three
grounds of the law of England maintain the plaintiff's
action.

And so it is in divers other cases that need not to be remembered now. And thus I make an end for this time to
speak any farther of the grounds of the law of England.

Doct. I thank thee for the great pain that thou hast taken
therein. Nevertheless, forasmuch as it appeareth that thou
hast said before that the learned men of the law of England pretend to verify that the law of England will nothing
do, ne attempt against the law of reason, nor the law of
God, I pray thee answer me to some questions grounded
upon the law of England, how, as thou thinkest, the law
may stand with reason or conscience in them.

Stud. Put the case, and I shall make answer therein, as
well as I can.

---

* Noy's Max. 19.

† Co. Litt. 257.

‡ See this statute explained and enforced by 31 Eliz., cap. 11, and 21 Jac.
1, cap. 15.

§ Upon an action of trespass, or an assize of novel disseisin, which is
the remedy given by the statute to recover the treble damages, and likewise
treble costs. Jenk. Cent. 197.

CHAP. XII.—*The first question of the doctor, of the law of England and conscience.*

I have heard say that if a man that is bound in an obligation pay the money, but he taketh no acquittance, or if he take one, and it happeneth him to leese it, that, in that case, he shall be compelled by the laws of England to pay the money again. And how may it be said then that that law standeth with reason and conscience? For as it is grounded upon the law of reason that debts ought of right to be payed, so it is grounded upon the law of reason (as it seemeth) that when they be payed, that he that payed them should be discharged.

Stud. First, Thou shalt understand that it is not the law of England that if a man that is bound in an obligation pay the money without acquittance, or if he take acquittance and leese it, that therefore the law determineth that he ought of right to pay the money eftsoons, for that law were both against reason and conscience. But though it is so, that there is a general maxim in the law of England that in an action of debt sued upon an obligation the defendant shall not plead that he oweth not the money, ne can in no wise discharge himself in that action, but he have acquittance, or some other writing sufficient in the law, or some other thing like, witnessing that he hath paid the money;* that is ordained by the law to avoid a great inconvenience that else might happen to come to many people; that is to say, that every·man by a nude parole and by a bare averment should avoid an obligation.† Wherefore, to avoid that inconvenience, the law hath ordained that as the defendant is charged by a sufficient writing, that so he must be discharged by sufficient writing or by some other thing of as high authority as the obligation is. And though it may follow thereupon that, in some particular case, a man by occasion of that general maxim may be

* Finch. 12.
† Fitzgib. 213; Finch. 11; Noy's Max. 4.

compelled to pay the money again that he payed before; yet, nevertheless, no default can be thereof assigned in the law. For like as makers of law take heed to such things as may oft fall, and do much hurt among the people, rather than to particular cases : so in likewise the general grounds of the law of England heed more what is good for many than what is good for one singular person only. And because it should be a hurt to many, if an obligation should be so lightly avoided by word; therefore the law especially preventeth that hurt under such manner as before appeareth; and yet intendeth not, nor commandeth not, that the money of right ought to be paid again, but setteth a general rule, which is good and necessary to all the people, and that every man may well keep, without it be through his own default. And if such default happen in any person, whereby he is without remedy at the common law, yet he may be holpen by a *subpœna;* and so he may in many other cases where conscience serveth for him, that were too long to rehearse now.*

Doct. But I pray thee shew me under what manner a man may be holpen by conscience; and whether he shall be holpen in the same court, or in another.

Stud. Because it cannot be well declared where a man shall be holpen by conscience, and where not, but it be first known what conscience is, therefore, because it pertaineth to thee most properly to treat of the nature and quality of conscience, therefore I pray thee that thou wilt make me some brief declaration of the nature and quality of conscience, and then I shall answer to thy question as well as I can.

Doct. I will with good-will do as thou sayest: and to the intent that thou mayest the better understand that I shall say of conscience, I shall first shew thee what *sinderesis* is, and then what reason is, and then what conscience is; and how these three differ among themselves, I shall somewhat touch.

---

* 1 Chanc. Cases, 78; 2 Comyn's Digest, 323.

CHAP. XIII.—*What sinderesis is.*

Sinderesis is a natural power of the soul, set in the highest part thereof, moving and stirring it to good and abhorring evil. And therefore *sinderesis* never sinneth nor erreth. And this *sinderesis* our Lord put in man, to the intent that the order of things should be observed. For, after St. Dionyse, the wisdom of God joined the beginning of the second things to the last of the first things : for angel is of a nature to understand without searching of reason, and to that nature man is joined by *sinderesis*, the which *sinderesis* may not wholly be extincted neither in man ne yet in damned souls. But nevertheless, as to the use and exercise thereof, it may be let for a time, either through the darkness of ignorance, or for undiscreet delectation, or for the hardness of obstinacy. First by the darkness of ignorance, *sinderesis* may be let that it shall not murmur against evil, because he believeth evil to be good, as it is in heretics, the which, when they die for the wickedness of their error, believe they die for the very truth of their faith. And by undiscreet delectation *sinderesis* is sometime so overlaid, that remorse or grudge of conscience for that time can have no place. For the hardness of obstinacy *sinderesis* is also let, that it may not stir to goodness, as it is in damned souls, that be so obstinate in evil, that they may never be inclined to good. And though *sinderesis* may be said to that point extinct in damned souls, yet it may not be said that it is fully extinct to all intents. For they alway murmur against the evil of the pain that they suffer for sin, and so it may not be said that it is universally, and to all intents, and to all times extinct. And this *sinderesis* is the beginning of all things that may be learned by speculation or study, and ministreth the general grounds and principles thereof; and also of all things that are to be done by man. An example of such things as may be learned by speculation appeareth thus : *sinderesis* saith that every whole thing is more than any one part of the same thing, and that is a sure ground that never faileth. And an example of things that are to be done, or not to be done: as where *sinderesis* saith no evil is to be done, but that goodness is to be done and followed, and evil to be fled, and such other.

And therefore *sinderesis* is called by some men the law of reason, for it ministreth the principles of the law of reason, the which be in every man by nature, in that he is a reasonable creature.

CHAP. XIV.—*Of reason.*

When the first man *Adam* was created, he received of God a double eye, that is to say, an outward eye, whereby he might see visible things, and know his bodily enemies, and eschew them: and an inward eye, that is, the eye of reason, whereby he might see his spiritual enemies that fight against his soul, and beware of them. And among all gifts that God gave to men, this gift of reason is the most noblest, for thereby man precelleth all beasts, and is made like to the dignity of angels, discerning truth from falsehood, and evil from good; wherefore he goeth far from the effect that he was made to, when he taketh not heed to the truth, or when he preferreth evil before good.

And therefore, after doctors, reason is the power of the soul that discerneth between good and evil, and between good and better, comparing the one with the other: the which also sheweth virtues, loveth good, and flieth vices. And reason is called righteous and good, for it is conformable to the will of God; and that is the first thing, and the first rule that all things must be ruled by. And reason that is not righteous nor strait, but that is said culpable, is either because she is deceived with an error that might be overcome, or else through her pride or slothfulness she enquireth not for knowledge of the truth that ought to be enquired. Also reason is divided into two parts, that is to say, into the higher part, and into the lower part.

The higher part hideth heavenly things and eternal, and reasoneth by heavenly laws or by heavenly reason what is to be done, and what is not to be done, and what things God commandeth, and what he prohibiteth. And this higher part of reason hath no regard to transitory things or temporal things, but that sometime, as it were by manner of counsel, she bringeth forth heavenly reasons to order well temporal things. The lower part of reason worketh most to govern well temporal things, and she groundeth her reasons much upon laws of man, and upon reason of man, whereby she concludeth that that is to be done that is honest and expedient to the commonwealth, or not to be done, that is not expedient to the commonwealth. And so that reason whereby I know God, and such things as pertain to God, belongeth to the highest part of reason; and the reason whereby I know creatures belongeth to the lower part of reason. And though these two parts, that is to say, the higher part and the lower part, be one in deed and essence, yet they differ by reason of their working, and of their office; as it is of one self eye, that sometime looketh upward, and sometime downward.

CHAP. XV.—*Of conscience.*

This word *conscience*, which in Latin is called *conscientia*, is compounded of this proposition *cum*, that is to say in English, *with;* and of this noun *scientia*, that is to say in English, *knowledge:* and so conscience is as much to say knowledge of one thing with another thing: and conscience so taken, is nothing else but an applying of any science or knowledge to some particular act of man. And so conscience may sometime err, and sometime not err. And of conscience thus taken, doctors make many descriptions. Whereof one doctor saith, that conscience is the law of our understanding. Another, that conscience is an habit of the mind discerning between good and evil. Another, that conscience is the judgment of reason judging on the particular acts of man. All which sayings agree in one effect, that is to say, that conscience is an actual applying of any cunning of knowledge to such things as are

to be done: whereupon it followeth, that upon the most
perfect knowledge of any law or cunning, and of the most
perfect and most true applying of the same to any particular act of man, followeth the most perfect, the most pure,
and the most best conscience. And if there be default in
knowing of the truth of such a law, or in the applying of
the same to particular acts, then thereupon followeth an
error or default in conscience. As it may appear by this
example: Sinderesis ministreth an universal principle that
never erreth, that is to say, that an unlawful thing is not to
be done. And then it might be taken by some men, that
every oath is unlawful, because the Lord saith, Mat. v.,
Ye shall in no wise swear; and yet he that by reason of the
said words will hold that it is not lawful in no case to
swear, erreth in conscience; for he hath not the perfect
knowledge and understanding of the truth of the said gospel, nor he reduceth not the saying of the scripture to other
scriptures, in which it is granted that in some case an oath
may be lawful. And the cause why conscience may so err
in the said case, and in other like, is because conscience is
formed of a certain proposition or question, grounded particularly upon universal rules ordained for such things as
are to be done. And because a particular proposition is
not known to himself, but must appear and be searched by
a diligent search of reason, therefore in search and in the
conscience that should be formed thereupon may happen
to be error, and thereupon it is said that there is error in
conscience: which error cometh either because he doth not
assent to that he ought to assent unto, or else because his
reason whereby he doth refer one thing to another is deceived. For farther declaration whereof it is to understand, that error in conscience cometh seven manner of
ways. First, through ignorance; and that is, when man
knoweth not what he ought to do: and then he ought to
ask counsel of them that he thinks most expert in that
science whereupon his doubt riseth. And if he can have
no counsel, then he must wholly commit him to God, and
he of his goodness will so order him, that he will save him

from offence. The second is through negligence; as when a man is negligent to search his own conscience, or to enquire the truth of other. The third is through pride; as when he will not meeken himself, ne believe them that be better and wiser than he is. The fourth is through singularity; as when a man followeth his own wit, and will not conform himself to other, nor follow the good common ways of men. The fifth is through an inordinate affection to himself, whereby he maketh conscience to follow his desire, and so he causeth her to go out of her right course. The sixth is through pusillanimity, whereby some person dreadeth ofttimes such things as of reason he ought not to dread. The seventh is through perplexity; and this is when a man believeth himself to be so set betwixt two sins, that he thinketh it unpossible but that he shall fall into the one: but a man can never be so perplexed indeed, but through an error in conscience; and if he will put away that error, he shall be delivered. Therefore I pray thee that thou wilt always have a good conscience; and if thou have so, thou shalt always be merry; and if thine own heart reprove thee not, thou shalt always have inward peace. The gladness of right wise men, is of God, and in God, and their joy is always in truth and goodness. There be many diversities of conscience, but there is none better than that whereby a man truly knoweth himself. Many men know many great and high cunning things, and yet know not themselves; and truly he that knoweth not himself, knoweth nothing well. Also he hath a good and clean conscience, that hath purity and cleanness in his heart, truth in his word, and right wiseness in his deed. And as a light is set in a lantern, that all that is in the house may be seen thereby; so Almighty God hath set conscience in the midst of every reasonable soul, as a light whereby he may discern and know what he ought to do, and what he ought not to do. Therefore forasmuch as it behoveth thee to be occupied in such things as pertain to the law; it is necessary that thou ever hold a pure and clean conscience, specially in such things as concern restitution: for the sin is not forgiven,

but if the thing that is wrongfully taken be restored. And
I counsel thee also that thou love that is good, and fly that
is evil; and that thou do to another, as thou wouldest
should be done to thee, and that thou do nothing to other,
that thou wouldest not should be done to thee, that thou do
nothing against truth, that thou live peaceably with thy
neighbour, and that thou do justice to every man as much
as in thee is: and also that in every general rule of the
law thou do observe and keep equity. And if thou do
thus, I trust the light of the lantern, that is, thy conscience,
shall never be extincted.

Stud. But, I pray thee, shew me what is that equity that
thou hast spoken of before, and that thou wouldest that I
should keep.

Doct. I will with good-will shew thee somewhat thereof.

CHAP. XVI.   *What is equity.*

Equity is a right wiseness that considereth all the particular circumstances of the deed, the which also is tem-
pered with the sweetness of mercy. And such an equity
must always be observed in every law of man, and in every
general rule thereof: and that knew he well that said thus,
Laws covet to be ruled by equity. And the wise man saith,
*Be not overmuch right wise; for the extreme right wise-
ness is extreme wrong:* as who saith, If thou take all that
the words of the law giveth thee thou shalt sometime do
against the law. And for the plainer declaration what
equity is, thou shalt understand, that sith the deeds and
acts of men, for which laws have been ordained, happen in
divers manners infinitely, it is not possible to make any
general rule of the law, but that it shall fail in some case:
and therefore makers of law take heed to such things as
may often come, and not to every particular case, for they
could not though they would. And therefore, to follow the
words of the law were in some case both against justice and
the commonwealth. Wherefore in some cases it is necessary to love the words of the law, and to follow that reason

and justice requireth, and to that intent equity is ordained; that is to say, to temper and mitigate the rigour of the law. And it is called also by some men *epieikeia;* the which is no other thing but an exception of the law of God, or the law of reason, from the general rules of the law of men, when they by reason of their generality, would in any particular case judge against the law of God or the law of reason : the which exception is secretly understood in every general rule of every positive law. And so it appeareth, that equity taketh not away the very right, but only that that seemeth to be right by the general words of the law. Nor it is not ordained against the cruelness of the law, for the law in such case generally taken is good in himself; but equity followeth the law in all particular cases where right and justice requireth, notwithstanding the general rule of the law be to the contrary. Wherefore it appeareth, that if any law were made by man without any such exception expressed or implied, it were manifestly unreasonable, and were not to be suffered : for such causes might come, that he that would observe the law should break both the law of God and the law of reason. As if a man make a vow that he will never eat white-meat, and after it happeneth him to come there where he can get no other meat : in this case it behoveth him to break his avow, for the particular case is excepted secretly from his general avow by his equity or *epicikeia,* as it is said before. Also if a law were made in a city, that no man under the pain of death should open the gates of the city before the sun-rising ; yet if the citizens before that hour flying from their enemies, come to the gates of the city, and one for saving of the citizens openeth the gates before the hour appointed by the law, he offendeth not the law, for that case is excepted from the said general law by equity, as is said before. And so it appeareth that equity rather followeth the intent of the law, than the words of the law. And I suppose that there be in like wise some like equities grounded on the general rules of the law of the realm.

Stud. Yea verily; whereof one is this. There is a

general prohibition in the laws of England, that it shall not be lawful to any man to enter into the freehold of another without authority of the owner or the law: but yet it is excepted from the said prohibition by the law of reason, that if a man drive beasts by the highway, and the beasts happen to escape into the corn of his neighbour, and he, to bring out his beasts, that they should do no hurt, goeth into the ground, and setteth out his beasts, there he shall justify that entry into the ground by the law.* Also notwithstanding the statute of Edw. 3, made the 14th year of his reign, whereby it is ordained, that no man, upon pain of imprisonment, should give any alms to any valiant beggar, that is well able to labour;† yet if a man meet with a valiant beggar in so cold a weather, and so light apparel, that if he have no clothes, he shall not be able to come to any town for succour, but is likely rather to die by the way, and he therefore giveth him apparel to save his life, he shall be excused by the said statute, by such an exception of the law of reason as I have spoken of.

Doct. I know well that, as thou sayest, he shall be excepted of the said statute by conscience, and over that, that he shall have great reward of God for his good deeds: but I would wit whether the party shall be so discharged in the Common law by such an exception of the law of reason, or not? For though ignorance invincible of a statute excuse the party against God, yet (as I have heard) it excuseth not in the laws of the realm, ne yet *Chancery*, as some say, although the case be so that the party to whom the forfeiture is given may not with conscience leave it.

Stud. Verily, by thy question thou hast put me in a great doubt; wherefore I pray thee give me a respite therein to make thee an answer: but, as I suppose for the time, (howbeit I will not fully affirm it to be as I say) it should seem that he should well plead it for his discharge at the Common law, because it shall be taken that it was the intent of the

---

* Viner's Abr., title Trespass, 466.
† Repealed by 1 Ed. 6, c. 13, and 21 Jac., 28; ante, 15.

makers of the statute to except such cases.* And the judges may many times judge after the mind of the makers as far as the letter may suffer, and so it seemeth they may in this case. And divers other exceptions there be also from other general grounds of the law of the realm by such equity as thou hast remembered before, that were too long to rehearse now.

Doct. But yet I pray thee shew me shortly somewhat more of the mind, under what manner a man may be holpen in this realm by such equity.

Stud. I will with good-will shew thee somewhat therein.

CHAP. XVII.—*In what manner a man shall be holpen by equity in the laws of England.*

First, It is to be understood, there be in many cases divers exceptions from the general grounds of the law of the realm by other reasonable grounds of the same law, whereby a man shall be holpen in the common law. As it is of this general ground, that it is not lawful for any man to enter upon a descent; yet the reasonableness of the law excepteth from that ground an infant that hath right, and hath suffered such a descent, and him also that maketh continual claim, and suffereth them to enter, notwithstanding the descent.† And of that exception they shall have advantage in the Common law. And so it is likewise of divers statutes; as of the statute whereby it is prohibited that certain particular tenants shall do no waste, yet if a lease for term of years be made to an infant that is within years of discretion, as of the age of five or six years, and a stranger do waste, in this case this infant shall not be punished for the waste, for he is excepted and excused by the law of reason.‡ And a woman covert, to whom such

---

* Noy's Max. 19.

† Litt., sec. 402, 414; Noy's Max. 7.

‡ But in 2 Inst. 303, it is said, that if an infant is tenant by the curtesy or lessee for life or years, he shall answer for waste done by a stranger, and have his remedy over. See likewise 1 Inst. 54.

a lease is made after the coverture, shall be also discharged
of waste after her husband's death, by a reasonable maxim
and custom of the realm.* And also for reparations to be
made upon the same ground, it is lawful for such particular tenants to cut down trees upon the same ground to make
reparations.† But the cause there, as I suppose, is, for
that the mind of the makers of the said statute shall be
taken to be, that that case should be excepted. And in all
these cases the parties shall be holpen in the same court,
and by the common law. And thus it appeareth, that
sometime a man may be excepted from the rigor of a maxim
of the law by another maxim of the law; and sometime
from the rigor of a statute by the law of reason, and sometime by the intent of the makers of the statute.‡ But yet
it is to be understood, that most commonly where any thing
is excepted from the general customs or maxims of the laws
of the realm by the law of reason, the party must have his
remedy by a writ that is called *subpœna*, if a *subpœna* lie
in the case.§ But where a *subpœna* lieth, and where not,
it is not our intent to treat of at this time. And in some
cases there is no remedy for such an equity by way of compulsion, but all remedy therein must be committed to the
conscience of the party.

Doct. But in case where a *subpœna* lieth, to whom shall
it be directed, whether to the judge or the party?

Stud. It shall never be directed to the judge, but to the
party plaintiff, or to his attorney ; and thereupon an injunction commanding them by the same, under a certain pain
therein to be contained that he proceed no farther at the
common law till it be determined in the king's *chancery*,
whether the plaintiff had title in conscience to recover, or

---

* This doctrine is denied in the authorities mentioned in the preceding
note, and it is there laid down, that the privilege of coverture shall not
prevail in this case against the wrong and disherison done to him that has
the inheritance, if the wife agrees to the estate, after the death of her husband, since she has a remedy over, and this seems to be the better law.

† Co. Litt. 53.

‡ 4 Bac. Abr. 649; Noy's Max. 19.

§ 1 Harr. Chan. Prac. 5.

not: and when the plaintiff, by reason of such an injunction, ceaseth to ask any farther process, the judges will in
like wise cease to make any farther process in that behalf.*

Doct. Is there any mention made in the law of England
of any such equities?

Stud. Of this term *equity*, to the intent that is spoken of
here, there is no mention made in the law of England : but
of an equity derived upon certain statutes mention is made
many times, and often in the law of England;† but that
equity is all of another effect than this. But of the effect
of this equity that we now speak of, mention is made many
times : for it is ofttimes argued in the law of England,
where a *subpœna* lieth, and where not, and daily bills be
made by men learned in the law of this realm to have *subpœnas.* And it is not prohibited by the law, but that they
may well do it, so that they make them not but in case
where they ought to be made, and not for vexation of the
party, but according to the truth of the matter. And the
law will in many cases, that there shall be such remedy in
the *chancery* upon divers things grounded upon such equities, and then the lord chancellor must order his conscience
after the rules and grounds of the law of the realm ; insomuch that it had not been inconvenient to have assigned
such remedy in the *chancery* upon such equities for the
seventh ground of the law of England. But forasmuch as
no record remaineth in the king's court of no such bill, ne
of the writ of *subpœna* or *injunction* that is used thereupon ;
therefore it is not set as for a special ground of the law,
but as a thing that is suffered by the law.

Doct. Then sith the parties ought of right in many cases
to be holpen in the *chancery* upon such equities ; it seemeth
that if it were ordained by statute, that there should be no
remedy upon such equities in the *chancery*, nor in none
other place, but that every matter should be ordained only

---

* 1 Harr. Chan. Prac. 212, 213.
† 4 New Abr. 649.

4

by the rules and grounds of the common law, that the statute were against right and conscience.

Stud. I think the same : but I suppose there is no such statute.

Doct. There is a statute of that effect, as I have heard say, wherein I would gladly hear thy opinion.

Stud. Shew me that statute, and I shall with good-will say as me thinketh therein.

CHAP. XVIII.—*Whether the statute hereafter rehearsed by the doctor be against conscience, or not.*

There is a statute made the fourth year of king Henry IV, cap. 22, whereby it is enacted, That judgment given by the king's courts shall not be examined in the *chancery, parliament,* nor elsewhere ; by which statute it appeareth, that if any judgment be given in the king's courts against an equity, or against any matter of conscience, that there can be had no remedy by that equity, for the judgment cannot be reformed without examination, and the examination is by the said statute prohibited : wherefore it seemeth that the said statute is against conscience. What is thine opinion therein?

Stud. If judgment given in the king's courts should be examined in the *chancery* before the king's council, or any other place, the plaintiffs or demandants should seldom come to the effect of their suit, ne the law should never have end. And therefore to eschew that inconvenience that statute was made. And though peradventure by reason of that statute some singular person may happen to have loss; nevertheless the said statute is very necessary, to eschew many great vexations and unjust expences that would else come to many plaintiffs that have right wisely recovered in the king's courts. And it is much more provided for in the law of England, that hurt nor damages should not come to many, than only to one. And also the said statute doth not prohibit equity,* but it prohibiteth only the examination of the judgment, for the eschewing of the inconvenience before rehearsed.† And it seemeth that the said statute standeth with good conscience. And in many other cases where a man doth wrong, yet he shall not be compelled by way of compulsion to reform it; for many times it must be left to the conscience of the party, whether he shall redress it or not. And in such case he is in conscience as well bound to redress it, if he will save his soul, as he were if he were compellable thereto by the law; as it may appear in divers cases, that may be put upon the same ground.

Doct. I pray thee put some of these cases for an example.

Stud. If the defendant wage his law in an action of debt brought upon a true debt, the plaintiff hath no means to come to his debt by way of compulsion, neither by *subpœna*, nor otherwise; and yet the defendant is bound in conscience to pay him. Also if the grand jury in attaint‡ affirm a false verdict given by the petty jury, there is no farther remedy but the conscience of the party. Also where there can be had no sufficient proof, there can be no remedy in the *chancery*, no more than there may be in the spiritual court. And because thou hast given an occasion to speak of conscience, I would gladly hear thy opinion, where conscience shall be ruled after the law, and where the law shall be ruled after conscience.

---

* That is, it does not extend to hinder the chancery from administering relief in cases where judgments at common law are obtained through fraud and false suggestions. That court, notwithstanding the statute, may prevent such judgments being put into execution. 3 P. Wms. 148. 'T is a power which seems necessarily inherent in the very constitution of a court of equity, and therefore one cannot help thinking Sir Edward Coke much to blame in the attempt he made in the time of Lord Ellesmere, to rob the chancery of this part of its jurisdiction. See 2 Whitlock of Parl. 390; 1 · Chan. Rep. Append. 11.

† Hetley, 20; Hard. 23.

‡ For the nature of an attaint, and how far it is in use at this day, see 3 B. C., cap. 25, p. 402.

Doct. And of that matter I would likewise gladly hear
thy opinion, specially in cases grounded upon the laws of
England, for I have not heard but little thereof in time past:
but before thou put any case thereof, I would that thou
wouldest shew me how these two questions after thy opinion
are to be understood.

CHAP. XIX.—*Of what law this question is to be understood, that is to say where conscience shall be ruled after
the law.*

The law whereof mention is made in this question, that
is to say, where conscience shall be ruled by the law, is
not, as me seemeth, to be understood only of the law of
reason, and of the law of God, but also of the law of man,
that is not contrary to the law of reason, nor the law of God,
but it is superadded unto them for the better ordering of the
commonwealth : for such a law of man is always to be set
as a rule in conscience, so that it is not lawful for a man to
frame it on the one side, ne on the other : for such a law
of man hath not only the strength of man's law, but also
the law of reason, or of the law of God, whereof it is derived. For laws made by men, which have received of
God power to make laws, be made by God. And therefore conscience must be ordered by the law, as it must be
upon the law of God and upon the law of reason. And
furthermore, the law whereof mention is made in the latter
end of the chapter next before, that is to say, in the question
wherein it is asked where the law is to be left and forsaken
for conscience, is not to be understood of the law of reason,
nor of the law of God; for those two laws may not be left.
Nor is it not to be understood of the law of man that is
made in particular cases, and that is consonant to the law
of reason, and to the law of God, that yet that law should
be left for conscience : for of such a law made by man, conscience must be ruled, as it is said before. Nor it is not to
be understood of a law made by man commanding or pro-
hibiting any thing to be done that is against the law of

reason or the law of God. For if any law made by him, bind any person to any thing that is against the said laws, it is no law, but a corruption, and manifest error. Therefore, after them that be learned in the laws of England, the said question, that is to say, where the law is to be left for conscience, and where not, is to be understood in divers manners, and after divers rules, as hereafter shall somewhat be touched.

First, Many unlearned persons believe that it is lawful for them to do with good conscience all things, which if they do them, they shall not be punished therefore by the law, though the law doth not warrant them to do that they do, but only, when it is done, doth not for some reasonable consideration punish them that do it, but leaveth it only to his conscience. And therefore many persons do ofttimes that they should not, and keep as their own that that in conscience they ought to restore. Wherefore there is the law of England in this case.

If two men have a wood jointly, and the one of them selleth the wood, and keepeth all the money wholly to himself;* in this case his fellow shall have no remedy against him by law :† for as they, when they took the wood jointly, put each other in trust, and were content to occupy together : so the law suffereth them to order the profits thereof according to the trust that each of them put the other in. And yet if one took all the profits, he is bound in conscience to restore the half to his fellow : for, as the law giveth him right only to half the land, so it giveth him right only in conscience to half the profits. And yet nevertheless, it cannot be said in that case, that the law is against conscience, for the law never willeth, ne commandeth that one should take all the profits, but leaveth it to their conscience ; so that no default can be found in the law, but in him that

---

*Co. Litt. 187; 1 Cro. 803.

† This is now altered by stat. 4 and 5 Ann., c.16, by which it is provided, that joint tenants, and tenants in common, and their executors and administrators, shall have an account against the others, as bailiffs for receiving more than their proportion, and against their executors and administrators.

taketh all the profits to himself may be assigned default, who is bound in conscience to reform it, if he will save his soul, though he cannot be compelled thereto by the law. And therefore in this case, and other like, that opinion which some have, that they may do with conscience all that they shall not be punished for by the law if they do it, it is to be left for conscience; but the law is not to be left for conscience.

Also many men think, that if a man have land that another hath title to, if he that hath the right shall not, by the action that is given him by the law to recover his right by, recover damages, that then he that hath the land is also discharged of damages in conscience; and that is a great error in conscience; for though he cannot be compelled to yield the damages by no man's law, yet he is compelled thereto by the law of reason, and by the law of God, whereby we be bound to *do as we would be done to*, and that we should *not covet our neighbour's goods*. And therefore if tenant in tail be disseised, and the disseisor dieth seised, and then the heir in the tail bringeth a *formedon*,* and recovereth the land, and no damages, for the law giveth him no damage in that case;† yet the tenant by conscience is bound to yield damages to the heir in tail from the death of his ancestor. Also it is taken by some men, that the law must be left for conscience, where the law doth not suffer a man to deny that he hath before affirmed in court of record, or for that he hath wilfully excluded himself thereof for some other cause: as if the daughter that is only heir to her father will sue livery with her sister that is a bastard, in that case he shall not be received to say that her sister is a bastard;‡ insomuch that if her sister take half the land with her, there is no remedy against her by

---

* The writ of formedon is now seldom brought, it being an easier method to try titles by *objectione firmæ*.

† 2 Danv. Abr. 455, 456.

‡ Co. Litt. 170.

the law.* And no more there is of diversity in other es-
topples, which were too long to rehearse now. And yet
the party that may take advantage by such an estopple, by
the law, is bound in conscience to forsake that advantage,
especially if he were so estopped by ignorance, and not by
his own knowledge and assent. For though the law in
such cases giveth no remedy to him that is estopped, yet
the law judgeth not that the other hath right unto the thing
that is in variance betwixt them.

And it is to be understood, that the law is to be left for
conscience, where a thing is tried and found by verdict
against the truth; for in the common law the judgment
must be given according as it is pleaded and tried, like as
it is in other laws, that the judgment must be given according to that that is pleaded and proved. And it is to be understood, that the law is to be left for conscience, where the
cause of the law doth cease : for when the cause of the law
doth cease, the law also doth cease in conscience, as appeareth by this case hereafter following.†

A man maketh a lease for term of life, and after a
stranger doth waste; wherefore the lessee bringeth an action of trespass, and hath judgment to recover damages,
having regard to the treble damages that he shall yield to
him in the reversion : and after he in the reversion, before
action of waste sued, dieth, so that the action of waste is
thereby extincted : then the tenant for term of life, though
he may sue execution of the said judgment by the law, yet
he may do it by conscience ; for in conscience he may take
no more than he is hurted by the said trespass, because he
is not charged over with treble damages to his lessor. Also
it is to be understood, where a law is grounded upon a presumption, if the presumption be untrue, then the law is not
to be holden in conscience. And now I have shewed thee
somewhat of the question, that is to say, where the law shall

---

* But this kind of estoppel will not bind in chancery. Cary's Rep. 26;
Pollexfen, 67.
† Noy's Max. 2.

be ruled after conscience, I pray thee shew me whether there be not like diversities in other laws, betwixt law and conscience.

Doct. Yes, verily, very many, whereof thou hast recited one before, where a thing that is untrue is pleaded and proved; in which case judgment must be given according, as well in the law civil as in the law canon. And another case is, that if the heir make not his inventory, he shall be bound after the law civil to all the debts, though the goods amount not to so much : and the law canon is not against that law, and yet in conscience, the heir, which in the laws of England is called an executor, is not in that case charged with the debts, but according to the value of the goods. And now I pray thee shew me some cases where conscience shall be ruled after law.

Stud. I will with good-will shew thee somewhat as methinketh therein.

CHAP. XX.—*Here follow divers cases where conscience is to be ordered after the law.*

The eldest son shall have and enjoy his father's lands at the common law in conscience, as he shall in the law.[*] And in Burgh-english [†] the younger son shall enjoy the inheritance, and that in conscience. And in Gavelkind[‡] all the sons shall inherit the land together, as daughters, at the common law;[§] and that in conscience. And there can be no other cause assigned why conscience in the first case is with the eldest brother, and in the second with the younger brother, and in the third case with all the breth-

---

[*] 2 B. C. 214.

[†] Ante, 35.

[‡] Ante, 34.

[§] See statute 31 H. 8, c. 3, whereby divers lands in the county of Kent are disgavelled and directed to descend in future like other lands; and Mr. Robinson, in his book on Gavelkind, 79, mentions six other statutes for disgavelling particular lands in Kent, though the statute 31 H. 8, is the only one in print.

ren; but because the law of England, by reason of divers customs, doth sometime give the land wholly to the eldest son, sometime to the youngest, and sometime to all. Also if a man of his mere motion make a feoffment of two acres of land lying in two several shires, and maketh livery of seisin in the one acre in the name of both; in this case the feoffee hath right but only in the acre whereof livery of seisin was made, because he hath no title by the law: but if both acres had been in one shire, he had had good right to both.* And in these cases the diversity of the law maketh the diversity of conscience.

Also, if a man of his mere motion make a feoffment of a manor, and saith not, *to have and to hold*, etc., with the appurtenances; in that case the feoffee hath right to the demesne lands, and to the rents, if there be atturnments, and to the common pertaining to the manor;† but he hath neither right to the advowsons, appendant, if any be, nor to the villeins regardant.‡ But if this term, with the appurtenances, had been in the deed, the feoffee had right in conscience, as well to the advowsons and villeins, as to the residue of the manor. But if the king, of his mere motion, give a manor with the appurtenances, yet the donee hath· neither right in law nor conscience to the advowsons nor villeins.§ And the diversity of the law, in these cases, makes the diversity of conscience.

Also, if a man make a lease for a term of years, yielding to him and to his heirs a certain rent, upon condition that if the rent be behind by forty days, etc., that then it

---

* And yet if the scite of the manor of Dale is in the county of Essex, and parcel of the same manor extends into the county of Middlesex, and a feoffment is made of the manor of Dale, and livery of seisin is made of the scite of the manor which lies in the county of Essex by this livery of seisin, the parcel of the manor which lies in Middlesex shall pass, because, says Perkins, it is parcel of the thing, viz: the manor of which the feoffment is made. Perk., sec. 227.

† 1 Co. 1S.

‡ But by the better opinion it seems they pass as incidents without the words with the appurtenances. Co. Litt. 121; 2 B. C. 22, 23; Shep. Touch. 186.

§ Wood's Inst. 153.

shall be lawful to the lessor and his heirs to re-enter ;* and after the rent is behind, the lessor asketh the rent according to the law, and it is not payed, the lessor dieth, his heir entereth ; in this case his entry is lawful both in law and conscience. But if the lessor had died before he had demanded the rent, and his heir demand the rent, and because it is not payed, he re-entereth ; in that case his re-entry is not lawful neither in law nor conscience.

Also, if the tenant in dower sow her land, and die before the corn is ripe ;† the corn in conscience belongeth to her executors, and not to him in reversion : but otherwise it is in conscience of grass and fruits. And the diversity of the law maketh there also the diversity in conscience. ·

Also, if a man seized of lands in his demesne as of fee bequeath the same by his last will to another, and to his heirs, and dieth ;‡ in this case the heir, notwithstanding the will, hath a right to the land in conscience. And the reason is, because the law judgeth that will to be void ;§ and as it is void in the law, so it is void in conscience.

---

* Shep. Touch. 147.

† 2 Inst. 80, 81.

·‡ Ante, 23.

§ Before the conquest, it is generally thought lands and tenements were devisable; but at that period, or soon after, probably in the reign of H. 2, the power of disposition ceased by consequence of the feudal tenure, except of socage lands, which in some cities and boroughs remained devisable, it being of very small consequence into whose power such tenures fell. But though the general rule of law was, that a man could not make a will of his lands, yet he might dispose of the use and profits to whom he pleased, for there was a clear distinction between the one and the other. Wright's Tenures, 172. A man might have made a feoffment of his property to another person, properly called the feoffee, to the use of the feoffor and his heirs. By this conveyance the whole legal estate was vested in the feoffee, and the feoffor had nothing, and could dispose of nothing but the mere simple usufructuary interest arising from the confidence and trust reposed in the feoffee. 4 Burn's Ecc. Law, 57; ante, 23.

Thus the land and the use were distinct, and the feoffor being, as we have seen, hindered from devising the one, he continued to dispose of the other till the twenty-seventh year of the reign of H. 8, when a statute was made, commonly called the statute of uses, which put a stop to the practice of devising uses by joining the possession and the use together in the feoffor.

Another statute was likewise made in the 34th and 35th of the same

Also, if a man grant a rent for term of life, and make a lease of land to the same grantee for term of life, and the tenant alieneth both in fee; in this case he in the reversion hath good title to the land both in law and conscience, and not to the rent. And the reason is, because the land by the alienation is forfeited by the law to him in the reversion, and not the rent.*

Also, if lands be given to two men, and to a woman in fee, and after one of the men enter-marrieth with the woman, and alieneth the land, and dieth; in this case the woman hath right but only to the third part: but if the man and the woman had been married together before the first feoff- ment, then the woman, notwithstanding the alienation of her husband, should have had right in law and conscience to the one half of the land.† And so in these two cases conscience doth follow the law of the realm. Also, if a man have two sons, one before espousals, and another after espousals, and after the father dieth seised of certain lands; in this case the younger son shall enjoy the lands in this realm, as heir to his father both in law and conscience. And the cause is, because that son born after espousals is by the law of this realm the very heir, and the elder son is a bastard.‡ And of these cases, and many other like in the laws of England, may be formed the *syllogism* of con- science, or the true judgment of conscience, in this man- ner. *Sinderesis* ministreth the major thus, Right wiseness is to be done to every man: upon which major the law of England ministereth the minor thus, The inheritance be- longeth to the son born after espousals, and not to the son

---

king's reign, which gave a testamentary power over lands subject only to certain conditions and restrictions with regard to the devising of lands holden by knight's service.

These restrictions were afterward taken away by statute 12 C. 2, c. 24, which abolished all tenures by knight's service; and now a man may dis- pose of his freehold lands at his free-will and pleasure. See stat. 29 Car. 2, c. 3.

* Wood's Con. 84; Roll. Abr. 854.

† Litt., sec. 291.

‡ 2 Inst. 96, 97; 2 B. C. 247.

born before espousals : then conscience maketh the conclusion, and saith, Therefore the inheritance is in conscience
to · be given to the son born after espousals. And so in
other cases infinite may be formed by the law, the syllogism
or the right judgment of conscience, wherefore they that be
learned in the law of the realm say, that in every case
where any law is ordained for the disposition of lands and
goods, which is not against the law of God, nor yet against
the law of reason, that the law bindeth all them that be under the law in the court of conscience, that is to say, in-
wardly in his soul. And therefore it is somewhat to marvel, that spiritual men have not endeavored themselves in
time past to have more knowledge of the king's laws than
they have done, or than they yet do : for by the ignorance
thereof they be ofttimes ignorant of that that should order
them according to right and justice, as well concerning
themselves, as other that come to them for counsel. And
now, forasmuch as I have answered to thy questions as well
as I can ; I pray thee that thou wilt shew me thy opinion
in divers cases formed upon the law of England, wherein
I am in doubt what is to be holden therein in conscience.

Doct. Shew me thy questions, and I will say as me
thinketh therein.

CHAP. XXI.—*The first question of the student.*

Stud. If any infant that is of the age of twenty years, and
hath reason and wisdom to govern himself, selleth his land,
and with the money thereof buyeth other land of greater value
than the first was, and taketh the profits thereof; whether
may the infant ask his first land again in conscience, as he
may by the law.

Doct. What thinkest thou in that question?

Stud. Me seemeth, that, forasmuch as the law of England* in this article is grounded upon a presumption, that is
to say, that infants commonly afore they be of the age of

---

* 3 New Abr. 128.

twenty-one years be not able to govern themselves, that yet, forasmuch as that presumption faileth in this infant, that he may not in this case with conscience ask the land again that he hath sold to his great advantage, as before appeareth.

Doct. Is not this sale of the infant, and the feoffment made thereupon, if any where, voidable in the law?

Stud. Yes, verily.

Doct. And if the feoffee have no right by the bargain,* nor by the feoffment made thereupon, whereby should he then have right thereto, as thou thinkest?

Stud. By conscience, as me thinketh, for the reason that I have made before.

Doct. And upon what law should that conscience be grounded that thou speakest of? for it cannot be grounded by the law of the realm, as thou hast said thyself. And methinketh, that it cannot be grounded upon the law of God, nor upon the law of reason: for feoffments nor contracts be not grounded upon neither of those laws, but upon the law of man.

Stud. After the law of property was ordained, the people might not conveniently live together without contracts; and therefore it seemeth that contracts be grounded upon the law of reason, or at least upon the law that is called *Jus gentium.*

Doct. Though contracts be grounded upon the law that is called *Jus gentium,* because they be so necessary, and so general among all people; yet that proveth not that contracts be grounded upon the law of reason :† for though the law called *Jus gentium* be much necessary for the people, yet it may be changed. And therefore if it were ordained by statute, that there should be no sale of land, ne no contract of goods, and if there were, that it should be void, so that every man should continue still seized of his lands, and possessed of his goods ; the statute were good.

---

* Litt., sec. 259; 2 Roll. Abr. 2.
† Post. 174.

And then if a man against that statute sold his land for a sum of money, yet the seller might lawfully retain his land according to the statute: and then he were bound to no more but to repay the money that he received, with reasonable expences in that behalf. And so in like wise me thinketh that in this case the infant may with good conscience re-enter into his first land; because the contract after the maxims of the law of the realm is void; for, as I have heard, the maxims of the law be of as great strength in the law as statutes. And some think that in this case the infant is bound to no more, but only to re-pay the money to him that he sold his land unto, with such reasonable cost and charges as he hath sustained by reason of the same. But if a man sell his land by a sufficient and lawful contract, though there lack livery of seisin or such other solemnities of the law, yet the seller is bound in conscience to perform the contract.* But in this case the contract is sufficient, and so me thinketh great diversity betwixt the cases.

Stud. For this time I hold me contented with thy opinion.

CHAP. XXII.—*The second question of the student.*

If a man that hath lands for term of life be impanelled upon an inquest, and thereupon leeseth issues and dieth;† whether may those issues be levied upon him in the reversion in conscience, as they may be by the law?

Doct. If they may be levied by the law, what is the cause why thou dost doubt whether they may be levied by conscience?

Stud. For there is a maxim in the laws of England,‡ that where two titles run together, the eldest title shall be preferred. And in this case the title of him in the reversion is before the title of the forfeiture of the issues. And

* See where, and in what cases, a court of equity will supply the want of livery and seisin in Vin. Abr., title Feoffment, 205.
† Noy's Max. 30.
‡ Ante, 32; Noy's Max. 15.

therefore I doubt somewhat whether they may be lawfully levied.

Doct. By that reason it seemeth thou art in doubt what the law is in this case; but that must necessarily be known, for else it were in vain to argue what conscience will therein.

Stud. It is certain that the law is such; and so it is like wise if the husband forfeit issues, and die, those issues shall be levied on the lands of the wife.*

Doct. And if the law be such, it seemeth that conscience is so in like wise: for sith it is the law, that for execution of justice every man shall be impanelled when need requireth; it seemeth reasonable, that if he will not appear, that he should have some punishment for his not appearance, for else the law should be clearly frustrate in that point. And the pain, as I have heard, is, that he shall lose issues to the king for his not appearance. Wherefore it seemeth not inconvenient, nor against conscience, though the law be, that those issues shall be levied of him in the reversion, for that the condition was secretly understood in the law to pass with the lease, when the lease was made. And therefore it is for the lessor to beware, and to prevent the danger at the making of the lease, or else it shall be adjudged his own default. And then this particular maxim, whereby such issues shall be levied upon him in the reversion, is a particular exception in the law of England, from the general maxim that thou hast remembered before, that is to say, that where two titles run together, that the eldest title shall be preferred;† and so in this case the general maxim in the point shall hold no place, neither in law nor in conscience, for by this particular maxim the strength of the general maxim is restrained to every intent, that is to say, as well in law as in conscience.

---

* Noy's Max. 30.
† Ante, 32.

CHAP. XXIII.—*The third question of the student.*

Stud. If a tenant for term of life, or for term of years, do waste, whereby they be bound by the laws to yield to him in the reversion treble damages, and so shall forfeit the place wasted :* whether he is also bound in conscience to pay those damages, and to restore that place wasted immediately after the waste done, as he is in the single damages, or that he is not bound thereto till the treble damages and place wasted be recovered in the king's court.

Doct. Before judgment given in the treble damages, and of the place wasted, he is not bound in conscience to pay them, for it is uncertain what he should pay : but it sufficeth that he be ready till judgment be given to yield damages according to the value of the waste ; but after the judgment given, he is bound in conscience to yield the treble damages, and also the place wasted. And the same law is in all statutes penal, that is to say, that no man is bound in conscience to pay the penalty till it be recovered by the law.†

Stud. Whether may he that hath offended against such a statute penal, defend the action, and hinder the judgment, to the intent he would not pay the penalty, but only single damages?

Doct. If the action be taken right wisely according to the statute, and upon a just cause, the defendant may in no wise defend the action, unless he have a true dilatory matter to plead, which should be hurtful to him if he pleaded not, though he be not bound to pay the penalty till it be recovered.

CHAP. XXIV.—*The fourth question of the student.*

Stud. If a man enfeoff other in certain land upon condition, that if he enfeoff any other, that it may be lawful for the feoffor and his heirs to re-enter, etc., whether is this condition good in conscience, though it be void in the law?

---

* 2 Inst. 146.
† Post. 71.

Doct. What is the cause why this condition is void in law?

Stud. The cause is this, by the law it is incident to every state of fee-simple, that he that hath the estate may lawfully by the law, and by the gift of the feoffor, make a feoffment thereof:* and then when the feoffor restraineth him after that he shall make no feoffment to no man against his own former grant, and also against the purity of the state of a fee-simple, the law judgeth the condition to be void :† but if the condition had been, that he should not have infeoffed such a man or such a man, that condition had been good, for yet he might infeoff other.‡

Doct. Though the said condition be against the effect of the state of a fee-simple, and also against the law; nevertheless it is not against the intent that the parties agreed upon, and that at the time of the livery. And forasmuch as the intent of the parties was, that if the feoffee infeoffed any man of the land, that the feoffor should enter, and to that intent the feoffee took the state, and after brake the intent: it seemeth that the land in conscience should return to the feoffor.

Stud. The intent of the parties in the laws of England is void in many cases :§ that is to say, if he be not ordered according to the law. And if a man of his mere motion, without any recompence, intending to give lands to another and to his heirs, make a deed unto him, whereby he giveth him those lands, to have and to hold to him for ever, intending that by the words *for ever* the feoffee should have the land to him and to his heirs ;‖ in this case his intent is void, and the other shall have the land only for term of life. Also, if a man give lands to another, and to his heirs for term of twenty years, intending that if the lessee die within

---

* Shep. Touch. 126; post. 84; 2 B. C. 147.
  † The law is the same in a devise in fee, upon condition that the devisee shall not alien. Co. Litt. 223.
  ‡ Vin. Abr., title Con. 103.
  § 2 Vez. 248.
  ‖ Litt., sec. 1.

5

the term, that then his heirs should enjoy the land during the term;* in this case his intent is void, for by the law of the realm all chattels real and personal shall go to the executors, and not to the heir. Also, if a man give lands to a man and to his wife, and to a third person, intending that every of them should take the third part of the land as three common persons should, his intent is void; for the husband and the wife, as one person in the law, shall take only the one half, and the third person the other half. But these cases be always to be understood where the said estates be made without any recompence. And forasmuch as in this principal case the intent of the feoffor is grounded against the law, and that there is no recompence appointed for the feoffment, methinketh that the feoffor hath neither right to the land by law nor conscience: for if he should have it by conscience, that conscience should be grounded upon the law of reason; and that it cannot, for conditions be not grounded upon the law of reason, but upon the maxims and customs of the realm; and therefore it might be ordained by statute, that all conditions made upon land should be void. And when a condition is void by the maxims of the law, it is as fully void to every intent, as if it were made void by statute: and so methinketh that in this case the feoffor hath no right to the land in law nor in conscience.

Doct. I am content thy opinion stand, till we shall have hereafter a better leisure to speak farther in this matter.

CHAP. XXV.—*The fifth question of the student.*

Stud. If a fine with proclamation be levied according to the statute,† and no claim made within five years, etc.,‡

* Godolph. 120; Off. of Exor. 53; 1 Vent. 161; Bac. El. 43.
† That is the statute 4 H. 7, c. 24, by which the common law, which gave only a year and a day to strangers, to make their claim, is altered. See likewise the statute 32 H. 8, c. 36, and 4 Ann., c. 16, s. 16. By the last mentioned act no claim or entry to avoid a fine with proclamation, shall be sufficient, unless an action is commenced within one year after such entry or claim, and prosecuted with effect; and this entry must, it seems, be an actual entry. 3 Burr. 1897; Doug. Rep. 468.
‡ Post. 110, 142; Bac. El. 51.

whether is the right of a stranger* extincted thereby in conscience, as it is in the law?

Doct. Upon what consideration was that statute made?

Stud. That the right of lands and tenements might be the more certainly known, and not to be so uncertain as they were before that statute.

Doct. And when any law of man is made for a commonwealth, or for the good peace and quietness of the people, or for any inconvenience or hurt to be saved from them, that law is good; though percase it extinct the right of a stranger, and must be kept in the court of conscience :† for, as it is said before in chap. 4, by laws right wisely made by man, it appeareth who hath right to the lands and goods : for whatsoever a man hath by such a law, he hath it right wisely ; and whatsoever he holdeth against such a law, he holdeth unrightwisely. And furthermore it is said there, all the laws made by man, which be not contrary to the law of God, must be observed and kept, and that in conscience, and he that despiseth them despiseth God, and he that resisteth them resisteth God. Also it is to be understood, that possessions and the right thereof are subject to the laws, so that they therefore with a cause reasonable may be translated and altered from one man to another by act of the law. And of this consideration that law is grounded, that by a contract made in fairs and markets the property is altered, except the property be to the king, so that the buyer pay toll, or do such other things as is accustomed there to be done upon such contracts, and that the buyer knoweth not the former property.‡ And in the law civil

---

* For the meaning and extent of the word " stranger," in this place, I must refer the reader to Shepherd's Touchstone of Assurances, 10 and 11, in which the different acceptations of the word as applied to fines are set down in regular order.

† Ante, 10.

‡ But there are many other exceptions to which the rule is liable; and as they are rather too numerous to fall conveniently within the compass of a note, I will direct the student to those authorities where he will find them enlarged upon. He may turn to 2 Black. Comm. 450, and 2 Inst. 713.

there is a like law, that if a man have another man's goods with a title three years, thinking that he hath right to it, he hath the very right unto the thing; and that was made for a law, to the intent that the property and right of things should not be uncertain, and that variance and strife should not be among the people.* And forasmuch as the said statute was ordained to give a certainty of title in the lands and tenements comprised in the fine, it seemeth that that fine extincteth the title of all other, as well in conscience, as it doth in the law. And sith I have answered to thy question, I pray thee let me know thy mind in one question concerning tailed lands, and then I will trouble thee no farther at this time.

CHAP. XXVI.—*A question made by the doctor, how certain recoveries that be used in the king's courts to defeat tailed land, may stand with conscience.*

I have heard say, that when a man that is seised of lands in the tail selleth the land, that it is commonly used, that he that buyeth the land, shall, for his surety, and for the avoiding of the tail in that behalf, cause some of his friends to recover the said lands against the said tenant in tail: which recovery, as I have been credibly informed, shall be had in this manner.† The demandants shall suppose in their writ and declaration, that the tenant had no entry but by such a stranger as the buyer shall list to name and appoint, where indeed the demandants never had possession thereof, nor yet the said stranger.‡ And thereupon the said tenant in tail shall appear in the court, and by assent of the parties shall vouch to warrant one that he knoweth well hath nothing to yield in value. And the vouchee shall appear, and the demandants shall declare against him; and thereupon he shall take a day to imparl at the same term,

---

* Wood's Civil Law, 167.
† Wood's Inst. 250; 2 B. C. 358.
‡ Cruise on Rec. 11, 12.

and at that day by assent and covin of the parties he shall make default; upon which default, because it is a default in despite of the court, the demandants shall have judgment to recover against the tenant in tail, and he over in value against the vouchee, and this judgment and recovery in value is taken for a bar of the tail for ever.* How may it therefore be taken, that the law standeth with conscience, that as it seemeth, alloweth and favoureth such feigned recoveries?

Stud. If the tenant in tail sell the land for a certain sum of money, as is agreed betwixt them, at such a price as is commonly used of other lands, and for the surety of the sale suffereth such a recovery as is aforesaid; what is the cause that moveth thee to doubt whether the said contract, or the recovery made thereupon, for the surety of the buyer that hath truly paid his money for the same, should stand with conscience? †

Doct. Two things cause me to doubt therein. One is, for that after our Lord had given the land of behest to Abraham and to his seed, that is to say, to his children, in possession alway to continue, he said to Moses, as it appeareth, Levit. 25, *The Land shall not be sold for ever, for it is mine:* and then our Lord assigned a certain manner how the land might be redeemed in the year of *Jubilee*, if it were sold before. And forasmuch as our Lord would that the land so given to Abraham, and his children, should not be sold for ever, it seemeth that he doth against the ensample of God that alieneth or selleth the land that is given to him and to his children, as lands entailed be given. Another cause is this: It appeareth by the commandment of God, that *Thou shalt not covet the house of thy neighbour*, etc. And if that concupiscence be prohibited, more stronger than the unlawful taking and withholding thereof is prohibited: and forasmuch as tailed land, when the ancestor is dead, is a thing that of right is belong-

---

* Piggot on Rec. 12.
† Wood's Inst. 250.

ing to his heir, for that he is heir according to the gift,
how may the land with right or conscience be holden from
him?

Stud. Notwithstanding the prohibition of Almighty God,
whereby the land that was given to Abraham, and to his
seed, might not be aliened for ever, yet land within walled
towns might lawfully be aliened for ever, except the lands
of the Levites, as appeareth in the said 25th chapter of
Leviticus. And so it appeareth, that the said prohibition
was not general for every place, and that among the Jews.
And it appeareth also, that it was given only to Abraham
and his children, and so it was not generally to all people.
And it appeareth also, that it extended not but only to the
land of promission, as it appeareth by the words of the said
chapter, where it is said thus, *All the region of our possession shall be sold under the condition of redeeming;*
whereby appeareth that lands in other countries be not
bound to that condition, and as they be not bound to that
condition, by the same reason it followeth that they be not
bound to the same succession. Therefore that said law,
that wills that the land given to Abraham, and to his
seed, shall not be sold for ever, bindeth no land out of
the land of promission; and some men will say, that
sithen the passion of our Lord was promulgate and known,
bindeth not there. And to the second reason, which is
grounded upon the commandment of God; it must needs
be granted that it is not lawful to any man unlawfully to
covet the house of his neighbour, and that then more
stronger he may not unlawfully take it from him. But
then it remaineth for thee yet to prove how in this case this
tailed land, that is sold by his ancestor, and whereof a recovery is had recorded in the king's court, may be said the
lands of the heir.

Doct. That may be proved by the law of the realm, that
is to say, by the statute of Westm. 2, cap. 1, where it is
said thus :* The will of the giver expressly contained in

---

* Wood's Inst. 250.

the deed of his gift shall be from henceforth observed, so
that they to whom the tenements be so given shall not have
power to alien, but that the lands after their death shall remain to the issue, or return to the donor, if the issue fail.*
By the which statute it appeareth† evidently, that though
they, to whom the tenements were so given, aliened them
away, that yet nevertheless they in law and conscience, by
reason of the said statute, ought to remain to their heirs,
according to the gift;‡ for it is holden commonly by all doctors, that the commandments and rules of the law of man,
or of a positive law that is lawfully made; bind all that be
subjects to the law according to the mind of the maker, and
that in the court of conscience.

Stud. Dost thou think that if a man offend against a
statute penal, that he offendeth in conscience? Admit that
he do it not of a wilful disobedience, or that he will not
obey the law : for if he do it of disobedience, I think he
offendeth.

Doct. If it be but only a statute that is called *Popular*,
it bindeth not in conscience to the payment of the penalty,
till it be recovered by the law, and then it doth bind in conscience : but if a statute be made principally to remedy the
hurt of one party, and for that hurt it giveth a penalty to
the party, in that case the offender of the statute is bound
immediately to restore the damages to the value of the hurt,
as it is upon the statute of waste ;§ but the penalty above
the hurt he is not bound to pay till judgment be given, as
it is said before. But statutes, by the which it is assigned
who shall have right or property to these lands and tenements,
or to these goods or chattels, if it be not against the law of
God nor against the law of reason, bind all them that be
subject to the law in law and conscience. And such a
statute is the statute of Westminster 2, whereof we have

---

* 2 Inst. 333.
† Post. 82.
‡ 2 Inst. 335.
§ Ante, 64.

treated before; wherefore it must be observed by conscience.

Stud. But some hold that the statute of Westm. 2 was
made of a singularity and presumption of· many that were
at the said parliament, for exalting and magnifying of their
own blood;* and therefore they say that that statute made
by such a presumption bindeth not in conscience.

Doct. It is very perilous to judge for certain that the
said statute was made of such presumption as thou speakest
of: for there be many considerations to prove that the said
statute was not made of such presumption, but rather of a
very good mind of all the parliament, or at the least of the
most part thereof, and for the commonwealth of all the
realm; and first in the king,† the which in the said parliament was the head, and most chief and principal part of
the parliament, (as he is in every parliament) cannot be
noted to be such intent: for it is not necessary, nor was it
not then in use, that lands of the crown should be entailed.
And in spiritual men, ne yet in certain burgesses and citizens of the said parliament, which at that time had no land,
there can be noted no such singularity; nor yet in the
noblemen and gentlemen, nor such other as were of the
said parliament, and had lands and tenements. It is not
good to judge in certain that they did it of such presumption; but it is good and expedient in this case, as it is in
other cases that be in doubt, to hold the surer way, and
that is, that it was made of charity, to the intent that he,
nor the heirs of him to whom the land was given, should
not fall into extreme poverty, and thereby haply run into
offence against God.‡ And though it were true, as they
say, that it was not made of charity, but of presumption
and singularity, as they speak of: nevertheless, forasmuch
as the statute is not against the law of God,§ nor against

* Lord Coke in particular is very severe in his animadversions upon this
act. Mildmay's Case, 6 Co. Rep. 40, 6, tho' in other places he seems to
commend it. Co. Litt. 19, 392.
† See section the second of this statute.
‡ 2 Inst. 334.
§ Post. 79.

the law of reason, it must be observed by all them that be subjects unto that law. For as John Gerson, in the treatise that he entitled in Latin, *De vita spirituali animæ*, the fourth lesson, and the third corollary, saith, that God wills that makers of laws judge only of outward things, and reserve secret things to him.' And so it appeareth. that man may not judge of the inward intent of the deed, but of such things as be apparent and certain: but it is not apparent that there was any such corrupt intent in the makers of the said statute: how may it therefore be said that the law is good or rightwise, that not only suffereth such things against the statute, but also against the commandment of God?

Stud. To that some answer and say, that when the land is sold, and a recovery is had thereupon in the king's court of record, that it sufficeth to bar the tail in conscience; for they say, that as the tail was first ordained by the law, so they say that by the law it is adnulled again.

Doct. Be thou thyself judge, if in that case there be like authority in the making of the tail as there is in the adnulling thereof: for it was ordained by authority of parliament,* the which is alway taken for the most high court in this realm before any other, and it is adnulled by a false supposal, for that, that they that be named demandants should have right to the land, where in truth they never had right thereto: whereupon followeth a false supposal in the writ, and a false supposal in the declaration, and a voucher to warrant by covin of such a person as hath nothing to yield in value ;† and thereupon by covin and collusion of the parties followeth the default of the vouchee, by the which default the judgment shall be given. And so all the judgment is derived and grounded of the untrue supposal and covin of the parties, whereby the law of the realm, that hath ordained such a writ of *entry* to help them that have rights to lands or tenements, is defrauded, the court is deceived,

---

* Co. Litt. 110; 4 Inst. 36.
† Piggot on Rec. 12. 19.

the heir is disherited, and, as it is to doubt, the buyer and the seller, their heirs and assigns, having knowledge of the tail, be bound to restitution. And verily I have heard many times, that after the law of the realm such recoveries should be no bar to the heir in the tail, if the law of the realm might be therein indifferently heard.

Stud. I cannot see but that after the law of the realm it is a bar of the tail ; for when the tenant in tail hath vouched to warranty, and the vouchee hath appeared and entered into the warranty, and after hath made default in despite of the court, whereupon judgment is given for the demandant against the tenant, and for the tenant that he shall recover in value against the vouchee ;* if the heir in the tail should after bring his *formedon*, and recover the lands entailed, and after the vouchee purchaseth lands, then should the heir also have execution against him to the value of the lands intailed, as heir to his ancestor that was tenant in the first action, and so he should have his own lands, and also the lands recovered in value. And therefore, because of the presumption that the vouchee may purchase lands after the judgment, some be of opinion that it is in the law a good bar of the tail.†

Doct. I suppose that in that case thou hast put that the vouchee may bar the heir in tail of his recovery in value, because he hath recovered the first lands. Nevertheless I will take a respite to be advised of that recovery in value. And if thou canst yet shew me any other consideration, why the said recoveries should stand with conscience, I pray thee let me hear thy conceit therein ;‡ for the multitude of the said recoveries is so great, that it were great pity that all should be bound to restitution that have lands by such recoveries, sith there is none (as far as I can hear) disposed them to restore.

Stud. Some men make another reason to prove that the

* 2 B. C. 360.
† Wood's Inst. 252.
‡ Post, 80.

said recoveries should be sufficient by the law to avoid the
statute of Westminster, and if they be sufficient thereto,
they be sufficient in conscience.

Doct. What is their reason therein?

Stud. In the seventh year of Henry VIII,* cap. 4,
among other things it is enacted, that all recoverers, their
heirs and assigns, may avow and justify for rents, services
and customs by them recovered, as they against whom
they recovered might have done. And then they say, that
when the parliament gavè to such recovérers authority to
avow and justify for such rents, customs, and services as
they recovered, that the intent of the parliament was, that
such recoverers should have right to that for the which they
should avow or justify : for else they say that it should be
in vain to give them such power, and that the parliament
should else be taken in manner as fortifiers of wrongful
titles : and so they say that such recoverers, by reason of
the said statute, have right by the law.

Doct. That statute, as it seemeth, was made only to give
to the recoverers a form to avow and justify, which they
had not before, though they had recovered upon a good
title. And the cause why they had no form to avow or justify before the said statute was, forasmuch as the recoverers
did not by the pretence of their action affirm the possession
of him or them against whom they recovered, nor claimed
not by them, but rather disaffirmed and destroyed their
estate. And therefore they cannot alledge any continuance
of their title by them, as they may that have rents or services,
or such other, of the grant of other by deed or by fine. And
therefore, as it seemeth, the most principal intent of the
statute was, that such recoverers should avow and justify
for rents, services and customs, as they should or might do
that had them by fine or deed ; not having any respect as
it seemeth whether they recovered against tenant in fee-
simple or in fee-tail ; nor whether the recoveries were had
upon a rightful title. And therefore, as me seemeth, the

* Piggot on Rec. 19.

said statute neither affirmeth nor disaffirmeth the title of recoverers, whereby they do avow: for if a man had right
before the recovery, the right should remain unto him notwithstanding the said statute; and so me seemeth that the
title of them that have the land entailed by such recoveries
is nothing fortified nor affirmed by the said statute, but that
they are in the same case as they were before. What
thinkest thou therein?

Stud. This matter is great; for, as thou sayest, there be
so many that have tailed lands by such recoveries, that it
were great pity and heaviness to condemn so many persons,
and to judge that they all were bound to restitution. For I
think there be but few in this realm that have lands of any
notable value, but that they or their ancestors, or some
other by whom they claim, have had part thereof by such
recoveries: insomuch that lords spiritual and temporal,
knights, 'squires, rich men and poor, monasteries, colleges
and hospitals have such land, for such recoveries have been
used of long time :* who may think therefore, without great
heaviness, that so many men should be bound to restitution,
and that yet, as thou sayest, no man disposeth him to make
restitution? And so I am in a manner perplexed, and wot
not what to say in this case, but that yet I trust that ignorance may excuse many persons in that behalf.

---

* The origin of common recoveries is a subject upon which there has
been a diversity of opinions. Some imagine that the æra of their commencement was in the reign of Edward the Third, and they adduce Octa-
vian Lombard's case, 44 Ed. 3, c. 21, in support of their opinion; whilst
others affirm that they were not introduced, nor so much as heard of before
Henry the VIII.'s time. Jenk. Cent. 250, pl. 4. Others again with more shew
of reason, and on better authority, suppose that common recoveries origi-
nated in Taltarun's case, in the 12th year of Edward the Fourth. Piggot on
Rec. 8. At that period, much distinguished for the wisdom of the prince
who sat upon the throne, it is probable that mankind, knowing that it
would be in vain to get the statute *de donis* repealed by any act of the legislature, on account of the great power of the barons, Cruise on Rec. 9, nat-
urally turned their attention to common recoveries, which being excepted
out of that statute, were found effectual to remedy the train of inconveniences which it had introduced. The judges have therefore invariably at-
forded them their countenance, and they are now become the common assurances of the kingdom.

Doct. Ignorance of the deed may excuse, but ignorance
of the law excuseth not,* but it be invincible, that is to say,
that they have done that in them is to know the truth :† as
to counsel with learned men, and to ask them what the law
is in that behalf; and if they answer them that they may
do this or that lawfully, then they be thereby excused in
conscience; but yet in man's law they be not thereby discharged : but they that have taken upon them to have
knowledge of the law, be not excused by ignorance of the
law; ne no more are they that have a wilful ignorance, and
that would rather be ignorant than to know the truth, and
therefore they will not dispose them to ask any counsel in
it.   And if it be of a thing that is against the law of God,
or the law of reason, no man shall be excused of ignorance; and so there be but few that be excused by ignorance.

Stud. What then?   Shall we condemn so many and so
notable men?

Doct. We shall not condemn them, but we shall give
them their peril.   -

Stud. Yet I trust their danger is not so great that they
should be bound to restitution : for John Gerson saith in his
said book called " De unitate ecclesiastica, consideratione
secunda," *Quod communis error facit jus,*‡ that is to say,
A common error maketh a right.   Of which words, as it
seemeth, some trust may be had, that though it were fully
admitted the said recoveries were first had upon an unlawful ground, and against the good order of conscience, that
yet nevertheless, forasmuch as they have been used of long
time, so that they have been taken of divers men that have
been right well learned, in manner as for a law, that the
buyers partly be excused, so that they be not bound to restitution.   And moreover, it is certain that the statute of
Westminster 2, nor none other statute made by man, cannot be of greater value or strength than was the bond of

---

* This was likewise a maxim of the Roman law. F. 22, C. 9.
† Douglas Rep. 471; post. 248.
‡ Shep. Touch. 39; Noy's Max. 27; Jenk. Cent. 250.

matrimony that was ordained ,of God. And though that
bond of matrimony was indissolvable, yet nevertheless
Moses suffered a bill of refusal of the Jews, which in Latin
is called *Libellum repudii*, and so they might thereby forsake their wives, as it appeareth Deut. 22. And therefore
like as a dispensation was suffered against that bond, so it
seemeth it may be against this statute.

Doct. As to that reason that thou hast last made of a bill
of refusal, let all purchasers of land hear what our Lord
saith in the Gospel of the Jews, of that bill of refusal;
Matthew 19, where he saith thus, *For the hardness of your
hearts Moses suffered you to leave your wives: for at the
beginning it was not so.* Of which words doctors hold
commonly, that though such a bill of refusal was lawful,
so that they that refused their wives thereby should be without pain in the law, that yet it was never lawful so that it
should be without sin. And so likewise it may be said in
this case, that such recoveries be suffered for the hardness
of the hearts of Englishmen, which desire land and possession with so great greediness, that they can not be with-
drawn from it neither by the law of God, nor of the realm.
And therefore the rich men should not take the possessions
of poor men from them by power, without colour of title,
that is to say, neither by open disseisin, or by the only sale
of the tenant in tail, and so to hold them against the express words of the statute; such recoveries have been suffered. And though for their great multitude they may
haply be without pain as to the law of the realm; yet it is
to fear that they be not without offence as against God.*
And as to the other reason, that a common error should
make a right, those words, as me seemeth, be to be thus
understood, that a custom used against the law of man shall
be taken in some countries for law, if the people be suffered so to continue. And yet some men`call such a cus-
tom an error, because that the continuance of that custom
against the law was partly an error in the people, for that

---

* Post. 80.

they would not obey the law that was made by their superiors to the contrary of that custom. But it is to be understood, that the said recoveries, though they have been long used, may not be taken to have the strength of a custom; for many, as well learned as unlearned, have always spoken against them and yet do.* And furthermore, as I have heard say, a custom or prescription in this realm against the statutes of the realm prevails not in the law.†

Stud. Though a custom in this realm prevaileth not against a statute as to the law, yet it seemeth that it may prevail against the statute in conscience: for though ignorance of a statute excuseth not in the law,‡ nevertheless it may excuse in conscience; and so it seemeth that it may do of a custom.

Doct. But if such recoveries cannot be brought into a lawful custom in the law, it seemeth they may not be brought into a custom in conscience; for conscience must alway be grounded upon the law, and in this case it cannot be grounded upon the law of reason, nor upon the law of God; and therefore if the law of man serve not, there is no ground whereupon conscience in this case may be grounded. And at the beginning of such recoveries, they were taken to be good, because the law should warrant them to be good, and not by reason of any custom : and so if the reason of the law will not serve in the recoveries, the custom cannot

---

* Cro. 347; Doug. 102; Cro. Car. 347.

† But a man may lawfully prescribe against a statute in the affirmative. Co. Lit. 115; 2 Buls. 36. And if a statute in the negative is declarative of the ancient law, that is in affirmance of the common law, there, a prescription may be alledged against it. As a man may prescribe to cut his own wood within a forest without the view of the forester, though the statute of 34 Edw. 1 provides that none shall cut any tree, though his own, within the forest, without the view of the forester; because this act is but in affirmance of the common law. Co. Lit. 115. So a man may prescribe to hold a leet oftener than twice a year, and that other days than are set forth in the statute of Magna Charta, cap. 35, because the statute, though in the negative, is still a confirmation of the ancient law. Cro. Eliz. 125. It therefore follows, that it is only against a statute which is introductive of a new law that a prescription can't be made.

‡ Ante, 46.

help; for an evil custom is to be put away. And therefore
me seemeth that the recoveries be not without offence
against God, though haply for their great multitude, and
that there should not be as it were a subversion of the inheritance of many in this realm, as well of spiritual as
.temporal, they be without pain in the law of the realm;*
except such recoveries as by the common course of the law
be voidable in the law by reason of some use, or of some
other special matter : but what pain that is, I will not tem-
'erously judge, but commit it to the goodness of our Lord,
whose judgment be very deep and profound : nor I will not
fully affirm that they that have lands by such recoveries
ought to be compelled to restitution : but this seemeth to
me to be good counsel, that every man hereafter hold that
is certain, and leave that is uncertain, and that is, that he
keep himself from such recoveries, and then he shall be
free from all scrupulousness of conscience in that behalf.

Stud. It seemeth that in this question thou ponderest
greatly the said statute of Westminster 2,† and that though
it be but only a law made by man, that yet, forasmuch as
it is not against the law of reason nor the law of God, thou
thinkest that it must be holden in conscience : and over that,
as it seemeth, thou art somewhat in doubt whether those
recoveries be any bar to the heir in the tail by the law of
the realm, unless that he have in value in deed upon the
vouchee;‡ and that thou wilt thereupon take a respite, or
thou shew thy full mind therein : and in likewise thou
thinkest, as I take it, that those recoveries cannot be brought
into a custom, but that the longer that they be suffered to
continue, if they be not good by the law, the greater is the
offence against God.§   And therefore thou ponderest little
that custom, but yet thou agreest that it is good to spare the
multitude of them that be past,‖ lest a subversion of the in-

---

* Ante, 78; post. 81.
† Ante, 72.
‡ Ante, 73.
§ Ante, 78.
‖ Ante, 74, 80.

heritance of many of this realm might follow, and great strife and variance also, if they should be adnulled for the time past, except there be any other special cause to avoid them by the law, as thou hast touched in the last reason :* but thou thinkest that it were good, that from henceforth such recoveries should be clearly prohibited, and not be suffered to be had in use, as they have been before; and thou counsellest all men therefore to refrain themselves from such recoveries hereafter.

Doct. Thou takest well that I have said, and according as I have meant it.

Stud. Now, I pray thee, sith I have heard thy question of these recoveries, according to thy desire, that thou wouldest answer me to some particular questions concerning tailed lands, whereof thou hast at this time given us occasion to speak.

Doct. Shew me these questions, and· I will shew thee my mind therein with good-will.

CHAP. XXVII.—*The first question of the student, concerning tailed lands.*

Stud. If a disseisor make a gift in tail to John at Stile, and John at Stile for the redeeming of the title of the disseisee agreeth with him, that he shall have a certain rent out of the same land to him and to his heirs, and for the surety of the rent it is devised that the disseisee shall release his right in the land, etc., and that such a recovery as we have spoken of before shall be had against the said John at Stile to the use of the payment of the said rent, and of the former tail: whether standeth that recovery well with conscience or not, as thou thinkest?

Doct. I suppose it doth, for it is made for the strength and surety of the tail, which the disseisee might have clearly defeated and avoided if he would: and therefore I think, if the said John at Stile had granted to the disseisee

* Piggot on Rec. 8.

6

only by his deed a certain rent for releasing of his title, that grant should have bound the heirs in the tail for ever. And then if the disseisee for his more surety, will have such a recovery, as before appeareth, it seemeth that recovery standeth with good conscience.

Stud. It seemeth that thy opinion is right good in this matter. And also it appeareth that with a reasonable cause some particular recoveries may stand both with law and conscience to bar a tail.

CHAP. XXVIII.—*The second question of the student, concerning tailed lands.*

If a tenant in tail suffer a recovery against him of his lands entailed, to the intent that the recoverer shall stand seised thereof to the use of a certain woman whom he intendeth to take to his wife, for term of life, and after to the use of the first tail, and after he marrieth the same woman : whether standeth that recovery with conscience, though other recoveries upon bargains and sales did not.

Doct. It seemeth yes; for though the statute be, that they to whom the tenements be so given should not have power to alien, but that the lands after their death should remain to their issues, or revert to the donors if the issues failed : yet if he to whom the lands were so given take a wife, and dieth seized without heir of his body, and the donor enter, the woman shall recover against him the third part, to hold in the name of her dowry for term of her life, though the tail be determined.* And the same law is of tenant by the courtesy, that is to say, of him that happeneth to marry one that is an inheritrix of the land entailed, and they have issue; the wife dieth, and the issue dieth ;† he shall have the lands for term of his life as tenant by the courtesy, notwithstanding the words of the statute, which say, that after the death of the tenant in tail without

* Litt., sec. 36, 53.
† Wood's Inst. 123.

issue, the lands shall revert to the donor;* and I think the cause is, because the intent of the statute shall not be taken that it intended to put away such titles as the law should give by reason of the tail; and so it seemeth that a like intent of the statute shall be so taken for jointures, for else the statute might be sometime a letting of matrimony, and it is not like that the statute intended so. And therefore it seemeth, that by the only deed of the tenant in tail a jointure may be made by the intent of the statute, though the words of the statute serve not expressly for it; for many times the intent of the letter shall be taken, and not the bare letter;† as it appeareth in the same statute, where it is said, that he to whom the lands be given shall have no power to alien; yet the same statute is construed, that neither he nor the heirs of his body shall have no power to alien: and so methinketh that such an intent shall be taken here for saving of jointures.

Stud. Truth it is, that sometime the intent of a statute shall be taken farther than the express letter stretcheth; but yet there may no intent be taken against the express words of the statute, for that should be rather an interpretation of the statute, than an exposition: and it cannot be reasonably taken, but that the intent of the makers of the said statute was, that the land should remain continually in the heirs of the tail, as long as the tail endureth; and there can no jointure be made neither by deed nor by recovery, but that the tail must thereby be discontinued. And therefore this case of jointure is not like to the said cases of tenant in dower, or tenant by the courtesy. For the title of dowry and of tenancy by the courtesy groweth most specially by the continuance of the possession in the heirs of the tail, but it is not so of jointures: and therefore by the only deed of the tenant in the tail, there may no jointures be lawfully made against the express words of the statute. And if there be any made by way of recovery,

---

* Ante, 70.

† 4 Bac. Abr. 643.

then it seemeth that it must be put under the same rule as other recoveries must be of lands entailed.

CHAP. XXIX.—*The third question of the student, concerning tailed lands.*

If John at Noke, being seised of land in fee, of his mere motion makes a feoffment of certain lands to the intent that the feoffees shall thereof make a gift to the said John at Noke, to have to him and to the heirs of his body, and they make the gift according; and after the said John at Noke falleth into debt, wherefore he is taken and put in prison, and thereupon for payment of his debts he selleth the same land, and for surety of the buyer he suffereth a recovery to be had against him in such a manner as before appeareth: whether standeth that recovery with conscience or not?

Doct. I would here make a little digression to ask thee another question, or that I make answer to thine; that is to say, to feel thy mind how the law by the which the body of the debtor shall be taken and cast into prison, there to remain till he have paid the debt, may stand with conscience, specially if he have nothing to pay it with; for as it seemeth if he will relinquish his goods, which in some laws is called in Latin, *Cedere bonis,* that he shall not be imprisoned; and that is to be understood most specially, if he be fallen into poverty, and not through his own default.*

Stud. There is no law in the realm that the defendant may in any case *Cedere bonis,* and, as me seemeth, if there were such a law, it should not be indifferent; for as to the knowledge of him that the money is owing to, the debtor might *Cedere bonis,* that is to say, relinquish his goods, and yet retain to himself secretly great riches. And therefore that law in such case seemeth more indifferent and righteous, that committeth such a debtor to the conscience of the plaintiff to whom the money is owing, than the com-

---

* The editor presumes that a reference is here made, principally to the imperial or civil law. Wood's Civil Law, 4th edition, p. 323.

mitting him to the conscience of him that is the debtor; for in the debtor some default may be assigned; but in him to whom the money is owing may be assigned no default.

Doct. But if he to whom the debt is owing knoweth that the debtor hath nothing to pay the debt with, and that he is fallen into poverty by some casualty, and not through his own default; doth the law of England hold that he may with good conscience keep the debtor still in prison till he be paid?

Stud. Nay verily, but it thinketh more reasonable to appoint the liberty and the judgment of conscience in that case to the debtee than to the debtor, for the cause before rehearsed. And then the debtee, if he knew the truth, is (as thou hast said) bound in conscience to let him go at liberty, though he be not compellable thereto by the law.* And therefore, admitting it for this time, that the law of England in this point is good and just, I pray thee that thou wilt make answer to my question.

Doct. I will with good-will: and therefore, as me seemeth, forasmuch as it appeareth that the said gift was made of the mere liberty and free-will of the said John at Noke, and without any recompence, that therefore it cannot be otherwise taken, but that the intent of the said John at Noke, as well at the time of the said feoffment, as at the time that he received again the said gift in the tail, was, that if he happened afterwards to fall into poverty, that he might alien the said land to relieve him with: for how may it be thought that a man will so much ponder the wealth of his heir, that he will forget himself? And so it seemeth, that not only the said recovery standeth with conscience, but also if he had made only a feoffment of the land, the feoffment should be in conscience a good bar of the tail: but if the said feoffment and gift had been made in consideration of any recompence of money, or for any matrimony, or such other, then the feoffment of the said

---

* See the statutes 18 Geo. 2, c. 13; 13 Geo. 2, c. 28; 1 Geo. 3, c. 17; 5 Geo. 3, c. 41, for the relief of insolvent debtors.

John at Noke should not bind his heir, and if he then
suffered any recovery thereof, then the recovery should be
of like effect as other recoveries whereof we have treated
before, and that which I said, it was good to favour rather
for their multitude, than for the conscience. And the
same law is, that if the son and the heir of the said John
at Noke, in case that the said gift was made without recompence, alien the land for poverty after the death of his
father; the recovery bindeth not but as other recoveries do.
For it cannot be thought that the intent of the father was,
that any of his heirs in tail should for any necessity disherit all other heirs in tail that should come after him, but
for himself, methinketh, it is reasonable to judge in such
manner as I have said before.

Stud. And though the intent of the said John at Noke,
when he made the said feoffment, and when he took again
the said gift in tail, were, that if he fell in need, that he
might alien : yet I suppose that he may not alien, though
percase for the more surety he declared his intent to be
such upon the livery of seisin : for that intent was contrary
to the gift that he freely took upon him ; and when any intent or condition is declared or reserved against the state
that any man maketh or excepteth, then such an intent or
condition is void by the law, as by a case that hereafter followeth will appear : that is to say, If a man make a feoffment in fee, upon condition that the feoffee shall not alien
to any man, that condition is void ;* for it is incident to
every state of the fee-simple, that he that is so seised
may alien. And like as in a fee-simple there is incident a power to alien, so in a state-tail, there is a secret
intent understood in the gift, that no alienation shall be
made.† And therefore though the intent of the said John
at Noke were, that if he fell into poverty, that he might
sell, and though he at the taking of the gift openly declared his intent to be so : yet the intent should be void by

---

* 2 B. C. 157; Co. Litt. 206; ante, 65.
† Post. 211.

the law, as me seemeth; and if it be void by the law, it is also void in conscience; and so the said recovery must be taken in this case to be of the same effect, as recoveries of other lands entailed be, and in no other manner.

CHAP. XXX.—*The fourth question of the student, concerning recoveries of inheritances entailed.*

Stud. If an annuity be granted to a man, to have and to perceive to the grantee, and to the heirs of his body, of the coffers of his grantor, and after the grantee suffereth a recovery against him in a writ of *Entry* by the name of a rent in Dale of a like sum as the annuity is of, with vouchers and judgment, after the common course, and both parties intend that the annuity shall be recovered: whether shall the recovery bind the heir in tail of his annuity?

Doct. What if it were a rent going out of land, of what effect should the recovery be then?

Stud. It should be then of like effect as if it were of land.*

Doct. And so it seemeth to be of this annuity; for, as me thinketh, a rent and annuity be of one effect; for the one of them shall be paid in ready money, as the other shall.

Stud. Truth, and yet there be many great diversities betwixt them in the law.

Doct. I pray you shew me some of these diversities.

Stud. Part I shall shew thee, but I wot not whether I can shew thee all. But first thou shalt understand, that one diversity is this: Every rent, be it rent-service, rent-charge, or rent-seck, is going out of land, but chargeth only the person, that is to say, the grantor, or his heirs that have assets.by discent, or the house, if it be granted by a house of religion to perceive of their coffers. Also of an annuity there lieth no action, but only a writ of *Annuity*,† against

---

* 1 Lec. 144; Pig. on Rec. 97; Sid. 285; Carter, 52.
† Co. Litt. 144; Finch. 161; 3 Cro. 171.

the grantor, his heirs or successors : and that a writ of *Annuity* lieth never against the pernor, but only against the grantor or his heirs. But of a rent the same action may lie as doth of land, as the case requireth : and it lieth sometime of rent against the pernor of the rent, that is to say, against him that taketh the rent wrongfully, and sometime against neither, as of a rent-service *Assise* may lie for the lord against the mesne and the disseisor, or sometime against the mesne only, if he did also the disseisin.* Also an annuity is never taken for assets, because it is no freehold in the law, ne it shall not be put in execution upon a statute-merchant, statute-staple, ne *Elegit*, as a rent may.† And because the said writ of *Entry* lay not in this case of this annuity,‡ and that it cannot be intended in the law to be the same annuity, though it be of like sum with the annuity, ne though the parties assented and meant to have the same annuity recovered by the said writ of *Entry;* therefore the said recovery is void in law and conscience. But if such a recovery be had of rent with the voucher over, then it shall be taken to be of like effect as recoveries of lands be, in such manner as we have treated of before.

CHAP. XXXI.—*The fifth question of the student, concerning tailed lands.*

If lands be given to a man and to his wife, in the name of her jointure, by the father of the husband, to have and to hold to them, and to the heirs of their two bodies begotten, and after they have issue, and the husband dieth, and

---

* Br. Assize, pl. 330.

† Br. Assets per Descent, pl. 26; Br. Execution, pl. 144; Co. Litt. 374.

‡ The reason is, because an annuity cannot be intailed, not being an inheritance within the statute *de donis*. In the case of the Earl of Stafford and Buckley, 2 Vez. 170, Lord Chief Justice Hardwicke held, that an annuity in fee granted by the crown out of the 4½ per cent. dut`es, payable for imports and exports at Barbadoes, was merely a personal inheritance, and not intailable. By a grant therefore of an annuity to the man and the heirs of his body, he has only a fee conditional at common law, and the true way to bar the heir is by a simple law conveyance, viz : by grant or release.

the wife alieneth the land,' and against the statute of 11 H. 7,* suffereth a recovery thereof to be had against her, to the use of the buyer, and after her son and heir apparent, that is heir to the tail, releaseth to the recoverers by fine, and dieth, having a brother alive, and after the mother dieth ; who hath right to the land, the buyer, or the brother of him that releaseth?

Doct. What is thine opinion therein? I pray thee shew me.

Stud. Me seemeth that the buyer hath.right; for by the said statute made in the 11th year of H. 7,† among other things it is enacted, that if any woman which hath lands of the gift of her husband, or of the gift of any of the ancestors of her husband, suffer any recovery thereof against her by covin, that then such recovery shall be void, and that it shall be lawful to him that should have the land after the death of the woman to enter, and it to hold as in his first right: provided alway that that statute shall not extend where he that should have the land after the death of the woman is agreeable to any such alienation or recovery, so that the agreement be of record.‡ And forasmuch as the heir in this case agreed to the said recovery and fine, which is one of the highest records in the law, it seemeth that the buyer hath right against that heir that agreed, and against all that shall be heir of the tail ; and that not only by the said recovery, but also by the said statute, whereby the said recovery, with assent of the heir is affirmed.

Doct. Though the buyer in this case have right during the life of 'the heir that released, yet nevertheless after his death his heir, as it seemeth, may lawfully enter : for the agreement whereof the statute speaketh, must, as I suppose, either be had before the recovery, or else at the time of the recovery. For if a title by reason of the said statute be once devolute to the heir in the tail, then the right,

* C. 20.
† Piggot on Rec. 77.
‡ 3 Rep. 58 : Cruise on Fines, 34.

as me seemeth, cannot be extinct, nor put away by the only
fine of the heir, no more than if he had died, and the next
heir to him had released to the buyer by fine, in which case
the release could not extinct the right of the title, nor the
right of entry that is given by the statute; and so, as me
seemeth, his next heir may therefore enter.

Stud. As I perceive, all thy doubt is in this case, because
the assent of the heir was after the recovery; for if it had
been at the time of the recovery, as if the heir had been
vouched to warrant in the same recovery, and he had entered, and thereupon the judgment had been given, thou
agreest well, that the recovery should have avoided the tail
for ever.

Doct. That is true, for it is in express words of the statute; but when the assent is after the recovery, then methinketh it is not so, ne that the right of the first tail, which
was revived by the said statute, shall not be extinct by his
fine, no more than it shall in other tail.

Stud. I will be advised upon thy opinion in this matter;
but yet one thing would I move farther upon this statute,
and that is this : Some say, that by this statute all other recoveries that have been had over beside these recoveries of
jointures be affirmed; for they say, that sith the parliament,
at the making of this statute, knew well that many other
recoveries were then used and had to defeat tails, that it
was like that they would so continue, which nevertheless
the parliament did not prohibit for the time to come, as it
did the said recoveries of jointures; that it is therefore to
suppose, that they thought that they should stand with law
and conscience : but because jointures were made rather
for the saving of the inheritance of the husband than to destroy the inheritance, they say that the parliament thought
and adjudged the alienations and recoveries of such jointures to be against the law and conscience, and not the alienations of other lands entailed; for if they had, they say
that the parliament would have avoided recoveries of tailed
lands generally, as well as it did of recoveries of jointures.

Doct. As to that opinion I will answer thee thus for this

time : That though that the makers of the said statute only put away recoveries of jointures, and not other recoveries ; that yet it cannot be taken therefore that their intent was that the other recoveries should stand good and perfect; for they spake then only of jointures, because there was no complaint made in the parliament at that time but against recoveries had of jointures, and therefore it seemeth that they intended nothing concerning other recoveries, but that they should be of the same effect as they were before, and no otherwise. And that will appear more plainly thus : Though the makers of the said statute intended to put away and annul such recoveries, as should be made of jointures after a certain day limited in the statute, that yet they intended not to avoid ne affirm such recoveries of jointures as were passed before that time ; and if they intended not to avoid ne affirm the recoveries had of jointures before that time, then how can it be taken that they intended to put away or affirm other recoveries that were passed before that time, and not of jointures, that would not affirm, ne put away recoveries passed of jointures before that time? And so, as it seemeth, they intended to spare the multitude of them that were passed of both, and not to comfort any to take them after that time.

Stud. I am content thy opinion stand for this time, and I will ask thee another question.

CHAP. XXXII.—*The sixth question of the student, concerning tailed lands.*

If tenant in tail be disseised, and die, and an ancestor collateral to the heir in tail release with a warranty, and die, and the warranty descendeth upon the heir in the tail ; whether is he thereby barred in conscience, as he is in the law ?*

Doct. Because your principal intent at this time is to speak of recoveries, and not of warranties, and also be-

---

* Post. 261; Viner's Abr., title Tayle, 165; 2 B. C. 303.

cause it hath been of long time taken for a principal maxim
of the law, that it should be a bar to the heirs as well that
claim by a fee-simple as by state-tail, and for that also that
it was not put away by the said stat. of Westm. 2,* which
ordained the tail; I will not at this time make thee an answer therein, but will take a respite to be advised.

Stud. Then, I pray thee, yet, or we depart, shew me
what was the most principal cause that moved thee to move
this question of recoveries had of tailed lands.

Doct. This moved me thereto : I have perceived many
times that there be many and divers opinions of these recoveries, whether they stand with conscience or not, and
that it is to doubt that many persons run into offence of conscience thereby ; and therefore I thought to feel thy mind
in them, whether I could perceive that it were clear that
they served to break the tail in law and conscience, or that
it were clearly against conscience so to break the tail, or
that it were a matter in doubt; and if it appeared a matter
in doubt, or that it appeared that the matter were used
clearly against conscience, then I thought to do somewhat
to make the matter appear as it is, to the intent that they
that have the rule and charge over the people, as well the
spiritual men as temporal men, should the rather endeavour
them to see it reformed, for the commonwealth of the people, as well in body as in soul.   For when anything is used
to the displeasure of God, it hurteth not only the body, but
also the soul : and temporal rulers have not only cure of
the bodies, but also of the souls, and shall answer for them
if they perish in their default.   And because it seemeth by
the more apparent reason that the tails be not broken, ne
fully avoided, by the said recoveries, and that yet nevertheless the great multitude of them that be passed is right
much to be pondered : therefore it were very good to prohibit them for time to come, to put away such ambiguities
and doubts as arise now by occasion of the said recoveries,
and so they be put as snares to deceive the people, and so

---

* 2 B. C. 303.   See stat. 4 and 5 Ann., c. 16.

will they be as long as they be suffered to continue. And methinketh verily that it were therefore right expedient, that tailed lands should from henceforth either be made so strong in the law that the tail should not be broken by recovery, fine with proclamation, collateral warranty, nor otherwise; or else that all tails should be made fee-simple, so that every man that list to sell his land, may sell it by his bare feoffment, and without any scruple or grudge of conscience : and then there should not be so great expences in the law, nor so great variance among the people, ne yet so great offence of conscience as there is now in many persons.

Stud. Verily methinketh that thy opinion is right good and charitable in this behalf, and that the rulers be bound in conscience to look upon it, to see it reformed and brought into good order. And verily, by that thou hast said therein, thou hast brought me into remembrance, that there be divers like snares concerning spiritual matters suffered among the people, whereby I doubt that many spiritual rulers be in great offence against God. As it is of the point that spiritual men have spoke so much of, that priests should not be put to answer before laymen, especially of felonies and murders ;* and of the statute of 45 E. 3, cap. 3, where it is said that a prohibition shall lie where a man is sued in the spiritual court for tithe of wood that is above the age of twenty years, by the name of *Sylva cædua*, as it was done before ;† and they have in open sermons, and in divers other open communications and counsels, caused it to be openly notified and known, that they should be all accursed that put priests to answer, or that maintain the said estatute, or any other like to it. And after, when they have right well perceived that, notwithstanding all that they have done therein, it hath been used in the same points through all the realm in like manner as it was before, then they have sat

---

* This point is fully treated upon in 2 H. P. C. 323, 324, and Hawkins P. C. 337, where the reader will find by what means the benefit of clergy was introduced, how it stood at common law, and how it stands at this day.

† 5 Inst. 642, 643; 12 Mod. 524; Cro. Eliz. 1.

still and let the matter pass ; and so when they have brought
many persons in great danger, but most specially them that
have given credence to their saying, and yet by reason of
the old custom have done as they did before, then there
they left them. But verily it is to fear, that there is to
themselves right great offence thereby, that is to say, to see
so many in so great danger as they say they be, and to do
no more to bring them out of it, than they have done for it.
If it be true, as they say, they ought to stick to it with effect in all charity, till it were reformed : and if be not as
they say, then they have caused many to offend that have
given credence to them, and yet contrary to their own conscience do as they did before, and that percase should not
have offended if such sayings had not been. And so it
seemeth that they have in these matters done either too
much or too little.

And I beseech Almighty God, that some good man may
so call upon all these matters that we have now communed
of, so that they that be in authority may somewhat ponder
them, and to order them in such manner, that offence of
conscience grow not so lightly thereby hereafter as it hath
done in times past. And verily He that on the cross knew
the price of man's soul, will hereafter ask a right strait
accompt of rulers for every soul that is under them, and
that shall perish through their default.

Thus I have shewn unto thee, in this little dialogue, how
the law of England is grounded upon the *law of reason*,[*]
the *law of God*, the *general customs* of the realm, and upon
certain *principles* that be called maxims, upon the *particular customs* used in divers cities and countries, and upon
statutes which have been made in divers parliaments by
our sovereign lord the king, and his progenitors, and by
the lords spiritual and temporal, and all the commons of
the realm.[†] And I have also shewed thee in the 9th
chapter of this book, under what manner the said general

---

[*] Ante, 5, 7, 12, 15, 17, 25, 34.
[†] Ante, 35.

customs and maxims of the law may be proved and affirmed, if they were denied :* and divers other things be contained in this present dialogue, which will appear in the table that is in the latter end in the book, as to the readers will appear. And in the end of the said dialogue I have at thy desire shewed thee my conceit concerning recoveries of tailed lands, and thou hast upon the said recoveries shewn me thine opinion. And I beseech our Lord set them shortly in a good clear way : for surely it will be right expedient for the well-ordering of conscience in many persons, that they be so. And thus the God of peace and love be alway with us. Amen.

{Here endeth the first dialogue in English, with new additions, betwixt a doctor of divinity and a student in the laws of England. And hereafter followeth the second.]

* Ante, 32.

DIALOGUE II.

THE PROLOGUE.

IN the beginning of this dialogue the doctor answereth to certain questions, which the student made to the doctor before the making of his dialogue concerning the laws of England and conscience, as appeareth in a dialogue made between them in Latin the twenty-fourth chapter. And he answereth also divers other questions, that the student maketh to him in his dialogue, of the law of England and conscience. And in divers other chapters of this present dialogue is touched shortly, how the laws of England are to be observed and kept in this realm, as to temporal things as well in law as in conscience, before any other laws. And in some of the chapters thereof is also touched, that spiritual judges in divers cases be bound to give their judgments according to the king's law. And in the latter end of the book the doctor moveth divers cases concerning the laws of England, wherein he doubteth how they may stand with conscience; whereupon the student maketh answer in such manner as to the reader will appear.

THE INTRODUCTION.

Stud. In the latter end of our first dialogue in Latin, I put divers cases grounded upon the laws of England, wherein I doubted, and yet do, what is to be holden therein in conscience. But forasmuch as the time was then far past, I shewed thee that I would not desire thee to make answer to them forthwith at that time, but at some better leisure; whereunto thou saidst thou wouldst· not only shew thine opinion in these cases, but also in such other cases as I would put. Wherefore pray thee now (forasmuch as methinketh thou hast good leisure) that thou wilt shew me thine opinion therein.

Doct. I will with good-will accomplish thy desire; but I would that when I am in doubt what the law of this realm is in such cases as thou shalt put, that thou wilt shew me what the law is therein; for though I have by occasion of our first dialogue in Latin learned many things of the laws of this realm which I knew not before, yet nevertheless, there be many more things that I am yet ignorant in, and that peradventure in these self cases that thou hast put, and intendest hereafter to put: and, as I said in the first dialogue in Latin the twentieth chapter, to search conscience upon any case of the law it is in vain, but where the law in the same case is perfectly known.

Stud. I will with good-will do as thou sayest, and I intend to put divers of the same questions that be in the last chapter of the said dialogue in Latin, and sometime I intend to alter some of them, and add some new questions to them as I shall be most in doubt of.

Doct. I pray thee do as thou sayest, and I shall with good-will either make answer to them forthwith as well as I can, or shall take longer respite to be advised, or else peradventure agree to thine opinion therein, as I shall see cause. But first, I would gladly know the cause why thou hast begun this dialogue in the English tongue, and not in the Latin tongue, as the first cases that thou desiredst to know mine opinion in, be; or in French, as the substance of the law.

Stud. The cause is this. It is right necessary to all men in this realm, both spiritual and temporal, for the good ordering of their conscience, to know many things of the law of England that they be ignorant in. And though it had been more pleasant to them that be learned in the Latin tongue to have had it in Latin rather than in English: yet nevertheless, forasmuch as many can read English that understand no Latin, and some that cannot read English, by hearing it read, may learn divers things by it, that they should not have learned if it were in Latin; therefore, for the profit of the multitude, it is put into the English tongue rather than into the Latin or French tongue. For if it had been in French, few should have understood it but they that be learned in the law, and they have least need of it; forasmuch as they know the law in the same cases without it, and can better declare what conscience will thereupon than

they that know not the law nothing at all. To them there--
fore that be not learned in the law of the realm this treatise
is specially made : for thou knowest well by such studies
thou hast taken to some knowledge of the law of the realm,.
that is to them most expedient.

Doct. It is true that thou sayest, and therefore I pray thee
now proceed to thy questions.

DIALOGUE II.

CHAP. I.—*The first question of the student.*

Stud. If tenant in tail after possibility of issue extinct do waste, whether doth he thereby offend in conscience,* though he be nòt punishable of waste by the law?

Doct. Is the law clear, that he is not punishable for the waste?†

Stud. Yes, verily.

Doct. And what is the law of tenants for term of life, or for term of years, if they do waste?

Stud. They be punishable of waste by the statutes, and shall yield treble damages;‡ but at the Common law before the statute they were not punishable.

Doct. But whether thinkest thou that before the statute they might have done waste with conscience, because they were not punishable by the law?

Stud. I think not, for, as I take it, the doing of waste of such particular tenant for term of life, for term of years, or of tenants in dower, or by the courtesy, is prohibited by the law of reason; for it seemeth of reason, that when such leases be made, or that such titles in dower, or by the courtesy be given by the law, that there is only given unto them

---

* Injunctions have been frequently granted by the court of chancery, against tenant in tail, after possibility of issue extinct, for committing wilful and malicious waste. 2 Frem. Rep. 278; 1 Cases in Equity abridged, 400.

† Shep. Touch. 145; Co. Litt. 27.

‡ Post. 106.

the annual profits of the land, and not the houses and trees,
and the gravel to dig and carry away, whereby the whole
profit of them in the reversion should be taken away for
ever. And therefore at the Common law, for waste done
by tenant in dower, or tenant by the courtesy, there was
punishment ordained by the law by a prohibition of waste,*
whereby they should have yielded damages to the value of
the waste. But against tenant for term of life, or for term
of years, lay no such prohibition,† for there was no maxim
in the law therein against them, as there was against the
other. And I think the cause was, forasmuch as it was
judged a folly in the lessor that made such a lease for term
of life, or for term of years, that at the time of the lease he
did not prohibit them, they should not do waste; and sith he
did not provide remedy to himself, the law would none
provide. But yet I think not that the intent of the law was,
that they might lawfully and with good conscience do waste;
but against tenants in dower, and by the courtesy, the law
provided remedy, for they had their title by the law.

Doct. And verily methinketh that this tenant in tail, as
to the doing of waste, should be like to a tenant for term
of life :‡ for he shall have the land no longer than for term
of his life, no more than a tenant for term of life shall,
and the waste of this tenant is as great hurt to him in the
reversion, or the remainder, as is the waste of a tenant for
term of life; and if he alien, the donor shall enter for the
forfeiture, as he shall upon the alienation of a tenant for
term of life; and if he make default in a *Præcipe quod
reddat*, the donor shall be received as he shall be upon the
default of a tenant for term of life; and therefore methinketh he shall also be punishable of waste, as tenant for
term of life shall.

Stud. If he alien, the donor shall enter, as thou sayest,
because the alienation is to his disheritance,§ and therefore

it is a forfeiture of his estate: and that is by an ancient maxim of the law, that giveth that forfeiture in the self case: and if he make default in a *Præcipe quod reddat,* he in the reversion, as thou sayest, shall be received, but that is by the statute of Westminster 2,* for at the Common law there was no such resceit. And as for the statute that giveth the action of waste against a tenant for term of life, and for term of years, it is a statute penal, and shall not be taken by equity :† and so there is no remedy given against him, neither by Common law nor by statute, as there is against tenant for term of life, and therefore he is unpunishable of waste by the law.

Doct And though he be unpunishable of waste by the law, yet nevertheless methinketh he may not by conscience do that that shall be hurtful to the inheritance after his time, sith he hath the land but for term of his life, no more than a tenant for term of life may, for then he should do as he would not be done unto.‡ For thou agreest thyself, that though a tenant for term of life was not punishable of waste before the statute, that yet the law judged not that he might rightfully and with good conscience do waste.§   And therefore at this day, if a feoffment be made to the use of man for term of life, though there lie no action against him for waste, yet he offendeth in conscience if he do waste, as tenant for term of life did afore the statute when no remedy lay against him by the law.

Stud. That is true; but there is great diversity between this tenant and a tenant for term of life: for this tenant hath good authority by the donor to do waste, and so hath not the tenant for term of life, as it is said before; for the

---

* 2 Inst. 345.

† This assertion of the student is too general, as the statute referred to, viz., the stat. of Marlebridge, is a remedial law, as well as a penal one, and has had an equitable construction. For instance, although the words in the act are "shall do waste," which literally import an active waste, yet they have been held to extend to waste omittendo. Hammond *v.* Webb, 10 Mod. 282.

‡ 2 B. C. 125; Co. Litt. 27, 28.

§ Post. 106; ante, 101.

estate of a tenant in tail after possibility of issue extinct is in this manner;* when lands be given to a man and to his wife, and to the heirs of their two bodies begotten, and after the one of them dieth without heirs of their bodies begotten, then he or she that overliveth is called tenant in tail after possibility of issue extinct, because there can never by no possibility be any heir that may inherit by force of the gift. And thus it appeareth that the donees at the time of the gift received of the donor an estate of inheritance, which by possibility might have continued for ever, whereby they had power to cut down trees, and to do all things that is waste, as tenant in fee-simple might.† And that authority was as strong in the law, as if the lessor that maketh a lease for term of life say by express words in the lease, that the lessee shall not be punishable of waste. And therefore if the donor in this case had granted to the donees that they should not be punishable of waste, that grant had been void, because it was included in the gift before, as it should be upon a gift in fee-simple.‡ And so forasmuch as by the first gift, and by the livery of seisin made upon the same, the donees had authority by the donor to do waste; therefore though that one of those donees be now dead without issue, so that it is certain that after the death of the other the land shall revert to the donor; yet the authority that they had by the donor to do waste continueth as long as the gift, and the livery of seisin made upon the same continueth. And I take this to be the reason why he shall not have in aid, as tenant for term of life shall, that is to say, for that he cannot ask help of that maxim, whereby it is ordained that a tenant for term of life shall have in aid: for he cannot say but that he took a greater estate by the livery of seisin that was made to him, which yet continueth, than for term of life: and so I think him not bound to make any restitution to him in the reversion in this case for the waste.

* Wood's Inst. 122; Litt., sec. 32.
† 1 Roll. Rep. 179; 4 Rep. 63.
‡ 2 New Abr. 269.

Doct. Is thy mind only to prove that this tenant is not bound to make restitution to him in the reversion for the waste? Or that thou thinkest that he may with clear conscience do all manner of waste?

Stud. I intend to prove no more but that he is not bound to make restitution to him in the reversion.

Doct. Then I will right well agree to thine opinion, for the reason that thou hast made; but if thy mind had been to have proved that he might with clear conscience have done all manner of waste, I would have thought the contrary thereto, and that the tenant in fee-simple may not do all manner of waste and destruction with conscience, as to pull down houses, and make pastures of cities and towns, or to do such other acts which be against the commonwealth. And therefore some will say, that tenant in fee-simple may not with conscience destroy his woods and coalpits, whereby a whole country for their money have had fuel; and yet though he do so, he is not bound by conscience to make restitution to no person in certain. But now I pray thee, ere thou proceed to the second case, that thou wilt somewhat shew me what thou meanest, when thou sayest, at the Common law it was thus or thus. I understand not fully what thou meanest by that term, *at the Common law*.

Stud. I shall with good-will shew thee what I mean thereby.

CHAP. II.— *What is meant by this term, when it is said " thus it was at the Common law."*

The Common law is taken three manner of ways. *First,* it is taken as the law of this realm of England, dissevered from all other laws. And under this manner taken it is oftentimes argued in the laws of England, what matters ought of right to be determined by the Common law, and what by the admiral's court, or by the spiritual court:* and

* See Comyn's Digest, and Bac. Abr., title Prohibition.

also if an obligation bear date out of the realm, as in Spain, France, or such other, it is said in the law, and truth it is, that they be not pleadable at the Common law.   * *Secondly*, the Common law is taken as the king's courts, of his *Bench*, or of the *Common Place:* and it is so taken when a plea is removed out of ancient demesne, for that the land is frank-fee, and pleadable at the Common law, that is to say, in the king's court, and not in ancient demesne.† And under this manner taken, it is oftentimes pleaded also in base courts, as in Courts-Barons, the County, and the court of Piepowders, and such other, this matter or that, etc., ought not to be·determined in that court, but at the Common law, that is to say, in the king's courts, etc.   *Thirdly,* by the Common law is understood such things as were law before statute made in that point that is in question ; so that that point was holden for law by the general or particular customs and maxims of the realm, or by the law of reason, and the law of God, no other law added to them by statute, nor otherwise, as is the case before rehearsed in the first chapter, where it is said, that at the Common law, tenant by the courtesy and tenant in dower were punishable of waste,‡ that is to say, that, before any statute of waste made, they were punishable of waste by the grounds and maxims of the law used before the statute made in that point.§   But tenant for term of life, ne for term of years, were not punishable by the said grounds and maxims, till by the statute remedy was given against them ; and therefore it is said,

---

* But if a bond bears date out of the realm, and is laid in the declaration *pro forma*, to have been made at Madrid in Spain, or Bourdeaux in France, viz., in London in parochia, etc., it is sufficient, and suable in the king's courts.   Str. 614, and vide the case of Mostyn *v.* Fabrigas, in Cow. Rep. 161, in which the whole learning upon this point seems to be summed up together.

† F. N. B. 13; 4 Inst. 270.

‡ 2 Inst. 299; ante, 103; post. 114.   See the stat. Marl. 5 H. 3, c. 23, and the stat. of Gloucester, 6 Edw. 1, c. 5.

§ It was a doubt whether tenant by the courtesy was punishable for waste at the Common law.   Reg. 72; Bro. Abr., title Waste, pl. 88; 2 Inst. 301.

that at the Common law they were not punishable of waste.

Doct. I pray thee now proceed unto the second question.

Chap. III.—*The second question of the student.*

Stud. If a man be outlawed, and never had knowledge of the suit, whether may the king take all his goods and retain them in conscience, as he may by the law?

Doct. What is the reason why they be forfeited by the law in that case?

Stud. The very reason is, for that it is an old custom, and an old maxim in the law, that he that is outlawed shall forfeit his goods to the king :*'and the cause why that maxim began was this, When a man had done a trespass to another, or another offence wherefore process of outlawry lay,† and he that the offence was done to had taken an action against him, according to the law, if he had absented himself, and had no lands, there had been no remedy against him : for, after the law of England no man shall be condemned without answer, or that he appear and will not answer, except it be by reason of any statute. Therefore, for the punishment of such offenders as will not appear to make answer, and to be justified in the king's courts, hath been used, without time of mind, that an attachment in that case should be directed against him returnable in the *King's Bench* or the *Common Place:* and if it were returned thereupon that he had nought whereby he might be attached, that then should go forth a *capias* to take his person, and after an *alias capias*, and then a *pluries;*‡ and if it were returned upon every of the said *capias*, that he

---

* The student may here be supposed to speak of an outlawry in a personal action; and though he only mentions a forfeiture of goods as the consequence of the offence, yet the outlawed person likewise forfeits the profits of his land, while the outlawry continues in force. Show. Pa. Ca. 73; 2 Roll. Abr. 806, 807.

† See where and in what cases process of outlawry lay at common law, and where it lies at this day, in 3 Bac. Abr., title Outlawry.

‡ 3 B. C. 283.

could not be found, and he appeared not, then should an
exigent be directed against him, which should have so long
a day of return, that five counties* might be holden before
the return thereof, and in every of the said five counties the
defendant to be solemnly called, and if he appeareth not,
then, for his contumacy and disobedience of the law, the
coroners to give judgment that he shall be outlawed,
whereby he shall forfeit his goods to the king, and leese
divers other advantages in the law, that needeth not here
to be remembered now. And so because he was in this
case called according to the law, and appeared not, it seemeth that the king hath good title to the goods both in law
and conscience.

Doct. If he had knowledge of the suit in very deed, it
seemeth the king hath good title in conscience, as thou
sayeth. But if he had no knowledge thereof, it seemeth
not so; for the default that is adjudged in him (as appeareth by thine own reason) is his contumacy and disobedience
of the law, and if he were ignorant of the suit, then there
can be assigned to him no disobedience, for a disobedience implieth a knowledge of that he should have obeyed
unto.

Stud. It seemeth in this case that he should be compelled
to take knowledge of this suit at his peril: for sith he hath
attempted to offend the law, it seemeth reason that he shall
be compelled to take heed what the law will do against him
for it; and not only that, but that he should rather offer
amends for his trespass, than to tarry till he were sued for
it. And so it seemeth the ignorance of the suit is of his
own default, specially sith in the law is set such order that
every man may know, if he will, what suit is taken against
him, and may see the records thereof when he will: and
so it seemeth that neither the party nor the law be not
bounden to give him no knowledge therein. And over this
I would somewhat move farther in this matter thus: that
though that action were untrue, and the defendant not

---

* That is, five county courts. 2 Black. Com. 285.

guilty, that yet the goods be forfeited to the king, for his
not appearance, in law, and also in conscience, and that
for this cause : the king, as sovereign and head of the law,
is bounden of justice to grant such writs, and such pro-
cesses, as be appointed in the law to every person that will
complain, be his surmise true or false; and thereupon the
king (of justice) oweth as well to make process to bring
the defendant to answer when he is not guilty, as when he
is guilty : and then when there is a maxim in the law, that
if a man be outlawed, in such manner as before appeareth,
that he shall forfeit all his goods to the king,* and maketh
no exception whether the action be true or untrue, it seemeth that the said maxim more regardeth the general ministration of justice, than the particular right of the party, and
therefore the property by the óutlawry, and by the said
maxim ordained for ministration of justice is altered, and is
given to the king, as before appeareth, and that both in law
and in conscience, as well as if the action were true.   And
then the party that is so outlawed is driven to sue for his
remedy against him that hath so caused him to be outlawed
upon an untrue action.

Doct. If he hath not sufficient to make him recompence,
or die before recovery can be had, what remedy is had
then ?

Stud. I think no remedy : and for a farther declaration
in this case, and in such other like cases, where the property of goods may be altered without consent of the owner,
it is to consider, that the property of goods is not given to
the owners directly by the law of reason, nor by the law
of God, but by the law of man, and is suffered by the law
of reason, and by the law of God so to be.   For at the beginning all goods were in common, but after they were
brought by the law of man into a certain property, so that
every man might know his own :† and then when such
property is given by the law of man, the same law may

* Ante, 107.
†2 B. C. 2, 3.

assign such conditions upon the property as it listeth, so they be not against the law of God, ne the law of reason, and may lawfully take away that it giveth, and ·appoint how long the property shall continue. And one condition that goeth with every property in this realm, is, If he that hath the property be outlawed according to such process as is ordained by the law, that he shall forfeit the property unto the king.* And divers other cases there be also, whereby property in goods shall be altered in the law, and the right in lands also, without assent of the owner, whereof I shall shortly touch some without saying any authority therein, for the more shortness.† *First*, By a sale in open market the property is altered. Also goods stolen and seised for the king, or waived, be forfeit, unless appeal or indictment be sued.‡ Also strays, if they be proclaimed, and be not after claimed by the owner within the year, be forfeit; and also a *deodand*§ is forfeit (to whomsoever the property was before, except it belonged to the king) and shall be disposed for the soul of him that was slain therewith; and a fine with a nonclaim at the Common law was a bar, if claim were not made within a year, as it is now by statute if the claim be not made within five years. And all these forfeitures were ordained by the law upon certain considerations, which I omit at this time : but certain it is that none of them were made upon a better consideration than this forfeiture of utlagary was. For if no especial punishment should have been ordained for offenders that would absent themselves, and not appear when they were sued in the king's courts, many suits in the king's courts

---

* Ante, 107.
† Post. 143.
‡ Finch. Law, 212; 1 B. C. 297; Wood's Inst. 212; ante, 65.
§ *Deodand* signifies accidental death, which happens without the intervention of human means, and induces a forfeiture which was formerly paid into the hands of the king's almoner, to be applied to pious uses for the soul of the deceased. But good sense having prevailed over ignorance and superstition, it is not now applied to superstitious uses, but remains part of the revenue of the crown, unless where lords of franchises are intitled to it by grant. Foster's Crown Law, 266.

should have been of small effect. And sith this maxim was ordained for the execution of justice, and as much done therein by the common law as policy of man could reasonably devise, to make the party have knowledge of the suit, and now is added thereto by the statute made the sixth year of H. VIII,* that a writ of proclamation shall be sued if the party be dwelling in another shire : it seemeth that such title, as is given to the king thereby, is good in conscience, especially seeing that the king is bound to make process upon the surmise of the plaintiff, and may not examine, but by plea of the party, whether the surmise be true or not. But if the party be returned five times called, where indeed he was never called (as in the second case of the last chapter of the said dialogue in Latin is contained), then it seemeth the party shall have good remedy by petition to the king, specially if he that made the return be not sufficient to make recompence, or die before recovery can be had.

Doct. Now sith I have heard thine opinion in this case, whereby it appeareth that many things must be seen, or a full and plain declaration can be made in this behalf, and seeing also that the plain answer to this case shall give a great light to divers other cases that may come by such forfeiture : I pray thee give me a farther respite ere that I shew thee my full opinion therein, and hereafter I shall right gladly do it. And therefore I pray thee, proceed now to some other case.

CHAP. IV.—*The third question of the student.*

Stud. If a stranger do waste in lands that another holdeth for term of life, without assent of the tenant for term of life, whether may he in the reversion recover treble damages, and the place wasted, against the tenant for term of life, according to the statute, in conscience, as he may by

---

* Cap. 4, to which may likewise be added the statute 31 Eliz., c. 3.

the law, if the stranger be not sufficient to make recompence for the waste done?*

Doct. Is the law clear in this case, that he in the reversion shall recover against the tenant for term of life, though that he assented not to the doing of waste?

Stud. Yea verily; and yet if the tenant for term of life had been bounden in an obligation in a certain sum of money, that he should do no waste, he should not forfeit his bond by waste of a stranger. And the diversity is this. It has been used as an ancient maxim of the law, that tenant by the courtesy and tenant in dower should take the land with this charge,† that is to say, that they should do no waste themselves, nor suffer none to be done : and when an action of waste was given after against a tenant for term of life, then he was taken to be in the same case, as to the point of waste, as tenant by the courtesy and tenant in dower was,‡ that is to say, that he shall do no waste, nor suffer none to be done; for there is another maxim in the law of England, that all cases like unto other cases shall be judged after the same law as other cases be : and sith no reason of diversity can be assigned why the tenant for term of life, after an action of waste was given against him, should have any more favour in the law than the tenant by the courtesy or tenant in dower should; therefore he is put under the same maxim as they be, that is to say, that he shall do no waste, ne suffer none to be done. And so it seemeth that the law in this case doth not consider the ability of the person that doth the waste, whether he be able to make recompence for the waste or not, but the assent of the said tenants, whereby they have wilfully taken upon them the charge to see that no waste shall be done.

Doct. I have heard that if houses of these tenants be destroyed with sudden tempest, or with strange enemies, that they shall not be charged with waste.§

---

*2 Inst. 306; ante, 101.
†3 Cro. 420.
‡ Ante, 102.
§ Co. Litt. 53 ; Noy's Max. 16; 2 Inst. 303.

Stud. Truth it is.

Doct. And I think the reason is, because they can have no recovery over.

Stud. I take not that for the reason, but that it is an old reasonable maxim in the law, that they should be discharged in these cases. Howbeit some will say, that in these cases the law of reason doth discharge them : and therefore they say, that if a statute were made that they should be charged in these cases of waste, that the statute were against reason, and not to be observed. But yet nevertheless I take it not so ; for they might refuse to take such estate if they would, and if they will take the estate after the law made, it seemeth reasonable that they take it with the charge, and with the condition that is appointed thereto by the law, though hurt might follow to them afterward thereby. For it is oftentimes seen in the law, that the law doth suffer him to have hurt without help of the law that will wilfully run into it of his own act, not compelled thereto, and judgeth it his folly so to run into it ; for which folly he shall also be many times without remedy in conscience. As if a man take land for term of life, and bindeth himself by obligation that he shall leave the land in as good case as he found it ;* if the houses be after blown down with tempest, or destroyed with strange enemies, as in the case that thou hast put before, he shall be bound to repair them, or else he shall forfeit his obligation in law and conscience : because it is his own act to bind him to it, and yet the law would not have bound him thereto, as thou hast said before. So methinketh that the cause why the said tenants be discharged in the law in an action of waste, when the houses be destroyed by sudden tempest, or by strange enemies, is by a special reasonable maxim in the law, whereby they be excepted from the other general bond before rehearsed, that is to say, they shall at their peril see that no waste shall be done, and not by the law of

---

* Noy's Max. 16.

8

reason : and sith there is no maxim in this case to help this tenant, ne that he cannot be holpen by the law of reason, it seemeth that he should be charged in this case by his own act both in law and ·conscience, whether the stranger be able to recompence him or not.

Doct. I doubt in this case whether the maxim that thou speakest of be reasonable or not, that is to say, that tenants by the courtesy, and tenants in dower, were bound by the common law, that they should do no waste themselves, and over that at their peril to see that no waste should be done by none other.* For that law seemeth not reasonable that bindeth a man to an impossibility :† and it is impossible to prevent that no waste should be done by strangers : for it may be suddenly done in the night, that the tenants can have no notice of, or by great power, that they be not able to resist : and therefore methinketh they ought not to be charged in those cases for the waste without they may have good remedy over ; and then percase the said maxim were sufferable, and else methinketh it is a maxim against reason.

Stud. As I have said before, no man shall be compelled to take the bond upon him, but he that will take the land ; and if he will take the land, it is reason he take the charge, as the law hath appointed it :‡ and then if any hurt grow to him thereby, it is through his own act, and his own assent, for he might have refused the lease if he would.§

Doct. Though a man may refuse to take estate for term of life, or for term of years, and a woman may refuse to take her dower ; yet tenant by the courtesy cannot refuse to take his estate, for immediately after the death of his wife the possession abideth still in him by the act of the law, without entry : and then I put the case, that after the death of his wife he would waive the possession, and after waste

---

* 2 Inst. 145; 3 Cro. 430; Co. Litt. 54; ante, 106.

† Lex cogit neminem ad vana aut impossibilia. 5 Rep, 21.

‡ Agreeable to the maxim, *Qui sentit commodum, debet sentire incom-modum sive onus.*

§ Post. 260.

were done by a stranger, whether thinkest thou that he should answer to the waste?

Stud. I think he should by the law.

Doct. And how standeth that with reason, seeing there is no default in him?

Stud. It was his default, and at his own peril, that he would marry an inheritrix, whereupon such danger might follow.

Doct. I put the case that he were within age at the marriage, or that the land descended to his wife after he married her.

Stud. There thou movest a farther doubt than the first question is : and though it were as thou sayest, yet thou canst not say but that there-is as great default in him, as in him in the reversion ; and that there is as great reason why he should be charged with the waste, as that he in the reversion should be disinherited, and have no manner of remedy, ne yet no profit of the land, as the other hath. And though the said maxim may be thought very strait to the said tenants ; yet it is to be favoured as much as may be reasonably, because it helpeth much the commonwealth ; for it hurteth the commonwealth greatly when woods and houses be destroyed ; and if they should answer for no waste, but for waste done by themselves, there might be wastes done by strangers by commandment or assent, in such colourable manner, that they in the reversion should never have proof of their assent.

Doct. I am content thine opinion stand for this time, and I pray thee now proceed to another question.

CHAP. V.—*The fourth question of the student.*

Stud. If he that is the very heir be certified by the ordinary, bastard, and after bring an action as heir against another person : whether may any man, knowing the truth, be of counsel with the tenant, and plead the said certificate against the demandant by conscience or not?

Doct. Is the law in this case, that all other against whom
the demandant hath title shall take advantage of this certificate, as well as he at whose suit he is certified bastard? ͵
Stud. Yea verily, and that for two causes, whereof the .
one is this. There is an old maxim in the law, that a
mischief shall be rather suffered than an inconvenience :*
and then in this case if another writ should afterward be
sent to another bishop in another action, to certify whether
he were a bastard or not: peradventure the bishop would
certify that he were *mulier*, that is to say, lawfully begot-.
ten, and then he should recover as heir : and so he should
in one self court be taken as *mulier* and bastard.† For
avoiding of which contrariosity, the law will suffer no more
writs to go forth in that case, and suffereth also all men to
take advantage of the certificate, rather than to suffer such ·
a contradiction in the court, which in the law is called an
inconvenience.‡ And the other cause is, because this
certificate of the bishop is the highest trial that is in the
law in this behalf : but this is not understood but where
bastardy is laid in one that is party to the writ;§ for if
bastardy be laid in one that is a stranger to the writ, as if ·
vouchee pray in aid for such other, then that bastardy shall
be tried by twelve men, by which trial he in whom the
bastardy is laid shall not be concluded, because he is not
privy to the trial, and may have no attaint ; but he that is
party to the issue may have attaint, and therefore he shall
be concluded, and none other but he. And forasmuch as
the said maxim was ordained to eschew an inconvenience
(as before appeareth) it seemeth that every man learned
may with conscience plead the said certificate for avoiding
thereof, and give counsel therein to the party according
unto the law, or else the said inconvenience must needs
follow. But yet nevertheless I do not mean thereby, that

* Wood's Inst. 5.
† 1 Roll. Abr. 361, 362.
‡ 1 Danv. Abr. 732.
§ 1 Burn's Ecc. Law, 119.

the party may after, when he hath barred the demandant. by the said certificate, retain the land in conscience by reason of the said certificate : for though there be no law to compel him to restore it, yet I think well that he in conscience is bound to restore it, if he knew that the demandant is the very true heir, whereof I have put divers cases like in the seventeenth chapter of our first dialogue in Latin.* But my intent is, that a man learned in the law, in this case, and other like, may with conscience give his counsel according to the law, in avoiding of such things as the law thinketh should for a reasonable cause be eschewed.

Doct. Though he that doth not know whether he be a bastard or not may give his counsel, and also plead the said certificate ; yet I think that he that doth know himself to be the very true heir may not plead it : and that is for two causes, whereof the one is this : every man is bound by the law of reason to do as he would be done to :† but I think that if he that pleadeth that certificate were in like case, he would think that no man, knowing the certificate to be untrue, might with conscience plead it against him, wherefore no more may he plead it against none other. The other cause is this : Although the certificate be pleaded, yet is the tenant bounden in conscience to make restitution thereof, as thou hast said thyself; and then in case that he would not make restitution, then he that pleadeth the plea should run thereby in l.ke offence, for he hath holpen to set the other man in such a liberty, that he may chuse whether he will restore the land or not; and so he should put himself to jeopardy of another man's conscience. And it is written, Eccl. 3, *Qui amat periculum peribit in illo*, that is, He that wilfully will put himself in jeopardy to offend, shall perish therein. And therefore it is the surest way, to eschew perils, for him that knoweth that he is heir, not to plead it. And as for the inconvenience that thou sayest must needs follow, but the

---

* Ante, 47.
† Post. 119.

certificate be pleaded; as to that it may be answered, that
it may be pleaded by some other that knoweth not that he
is very heir: and if the case be so far put, that there is
none other learned there but he, then methinketh that he
shall rather suffer the said inconvenience, than to hurt his
own conscience; for always charity beginneth at himself,
and so every man ought to suffer all other offences rather
than himself would offend. And now that thou knowest
mine opinion in this case, I pray thee proceed to another
question.

CHAP. VI.—*The fifth question of the student.*

Stud. Whether may a man with conscience be of counsel
with the plaintiff in action at the common law, knowing
that the defendant hath sufficient matter in conscience
whereby he may be discharged by a *subpœna* in the chancery, which he cannot plead at the common law, or not?

Doct. I pray thee put a case thereof in certain, for else
the question is very general.

Stud. I will put the same case that thou puttest in our
first dialogue in Latin, the twelfth chapter, that is to say,
If a man bound in an obligation pay the money, and taketh
no acquittance, so that by the common law he shall be
compelled to pay the money again,* for such consideration
as appeareth in the fifteenth chapter of the said dialogue
where it is shewed evidently how the law in that case is
made upon a good reasonable ground, much necessary for
all the people, howbeit that a man may sometime, through
his own default, take hurt thereby : herein I pray thee shew
me thine opinion.

Doct. This case seemeth to be like to the case that thou
hast next before this,† and that he that knoweth the payment to be made doth not as he would be done to, if he

---

* Ante, 37.
† Ante, 115.

gave counsel that an action should be taken to have it payed again.

Stud. If he be sworn to give counsel according to the law,* as serjeants at the law be, it seemeth he is bound to give counsel according to the law, for else he should not perform his oath.

Doct. In these words (according to the law) is understood the law of God, and the law of reason, as well as the law and customs of the realm : for as thou hast said thyself, in our first dialogue in Latin,† that the law of God, and the law of reason, be two special grounds of the laws of England, wherefore (as methinketh) he may give no counsel (saving his oath) neither against the law of God, nor the law of reason. And certain it is, that this article, that is to say, that a man shall do as he would be done to, is grounded upon both the said laws. And first that it is grounded upon the law of reason, it is evident of itself. And in the sixth chapter of St. Luke it is said, *Et prout vultis ut faciant vobis homines, et vos facite illis similiter;* that is to say, All that other men should do to you, do you to them :‡ and so it is grounded upon the law of God. Wherefore if he should give counsel against the defendant in that case, he should do against both the said laws.

Stud. If the defendant had no other remedy but the common law, I would agree well it were as thou sayest, but in this case he may have good remedy by a *subpœna:* and this is the way that shall induce him directly to his *subpœna,* that is to say, when it appeareth that the plaintiff shall recover by law.

Doct. Though the defendant may be discharged by *subpœna,* yet the bringing in of his proofs there will be to the charge of the defendant, and also the proofs may die or they come in. Also there is a ground in the law of reason, *Quod nihil possimus contra veritatem,* (that is) We

* 2 Inst. 214.
† Ante, 5, 7.
‡ Ante, 117.

may do nothing against the truth; and sith he knoweth it is truth that the money is payed, he may do nothing against the truth; and if he should be of counsel with the plaintiff, he must suppose and aver that it is the very due debt of the plaintiff, and that the defendant with-holdeth it from him unlawfully, which he knoweth himself to be untrue: wherefore he may not with conscience in this case be of counsel with the plaintiff, knowing that the plaintiff is paid already. Wherefore if thou be contented with this answer, I pray thee proceed to some other question.

Stud. I will with good-will.

Chap. VII.—*The sixth question of the student.*

A man maketh a feoffment to the use of him and of his heirs, and after the feoffor putteth in his beasts to manure the ground, and the feoffee taketh them as damage-feasant, and putteth them in pound, and the feoffor bringeth an action of trespass against him for entering into his ground, etc. Whether may any man, knowing the said use, be of counsel with the feoffee to avoid the action?

Doct. May he by the common law avoid that action, seeing that the feoffor ought in conscience to have the profits?

Stud. Yes, verily; for as to the common law the whole interest is in the feoffee,* and if the feoffee will break his conscience, and take the profits, the feoffor hath no remedy by the common law, but is driven in that case to sue for his remedy by *subpœna* for the profits, and to cause him to enfeoff him again :† and that was sometime the most common case where the *subpœna* was sued, that is to say, before the statute of R. 3. but sith the statute, the feoffor may lawfully make a feoffment.‡ But nevertheless, for the profits received, the feoffor hath yet no remedy but by *subpœna* as he had before the said statute. And so the supposal of this

---

* See note, p. 58.
† Wood's Inst. 256; Kelw. 42, b.; 1 Rep. 121.
‡ Godbolt, 303; Gilbert, Law of Uses, 27.

action of trespass is untrue in every point as to the common law.

Doct. Though the action be untrue as to the law, yet he that sueth it ought in conscience to have that he demandeth by the action, that is to say, Damages for his profits; and as it seemeth, no man may with conscience give counsel against that he knoweth conscience would have done.

Stud. Though conscience would he should have the profits, yet conscience will not that for the attaining thereof the feoffor should make an untrue surmise. Therefore against the untrue surmise every man may with conscience give his counsel; for in that doing he resisteth not the plaintiff to have the profits, but he withstandeth him that he should not maintain an untrue action for the profits. And it sufficeth not in the law, ne yet in conscience, as me seemeth, that a man have right to that he sueth for, but that also he sue by a just means, and that he have both good right, and also a good and true conveyance to come to his right. For if a man have a right to lands as heir to his father, and he will bring an action as heir to his mother, that never had right, every man may give counsel against the action, though he know he have right by another means; and so, as methinketh, he may do in dilatories, whereby the party may take hurt if it were not pleaded, though he know the plaintiff have right; as if the party or the town be misnamed, or if the degrees in writs of *Entry* be mistaken; but if the party should take no hurt by admitting of a dilatory, there he that knoweth that the plaintiff hath right, may not plead that dilatory with conscience. As in a *Formedon* to plead in abatement of the writ, because he hath not made himself heir to him that was the last seised;* for in a writ of right, for that the demandant had omitted one that tended right, ne such other. Ne he may not assent to the casting of an essoin nor protection for him, if he know that the demandant hath right; ne he may not vouch for him, except it be that he knoweth that the tenant hath

---

* Het. 78; 8 Co. 88; Hob. 51, 52.

a true cause of a voucher and of lien, and that he doth it to bring him thereto. And in like wise he may not pray in aid for him, unless he know the prayee have good cause of voucher and lien over; or that he knew that the prayee hath somewhat to plead that the tenant may not plead, as villeinage in the demandant, or such other.

Doct. Though the plaintiff hath brought an action that is untrue, and not maintainable in the law, yet the defendant doth wrong to the plaintiff in the with-holding of the profits as well before the action brought, as hanging the action; and that wrong, as it seemeth, the counsellor doth maintain, and also sheweth himself to favour the party in that wrong, when he giveth counsel against the action.

Stud. If the plaintiff do take that for a' favour, and a maintenance of his wrong, he judgeth farther than the cause is given, so that the counsellor do no more but give counsel against the action: for though he give him counsel to withstand the action for the untruth of it, and that he should not confess it, and to make thereby a fine to the king without cause; yet it may not stand with reason that he may give counsel to the party to yield the profits.* And therefore I think he may in this case be of counsel with him at the Common law, and be against him in *Chancery*, and in either court give his counsel, without any contrariosity or hurt of conscience. And upon this ground it is, that a man may with good conscience be of counsel with him that hath land by descent, or by a discontinuance without title, if he that hath the right bring not his action according to the law, for the recovering of his right in that behalf.

CHAP. VIII.—*The seventh question of the student.*

If a man take distress for debt upon an obligation † or upon a contract, or such other thing that he hath right title to have, but that he ought not by the law to distrain for it,

* 2 B. 398.
† Ante, 23; post. 127.

and nevertheless he keepeth the same distress in pound till
he be paid of his duty, what restitution is he bound to make
in this case? Whether shall he repay the money, because
he is come to it by an unlawful means, or only restore the
party for the wrongful taking of the distress, or for neither?
I pray you shew me?

Doct. What is the law in this case?

Stud. That he that is distrained* may bring a special
action of trespass against him that distrained,† for that he
took his beasts wrongfully, and kept them till he made a
fine; and therefore he shall recover the fine in damages, as
he shall do for the residue of trespass: for the taking of the
money by such compulsion, is taken in the law but as a
fine wrongfully taken, though it be his duty to have it.

Doct. Yet though he may so recover, methinketh that as
to the repayment of the money, he is not bound thereto in
conscience, so that he take no more than of right he ought
to have: for though he came to it by unjust means, yet
when the money is paid him, it is his of right, and he is
not bound to repay it, unless it be recovered as thou said'st;
and then when he hath repayed it, he is, as methinketh,
restored to his first action. But to the redelivery of the
beasts, with such damages and such hurt as he hath by the
distress, I suppose he is bound to make recompence of
them in conscience without compulsion or suit in the law:
for though he might lawfully have sued for his duty in such
manner as the law hath ordered; yet I agree well that he
may not take upon him to be his own judge, and to come
to his duty against the order of the law. And therefore if
any hurt come to the party by the disorder, he is bound to
restore it. But I would think it were the more doubt, if a
man took such a distress for a trespass done to him, and
keepeth the distress till amends be made for the trespass:†

---

* Sayer's Rep. 148.

† Or he may have a replevin, and if the distress had not been impounded,
he might have made a rescue. Co. Litt. 47.

‡ 2 New Abr. 2.

for in that case the damages be not in certain, but be arbitrable either by the assent of the parties, or by twelve men.
And it seemeth that there is no assent of the party in this
case, especially no free assent, for that he doth is by compulsion, and to have his distress again, and so his assent is
not much to be pondered in that case, for all his assessing
of him that took the distress, and so he hath made himself
his own judge, and that is prohibited in all laws: but in
that case where the distress is taken for debt, he is not his
own judge; for the debt was judged in certain before the
first contract, and therefore some think great diversity
betwixt the cases.

Stud. By that reason it seemeth, that if he that distrained
in the first case for the debt take any thing for his damages,
that he is bound in conscience to restore it again; for
damages be arbitrable, and not certain, no more than
trespass is; and me seemeth that both in the case of trespass* and debt, he is bound in conscience to restore that
he taketh: for, though he ought in right to have like sum
as he receiveth, yet he ought not to have the money that he
receiveth, for he came to the money by an unjust means:
wherefore it seemeth he ought to restore it again.

Doct. And if he should be compelled to restore it again,
should he not yet (for that he received it once) be barred
of his first action notwithstanding the payment?

Stud. I will not at this time clearly assoil thee that question; but this I will say, That if any hurt come to him
thereby, it is through his own default, for that he would do
against the law: but nevertheless a little I will say to thy
question, that, as me seemeth, when he hath repaid the
money, that he is restored to his first action. As if a man
condemned in an action of trespass pay the money, and
after the defendant reverse the judgment by a writ of error,

---

* This cannot be understood of a trespass damage feasant, for in that
case it is clear that a man may lawfully distrain the beasts of a stranger
which come upon his premises; and if reasonable tender of amends is
made him by the owner of the beasts before they are impounded, and he
accepts it, he is not bound to repay the money either in law or equity.

and have his money repaid, then the plaintiff is restored to his first action. And therefore if he that in this case took the money, restore that he took by the wrongful distress, or that he ordered the matter so liberally that the other murmur not, he complain not at it, me seemeth he did very well to be sure in conscience : and therefore I would advise every man to be well aware how he distraineth in such case against the law.

Doct. Thy counsel is good, and I note much in this case, That the party may have an action of trespass against him that distraineth, so that he is taken in the law but as a wrong-doer; and therefore to pay the money again is the sure way, as thou hast said before. And I pray thee now shew me for what a man may lawfully distrain, as thou thinkest.

CHAP. IX.—*For what things a man may lawfully distrain.*

Stud. A man may lawfully distrain for a rent-service, and for all manner of services,* as homage, fealty, escuage,† suit of court, reliefs, and such other. Also for a rent reserved upon a gift in tail, a lease for term of life, for years, or at will, if he reserve the reversion, the feoffor shall distrain of common right, though there be no distress spoken of.‡ But in case a man make a feoffment, and that in fee by indenture, reserving a rent, he shall not distrain for that rent, unless a distress be expressly reserved :§ and if the feoffment be made without a deed reserving a rent, that reservation is void in law, and he shall have the rent only in conscience, and shall not distrain for it. And

---

* 2 Inst. 118; Noy's Max. 42; Gilbert's Distresses, 7, 8.

† As the service of escuage was *peculiarly* incident to knight service, it is entirely abolished by the statute of 12 Car. 2, ante, 26, and does not rank among the modern English tenures, like suit of court, fealty, and relief.

‡ Co. Litt. 142.

§ But it seems to be good to bind the feoffee by way of contract. 2 New Abr. 106.

like law is where a gift in tail, or a lease for term of life is
made, the remainder over in fee, reserving a rent, that reservation is void in the law.*

Also, if a man seised of land for term of life granteth
away his whole estate, reserving a rent,† that reservation is
void in the law, without it be by indenture; and if it be by
indenture, yet he shall not distrain for the rent, but a distress
be reserved.‡ And for amerciaments in a leet the lord
shall distrain;§ but for amerciaments in a Court-Baron he
shall not distrain.‖

Also, if a man make a lease at Michaelmas for a year,
reserving rent payable at the feasts of the Annunciation of
our lady, and St. Michael the arch-angel; in that case he
shall distrain for the rent due at our *Lady-day*, but not for
the rent due at Michaelmas,¶ because the term is expired.**

But if a man make a lease at the feast of *Christmas*, for
to endure to the feast of *Christmas* next following, that is
to say, for a year, reserving a rent at the aforesaid feasts
of the Annunciation of our lady, and St. Michael the arch-
angel; there he shall distrain for both the rents as long as
the term continued, that is to say, till that aforesaid feast
of *Christmas*.

And if a man hath land for term of life†† of John at Noke,
and maketh a lease for term of years, reserving a rent, the
rent is behind, and John at Noke dieth; there he shall not
distrain, because his reversion is determined.

Also, if he to whose use feoffees been seised maketh a

* Litt., sec. 215.
† Br. Reservation, pl. 8.
‡ Br. Distress, pl. 8; 8 Co. 41; 1 Roll. Rep. 201; Cro. Eliz. 748.
§ Or he may have an action of debt. Cro. Jac. 382; 1 Wils. 243.
‖ But if the lord can prescribe in a distress for the amerciament, then it
becomes lawful. Gilbert Law of Distresses, 16.
¶ Co. Litt. 47; 2 Cro. 442; 1 Roll. 672.
** By the 8 Ann., c 14, rent may be distrained for after determination
of the lease, in the same manner as before, if the distress is made within
six calendar months afterward, and during the continuance of the landlord's title, and the possession of the tenant from whom the arrears are
due.
†† Br. Distress, pl. 74.

lease for term of years, or for term of life, or a gift in tail reserving a rent; there the reservation is good, and the lessor shall distrain.

And if a township be amerced, and the neighbours by assent assess a certain sum upon every inhabitant,* and agree that if it be not paid by such a day, that certain persons thereto assigned shall distrain; in this case the distress is lawful. If lord and tenant be, and if the tenant do hold of the lord by fealty and rent;† and the lord doth grant away the fealty, reserving the rent, and the tenant atturneth; in this case he that was lord may not distrain for the rent, for it is become a rent-seck.‡ But if a man make a gift in tail to another, reserving fealty and certain rent, and after that he granteth away the fealty, reserving the rent and the reversion to himself; in this case he shall distrain for the rent, for the grant of the fealty is void, for the fealty cannot be severed from the reversion.§ Also, for heriot-service the lord shall distrain;‖ and for heriot-custom he shall seise, and not distrain.¶ Also, if rent be assigned, to make a partition or assignment of dower legal, he or she to whom the rent is assigned may distrain. And in all these cases abovesaid, where a man may distrain, he may not distrain in the night,** but for damage feasant;†† that is to say, where beasts do hurt in his ground, he may distrain in the night. Also for wastes, for reparations, for accompts, for debts upon contracts, or such other, no man may lawfully distrain.

---

* Gilb. Law of Distresses,·31.

† Litt., sec. 226.

‡ By stat. 4 Geo. 2, c. 28, the like remedy is given by distress for rent-seck as for any other rent.

§ Co. Litt. 143.

‖ Or he may seize at his election. Cro. Eliz. 32; Cro. Jac. 260; 3 Mod. 231.

¶ Kelw. 82; Bro., tit. Heriot, 2; Noy's Max. 25.

** Which according to the author of the Mirror and construction of law, is after sun-set, and before sun-rising. Mirr., c. 2, sec. 6.

†† Co. Litt. 142.

CHAP. X.—*The eighth question of the student..*

If a man do a trespass, and after make his executors, and die before any amends made; whether be his exec‑utors bound in conscience to make amends for the trespass, if they have sufficient goods thereto, though there be no remedy against them by the law to compel them to it?

Doct. It is no doubt but they are bound thereto in con‑science, before any other deed in charity that they may do for him of their own devotion.

Stud. Then would I wit, if the testator made legacies by his will, whether the executors be bound to do first, that is to say, to make amends for the trespass, or to pay the leg‑acies, in case they have no goods to do both?

Doct. To pay legacies: for if they should first make recompence for the trespass, and then have not sufficient to pay the legacies;* they should be taken in the law as wasters of their testator's goods; for they were not com‑pellable by no law to make amends for the trespass, because every trespass dieth with the person;† but the legacies they should be compelled by the law spiritual to fulfil, and so they should be compelled to pay the legacies of their own goods, and they shall not be compelled thereto by no law ne conscience: but if the case were, that he leave sufficient goods to do both, then methinketh they be bound to do both, and that they be bound to make amends for the trespass, before they may do any other charitable deed for the testa‑tor of their own mind, as I have said before, except the

---

* Office of Executor, 292; Noy's Max. 5; Office of Executor, 126.

† This maxim not being generally true, but liable to many exceptions, leaves the law undefined as to the kind of personal actions which die with the person or survive against the executor. However, it may be affirmed with certainty, that where the cause of action is a tort, or arises *ex delicto*, supposed to be by force and battery, against the king's peace; there the action dies, as trover, battery, false imprisonment, words, nuisance, ob‑structing lights, diverting a water‑course, etc. Cow. Rep. 374, 375.

funeral expenses* that be necessary, which must be al-' lowed before all other things.†

Stud. And what the proving of the testament?

Doct. The ordinary may nothing take by conscience, therefore, if there be not sufficient goods besides for the funerals,‡ to pay the debts, and to make restitution. And in like wise the executors be bound to pay debts upon a simple contract, before any other deed of charity that they may do for the testator of their own devotion, though they shall not be compelled thereto by the law.

Stud. And whether thinkest thou that they be bound to do first, that is to say, to make amends for the trespass, or to pay the debts upon a simple contract?

Doct. To pay the debts, for that is certain, and the trespass is arbitrable.

Stud. Then for the plainer declaration of this matter, and other like, I pray thee shew me thy mind, by what law it is, that if a man make executors, that the executors, if they take upon them, be bound to perform the will, and dispose the goods that remain for the testator?

Doct. I think that it is best by the law of reason.

Stud. And methinketh that it should be rather by the custom of the realm.

Doct. In all countries, and in all lands, they make executors.

Stud. That seemeth to be rather by a general custom, after that the law and custom of property was brought in, than by the law of reason, for as long as all things were in common, there were no executors ne wills, ne they needed not them: and when property was after brought in, methinketh that yet making of executors, and disposing of goods by will, after a man's death, followeth not necessarily thereupon: for it might have been made for a law, that a

---

* Office of Executor, 129, 130; 2 B. C. 508.

† And see what expences and articles will be allowed against creditors in Wentworth's Office of Exec. 292, 173; 2 Salk. 296; 3 Atk. 249.

‡ Office of Executor, 130, 131.

man should have had the property of his goods only during
his life, and that then, his debts paid, all his goods to have
been left to his wife and children, or next of his kin, without any legacies making thereof; and so it might now be
ordained by statute, and the statute good, and not against
reason. Wherefore it appeareth that executors have no
authority by the law of reason, but by the law of man.
And by the old law and custom of the realm a man may
make executors, and dispose his goods by his will, and then
his executors shall have the execution thereof, and his heirs
shall have nothing, but if any particular custom help :* and
the executors shall also have the whole possession and disposition of all his goods and chattels, as well real as personal, though no word be expressly spoken in the will, that
they shall have them : and they shall have also actions to
recover all debts due to the testator,† though all debts and
legacies of the testator be paid before, and shall have the
disposition of them to the use of the testator, and not to
their own use. And so methinketh that the authority to
make executors, and that they shall dispose the goods for
the testator, is by the custom of this realm : but then, I
think, as thou sayest, that by the law of God they shall be
bound to do the first, that is, to the most profit of the soul
of their testator, where the disposition thereof is left to their
discretion ;‡ and that, I agree well, is to pay debts upon
contracts, and to make amends for wrong done by the testator, though they be not compelled thereto by the law and
custom of the realm, if there be none other debt nor legacy
that they be bound to pay by the law ; but if two several
debts be payable by the law, then which debt they shall do
first in conscience, I am somewhat in doubt.

Doct. Let us first know what the Common law is therein.

Stud. The Common law is, That if the testator owe 10*l.*
to two men severally by obligation, or by such other manner that an action lieth against his executors thereof by the

* Office of Executor, 53, 57, 58, 59; ante, 22.
† Lovelass on Intestacy and Wills, 43.
‡ Office of Executor, 155.

law, and he leaveth goods to pay the one, and not both;* that in that case he that can first obtain his judgment against the executors, shall have execution of the whole, and the other shall have nothing: but to which of them he shall in conscience owe his favour, the Common law teacheth not.

Doct. Therein must be considered the cause why the debts began, and then he must after conscience bear his lawful favour to him that hath the clearest cause of debt: and if both have like cause, then in conscience he must bear his favour where is most need and greatest charity.

Stud. May the executors in that case delay that action that is first taken, if it stand not with so good conscience to be paid as another debt whereof no action is brought, and procure that an action may be brought thereof, and then to confess that action, that he may so have execution, and then the executors to be discharged against the other?

Doct. Why may he not in that case pay the other without action, and so be discharged in the law against the first?

Stud. No verily, for after an action is taken, the executor may not minister the goods so, but that he leave so much as shall pay the debt whereof the action is taken:† and if he do not, he shall pay it of his own goods, except another recover and have judgment against him hanging that action, and that without covin.

Doct. Then to answer to thy question, I think, that by delays that be lawful, as by essoin, imparlance, or by dilatory plea in abatement of the writ, that is true he may delay it:‡ but he may plead no untrue plea to prefer the other to his duty. But, I pray thee, what is the law of legacies, restitution, and debts upon contracts, that percase ought rather after charity to be paid than a debt upon an obligation? What may the favour of the executor do in these cases?

---

* Office of Exec. 144; Swin. 457, 458.
† Office of Exec. 144.
‡ Ib. 144.

Stud. Nothing : for if they either perform legacies, make restitutions, or pay debts upon contracts,* and keep not sufficient to pay debts which they are compelled by the law to pay, that shall be taken as a *devastaverunt bona testatoris*,† that is to say, that they have wasted the goods of their testator ; and therefore they shall be compelled to pay the debts of their own goods ;‡ and so it is, if they pay a debt upon an obligation, whereof the day is yet to come, though it be the clearer debt, and that be the more charity to have it paid. §

Doct. Yet in that case, if he to whom the debt is already owing forbear till after the day of the other obligation is past, then he may pay him without danger. ||

Stud. That is true, if there be no action taken upon it ;. and though there be, yet if that action may be delayed by lawful means as thou hast spoken of before, till after the day, and that an action is taken upon it, then may the executor confess the action, and then after judgment he may pay the debt without danger of the law.

Doct. Is not that confessing of the action so done of purpose a covin in the law?

Stud. No, verily ; for covin is where the action is untrue,. and not where the executors bear a lawful favour.¶

Doct. The ordinary, upon the accompt in all the cases before rehearsed, will regard much what is best for the testator.

Stud. But he may not drive them to accompt against the order of the Common law.**

---

* Lovelass on Intestacy and Wills, 186, 187.
† Office of Exec. 292, 157.
‡ Noy's Max. 104.
§ Office of Exec. 292.
|| Ib. 142.
¶ Swin a, 459.
** Office of Exec. 21.

CHAP. XI.—*The ninth question of the student.*

A man is indebted to another upon a simple contract in
20*l.* and he maketh his will, and bequeatheth 20*l.* to H.
Hart, and dieth, and leaveth goods to his executors only to
bury him with, and to perform the said legacy, and after
the said executors deliver the goods of their testator in performance of the said bequest: whether is he to whom the
bequest is made bound in conscience to pay the said debt
upon the simple contract, or not?

Doct. Is he not bound thereto by the law?

Stud. No, verily.

Doct. And what thinkest thou he is in conscience?

Stud. I think that he is not bound thereto in conscience,
for he is neither ordinary, administrator, nor executor.
And I have not heard that any man is bound to pay debts
of any man that is deceased, but he be one of those three.
For the goods that the testator left to the executors were
never charged with the debt, but the person of the testator
while he lived was only charged with the debt, and not his
goods ; and his executors, that represent his estate after his
death, having goods thereto of the testator's, be charged
also with the debts, and not the goods.   And therefore if
an executor give away or sell all the goods of the testator,
or otherwise waste them, he that hath the goods is not
charged with the debts in law nor conscience, but the
executors shall be charged of their own goods.*   And in
like wise, if John at Noke owe to A. B. 20*l.* and A. B.
oweth to C. D. 20*l.*, and after A. B. dieth intestate, having
none other goods but the said 20*l.* which the said John at
Noke oweth him ; yet the said C. D. shall have no remedy
against the said John at Noke, for he standeth not charged
to him in law nor conscience.   But the ordinary in that
case must commit administration of the goods of the said
A. B., and the said administrator must levy the money of

---

* Ante, 132.

the said John at Noke, and pay it to the said C. D., and the
said John at Noke shall not pay it himself, because he is
not charged therewith to him : and no more methinketh in
this case, that he to whom the bequest is made, is neither
charged to him that the money was owing to, in the law or
conscience.

Doct. Then shew me thy mind, by what law it was
grounded, as thou thinkest, that executors be bound to pay
debts before legacies; whether it is by the law of God, or
by the law of reason, or by the law of man, as thou
thinkest?

Stud. I think that it is both by the law of reason and by
the law of God. For reason wills that they shall do first
that is best for the testator, and that is to pay debts, that
their testator is bound to pay, before legacies that he is
not bound to.* And also by the law of God they are
bound to pay the debts first : for sith they are bound by the
law of God to love their neighbour, they are bound to do for
him that shall be best for him, when they have taken the
charge thereto, as executors do when they agree to take
the charge of the will of their testator upon them ; and it is
better for the testator that his debts be paid, (wherefore his
soul shall suffer pain) than that his legacies be performed,
wherefore he shall suffer no pain for the performing of
them.†

And that is to be understood, where the legacy is made
of his own free-will, and not where it is made as a satisfaction of any duty. And after the saying of St. Gregory, the
very true proof of love is the deed. But this man is not in
that case, for he took never the charge upon him to pay
the debts of the testator, and therefore he is not bound to
them in law nor conscience, as me seemeth : but rather the
executors should have been ware ere they had paid the
legacies, seeing there were debts to pay.

Doct. The executors might no otherwise have done in

---

* Office of Exec. 27.
† Ib. 155.

this case, but to pay the legacies: for them they should have been compelled by the law to have paid, and so they could not have been to have paid the debt upon a contract,* and therefore they did well in performing of that legacy; but he to whom the 'legacy was made ought not to have taken them, but ought in conscience to have suffered them to have gone to the payment of the debt. And sith he did not so, but took them where he had no right to them, it seemeth that when he took them, he took with them the charge in conscience to pay the debt: for sith the executors were compellable by the law to perform that bequest, and not to pay the debt, therefore when they performed that bequest, they were discharged thereby against him that the debt was owing to, in the law and conscience; and then the charge rested upon him that took the goods, where he ought not in conscience to have taken them : but if it had been a debt upon an obligation, or such other debt, where-upon remedy hath been had against the executors by the law, I there suppose, though that the executors had performed the legacy, that yet he to whom the legacy was made and performed, had not been charged in conscience to the payment of the debt, for the executors stood still charged thereto of their own goods; and he to whom the bequest was made was only bound in conscience to repay that he received to the executors, because he had no right to have received it, for against the executors he had no right thereto.

Stud. Then it seemeth in this case, that in like wise he to whom the bequest was made should repay that he received to the executors, and then they to pay it rather than he.†

---

* But the old law is now altered, and an action will lie against the executor upon the assumpsit of the testator implied in a simple contract. Lev. 200, 201; 2 Cro. 293. And therefore an executor should be very careful how he pays legacies pecuniary or specific, especially where his testator dies much indebted, without taking securities from the different legatees to refund in case debts of any kind shall appear, or putting himself under the direction of a court of equity.

† 2 Vern. 205; 1 Chan. Ca. 136.

Doct. The executors have no farther meddling with it, as this case is: for when they performed the bequest, they were discharged against both the other in law and conscience: and also he to whom the bequest was made stood not in this case charged to the executors; for against them he had good title by the law: and so this charge standeth only against him that the debt is owing to. And the same law, that is in this case upon a debt upon a contract, as if the testator had done a trespass whereupon he ought to have made restitution, that is to say, that he to whom the bequest is made, is bound to make the amends for the trespass: for it should be no discharge to him to pay it again to the executors without they paid it over, and it were uncertain to him whether they should pay it or not. And therefore to be out of peril, it is necessary that he pay it himself, and then he is surely discharged against all men.

CHAP. XII.—*The tenth question of the student.*

A man seised of certain land in his demesne as of fee, hath issue two sons, and died seised, after whose death a stranger abateth, and taketh the profits, and after the eldest son dieth without issue, and his brother bringeth an *assize of mortdancestor* as son and heir to his father, not making mention of his brother, and recovereth the land with damages from the death of his father, as he may well by the law:* whether in this case is the younger brother bound in conscience to pay to the executors of the eldest brother the value of the profits of the said land that belonged to the eldest brother in his life, or not?

Doct. What is thine opinion therein?

Stud. That like as the said profits belonged of right to the eldest brother in his life, and that he had full authority to have released as well the right of the said land as of the said profits, which release should have been a clear bar to the younger brother for ever; that the right of the said

* 2 Inst. 287.

damages, which be in the law but a chattel, belong to his executors, and not to the heir :* for no manner of chattel, neither real nor personal, shall after the law of the realm descend unto the heir.

Doct. Thou saidest in the case next before, that it is not of the law of reason, that a man shall make executors, and dispose of his goods by his will, and that the executors shall have the goods to dispose, but by the law of man ; and if it be left to the determination of the law of man, that in such cases as the law giveth such chattels unto the executors, they shall have good right unto them, and in such cases as the law taketh such chattels from them, they been rightfully taken from them : and therefore it is thought by many, that if a man sue a writ of *Right of Ward* of a ward, that he hath by his own fee, and dieth hanging the writ, and his heir sue a re-summons, according to the statute of Westminster 2, and recovereth ;† that in that case the heir shall enjoy the wardship against the executors, and yet it is but a chattel. And they take the reason to be, because of the said statute. And so it might be ordained by statute, that all wards shall go to the heirs, and not to the executors. Right so in this case, sith the law is such, that the younger brother shall in this case have an *assize of mortdancestor*‡ as heir to his father, not making any mention of his elder brother, and recover damages as well in

---

* Ante, 21; Office of Exec. 53, 57, 58, 59.

† 2 Inst, 441; ante, 27.

‡ On an assize of *mortdancestor*, Mr. Justice Blackstone has the following observation (3 B. C. 187): "It was always (says he) held to be law, that where lands were devisable in a man's last will by the custom of the place, there an assize of *mortdancestor* did not lie. For where lands were so devisable, the right of possession could never be determined by a process which enquired only of these two points, the seisin of the ancestor and the heirship of the demandant, and hence it might be reasonable to conclude, that when the statute of Wills, 32 H. S, c. 1, made all socage lands devisable, an assize of *mortdancestor* no longer could be brought of lands held in socage; and that now since the stat. 12 Cha. 2, c. 24, which converts all tenures (a few only excepted) into free and common socage, it should follow that no assize of *mortdancestor* can be brought of any lands in the kingdom."

the time of his brother as in his own time ;* it appeareth that the law giveth the right of these damages to the heir, and therefore no recompence ought to be made to the executors, as me seemeth. And it is not like to the writ of Aiel,† where, as I have learned in Latin, (sith our first dialogue) the demandant shall recover damages only from the death of his father, if he overlive the Aiel :† and the cause is, for that the demandant, though his Aiel overlived his father, must of necessity make his conveyance by his father, and must make himself son and heir to his father, and cousin and heir to his Aiel ;§ and therefore in that case, if the father overlived the Aiel, the abator were bounden in conscience to restore to the executors of the father the profits run in his time (for no law taketh them from him) ; but otherwise it is in this case as me seemeth.

Stud If the younger brother in this case had entered into the land without taking any *assize of mortdancestor*, as he might if he would, to whom were the abator then bounden to make restitution for those profits, as thou thinkest?

Doct. To the executors of the eldest brother ; for in that case there is no law that taketh them from them, and therefore the general ground, which is that all chattels shall go to the executors, holdeth in that case ; but in this case that ground is broken and holdeth not, for the reason that I have made before. For commonly there is no general ground in the law so sure, but it faileth in some particular case.

CHAP. XIII.—*The eleventh question of the student*

Stud. A man seised of land in fee taketh a wife, and after alieneth the land, and dieth, after whose death his wife asketh her dower, and the alienee refuseth to assign it unto

---

* 2 Inst. 287.

† Since an ejectment has been introduced, the writ of Aiel has fallen into disuse.

‡ 2 Inst. 288.

§ Ib.

her, but after she asketh her dower again, and he assigneth it unto her : whether is the alienee in this case bound in
conscience to give the woman damages for the profits of the
land after her third part from the death of her husband, or
from the first request of her dower, or neither the one nor
the other.

Doct. What is the law in this case?

Stud. By the law the woman shall recover no damages ;[*]
for at the common law the demandant in a writ of dower
should never have recovered damages; but by the statute
of Merton,[†] it is ordained, that where the husband dieth
seised, that the woman shall recover damages,[‡] which is
understood the profits of the land sith the death of her husband, and such damages as she hath by the forbearing of
it.[§] But in this case the husband died not seised, where-
fore she shall recover no damages by the law.[||]

Doct. Yet the law is, that immediately after the death of
her husband the wife ought of right to have her dower, if
she ask it; though her husband die not seised.

Stud. That is true.

Doct. And sith she ought to have her dower from the
death of her husband, it seemeth that she ought in conscience to have also the profits from the death of her husband, though she have no remedy to come to them by the
law ;[¶] for methinketh that this case is like to a case that thou
puttest in our first dialogue in Latin, the seventeenth chapter.
That if a tenant for term of life be disseised and die, and
the disseisor dieth, and his heir entereth and taketh the
profits, and after he in the reversion recovereth the lands
against the heir, as he ought to do by the law, that in that
case he shall recover no damages by the law ; and yet thou
didst agree, that in that case the heir is bound in conscience

[*] 2 Inst. 30; Co. Litt. 33.
[†] 20 H. 3, c. 1.
[‡] Dyer, 284.
[§] And by the statute of Gloucester, 6 Ed. 1, c. 1, she is intitled to costs
as well as damages.
[||] Co. Litt. 32.
[¶] Ib.

to pay the damages to the demandant: and so methinketh
in this case that the feoffee ought in conscience to pay the
damages from the death of her husband, seeing that immediately after his death she ought to have her dower.

Stud. Though she ought to be indowed immediately
after the death of her husband, yet she can lay no default
in the feoffee till she demand her dower upon the ground,
and that the tenant be not there to assign it, or if he be
there, that he will not assign it;* for he that hath the possession of land whereunto any woman hath title of dower,
hath good authority as against her to take the profits till she
require her dower; for every woman that demandeth dower
affirmeth the possession of the tenant as against her: and
therefore although she recover by action, she leaveth the
reversion alway in him against whom she recovereth,
though he be a disseisor, and bringeth not the reversion by
her recovery to him that hath right, as other tenants for
term of life do.   And for this reason it is that the tenant in
a writ of dower, where the husband died seised, if he appear the first day, may say, to excuse himself of damages,†
that he is, and all times hath been ready to yield dower if
it had been demanded; and so he shall not be received to
do in a writ of coisnage,‡ neither in the case that thou re-
memberest above: for in both cases the tenants be supposed
by the writ to be wrong-doers, but it is not so in this case;
and so methinketh it is quite clear that the feoffee in this
case shall never be bound by law nor conscience to yield
damages for the time that passed before the request, but for
the time after the request is greater doubt;§ howbeit some
think him there not bound to yield damages, because his
title is good, as is said before, and that it is her default that
she brought not her action.

Doct. As unto the time before the request I hold me content with thine opinion, so that he assign the dower when

* Co. Litt. 32.
† Br. Damages, pl. 79; Co. Litt. 32, 33.
‡ This writ, like that of Aiel, is now grown quite out of use.
§ Jenk. 45, pl. 85; Co. Litt. 32.

he is required : but when he refuseth to assign it, then I think him bound in conscience to yield damages for both times, though she shall none recover by the law. And first, as for the time after the refusal, it appeareth evidently, that when he denied to assign her dower he did against conscience ; for he did not that he ought to have done by the law, ne as he would should have been done to him : and so after the request he holdeth her dower from her wrongfully, and ought in conscience to yield damages therefore. And as to the default that thou assignest in her, that she took not her action, that forceth little ; for actions need not but where the party will not do that he ought to do of right; and for that he ought of right to have done, and did it not, he can take no advantage. And then as to the damages before the request, methinketh him also bounden to pay them ; for when he was required to assign dower, and refused, it appeareth that he never intended to yield dower from the beginning, and so he is a wrong-doer in his own conscience. And moreover, if the husband die seised, the law is such, that if the tenant refuse to assign dower when he is required, wherefore the woman bringeth a writ of dower against him, that in that case the woman shall recover damages as well for the time before the request as after ; and yet he ought not in that case, after thine opinion, to have yielded any manner of damages, if he had been ready to assign dower when it was demanded, as some think here.

Stud. The cause in the case that thou hast put is, for that the statute is general, that the demandant shall recover damages where the husband died seised, and that statute hath been alway construed, that where the tenant may not say that he is and hath been ready alway to yield dower, etc., that the demandant shall recover damages from the death of her husband.* But in that case there is no law of the realm that helpeth for the demandant, neither common law nor statute. And furthermore, though it might be proved by his refusal, that he never intended from the

---

* Co. Litt. 32.

death of the husband to assign her dower; yet that proveth
not but that he had good right to take the profits of her
third part for the time, as well as he had of his own two
parts, till request be made, as is aforesaid: and 'so methinketh that, notwithstanding the denial, he is not bound
to yield damages in this case, but for the time of the request, and not for the time before.

Doct. For this time I am content with thy reason.

CHAP. XIV.—*The twelfth question of the student.*

Stud. A man seised of certain lands, knowing that another hath good right and title to them, levieth a fine with
proclamation, to the intent he would extinct the right of the
other man, and the other man maketh no claim within the
five years : whether may he that levied the fine hold the
land in conscience, as he may do by the law?*

Doct. By this question it seemeth that thou dost agree,
that if he that levied the fine had no knowledge of the other
man's right, that his right should then be extincted by the
fine in conscience.

Stud. Yes, verily; for thou didst shew a reasonable
cause why it should be so, in our first dialogue in Latin,
the twenty-fourth chapter, as there appeareth. But if he
that levied a fine, and that would extinct the right of another, knew that the other had more right than he, then I
doubt therein : for I take thine opinion in the first dialogue
to be understood in conscience, where he that would extinct former rights by such a fine by proclamation, knoweth
not of any former title, but for his more surety, if any such
former right be, taketh the remedy that is ordained by the
law.

Doct. Whether dost thou mean in this case that thou
puttest now, that he that hath right knoweth of the fine,
wilfully letting the five years pass without claim, or that he
knoweth not anything of the fine?

* Ante, 65, 110.

Stud. I pray thee let me know thine opinion in both cases, and whether thou think that he that hath right be barred in either of the said cases by conscience, as he is by the law, or not?

Doct. I will with good-will hereafter shew thee my mind therein : but at this time I pray thee give a little sparing, and proceed now for this time to some other question.

CHAP. XV.—*The thirteenth question of the student.*

Stud. A man seised of certain land, in fee hath a daughter, which is his heir apparent, the daughter taketh an husband, and they have issue ; the father dieth seised, and the husband as soon as he heareth of his death goeth toward the land to take possession, and before he can come there his wife dieth : whether ought he to have the land in conscience for term of his life as tenant by the courtesy,* because he hath done that in him was, to have had possession in his wife's life, so that he might have been tenant by the courtesy according to the law ; or that he shall neither have it by the law nor conscience ?

Doct. Is it clearly holden in the law, that he shall not be tenant by the courtesy in this case, because he had not possession in deed ?

Stud. Yea, verily, and yet upon a possession in law a woman shall have her dower ;† but no man shall be tenant by the courtesy of land without his wife have possession in deed.‡

Doct. A man shall be tenant by the courtesy of a rent though his wife die before the day of payment,§ and in like wise of an advowson‖ though she die before the avoidance.¶

---

* Perk., sec. 458.
† Co. Litt. 31.
‡ Finch Law, 129.
§ Co. Litt. 29.
‖ 2 B. C. 127.
¶ And Mr. Perkins thinks that notwithstanding the advowson becomes void during the coverture, and the wife dies after the six months past, and

Stud. That is truth; for the old custom and maxim of the law is, that he shall be so: but of land there is no maxim that serveth him, but his wife have possession in deed.

Doct. And what is the reason that there is such a maxim in the law of the rent, and of the advowson, rather than of land, when the husband doth as much as in him is, to have possession, and cannot?

Stud. Some assign the reason to be, because it is impossible to have possession in deed of the rent, or of advowson,* before the day of payment of the rent, or before the avoidance of the advowson.

Doct. And so it is impossible that he should have possession in deed of land, if his wife die so soon that he may not by a possibility come to the land after his father's death, and in her life, as the case is.

Stud. The law is such as I have shewed thee before: and I take the very cause to be, for that there is a maxim serveth for the rent and the advowson, and not for the lands, as I have said before: and, as it is said in the eighth chapter of our first dialogue,† it is not alway necessary to assign a reason or consideration why the maxims of the law of England were first ordained and admitted for maxims; but it sufficeth that they have been always taken for law, and that they be neither contrary to the law of reason, nor to the law of God, as this maxim is not:‡ and therefore, if the husband in this case be not holpen by conscience, he cannot be holpen by the law.

Doct. And if the law help him not, conscience cannot help him in this case; for conscience must always be grounded upon some law; and it cannot in this case be

before any presentment by the husband, and the ordinary presents by lapse unto the advowson, that the husband shall still be tenant by courtesy, Perk., sec. 468, but I do not apprehend there is any authority in support of this opinion. Indeed it seems to be rather an extraordinary one, as the laches of the husband must certainly be a capital objection against his claim.

* Kelw. 104; 1 Co. 97.
† Ante, 26.
‡ Ante, 79.

grounded upon the law of reason, nor upon the law of God ; for it is not directly by those laws that a man shall be tenant by courtesy, but by the custom of the realm ;* and therefore if the custom help him not, he can nothing have in this case by conscience ; for conscience never resisteth the law of man, nor addeth nothing to it, but where the law of man is in itself directly against the law of reason, or else the law of God, and then properly it cannot be called a law, but a corruption ;† or where the general grounds of the law of man work in any particular case against the said laws, as it may do, and yet the law good, as it appeareth in divers places in our first dialogue in Latin ; or else where there is no law of man provided for him that hath right to a thing by the law of reason, or by the law of God : and then sometime there is remedy given to execute that in conscience, as by a subpœna, but not in all cases ;‡ for sometime, it shall be referred to the conscience of the party, and upon this ground, that is to say, that when there is no title given by the Common law, that there is no title by conscience. There be divers other cases, whereof I shall put some for an example : As if a reversion be granted unto one, but there is no attornment, or if a new rent be granted by word without deed ;§ there is no remedy by conscience, unless the said grants were made upon consideration of money, or such other. And in like wise where he that is seised of lands in fee-simple maketh a will thereof,‖ that will is void in conscience, because the ground serveth not for him whereby the conscience should take effect, that is to say, the law. And if the tenant make a feoffment of the land that he holdeth by priority, and taketh estate again and dieth, (his heir within age) the lord of whom the land was first holden by priority shall have no remedy for the

* Ante, 20.
† Ante, 11, 53.
‡ Ante, 39.
§ Litt., sec. 567, 568; ante, 30.
‖ Ante, 23, 58.
10

body by conscience ;* for the law that first was with him, is now against him, and therefore conscience is altered in like wise as the law altereth. And divers and many cases like be in the law, that were too long to rehearse now. And thus methinketh, that if the law be as thou sayest, the husband in this case hath neither right by the law nor conscience.

CHAP. XVI.—*The fourteenth question of the student.*

Stud. A rent is granted to a man in fee to perceive of two acres of land, and after the grantor enfeoffeth the grantee of one of the said acres ;† whether is the whole rent extinct thereby in conscience, as it is in the law?

Doct. This case is somewhat uncertain : for it appeareth not whether the grantor enfeoffed him on ·trust, or that he gave the acre to him of his mere motion to the use of the said feoffee ;‡ or else that the feoffment was made upon a bargain : and if it were but only a feoffment of trust, then I think the whole rent abideth in conscience, though it be extincted in law. And first, That it continueth in that case in conscience for the part that the grantee hath to the use of the grantor, it is evident, for he may take the profits of the land, and it is against conscience that he should leese both. And in like wise it abideth in conscience for the acre that remaineth in the hands of the grantor, though it be extinct in the law : for there was a default in the grantor that he would make a feoffment to the grantee, as well as there was in the grantee, to take it ; and it is no conscience that of his own default he should take so great avail, to be discharged of the whole rent, seeing that the feoffment was made to his own use. And if the feoffment were made upon a bargain, and a contract between them, then it is to see whether they remembered the rent in their bargain, or

---

* Vin. Abr., title Guardian and Ward, 166; ante, 27.
† Litt., sec. 222; Wood's Inst. 205;
‡ Post. 152.

that they remembered it not; and if they remembered it in their bargain and contract, then conscience must follow the bargain: and thus, If they agreed that the grantee should have the rent after the portion in the other acre, then by conscience he ought to have it, though it be extincted in the law; and if they agreed that the whole rent should be extinct, and made their price according, then it is extinct in law and conscience; and if they clearly forgot it, and made no mention of it, or, for lack of cunning, took the law to be that it should continue in the other acre after the portion, and made their price according, pondering only the value of the acre that was sold, then methinketh it doth continue in conscience after the portion; and if the feoffment were made to the use of the grantee, then it seemeth the whole rent is extinct in law and conscience.

Stud. Then take this to be the case, that·is to say, that the feoffment was made to the use of the grantee.

Doct. What is thine opinion therein?

Stud. Then the rent should abide in conscience after the portion of the acre remaining in the hands of the grantor, notwithstanding it be extinct in the law.

Doct. Then shew me thine opinion in this that I shall ask thee: Of what law is it, that grants of rent, and of such other profits out of lands may be made, and that they shall be good and effectual to the grantees? Whether it be by the law of reason, or by the law of God, or by the custom and law of the realm?

Stud. I think it is by the law of reason: for by the same reason that a man may give away all his lands, he may, as it seemeth, give away the profits thereof, or grant a rent out of the land, if he will.

Doct. But then by what law is it that a man may give away his lands? I trow by none other law but by the custom of the realm; for by statute all alienations and grants of lands may be prohibited; and then that reason proveth not that grants of the profits of land, or of a rent, should be good, because he may alien the land, if alienation of land be by custom, and not by the law of reason,* as I suppose it is, whereof I have touched somewhat in our first dialogue in Latin, the nineteenth chapter. And also if grants should have their effect by the law of reason, then reason would they should be good by the only word of the grantor, as well as by his deed; and that is not so, for without deed the grant of rent is void in law; and so methinketh, that grants have their effects only by the law of the realm.†

Stud. Admit it be so, what meanest thou thereby?

Doct. I shall shew thee hereafter, as I shall shew thee the cause why I think the rent is ext.nct in conscience as well as in law. And first, as I take it, the reason why it is extinct in the law, is because the rent by the first grant was going out of both acres, and was not going part out of the one acre, and part out of the other, but the whole rent was going out of both;‡ and then when the grantee of his own folly will take estate in the one acre, whereby that acre be discharged, then the other acre also must be discharged, unless it should be apportioned; and the law will not that any apportionment should be in that case;§ but rather insomuch as the party hath by his own act discharged the one acre, the law discharged also the other, rather than to suffer the other acre to be charged contrary to the form of the grant:|| for this rent beginneth all by the act of the party; and, as I have heard, it is called, *A rent against common right.*¶ Wherefore it is not favoured in the law, as a rent-service is: and then methinketh, that forasmuch

---

* Post. 155.

† 2 Roll. Abr. 62; Shep. Touch. 228.

‡ Co. Litt. 147.

§ Yet it seems that a rent-charge may be apportioned by the act of the party, as if a man hath a rent-charge of 20s. he may release to the tenant of the land 10s. or more or less, and reserve part; for the grantee meddles only with that which is his own, viz., the rent and not with the land. Co. Litt. 148.

|| But if the grantor by deed reciting the purchase had granted that the grantee should distrain for the same rent in the residue of the land, the whole rent-charge had been preserved, because such power of distress had amounted to a new grant. Co. Litt. 147.

¶ Litt., sec. 222.

as it is not grounded by the law of reason, that grants of rent should be made out of land, but by custom and law of the realm, as I have said before, that so in like wise it remaineth to the law and custom of the realm to determine how long such rents shall continue.* And when the law judgeth such rent to be void, I suppose that so doth conscience also, except the judgment of the law be against the law of reason, or the law of God, as it is not in this case. For in this case, he that taketh the feoffment hath profit by the feoffment, and knoweth that he hath such a rent out of the land, and that this purchase should extinct it, whereby it appeareth that he assented unto the law, whereto he was not compelled, and that is his own act, and his own default so to do, which shall extinct his whole rent as well in conscience as in law. But if he have no profit of the land, or be ignorant that he hath such a rent out of the land, which is called *Ignorance of the deed*, or if he be ignorant that the law would extinct his whole rent thereby, which is called *Ignorance of the law*, then methinketh it remaineth in conscience after the portion.

Stud. Ignorance of the law,† or of the deed, helpeth not. but in few cases in the law of England.‡

Doct. And therefore it must be reformed by conscience, that is to say, by the law of reason. For when the general maxims of the law be in any particular cases against the law of reason, as this maxim seemeth to be, because it excepteth not them that be ignorant, though it be an ignorance invincible ;§ then doth it not agree with the law of reason.

Stud. Methinketh that ignorance in this case helpeth little. For when a man buyeth any land, or taketh it of the gift of any other, he taketh it at his peril, so that if the title be no good, ignorance cannot help,‖ for the buyer

* Ante, 148.
† Douglas Rep. 471;
‡ Ante, 77; post., chap. 46.
§ Ib.
‖ *Tamen quære*, whether a court of equity will not relieve a purchaser for a *valuable consideration*, who used all possible means to find out in-

must beware what he buyeth : and so in this case, if the
taking of an acre should extinct the whole rent in conscience, if he were not ignorant, so methinketh it should in
like wise extinct it also, though he be ignorant of the law,
or of the deed ; for every man must be compelled to take
notice of his own title, and out of what land his rent is
going, and so methinketh ignorance is but little to be considered in this case.

Doct. If a man buy land, or taketh it of the gift of another, it is reason that he take it with the peril, though he
be ignorant that another hath right ;* for it were not standing with reason that his ignorance should extinct the right
of another : but in this case there is no doubt of the right
ot the land, but all the doubt is how the rent shall be ordered in conscience, if he that hath the rent take part of
the land ; and therein is great diversity between him that
is ignorant in the law, and him that knoweth the law, and
knoweth well also that he hath a rent out of the land, and
other. For I put case, he asked counsel of the grantor
himself therein, and he saying as he thought, told him, that
the taking of the one acre should not extinct the rent but
for the portion, and so he thinking the law to be, took the
other acre of his gift : is it not reasonable in that case, that
the ignorance should save the rent in conscience?

Stud. Yes, for there the grantor himself is party to his
ignorance, and in manner the cause thereof.

Doct. And methinketh all is one if any other had shewed
him so, or if he asked no counsel at all ; for methinketh it
sufficeth in this case that he be ignorant of the law : for
why? it is more hard in this case to prove the rent should
be extinct in conscience, tho' he knew it should be extinct
in the law, than to prove that it continueth in conscience
after the portion, if he be ignorant ; and thou thyself wert
of the same opinion, as it appeareth in the beginning of

cumbrances affecting his title, but it afterward proves to be bad through
some *latent* circumstances which he could not well inform himself of. See
2 Lev. 152 ; R. Eq. Ca. 37 ; Cary's Rep. 132, 133.
   * Ante, 149.

this present chapter.* But if the opinion were true, it would be hard to prove but that the said general maxim were wholly against reason, and then it were void. But I have sufficiently answered thereto, as me seemeth, and that it is extinct in the law, and also in conscience, except ignorance help it to be apportioned. And moreover, forasmuch as apportionment is suffered in the law, where part of the land descendeth to the grantee, because no default can be assigned in him :† some think no default can be assigned in him in conscience, when he is ignorant of the law, or of the deed, though such ignorance do not excuse in the law of the realm.

Stud. I am content with thy opinion in his behalf at this time.

CHAP. XVII.—*The fifteenth question of the student.*

A man granteth a rent-charge out of two acres of land, and after the grantor enfeoffeth H. H. in one of the said two acres to the use of the said H. H. and of his heirs,‡ and after the said H. Hart, intending to extinct all the rent causeth the said acre to be recovered against him to his own use in a writ of *Entry in le post*, in the name of the grantee, and of others, after the common course, the grantee not knowing of it, and by force of the said recovery the other demandants enter, and die living the grantee, so that the grantor is seised of all by the survivor to the use of the said H. H., whether is the said rent extinct in conscience in part or in all, or no part?

Doct. I am in doubt of the law in this case.

Stud. In what point?

Doct. Whether the whole rent be going out of the acre that remaineth in the hands of the grantor, because the grantee cometh to the land by way of recovery; or that it shall be extinct in law but after the portion, because the

* Ante, 146.
† Litt., sec. 224.
‡ Co. Litt. 148.

grantee hath not the acre to his own use ; or that the whole
rent shall be extinct in the law?

Stud. The rent cannot be whole going out of the acre
that the grantor hath :* for this recovery is upon a feigned
title ; and the grantor, because he is a stranger to it, shall
be well received to falsify it.† But if the recovery had been
upon a true title, then it had been as thou sayest; if the
grantee recover the one acre against the grantor upon the
true title, the grantor shall pay the whole rent out of the
land that remaineth in his hands.‡ And as to the use, it
maketh no matter to the grantor, as to the law, in whom
the use be; for the possession without the use extinguisheth
the whole rent as against him, in the law, as well as if the
possession and use were both joined together in the grantee.

Doct. Then methinketh that the said Henry Hart is bound
in conscience to pay the grantee the rent after the portion
of that acre that was recovered ; for it cannot stand with
conscience that he should lose his rent, and have no profits
of the land?

Stud. Then of whom shall he have the other portion of
his rent?

Doct. Is the law clear, that the acre that the grantor hath
shall be in this case discharged in the law?

Stud. I take the law so.

Doct. And what in conscience?

Stud. As against the grantor, methinketh also it is extinct in conscience, for the reason that thou hast made in
the sixteenth chapter.§ For it is all one in conscience in
this case as against the grantor, whether the recovery were
to the use of the grantee or not, especially seeing that the
grantor is not privy to the recovery : for the unity of possession is the cause of extinguishment of the rent against
the grantor, both in law and conscience, wheresoever the use

---

* Co. Litt. 148.
† Piggot on Rec. 165.
‡ Co. Litt. 148.
§ Ante, 146.

be.* But if the grantor hath been privy to the cause of the extinguishment, as he was in the case that I put in the last chapter, where the grantor enfeoffed the grantee of one of the acres to the use of the grantee;† there it is not extinct in conscience in that acre that remaineth in the hands of the grantor, though it be extincted in the law, because he was privy to the extinguishment himself: but he is not in this case, and therefore it is extinct against him in law and conscience. And therefore methinketh that the grantee shall in conscience have the whole rent of the said Henry Hart, that causeth the said recovery to be had in his name, for in him was all the default. But it is to be understood, that in all the cases where it is said before in this chapter, or in the chapter next before,‡ that the rent is extinct in the law, and not in conscience, that in such case all the remedies that the party might first have had for the rent at the Common law by distress, assise, or otherwise, are determined, and the party that ought to have the rent in conscience shall be driven to sue for his remedy by *subpœna*.

Doct. I am content with thy conceit in this matter for this time.

CHAP. XVIII.—*The sixteenth question of the student.*

Stud. A villein is granted to a man for term of life, the villein purchaseth lands to him and to his heirs, the tenant for term of life entereth;§ in this case by the law he shall enjoy the lands to him and to his heirs; whether shall he do so in like wise in conscience?

Doct. Methinketh it first good to see whether it may stand with conscience, that one man may claim another to be his villein, and that he may take from him his lands and goods, and put his body in prison if he will:‖ it seemeth he loveth not his neighbour as himself that doth so to him.

* Ante, 33.
† Ante, 146.
‡ Ib.
§ Perk., sec. 94; Co. Litt. 124.
‖ 26 E. 3, c. 24.

Stud. That law hath been so long used in this realm, and in other also, and hath been admitted so long in the laws of this realm, and in divers other laws also, and hath been affirmed by bishops, abbots, priors;* and many other men both spiritual and temporal, which have taken advantage by the said laws, and have seized the lands and goods of their villeins thereby, and call it their right inheritance so to do :† that I think it not good now to make doubt, ne to put it in argument, whether it stand with conscience, or not? And therefore I pray thee, admitting the law in that behalf to stand in conscience, shew me thine opinion in the question that I have made.

Doct. Is the law clear, that he that hath the villein but only for term of life, shall have the lands that that villein purchaseth in fee to him and to his heirs?

Stud. Yes, verily I take it so.

Doct. I should have taken the law otherwise : for if a seigniory be granted to a man for term of life,‡ and the tenant attourn, and after the land escheat, and the tenant for term of life, entereth, he shall have there none other estate in the land than he had in the seigniory : and methinketh that it should be like law in this case, and that the lord ought to have in the land but such estate as he hath in the villein.

Stud. The cases be not alike : for in the case of the escheat the tenant for term of life of the seigniory hath the lands in lieu of the seigniory,§ that is to say, in the place of the seigniory, and the seigniory is clearly extinct : but in this case he hath not the land in lieu of the villein ;|| for he shall have the villein still as he had before, but he hath the lands as a profit come by means of the villein, which he shall have in like case as the villein had them,¶ that is to

---

* Br. Villeinage, pl. 70.
† Ante, 29.
‡ Br. Villeinage, pl. 70.
§ Co. Litt. 99.
|| Perk., sec. 94.
¶ See post., cap. 43; Finch Law. 159.

say, of all goods and chattels he shall have the whole
property, and of a lease for term of years he shall have the
whole term, and for term of life he shall have the same estate, the lord shall have in the villein during the life of the
villein, and of land in fee-simple;* and of an estate-tail
that the villein hath, the lord shall have the whole fee-simple,
although he had the villein but only for term of years, so
that he enter or seise according to the law before the villein alien, or else he shall have nothing.†

Doct. Verily, and if the law be so, I think conscience
followeth the law therein. For admitting that a man may
with conscience have another man to be his villein, the
judgment of the law in this case (as to determine what estate the lord hath in the land by his entry) is neither against
the law of reason nor against the law of God, and therefore conscience must follow the law of the realm. But I
pray thee let me make a little digression, to hear thine
opinion in another case somewhat pertaining to the question, and it is this : If an executor have a villein that his
testator had for term of years, and he purchaseth lands in
fee, and the executor entereth into the land, what estate
hath he by his entry ?.

Stud. A fee-simple,‡ but that shall be to the behoof of
the testator, and shall be an asset in his hands.§

---

* Co. Litt. 117.
† Ante, 29.
‡ Br. Villeinage, pl. 46.
§ On this chapter I beg leave to offer the following brief observation;
which is, that although villeinage, properly so called, was happily for this
country, and the cause of civil liberty, abolished by the memorable statute
of 12 Car. 2, c. 24, which we have had occasion to mention in another
place; yet there is a proviso in that statute, which declares that it shall
not be construed to extend to change or alter any tenure by copy of court
roll, or any services incident to that tenure; and from this proviso we may
learn, that in the opinion of the legislature copyholds had some connec-
tion with the feudal system. Indeed the fact was so; and at this day it
may perhaps be said, that copyhold tenure is nothing but pure villeinage
divested of its servile appendages by the hand of time. F. N. B. 25.
Custom or prescription is the principal foundation of the immunities which
copyholders now enjoy, and is the life of their estates. Co. Com. Co. 204.
For though they hold them at *the will of the lord* like their ancestors the

Doct. Well then, I am content with thy conceit at this time in this case, and I pray thee proceed to another question.

Stud. Forasmuch as it appeareth in this case, and in some other before, that the knowledge of the law of England is right necessary for the good ordering of conscience; I would hear thine opinion, if a man mistake the law, what danger it is in conscience for the mistaking of it.

Doct. I pray thee put some case in certain thereof that thou doubtest in, and I will with good-will shew thee my mind therein, or else it will be somewhat long, or it cannot be plainly declared, and I would not be tedious in this writing.

CHAP. XIX.—*The seventeenth question of the student.*

Stud. A man hath a villein for term of life, the villein purchaseth lands in fee,* as in the case of the last chapter, and the tenant for term of life entereth, and after the villein dieth: he in the reversion pretending that the tenant for term of life hath nothing in the land but for term of life of the villein, asketh counsel of one that sheweth him that he hath good right to the land, and that he may lawfully enter, and through that counsel he in the reversion entereth, by reason of the which entry great suits and expenses follow in the law, to the great hurt of both parties: what danger is this to him that gave the counsel?

Doct. Whether meanest thou that he that gave the counsel gave it willingly against the law, or that he was ignorant of the law?

Stud. That he was ignorant of the law: for if he knew the law, and gave counsel to the contrary, I think him bound to restitution, both to him against whom he gave the

villeins, yet observe, it is *according to the custom of the manor.* Ib. And while they perform the services which that custom imposes upon them, (light a nd easy as they are compared with the drudgery of pure villeinage in its original state,) their property is secure from the invasions of the lord, they have a permanency in it, and can call it their own. Co. Co. 58.

* Perk., sec. 94; ante, 153.

counsel, and also to his client, (if he would not have sued
but for his counsel) of all that they be damnified by it.

Doct. Then will I yet farther ask thee this question;
whether he of whom he asked counsel gave himself to
learning and to have knowledge of the law after his capac-
ity? Or that he took upon him to give counsel, and took
no study competent to have learning? For if he did so, I
think he be bounden in conscience to restitution of all the
costs and damages that he sustained to whom he gave
counsel, if he would not have sued but through his counsel,
and also to the other party. But if a man that hath taken
sufficient study in the law mistake the law in some point
that it is hard to come to the knowledge of, he is not
bounden to such restitution, for he hath done that in him
is: but if such a man knowing the law give counsel
against the law, he is bound in conscience to restitution of
costs and damages, (as thou hast said before) and also to
make amends for the untruth.*

Stud. What if he ask counsel of one that he knoweth is
not learned, and he giveth him counsel in this case to enter,
by force whereof he entereth?

Doct. Then be they both bound in conscience to restitution; that is to say, the party, if he be sufficient, and else
the counsellor, because he assented, and gave counsel to
the wrong.

Stud. But what is the counsellor in that case bounden to
him that he gave counsel to?

Doct. To nothing: for there was as much default in him
that asked the counsel as in him that gave it; for he asked
counsel of him that he knew was ignorant; and in the
other was default for the presumption, that he would take
upon him to give counsel in that he was ignorant in.

Stud. But what if he that gave the counsel knew not but
that he that asked it had trust in him, that he could and
would give him good counsel, and that he asked counsel

---

* And it seems that he is liable to answer in an action of disceit.

for to order well his conscience, howbeit that the truth was that he could not so do?

Doct. Then is he that gave the counsel bounden to offer to the other amends, but yet the other may not take it in conscience.

Stud. That were somewhat perilous; for haply he would take it, though he have no right to it, except the world be well amended.

Doct. What thinkest thou in that amendment?

Stud. I trust every man will do now in this world as they would be done to, speak as they think, restore where they have done wrong, refuse money if they have no right to it, though it be offered them, do that they ought to do by conscience, and though that they cannot be compelled to it by no law; and that none will give counsel but that they shall think to be according to conscience, and if they do, to do what they can to reform it, and not to intermit themselves with such matters as they be ignorant in, but in such cases to send them that ask the counsel to other that they shall think be more cunning than they are.

Doct. It were very well if it were as thou hast said, but, the more pity, it is not alway so; and especially there is great default in givers of counsel: for some, for their own lucre and profit, give counsel to comfort other to sue that they know have no right, but I trust there be but few of them; and some 'for dread, some for favour, some for malice, and some upon confederacies, and to have as much done for them another time to hide the truth. And some take upon them to give counsel in that they be ignorant in, and yet when they know the truth will not withdraw that they have misdone, for they think it should be greatly to their rebuke; and such persons follow not this counsel, that saith, "That we have unadvisedly done, let us with good advice revoke again."

Stud. And if a man give counsel in this realm after as his learning and conscience giveth him, and regardeth the laws of the realm, giveth he good counsel?

Doct. If the law of the realm be not in that case against

the law of God, nor against the law of reason, he giveth good counsel : for every man is bound to follow the law of the country where he is, so it be not against the said laws ;* and so may the cases be, that he may bind himself to restitution.

Stud. At this time I will no farther trouble thee in this question.

CHAP. XX.—*The eighteenth question of the student.*

If a man of his mere motion give lands to H. Hart, and to his heirs, by indenture, upon a condition, that he shall yearly, at a certain day, pay to John at Stile out of the same land a certain rent, and if he do not, that then it should be lawful to the said John at Stile to enter, etc., if the rent in this case be not payed to John at Stile, whether may the said John at Stile enter into the lands by conscience, though he may not enter by the law?

Doct. May he not enter in this case by the law, sith the words of the indenture be that he shall enter?

Stud. No, verily ; for there is an ancient maxim in the law, that no man shall take advantage in a condition, but he that is party or privy to the condition ;† and this man is not party or privy, wherefore he shall have no advantage of it.

Doct. Though he can have no advantage of it as party, yet because it appeareth evidently that the intent of the giver was, that if he were not payed of the rent, that he should have the land, it seemeth that in conscience he ought to have it, though he can not have it by the law.

Stud. In many cases the intent of the party is void to all intents, if it be not grounded according to the law ;‡ and therefore if ·a man make a lease to another for term of life, and after of his mere motion he confirmeth his estate for

* Ante, 77.
† Litt., sec. 347; Dyer, 6, pl. 2; post. 170.
‡ 2 Vezey, 248; ante, 65.

term of life to remain after his death to another, and to his
heirs; in this case that remainder is void in law and conscience: for by the law there can no remainder depend
upon an estate, but that the same estate beginneth at the
same time that the remainder doth;* and in this case the
estate began before, and the confirmation enlarged not his
estate, nor gave him no new estate. But if a lease be
made to a man for term of another man's life, and after the
lessor only of his mere motion confirmeth the land to the
lessee for the term of his own life, the remainder over in
fee; that is a good remainder in the law and conscience.
And so methinketh the intent of the party shall not be regarded in this case.

Doct. And in the first case that thou hast put, methinketh
though it pass not by way of remainder of that, yet shall it
pass as by the way of grant of the reversion;† for every
deed shall be taken most strong against the grantor, and
the taking of a deed in this case is an attornment in itself.

Stud. That cannot be, for he in the remainder is not
party to the deed, and therefore it cannot be taken by the
way of grant of the reversion; for no grant can be made
but to him that is party to the deed, except it be by way of
remainder.‡ And therefore if a man make a lease for
term of life, and after the lessor grant to a stranger that the
tenant for term of life shall have the land to him, and to
his heirs, that grant is void, if it be made only of his mere
motion without recompence. And in like wise, if a man
make a lease for term of life, and after grant the reversion
to one for term of life, the remainder over in fee, and the
tenant attorneth to him that hath the estate for term of life
only, intending that he only should have advantage of the
grant;§ his intent is void, and both ‖ shall take advantage

* 2 B. C. 167.
† 2 Roll. Abr. 56.
‡ 2 Roll. Abr. 68; Hob. 313; Hutt. 88.
§ Co. Litt. 310.
‖ Attornment is now almost rendered unnecessary by statute. The act
of 4 Ann., c. 16, s. 9, enacts that all grants or conveyances, by fine or

thereof, and the attornment shall be taken good, according to the grant. And so in this case, though the feoffor intended, that if the rent were not payed, that the stranger should enter; yet because the law giveth him no entry in that case, that intent is void, and the same stranger shall neither enter into the land by law nor conscience.

Doct. What shall then be done with that land, as thou thinkest, after the condition broken?

Stud. I think the feoffor in this case may lawfully re-enter; for when the feoffment was made upon condition that the feoffee would pay a rent to a stranger, in those words is concluded in the law, that if the rent were not paid to the stranger, that the feoffor should re-enter; for those words, *upon condition*, imply so much in the law, though it be not expressed. And then when the feoffor went farther, and said that if the rent were not paid, that the stranger should enter, those words were void in the law; and so the effect of the deed stood upon the first words, whereby the feoffor may re-enter in law and conscience: but if the first words had not been conditional, I would have holden it the greater doubt.

Doct. I pray thee put the case thereof in certain with such words as be not conditional, that I may the better perceive what thou meanest therein.

otherw se, of any manors, rents, reversions, or remainders, shall be effectual without the attornment of any of the tenants, but it provides that no tenant shall be prejudiced by payment of rent to any grantor or conusor, or by breach of any condition for non-payment of rent, before notice shall be given to him of such grant by the conusee or grantee. And the statute 11 Geo. 2, c. 19, s. 11, after reciting that the possession of estates is rendered very precarious by the frequent and fraudulent practice of tenants in attorning to strangers, who claim title to the estates of their respective landlords or lessors, who are thereby put out of the possession of their respective estates, and put to the difficulty of recovering the same at law, enacts that all such attornments shall be void, and the possession not altered; but it provides that the said act shall not extend to affect any attornment made pursuant to any judgment at law, or decree, or order of a court of equity, or made with the privity and consent of the landlord or landlords, lessor or lessors, or to any mortgagees after the mortgage is become forfeited.

11

CHAP. XXI.—*The nineteenth question of the student.*

A man maketh a feoffment by deed indented, and by the same deed it is agreed, that the feoffee shall pay to A. B. and to his heirs, a certain rent yearly at certain days, and that if he pay not the rent, then it is agreed that A. B. or his heirs, shall enter into the land; and after the feoffee payeth not the rent; then the question is, who ought in conscience to have this land and rent?

Doct. Ere we argue what conscience will, let us know first what the law will therein.

Stud. I think that by the law neither the feoffor ne yet the said A. B. shall ever enter into the land in this case for non-payment of the rent, for there is no re-entry in this case given to the feoffor for not payment of the rent, as there is in the case next before, and the entry that is given to the said A. B. for not payment thereof is void in the law, because he is estrange to the deed, as it appeareth also in the next chapter before.* And therefore methinketh that the greatest doubt in this case is, to see what use this feoffment shall be taken.

Doct. There appeareth in this case as thou hast put it, no consideration ne recompence given to the feoffor, whereupon any use may be derived; and if the case be so indeed, and the feoffor declared never his mind therein, to what use shall it then be taken?

Stud. I think it shall be taken to be to the use of the feoffee, as long as he payeth the rent: for there is no reason why the feoffee should be busied with payment of the rent, having nothing for his labour: ne it may not conveniently be taken that the intent of the feoffor was so, except he expressed it; and then it must be taken that he intended to recompence the feoffee for the business that he should have in the payment over, and by the words following his intent it appeareth to be so, as methinketh; for if the rent were not payed, he would that A. B. should enter, and so

* Co. Litt. 213; Dyer, 127; ante, 160; Cro. Eliz. 727.

it seemeth he intended not to have any use himself. And thus, me seemeth, this case should vary from the common case of uses; that is to say, if a man seised of land make a feoffment thereof, and it appeareth not to what use the feoffment was made, ne it is not upon any bargain or other recompence, then it shall be taken to be to the use of the feoffor;* except the contrary can be proved by some bargain, or other like : or that his intent at the time of the delivery of seisin was expressed that it should be to the use of the feoffee, or of some other; and then it shall go according to his intent: but in this case methinketh it shall be taken that his intent was, that it should first be to the use of the feoffee, for the cause before rehearsed, except the contrary can be proved; and so that knowledge of the intent of the feoffor is the greatest certainty for knowledge of the use in this case, as me seemeth. But when the feoffor goeth farther, and saith, That if the rent be not paid, that then the said A. B. should enter into the land; then it appeareth that his intent was that the rent should cease, and that A. B. should enter into the land : and though he may not by those words enter into the land after the rules of the law, and to have freehold, yet those words seem to be sufficient to prove that the intent of the feoffor was that he should have the use of the land :† for sith he had the rent to his own use, and not to the use of the feoffor; so it seemeth he shall have the use of the land that is assigned to him for the payment of the rent.

Doct. But I am somewhat in doubt, whether he had the rent to his own use : for the intent of the feoffor might be, that he should pay the rent for him to some other, or some other use might be appointed thereof by the feoffor.

Stud. If such an intent can be proved, then the intent must be observed; but we be in this case to wit to what use it shall be taken, if the intent of the feoffor cannot be

---

* Br. Feoffment to uses, pl. 10; Shep. Touch. 477; And. 37, pl. 95; post. 163.

† Post. 170, 172.

proved :* and then methinketh it cannot be otherwise taken, but it shall be to the use of him to whom it should be paid. For though it be called a rent, yet it is no rent in law, ne in the law he shall never have remedy for it, though it were assigned to him, and to his heirs, without condition, neither by distress, by assise, by writ of annuity, nor otherwise; but he shall be driven to sue in the Chancery for his remedy :† and then when he sueth in the Chancery, he must surmise that he ought to have it by conscience, and that he can have no remedy for it in the law. And then, sith he hath no remedy to come to it but by the way of conscience, it seemeth it shall be taken that when he hath recovered it, that he ought to have it in conscience, and that to his own use, without the contrary can be proved: and if the contrary can be proved, and that the intent of the feoffor was, that he should dispose it for him as he should appoint, then hath he the rent in use to another use, and so one use should be depending upon another use, which is seldom seen, and shall not be intended till it be proved: and so, sith no matter is here expressed, methinketh the rent shall be taken to be to the use of him that it is paid to, and the land in like wise that is appointed to him for not payment of the said rent shall be also to his use: how thinkest thou will conscience serve therein?

Doct. I think that as thou takest the law now, that conscience (in this case) and the law be all one: for the law seercheth the same thing in this case, to know the case that conscience doth, that is to say, the intent of the feoffor. And therefore I would move thee farther in one thing.

Stud. What is that?

Doct. That sith the intent of the feoffor shall be so much regarded in this case, why it ought not also to be as much regarded in the case that is in the last chapter next before this, where the words be conditional, and give the feoffor a title to re-enter. For methinketh, that though the feoffor

---

* Shep. Touch. 80; post. 172.
† Litt., sec. 345.

may in that case re-enter for the condition broken, that yet
after this entry he shall be seised of the land after his entry
to the use of him to whom the land was assigned by the
said indenture for lack of payment of the rent, because the
intent of the feoffor shall be taken to be so in that case as
well as in this. And I pray thee let me know thy mind
what diversity thou puttest between them.

Stud. Thou drivest me now to a narrow diversity, but
yet I will answer thee therein as well as I can.

Doct. But first, ere thou shew me that diversity, I pray
thee shew me how uses began, and why so much land hath
been put in use in this realm as hath been.

Stud. I will with good-will say as methinketh therein.

CHAP. XXII.—*How uses of land first began, and by what
law; and the cause why so much land is put in use.*

Uses were reserved by a secondary conclusion of the
law of reason in this manner: When the general custom
of property, whereby every man knew his own goods from
his neighbours, was brought in among the people, it followeth of reason, that such lands and goods as a man had,
ought not to be taken from him but by his assent, or by
order of the law: and then sith it be so, that every man
that hath lands hath hereby two things in him, that is to
say, the possession of the land, which after the law of England is called the frank-tenement, or the freehold, and the
other is authority to take thereby the profits of the land;*
wherefore it followeth, that he that hath land, and intendeth to give only the possession and freehold thereof to another, and keep the profits to himself, ought in reason and
conscience to have the profits, seeing there is no law made
to prohibit, but that in conscience such reservation may be
made.† And so when a man maketh a feoffment to another,
and intendeth that he himself shall take the profits; then

* 2 C. B. 104.
† Gilb. Law of Uses, 175.

the feoffee is said seised to his use that so enfeoffed him, that is to say, to the use that he shall have the possession and freehold thereof, as in the law ;* to the intent that the feoffor shall take the profits.† And under this manner, as I suppose, uses of land first began.

Doct. It seemeth that the reserving of such use is prohibited by the law :‡ for if a man make a feoffment, and reserve the profits, or any part of the profit, as the grass, wood, or such other ; that reservation is void in the law : and methinketh it is all one to say, that the law judgeth such a thing, if it be done, to be void, and that the law prohibiteth that the thing shall not be done.

Stud. Truth it is, that such reservation is void in the law, as thou sayest :§ and that is by reason of a maxim in the law, that willeth that such reservation of part of the same thing shall be judged void in the law. But yet the law doth not prohibit that no such reservation shall be made, but if it be made it judgeth of what effect it shall be ; that is to say, that it shall be void ; and so he that maketh such reservation offendeth no law thereby, ne breaketh no law thereby, and therefore the reservation in conscience is good. But if it were prohibit by statute that no man should make such a reservation, ne that no feoffment of trust should be made, but that all the feoffments should be to the use of him to whom possession of the land is given ; then the reservation of such uses against the statute should be void, because it were against the law : and yet such a statute should not be a statute against reason, because such uses were first grounded and reserved by the law of reason ; but it should prevent the law of reason, and should put away the con-

---

* Gilb. Law of Uses, 178.

† As for example, if a feoffment was made to John at Stile and his heirs, to the use and behoof of William at Stile and his heirs, in this case heretofore John at Stile had the estate and property in the land; but William at Stile had and was to have the profits in equity. Shep. Touch. 477 ; ante, 58, 120.

‡ Co. Litt. 142.

§ Shep. Touch. 78.

sideration whereupon the law of reason was grounded before the statute made. And then to the other question, that is to say, why so much land hath been put in use? It will be somewhat long, and peradventure to some tedious, to shew all the causes particularly : but the very cause why the use remained to the feoffor, notwithstanding his own feoffment or fine, and sometime notwithstanding a recovery against him, is all upon one consideration after the cause and intent of the gift; fine or recovery, as is aforesaid.

Doct. Though reason may serve that upon a feoffment a use may be reserved to the feoffor by the intent of the feoffor against the form of his gift, as thou hast said before ; yet I marvel much how an use may be reserved against a fine, that is one of the highest records that is in the law, and is taken in the law of so high effect, that it should make an end of all strifes ;* or against a recovery, that is ordained in the law for them that be wronged to recover their right by. And methinketh, that great inconvenience and hurt may follow, when such records may so lightly be avoided by a secret intent or use of the parties, and by a nude and bare averment and matter in deed, and specially sith such a matter in deed may be alledged that is not true, whereby may rise great strife between the parties, and great confusion and uncertainty in the law. But nevertheless, sith our intent is not at this time to treat of that matter, I pray thee touch shortly some of the causes why there hath been so many persons put in estate of lands to the use of others as there have been ; for, as I hear say, few men be sole seised of their own land.

Stud. There have been many causes thereof, of the which some be put away by divers statutes, and some remain yet.†
Wherefore thou shalt understand, that some have put their land in feoffment secretly, to the intent that they that have right to the land should not know against whom to bring

---

* Cruise on Fines, 4; ante, 89.

‡ 2 B. C. 331, 322; Gilb. Law of Uses, 72, 73; stat. 7 Ric. 2, c. 9; 4 H. 4, c. 7; 11 H. 6, c. 31; stat. 27 H. 8, c. 10.

their action, and that is somewhat remedied by divers statutes that give actions against pernors and takers of the profits. And sometime such feoffments of trust have been made to have maintenance and bearing of their feoffees, which peradventure were great lords or rulers in the country :* and therefore to put away such maintenance, treble damages be given by statute against them that make such feoffments for maintenance. And sometime they were made to the use of mortmain, which might then be made without forfeiture, though it were prohibited that the freehold might not be given in mortmain ; but that is put away by the statute of R. 2.† And sometime they were made to defraud the lords of wards, reliefs, heriots, and of the lands of their villeins ; but those points be put away by divers statutes made in the time of king H. the 7th. Sometime they were made to avoid executions upon a statute-staple, statute-merchant, and recognisance : and remedy is provided for that, that a man shall have execution of all such lands as any person is seised of to the use of him that is so bound at the time of execution sued, in the 19th year of H. 7.‡ And yet remain feoffments, fines, and recoveries in use for many other causes, in manner as many as there did before the said estatute. And one cause why they be yet thus used is, to put away tenancy by the courtesy and titles of dower.§ Another cause is, for that the lands in use shall not be put in execution upon a statute-staple, statute-merchant, nor recognisance, but such as be in the hands of the recognisor at the time of the execution sued. And sometime lands be put in use, that they should not be put in execution upon a writ of *extendi facias ad valentiam*. And sometime such uses be made that he to whose use, etc., may

---

* Gilb. Law of Uses, 72, 73.

† 2 B. C. 272; Wood's Inst. 255; Popham, 73; Bac. Use of the Law, 153; Gilb. Law of Uses, 38.

‡ See stat. 27 H. 8, c. 10.

§ Perk., sec. 463; 3 Bac. Abr. 221; Shep. Touch. 479; 1 Co. 131, Chudleigh's Case.

declare his will thereon :* and sometime for surity of divers covenants in indentures of marriage and other bargains. And these two last articles be the chief and principal cause why so much land is put in use. Also lands in use be not assets neither in a *Formedon*, nor in an action of debt against the heir :† ne they shall not be put in execution by an *elegit* sued upon a recovery, as some men say.‡ And these be the very chief causes, as I now remember, why so much land standeth in use as there doth :§ and all the said uses be reserved by the intent of the parties understood or agreed between them, and that many times directly against the words of the feoffment, fine, or recovery : and that is done by the law of reason, as is aforesaid.

Doct. May not a use be assigned to a stranger as well as to be reserved to the feoffor, if the feoffor so appointed it upon his feoffment?

Stud. Yes, as well, and in like wise to the feoffee, and upon that a free gift, without any bargain or recompence, if the feoffor so will.

Doct. What if no feoffment be made, but that a man grant to his feoffee, that from henceforth he shall stand seised to his own use? Is not that use changed, though there be no recompence?

Stud. I think yes, for there was an use *in esse* before

---

* 2 B. C. 328.
† 1 Cham. Rep. 148.
‡ Shep Touch. 478; Gilb. Law of Uses, 37.
§ It was evidently the intention of the legislature when they made the statute 27 H. 8, c. 10, to abolish uses by transferring the possession to the use; but the strict construction of that statute defeated the intent of it, and gave rise to trusts of land too tedious to be here enumerated, exactly of the same nature as uses were at Common law. Shep. Touch. 482; Allen, 15; Stile, 40. Of these uses, which may properly be called chancery trusts, intails may be made, fines levied, recoveries suffered, and husbands be tenants by the courtesy. In short, they are governed nearly by the same rules, and liable to every charge in equity which the legal ownership is subject to in law. 2 Wms. Rep , c 49, in the case of Sutton against Sutton. They may be aliened, or liable to debts, to leases and other incumbrances. They have not yet indeed been held subject to dower, nor are they liable to escheat to the lord.

the gift, which he might as lawfully give away, as he might the land if he had it in possession.*

Doct. And what if a man being seised of land in fee, grant to another of his mere motion, without bargain or re-compence, that he from thenceforth shall be seised to the use of the other; is not that grant good?

Stud. I suppose that it is not good; for, as I take the law, a man cannot commence an use but by livery of seisin, or upon a bargain, or some other recompence.†

Doct. I hold me contented with that thou hast said in this chapter for this time; and I pray thee shew me what diversity thou puttest between those two cases that thou hast before rehearsed in the 20th chapter, and in the 21st chapter of this present book.

Stud. I will with good-will.

CHAP. XXIII.—*The diversity between two cases hereafter following, whereof one is put in the 20th chapter, and the other in the 21st chapter of this present book.*

The first case of the said two cases is this.‡ A man maketh a feoffment by a deed indented, upon a condition that the feoffee shall pay certain rent yearly to a stranger, etc., and if he pay it not, that it shall be lawful to the stranger to enter into the land. In this case, I said before in the 20th chapter, that the stranger might not enter, because that he was not privy unto the condition. But I said, that in that case the feoffor might lawfully re-enter by the first words of the indenture, because they imply a condition in the law, and that the other words, that is to say, that the stranger should enter, be void in law and conscience. And therefore I said farther that when the feoffor had re-entered, that he was seised of the land to his own use, and not to the use of the stranger, though his intent at the making of the feoffment were, that the stranger, after his entry, should

---

* Post. 171.

†Shep. Touch. 485.

‡Perk., sec. 531; Co. Litt. 214; 2 Inst. 516; ante, 159.

have had the land to his own use, if he might have entered
by the law. And the cause why I think that the feoffor
was seised in that case to his own use, I shall shew thee
afterward. The second case is this; a man maketh a feoffment in fee, and it is agreed upon the feoffment, that the
feoffor shall pay a yearly rent to a stranger, and if he pay
it not, that then the stranger shall enter into the land.* In
this case I said, as it appeareth in the said twenty-first
chapter,† that if the feoffor paid not the rent, that the
stranger should have the use of the land, though he may
not by the rules of the law enter into the land. And the
diversity between the cases methinketh to be this. In the
first case it appeareth, as I have said before in the said
twentieth chapter,‡ that the feoffor might lawfully re-enter
by the law for not payment of rent; and then when he
entered according, he by that entry avoided the first livery
of seisin, insomuch that after the re-entry he was seised of
the land of like estate as he was before the feoffment;§ and
so remaineth nothing whereupon the stranger might ground
his use, but only the bare grant or intent of the feoffor, when
he gave the land to the feoffee upon condition that he should
pay the rent to the stranger, and if not, that it should be
lawful to the stranger to enter : for the feoffment is avoided
by the re-entry of the feoffor, as I have said before : and as
I said in the last chapter, as I suppose, a nude or bare
grant of him that is seised of land is not sufficient to begin
an use upon.

Doct. A bare grant may change an use, as thou thyself
agreed in the last chapter : why then may not an use as well
begin upon a bare grant?

Stud. When a use is *in esse*, he that hath the use may
of his mere motion give it away, if he will, without recompence, as he might the land, if he had it in possession :‖

* Ante, 162, 164.
† Post. 172; ante, 163.
‡ Ante, 161.
§ Post. 172, 173.
‖ Ante, 169.

but I take it for a ground, that he cannot so begin an use without livery of seisin, or upon a recompence or bargain. And that there is such a ground in the law, that it may not so begin, it appeareth thus. It hath been alway holden for law, that if a man make a deed of feoffment to another, and deliver the deed to him as his deed, that in this case he to whom the deed is delivered hath no title ne meddling with the land afore livery of seisin be made to him, but only that he may enter and occupy the land at the will of the feoffor.* And there is no book saith that the feoffee in that case is seised thereof, before livery to the use of the feoffee. And in like wise, if a man make a deed of feoffment of two acres of land that lie in two shires, intending to give them to the feoffee, and maketh livery of seisin in the one shire, and not in the other;† in this case it is commonly holden in books, that the deed is void to the acre, where no livery is made, except it lie within that view, save only that he may enter and occupy at will, as is aforesaid :‡ and there is no book that saith that the feoffee should have the use of the other acre; for if an use passed thereby, then were not the deed void unto all intents ; and yet it appeareth by the words of the deed, that the feoffor gave the lands to the feoffee, but for lack of livery of seisin the gift was void :§ and so methinketh it is here, without livery of seisin be made according. But in the second case of the said two cases, the feoffor may not re-enter for non-payment of the rent, and so the first livery of seisin continueth and standeth in effect; and•thereupon the first use may well begin and take effect in the stranger of the land, when the rent is not paid unto him according to the first agreement. And so methinketh that in the first case ‖ the use is determined, because the livery of seisin whereupon it commenced is determined : and that in the second case ¶ the use of the land taketh

* Shep. Touch. 281.
† Perk., séc. 127; 2 Roll. Abr. 11.
‡ Shep. Touch. 281; ante, 171.
§ Ante, 23.
‖ Ante, 171.
¶ Ante, 163, 170.

effect in the stranger for not payment of the rent by the grant made at the first livery, which yet continueth in his effect: and this methinketh is the diversity between the cases.

Doct. Yet, notwithstanding the reason that thou hast made, methinketh that if a man seised of lands make a gift thereof by a nude promise, without any livery of séisin, or recompence to him made, and grant that he shall be seised to his use, that though the promise be void in law, that yet nevertheless it must hold and stand good in conscience, and by the law of reason. For one rule of the law of reason is, That we may do nothing against the truth : and sith the truth is, that the owner of the ground hath granted that he shall be seised to the use of the other, that grant must needs stand in effect, or else there is no truth in the grantor.

.Stud. It is not against the truth of the grantor in this case, though by the grant he be not seised to the use of the other; but it proveth that he hath granted that the law will not warrant him to grant, wherefore his grant is void. But if the grantor had gone farther and said, That he would also suffer the other to take the profits of the lands without lett or other interruption, or that he would make him estate in the land when he should be required : then I think in those cases he were bound in conscience, by that rule of the law of reason that thou hast remembered, to perform them, if he intend to be bounden by his promise ; for else he should go against his own truth, and against his own promise. But yet it shall make no use in that case, nor he to whom the promise is made shall have no action in the law upon that promise, though it be not performed :* for it is called in the law a *nude, or naked promise.* And thus, methinketh, that in the first case† of the said two cases, the grant is now avoided in the law by the re-entry of the feoffor, and that the feoffor is not bounden by his grant, neither in law nor conscience : but in that second case he

* Post. 174; Burr. Rep., part 4, vol. 3.
† Ante, 171, 172.

is bound, so that the use passeth from him, as I have said before.

Doct. I hold me content with thy conceit for this time, but I pray thee shew me somewhat more at large what is taken for a nude contract, or naked promise, in the laws of England, and where an action may lie thereupon, and where not.

Stud. I will with good-will say as methinketh therein.

CHAP. XXIV.—*What is a nude contract, or naked promise, after the laws of England, and whether any action may lie thereon.*

First, it is to be understood, that contracts be grounded upon a custom of the realm, and by the law that is called *Jus gentium*, and not directly by the law of reason :* for when all things were in common, it needed not to have contracts, but after property was brought in, they were right expedient to all people, so that a man might have of his neighbour that he had not of his own; and that could not be lawfully but by his gift, by way of lending, concord, or by some lease, bargain, or sale; and such bargains and sales be called contracts, and be made by assent of the parties upon agreement between them, of goods or lands, for money, or for other recompence, but only of money usual, for money usual is no contract. And also a concord is properly upon an agreement between the parties, with divers articles therein, some rising on the one part, and some on the other. As if John at Stile letteth a chamber to Henry Hart, and it is farther agreed between them, that the said Henry Hart should go to board with the said John at Stile, and the said Henry Hart to pay for the chamber and boarding a certain sum, etc., this is properly called a *Concord;* but it is also a contract, and a good action lieth upon it. Howbeit it is not much argued in the laws of England what diversity is between a contract, a concord, a

---

† Ante, 61.

promise, a gift, a loan, or a pledge, a bargain, a covenant, or such other. For the intent of the law is to have the effect of the matter argued, and not the terms. And a nude contract is, when a man maketh a bargain, or a sale of his goods or lands, without any recompence appointed for it:* as if I say to another, I sell thee all my land, or else my goods, and nothing is assigned that the other shall give or pay for it; this is a nude contract, and, as I take it, it is void in the law and conscience.† And a nude or naked promise is, where a man promiseth another to give him certain money such a day, or to build an house, or to do him such certain service, and nothing is assigned for the money, for the building, nor for the service; these be called naked promises, because there is nothing assigned why they should be made; and I think no action lieth in those cases, though they be not performed. Also if I promise to another to keep him such certain goods safely to such a time, and after I refuse to take them, there lieth no action against me for it. But if I take them, and after they be lost or impaired through my negligent keeping, there an action lieth.‡

Doct. But what opinion hold they that be learned in the law of England in such promises that be called naked or nude promises? Whether do they hold that they that make the promise be bounden in conscience to perform their promise, though they cannot be compelled thereto by the law, or not.

Stud. The books of the law of England entreat little thereof, for it is left to the determination of doctors; and therefore I pray thee shew me somewhat now of thy mind therein, and then I shall shew thee somewhat therein of the minds of divers that be learned in the law of the realm?

Doct. To declare the matter plainly after the saying of doctors, it would ask a long time, and therefore I will touch it briefly, to give thee occasion to desire to hear more

---

* Ante, 173; Dyer, 336.
† 2 B. C. 445; Salk. 129, 24; 1 Roll. Abr. 9, 10; 1 Danv. Abr. 32.
‡ Lord Raym. 909; 12 Mod. 487.

therein hereafter.   First thou shalt understand, that there
is a promise that is called an *Advow*, and that is a promise
made to God; and he that doth make such a vow upon a
deliberate mind, intending to perform it, is bound in conscience to do it, though it be only made in the heart,
without pronouncing of words.   And of other promises
made to a man upon a certain consideration, if the promise
be not against the law, as if A. promise to give B. 20*l.* because he hath made him such a house, or hath lent him
such a thing, or other such like, I think him bound to keep
his promise.*   But if his promise be so naked, that there is
no manner of consideration why it should be made, then I
think him not bound to perform it : for it is to suppose that
there were some error in the making of the promise.   But
if such a promise be made to an university, to a city, to
the church, to the clergy, or to poor men of such a place,
and to the honor of God, or such other cause like, as for
maintenance of learning, of the commonwealth, of the
service of God, or in relief of poverty, or such other ; then
I think that he is bounden in conscience to perform it,
though there be no consideration of worldly profit that the
grantor hath had or intended to have for it.   And in all
such promises it must be understood, that he that made the
promise intended to be bound by his promise ; for else
commonly, after all doctors, he is not bound unless he were
bound to it before his promise : as if a man promise to give
his father a gown that hath need of it to keep him from
cold, and yet thinketh not to give it him, nevertheless he is
bound to give it, for he was bound thereto before.   And,
after some doctors, a man may be excused of such a
promise in conscience by casualty that cometh after the
promise, if it be so, that if he had known of the casualty at
the making of the promise he would not have made it.
And also such promises if they shall bind, they must be
honest, lawful, and possible, and else they are not to be
holden in conscience, though there be a cause, etc.   And

---

*Post. 179.

if the promise be good, and with a cause, though no
worldly profit shall grow thereby to him that maketh the
promise, but only a spiritual profit, as in the case before rehearsed of a promise made to an university, to a city, to
the church, or such other, and with a cause, as to the honor
of God, there it is most commonly holden that an action
upon those promises lieth in the law canon.

Stud. Whether dost thou mean in such promises made to
an university, to a city, or to such other as thou hast rehearsed before, and with a cause, as to the honor of God,
or such other, that the party should be bound by his
promise, if he intended not to be bound thereby yea or
nay?

Doct. I think nay, no more than upon promises made
unto common persons.

Stud. And then methinketh clearly, that no action can
lie against him upon such promises, for it is secret in his
own conscience whether he intended for to be bound or nay.
And of the intent inward in the heart, man's law cannot
judge, and that is one of the causes why the law of God is
necessary, (that is to say) to judge inward things: and if
an action should lie in that case in the law canon, then
should the law canon judge upon the inward intent of the
heart, which cannot be, as me seemeth. And therefore,
after divers that be learned in the laws of the realm, all
promises shall be taken in this manner: that is to say, if
he to whom the promise is made have a charge by reason
of the promise, which he hath also performed, then in that
case he shall have an action for that thing that was promised,
though he that made the promise have no worldly profit by
it. And if a man say to another, heal such a poor man of
his disease, or make an highway, and I will give thee thus
much,* and if he do it, I think an action lieth at the Common law,† and moreover, though the thing that he should

---

* Noy's Max. 91.

† This is not a promise within the statute 29 Car. 2, c. 3, s. 4, of frauds
and perjuries; for in this case the entire credit is given to the person mak-

12

do be all spiritual, yet if he perform it, I think an action lieth at the Common law. As if a man say to another, fast for me all the next Lent, and I will give thee twenty pounds, and he performeth it; I think an action lieth at the Common law. And likewise if a man say to another, marry my daughter,* and I will give thee twenty pounds;† upon this promise an action lieth, if he marry his daughter. And in this case he cannot discharge the promise though he thought not to be bound thereby: for it is a good contract, and he may have *quid pro quo*, that is to say, the preferment of his daughter for his money.‡   But in those promises made to an university, or such other as thou hast remembered before, with such causes as thou hast shewed, that is to say, to the honor of God, or to the increase of learning, or such other like where the party to whom the promise was made is bound to no new charge by reason of the promise made to him, but as he was bound to before; there they think that no action lieth against him, though he perform not his promise, for it is no contract, and so his own conscience must be his* judge whether he intended to be bound by his promise or not.   And if he intended it not, then he offended for his dissimulation only; but if he intended to be bound, then if he perform it not, untruth is in him, and he proveth himself to be a liar, which is prohibited as well by the law of God as by the law of reason. · And furthermore, many that be learned in the law of England hold, that a man is as much bounden in conscience by

ing the promise, and·he alone is liable to be sued, whereas the undertaking within the statute signifies a collateral engagement which subjects the party to an action if the person for whom he undertakes does not perform the agreement; as if two come to a shop, and one of them contracts for goods, and the seller does not care for trusting him, whereupon the other says, Let him have them, and I will undertake he shall pay you; this is an agreement within the statute,·and must be reduced into writing.   Ld. Raym. 224, 1085, 1087; Fitzgib. 302; Salk. 27.

* 1 Roll. Abr. 19; Moor, 857:

† This promise is within the statute, and must be in writing.   1 Danv. Abr. 69.   It being a contract in consideration of marriage.   1 Str. 34.

‡ Co. Litt. 47.

-a promise made to a common person, if he intended to be bound by his promise, as he is in the other cases that thou hast remembered of a promise made to the church, or the clergy, or such other: for they say as much untruth is in the breaking of the one as of the other; and they say that the untruth is more to be pondered than the person to whom the promises be made.

Doct. But what hold they if a promise be made for a thing past, as I˙ promise thee xl. li., for that thou hast builded me such a house, lieth an action there?

Stud. They suppose nay,* but he shall be bound in con-science to perform it after his intent, as is before said.†

Doct. And if a man promise to give another xl. l. in re-compence for such a trespass that he hath done him, lieth an action there?

Stud. I suppose nay, and the cause is, for that such promises be no perfect contracts. For a contract is prop-erly where a man for his money shall have by assent of the other party certain goods, or some other profit at the time of the contract or after ;‡ but if the thing be promised for a cause that is past, by way of recompence, then it is rather an accord than a contract; but then the law is that upon such accord the thing that is promised in recompence must be paid, or delivered in hand, for upon an accord there lieth no action.

Doct. But in the case of trespass, whether hold they, that he be bound by his promise, though he intended not to be bound thereby?

Stud. They think nay, no more than in the other cases that be put before.

Doct. In the other cases he was not bound to that he promised, but only by his promise; but in this case of tres-

---

* But if there had been a precedent request to build the house on the part of him who made the promise, the action would lie, although the consideration was executed. Cro. Car. 409; Townsend *v.* Hunt, Cro. Eliz. 282.

† Cro. Eliz. 741; 1 Roll. Abr. 11, 12.

‡ 2 B C. 442; 1 New Abr. 23; 1 Comyn's Digest, 99.

pass he was bound in conscience, before the promise, to
make recompence for the trespass : and therefore it seemeth
that he is bound in conscience to keep his promise, though
he intended not to be bound thereby.

Stud. Though he were bound before the promise to
make recompence for his trespass, yet he was not bound to
no sum in certain but by his promise : and because that the
sum may be too much or too little, and not egal to the trespass, and that the party to whom the trespass was done,
notwithstanding the promise, is at liberty to take his action
of trespass if he will ; therefore they hold that he may be
his own judge in conscience whether he intended to be
bound by his promise or not, as he may in other cases ; but
if it were of a debt, then they hold that he is bound to perform his promise, in conscience.

Doct. What if in the case of trespass he affirmeth his
promise with an oath ?

Stud. Then they hold that he is bound to perform it for
saving of his oath, though he intended not to be bound : but
if he intended to be bound by his promise, then they say
that an oath needed not but to enforce the promise ; for they
say, he breaketh the law of reason, which is, that we may
do nothing against the truth, as well when he breaketh his
promise that he thought in ·his own heart to be bound by, as
he doth when he breaketh his oath, though the offence be
not so great, by reason of the perjury.   Moreover to that
thou sayest, that upon such promises as thou hast rehearsed
before, shall lie an action after the law canon ; verily as to
that in this realm there can no action lie thereon in the ·
spiritual court, if the promise be of a temporal thing ; for a
prohibition or a *præmunire facias* should lie in that case.*

Doct. That is marvel, sith there can no action lie thereon
in the king's court, as thou sayest thyself.

Stud. That maketh no matter : for though there lie no
action in the king's court against executors upon a simple

---

* Br. Præmunire, pl. 16.

coatract;* yet if they be sued in that case for the debt in the spiritual court, a prohibition lieth. And in like wise, if a man wage his law untruly in an action of debt upon a contract in the king's court, yet he shall not be sued for the perjury in the spiritual court, and yet no remedy lieth for the perjury in the king's courts;† for the prohibition lieth not only where a man is sued in the spiritual court of such things as the party may have his remedy in the king's court, but also where the spiritual court holdeth plea, in such case where they by the king's prerogative, and by the ancient custom of the realm, ought none to hold.‡

Doct. I will take advisement upon that thou hast said in this matter till another time, and I pray thee now proceed to another question.

CHAP. XXV.—*The twentieth question of the student.*

Stud. A man hath two sons, one born before espousals, and the other after espousals, and the father by his will bequeatheth to his son and heir all his goods : which of these two sons shall have the goods in conscience?

Doct. As I said in our first dialogue in Latin, the last chapter, the doubt in this case dependeth not in the knowing what conscience will in this case, but rather the knowing which of the sons shall be judged heir, (that is to say) whether he shall be taken for heir, that is heir by the spiritual law, or he that is heir by the law of the realm, or else that it shall be judged for him that the father took for heir.§

Stud. As to that point, admit the father's mind not to be known, or else that his mind was that he should be taken for heir that should be judged for heir by the law, that in this case it ought to be judged by; and then I pray thee, shew me thy mind therein : for though the question be not directly depending upon the point to see what conscience

---

* Ante, 135; 2 Cro. 293; F. N. B. 95; Br. Præmunire, pl. 16.
† 3 New Abr. 317.
‡ 3 B. C. 112; 2 Inst. 601, 602.
§ Perk., sec. 49; 2 Inst. 96, 97.

will in this case, yet it is right expedient for the well ordering of conscience, that it be known after what law it shall be judged; for if it ought to be judged after the temporal law who should be heir, then it were against conscience, if the judges in the spiritual law should judge him for heir that is the heir by the spiritual law, and I think they should be bound to restitution thereby. And therefore, I pray thee, shew me thine opinion, after what law it shall be judged.

Doct. Methinketh that in this case it shall be jndged after the law of the church; for it appeareth that the bequest is of goods : and therefore if any suit shall be taken upon the execution of the will for the bequest, it must be taken in the spiritual court;* and when it is depending in the spiritual court, methinketh it must be judged after the spirituĂl law; for of the temporal law they have no knowledge, nor they are not bound to know it, as methinketh; and more stronger not to judge after it. But if the bequest had been of a chattel real, as of a lease for term of years, or of a ward, or such other, then the matter should have come in debate in the king's court;† and then I think the judges there should judge after the law of the realm, and that is, that the younger brother is heir : and so methinketh the diversity of the courts shall make the diversity of judgment.

Stud. Of that might follow a great inconvenience, as me seemeth, for it might be such a case that both chattels real and chattels personal were in the will, and then, after thine opinion, the one son shall have the chattels personal, and the other son the chattels real; and it cannot be conveniently taken, as methinketh, but that the father's will was, that the one son should have all, and not be divided. Therefore methinketh that he shall be judged for heir that is heir by the Common law, and that the judges spiritual in this case be bound to take notice what the Common law is :‡ for sith the things that be in variance be temporal, that is to say, the

* F. N. B. 102.
* Ib. con.
† Ante, 17, 18.

goods of the father, it is reason that the right of them in this realm shall be determined by the law of the realm.

Doct. How may that be? For the judges spiritual know not the law of the realm, ne they cannot know it as to the most part of it; for much part of the law is in such speech that few men have the knowledge of it, and there is no means, ne familiarity of study between them that learn the said laws; for they be learned in several places, and after divers ways, and after divers manners of teachings, and in divers speeches, and commonly the one of them have none of the books of the other: and to bind the spiritual judges to give judgment after the law that they know not, ne that they cannot come to the knowledge of it, seemeth not reasonable.

Stud. They must do therein as the king's judges must do when any matter cometh before them that ought to be judged after the spiritual law, whereof I put divers cases in our first dialogue in English, the sixth chapter;* that is to say, they must either take knowledge of it by their own study, or else they must enquire of them that be learned in the law of the church, what the law is; and in like wise must they do. But it is to doubt, that some of them would be loth to ask any such question in such case, or to confess that they are bound to give their judgment after the temporal law: and surely they may lightly offend their conscience.

Doct. I suppose that some be of opinion that they are not bound to know the law of the realm; and verily, to my remembrance, I have not heard that judges of the spiritual law are bound to know the law of the realm.

Stud. And I suppose that they are not only bound to know the law of the realm, or to do that in them is to know it, when the knowledge of it openeth the right of the matter that dependeth before them: but that they be also bound to know where, and in what case they ought to judge after it: for in such cases they must take the king's law as the

---

* Ante, 18.

law spiritual to that point, and are bound in conscience to follow it, as it may appear by divers cases, whereof one is this.* Two joint-tenants be of goods, and the one of them by his last will bequeathed all his part to a stranger, and maketh the other joint-tenant his executor, and dieth : if he to whom the bequest is made sue the other joint-tenant upon the legacy as executor, etc., upon this matter shewed, the judges of the spiritual law are bound to judge the will to be void, because it is void by the law of the realm, whereby the joint-tenant hath right to the whole goods by the title of the survivor, and is judged to have the goods as by the first gift, which is before the title of the will, and must therefore have preferment as the eldest title ;† and if the judges of the spiritual court judge otherwise, they are bound to restitution. And by like reason the executors of a man that is outlawed at the time of his death, may discharge themselves in the spiritual court of the performing of the legacies, because they be chargeable to the king ;‡ and yet there is no such law of utlagary in the spiritual law.

Doct. By occasion of that thou hast said before, I would ask of thee this question.§ If a parson of a church alien a portion of dismes according as the spiritual law hath ordained, is not that alienation sufficient, though it have not the solemnities of the temporal law?

Stud. I am in doubt therein,‖ if the portion be under the fourth part of the value of the church; but if it be to the value of the fourth part of the church or above, it is not sufficient, and therefore was the writ of right of dismes ordained.¶ And if in a writ of right of dismes it be adjudged in the king's court for the patron of the successor of him that alieneth, because the alienation was not made according to the Common law: then the judges of the spiritual

---

* Ante, 18.
† Perk., sec. 500; Litt., sec. 287; 2 Cro. 106.
‡ Ante, 18.
§ Ib.
‖ F. N. B. 70.
¶ 2 Inst. 364; Br. Prohibition, pl. 7.

law are bound to give their judgment according to the judgment given in the king's court. And in like wise, if a parson of a church agree to take a pension for the tythe of a
mill, or if the pension be to the fourth part of the value of
the church, or above, then it must be aliened after the
solemnities of the king's laws, as lands and tenements must;
or else the patron of the successor of him that alieneth may
bring a writ of right of dismes, and recover in the king's
court; and then the judges of the spiritual court are bound
to give judgment in the spiritual courts accordingly, as is
aforesaid.

Doct. I have heard say, that a writ of right of dismes is
given by the statute of Westm. 2, and that speaketh only
of dismes, and not of pensions.

Stud. Where a parson of a church is wrongfully de-
forced of his dismes,* and is let by an *indicavit* to ask his
dismes in the spiritual court, then the patron may have a
writ of right of dismes by the statute that thou speakest of,
for there lay none at the common law; for the parson had
there good right, though he were let by the *indicavit* to sue
for his right.† But when the parson had no remedy at the
spiritual law, there a writ of right of dismes lay for the
patron by the common law, as well of pensions as of
dismes; and some say that in such case it lay of less than
of the fourth part, by the common law, but that I pass over.
And the reason why it lay at the common law, if the dismes
or pensions were above the fourth part, etc., was this: By
the spiritual law the alienation of the parson with the assent of the bishop, and of the chapter, shall bar the successor without assent of the patron, and so the patron might
leese his patronage, and be not assenting thereto: for his
incumbent might have no remedy but in the spiritual court,
and there he was barred: wherefore the patron in that case
shall have his remedy by the common law, where the assent of the ordinary and chapter without the patron shall

* F. N. B. 70.
† 2 Inst. 364; Booth on Real Actions, 123; F. N. B. 70.

186 Doctor and Student.

not serve, as it is said before. But where the incumbent had good right by the spiritual law, there lay no remedy for the patron by the common law, though the incumbent were let by an *indicavit*. And for that cause was the said statute made, and it lieth as well by the equity for offerings and pensions, as for dismes. Then, farther, I would think that where the spiritual court may hold plea of a temporal thing, that they must judge after the temporal law, and that ignorance shall not excuse them in that case ;* for by taking of their office they have bound themselves to have knowledge of as much as belongéth to their office, as all judges be, spiritual and temporal. But if it were in argument in this case, whether the eldest son might be a priest, because he is a bastard in the temporal law, that should be judged after the spiritual law, for the matter is spiritual.

Doct. Yet notwithstanding all the reasons that thou hast made, I cannot see how the judges of the spiritual law · shall be compelled to take notice of the temporal law ; seeing that the most part of it is in the French tongue ; for it were hard that every spiritual judge should be compelled to learn the tongue. But if the law of the realm were set in such order, that they that intend to study the law canon might first have a sight of the law of the realm, as they have now of the law civil, and that some books and treatises were made of cases of conscience concerning those two laws, as there be now concerning the law civil and the law canon ; I would assent that it were right expedient, and then reason might serve the better, that they should be compelled to take notice of the law of the realm, as they be now bound in such countries as the law civil is used to take notice of that law.

Stud. Methinketh thine opinion is right good and reasonable : but till such an order be taken, they are bound, as I suppose, to enquire of them that be learned in the Common law, what the law is, and so to give their judgment according, if they will keep themselves from offence

---

* Het. 87.

of conscience.* And forasmuch as thou hast well satisfied my mind in all the questions before, I pray thee now that I may somewhat feel thy mind in divers articles that be written in divers books for the ordering of conscience upon the law canon or civil: for methinketh that there be divers conclusions put in divers books, as in the sums called *summa angelica* and *summa rosella*, and divers other for the good order of conscience, that be against the law of this realm, and rather bind conscience, than do give any light to it.

Doct. I pray thee shew me some of these cases.

Stud. I will with good-will.

CHAP. XXVI.—*Whether the abbot may with conscience present to an advowson of a church that belongeth to the house, without assent of the covent?*

It appeareth in the chapter, *Et agnoscitur de his quæ fiunt a prælatis*, the which chapter is recited in the sum called *summa angelica*, in the title *abbas*, the twenty-seventh article, that he may not, without any custom, or any special privilege to help therein.

Stud. Truth it is, that there is such a decretal; but they that be learned in the law of England hold the decretal bindeth not in this realm: and this is the cause why they do hold that opinion. By the law of the realm the whole disposition of lands and goods of the abbey is the abbot's only for the time that he is abbot, and not in the covent, for they be but as dead persons in the law;† and therefore the abbot shall sue and be sued only without the covent, do homage, fealty, atturn, make leases, and present to advowsons only in his own name. And they say, farther, that this authority cannot be taken from him but by the law of the realm; and so they say, that the makers of the decretal exceed their power; wherefore they say it is not to be holden in conscience, no more than if a decree were made that a lease for a term of years, or at will, made by the

---

* Ante, 18, 19.
† Co. Litt. 94; ante, 31.

.abbot without the covent, should be immediately void : and
so they think that the abbot may in this case present in his
own name without offence of conscience, because the said
decretal holdeth not in this realm.

Doct. But many be of opinion, that no man hath authority to present in right and conscience to any benefice
with cure but the pope, or that he hath his authority therein
derived from the pope;* for they say, that forasmuch as
the pope is the vicar general under God, and hath the
charge of the souls of all people that be in the flock of
Christ's church, it is reason that, sith he cannot minister to
all, ne do that is necessary to all people for their soul's
health in his own person, that he shall assign deputies for
his discharge in that behalf. And because patrons claim
to present to churches in this realm by their own right,
without title derived from the pope, they say, that they
usurp upon the pope's authority. And therefore they conclude, that though the abbot have title by the law of the
realm to present in this case in his own name, that yet, because that title is against the pope's prerogative, that that
title, ne yet the law of the realm that maintaineth that title,
holdeth not in conscience. And they say also, that it belongeth to the law canon to determine the right of presentment to benefices, for it is a thing spiritual, and belongeth
to the spiritual jurisdiction, as the deprivation from a
benefice doth;† and so they say the said decretal bindeth in
conscience, though in the law of the realm it bindeth not.

Stud. As to the first consideration, I would right well
agree, that if the patrons of churches in this realm claimed
to put incumbents into such churches as should fall void of
their patronage, without presenting them to the bishop, or
if they claimed that the bishop should admit such incumbent as they should present, without any examination to be

* But *vide* the statutes 25 Ed. 3, st. 6; 38 Ed. 3, st. 2; 12 R. 2, c. 15; 13
R. 2, st. 2; 7 R. 2, c. 12; 16 R. 2, c. 5, and 21 Ed. 3, c. 1, which entirely
take away the power of the pope to present to any benefice within this
realm, and see post., c. 37.

† Post., c. 36; Br. Trials, pl. 47.

made of his ability in that behalf, that that claim were against reason and conscience, for the cause that thou hast rehearsed : but forasmuch as the patrons in this realm claim no more but to present their incumbents to the bishop, and then the bishop to examine the ability of the incumbent, and if he find him by examination not able to have cure of souls, he then to refuse him, and the patron to present another that shall be able, and if he be able, then the bishop to admit him, institute him and induct him ;* I think that this claim, and their presentments thereupon, stand with good reason and conscience.† As to the second consideration, it is holden in the laws of the realm, that the right of presentment to a church is a temporal inheritance, and shall descend by course of inheritance from heir to heir, as lands and tenements shall, and shall be taken as assets, as lands and tenements be : and for the trial of the right of patronages be ordained in the law divers actions for them that be wronged in that behalf, as writs of right of advowson, assises of *Darrein presentment*, *Quare impedit*, and divers others,‡ which alway without time of mind have been pleaded in the king's courts as things pertaining to his crown and royal dignity : and therefore they say that in this case his laws ought to be obeyed in law and conscience.

Doct. If it come in variance whether he that is so presented be able or not able, by whom shall the ability be tried?

Stud. If the ordinary be not party to the action, it shall be tried by the ordinary ; but if he be party, it shall be tried by the metropolitan.

Doct. Then the law is more reasonable in that point than I thought it had been : but in the other point I will take advisement in it till another time, and I pray thee shew me

---

* Watson's Clergyman's Law, 212; 1 Burn's Ecl. Law, 127.

† Co. Litt. 374; post., c. 36.

‡ For the nature and use of these different actions see Vin. Abr., title Presentation, 411, 473, 481, etc.

thy mind in this point. If an abbot name his covent with him in his presentation, doth that make the presentation void in the law? Or is the presentation good notwithstanding?

Stud. I think it is not void therefore, but the naming of them is void, and a thing more than needeth. For if the abbot be disturbed, he must bring his action in his own name, without the covent.

Doct. Then I perceive well that it is not prohibited by the law of England, but that the abbot may name the covent in his presentation with him, and also take their assent whom he shall present, if he will: and then I hold it the surest way that he so do, for in so doing he shall not offend neither in law nor conscience.

Stud. To take the assent of the covent whom he shall present, and to name them also in the presentation, knowing that he may do otherwise both in law and conscience, if he will, is no offence: but if he take their assent, or name them with him in the presentation, thinking that he is so bound to do in law and conscience, setting a conscience where none is, and regardeth not the law of the realm, that will discharge his conscience in this behalf, if he will, so that he present an able man, as he may do without their assent; there is an error and offence of conscience in the abbot. And in like wise, if the abbot present in his own name, and therefore the covent saith that he offendeth in conscience, in that he observeth not the law of the church, for that he taketh not their assent;* then they offend in judging him to offend that offendeth not. And therefore the sure way is in this case to judge both the said laws of such effect as they be, and not to set an offence of conscience by breaking of the said decree, which standeth not in effect in this behalf within this realm.

* Ante, 187.

CHAP. XXVII.—*If a man find beasts in his ground doing hurt, whether may he by his own authority take them, and keep them till he be satisfied of the hurt.*

This question is made in the sum called *summa rosella* in the title of *restitution*, that is to say, *restitutio* 13, the ninth article : and there it is answered, that he may not take them for to hold them as a pledge till he be satisfied for the hurt; but that he may take them, and keep them till he know who oweth them, that he may thereby learn against whom to have his remedy.   Is not the law of the realm so in like wise?

Stud, No verily, for, by the law of the realm, he that in that case hath the hurt may take the beasts as a distress,* and put them in a pound overt, so it be within the said shire,† and there let them remain till the owner will make him amends for the hurt.

Doct. What callest thou a pound overt?

Stud. A pound overt is not only such a pound as is commonly made in towns and lordships, for to put in beasts that be distrained, but it is also every place where they may be in lawfully, not making the owner an offender for their being there :‡ and that it be there also, that the owner may lawfully give the beasts meat and drink while they be in pound.

Doct. And if they die in the pound for lack of meat, whose jeopardy is it?

Stud. If it be such a pound overt as I speak of, it is at the peril of him that oweth the beasts, so that he that had the hurt shall be at liberty to take his action for the trespass, if he will : and if it be not a lawful pound, then it is at the

---

* 3 Lev. 48; 2 Inst. 106, 107: ante, 14.

† According to the statute of Marlbridge, 52. H. 3, 4, and *vide* the statute 1 and 2 P. & M., c. 12, which says that no distress of cattle shall be driven out of the hundred where it is taken unless to a pound overt in the same county, within three miles distance.

‡ 3 B. C. 12; Co. Litt. 47.

peril of him that distrained; and so it is if he drive them,, out of the shire, and they die there.*

Doct. I put the case that he that owneth the beasts offer sufficient amends, and the other will not take it, but keepeth the beasts still in pound, may not the owner take them. out?

Stud. No, for he may not be his own judge; and if he do, an action lieth against him for breaking of the pound;† but he must sue a replevin, to have his beast delivered him out of the pound, and thereupon it shall be tried by twelve men, whether the amends that was offered were sufficient or not?‡   And if it be found that the offer was not sufficient. then he that hath the hurt shall have such amends as the twelve men shall assess.

Doct. If it be found by the twelve men that the amends were sufficient, shall he that refuseth to take it have no punishment for his refusal, and for keeping of the beasts in pound after that time?

Stud. I think no, but that he shall yield damages in the *replevin,* because the issue is tried against him.§

Doct. I put the case that the beasts after the refusal die in pound for lack of meat, at whose jeopardy is it then?

Stud. At the jeopardy of him that owned the beasts, as it was before;|| for he is bound at his peril by reason of the wrong that was done at the beginning, to see that they have meat as long as they shall be in pound, unless the king's writ come to deliver them, and he resisteth it; for after that time it will be at his jeopardy if they die for lack of meat, and the damage shall be recovered in an action brought upon the statute for disobeying the king's writ.

---

* Finch Law, 137; 3 B. C. 13.

† If the owner of the beasts break the pound, the distrainer may either have a writ of pound breach, in which he shall recover damages, F. N. B. 101, or he may have an action upon the case, and if the distress is for rent shall therein recover treble damages by virtue of the statute of 1 and 2 W. & M., sess. 1, c. 5.

‡ 3 B. C. 147; Viner's Abr., title Tender, 188, 189.

§ Vin. Abr., title Replevin, 22.

|| Ante, 14; Finch Law, 137.

CHAP. XXVIII.— *Whether a gift made by one under the age of twenty-five years be good.*

Doct. It appeareth in *summa angelica* in the title *donatio prima*, the 7th article, that a man before the age of twenty-five years may not give, without it be with the authority of his tutor; is it not so likewise at the Common law?

Stud. The age of infants to give or sell their lands and goods in the law of England is at twenty-one years, or above;* so that after that age the gift is good, and before that age it is not good, by whose assent soever it be, except it be for his meat, and his drink, or apparel,† or that he do it as executor, in performance of the will of his testator,‡ or in some other like cases, that need not to be rehearsed here : and that age must be observed in this realm in law and conscience, and not the said age of twenty-five years.§

Doct. I put the case it were ordained by a decree of the church, that if any man by his will bequeatheth goods to another, and willeth that they shall be delivered to him at his full age, and that in that case twenty-five years shall be taken for the full age; shall not that decree be observed and stand good after the law of England?

Stud. I suppose it shall not. For though it belong to the church to have the probate and the execution of testaments made of goods and chattels, except it be in certain lordships and seigniories that have them by prescription;‖ yet the church may not, as me seemeth, determine what shall be the lawful age for another person to have the goods, for that belongeth to the king and his laws to determine. And therefore if it were ordained by a statute of the realm, that he should not in such case have the goods till he were of

---

* Ante, 61.

† 1 B. C. 466; Co. Litt. 172.

‡ And then he must be of the age of seventeen years, for before that age he cannot act as executor. Went. Off. of Executor, 213.

§ Which in the civil law is the full age of infants. Wood's Civil Law, 101.

‖ Perk., sec. 486; Godolph. 58; 1 Salk. 41; Office of Exec. 43.

13

the age of twenty-five years, that statute were good, and to
be observed as well in the spiritual law as in the law of the
realm : and if a statute were good in that case, then a decree made thereof is not to be observed ; for the ordering
of the age may not be under two several powers ; and one
property of every good law of man is, that the maker exceed not his authority : and I think that the spiritual judge
in that case ought to judge the full age after. the law of the
realm, seeing that the matter of the age concerneth temporal goods. And I suppose farther, that as the king by
authority of his. parliament may ordain that all wills shall
be void, and that the goods of every man shall be disposed
in such manner as by statute should be assigned, that more
stronger he may appoint at what age such wills as be made
shall be performed.

Doct. Thinkest thou then that the king may take away
the power of the ordinary, that he shall not call executors
to account?

Stud. I am somewhat in doubt therein : but it seemeth
that if it might be enacted by statute, that all wills should
be void, as is aforesaid, that then it might be enacted, that
no man should have authority to call none to account upon
such wills, but such as the statute shall therein appoint, for
he that may do the more may do the less. Notwithstanding I will nothing speak determinately in that point at this
time; ne I mean not that it were good to make a statute
that all wills should be void, for I think them right expedient : but mine intent is, to prove that the Common law
may ordain the time of the full age, as well in wills of
temporal things as otherwise, and also that wills shall be
made ; and if it may so do, then much stronger it belongeth
to the king's law to interpret wills concerning temporal
things, as well when they come in argument before his
judges as when they come in argument before spiritual
judges, and that they ought not to be judged by several
laws, (that is to say) by the spiritual judges in one manner,
and by the king's judges in another manner.

CHAP. XXIX.—*If a man be convict of heresy, before the ordinary, whether his goods be forfeited.*

Doct. It appeareth in *summa angelica*, in the title *donatio prima*, the 13th article, that he that is a heretick may not make executors;* for in the law his goods be forfeit: what is the law of the realm therein?

Stud. If a man be convict of heresy, and abjure, he hath forfeit no goods; but if he convicted of heresy, and be delivered to laymen's hands, then hath he forfeit all his goods that he hath at that time that he is delivered to them, though he be not put in execution for the heresy: but his lands he shall not forfeit except he be dead for the heresy, and then he shall forfeit them to the lords of the fee, as in case of felony, except they be holden of the ordinary, for then the king shall have the forfeiture; as it appeareth by the statute made the second year of H. 5, c. 7.

Doct. Methinketh that, as it belongeth only to the church to determine heresies, that so it belongeth to the church to determine what punishment he shall have for his heresy, except death; which they may not be judges in: but if the church decree that he shall therefore forfeit his goods, methinketh that they be forfeit by that decree.

Stud. Nay, verily, for they be temporal, and belong to the judgment of the king's court: and I think the ordinary might have set no fine upon one impeached of heresy, till it was ordained by the statute of H. 4, that he may set a fine in that case, if he see cause; and then the king shall have that fine, as in the said statute appeareth.†

---

* Godolphin's Orphan's Legacy, 36.

† By the statute 1 Eliz., c. 1, all former statutes relating to heresy are repealed, and it is now agreed that the ordinary may proceed to punish the offence by ecclesiastical censures. 4 B. C. 48. And if an heretic in maintenance of his errors set up conventicles, and raises factions which may tend to the disturbance of the public peace, he may be fined and imprisoned upon an indictment at common law. 1 Haw. P. C. 4. But the common law has no power to punish *merely* for heresy. Ib. Nor is the offender amenable to the statute law, but for one species of heresy, in which the civil magistrate is enabled to shew his authority; for by the act of 9 and

CHAP. XXX.— *Where divers patrons of an advowson, and the church voideth, the patrons vary in their present-ments, whether the bishop shall have liberty to present such of the incumbents that he will, or not?*

Doct. This question is asked in *summa rosella*, in the title *patronus*, the 9th article; and there it appeareth by the better opinion, that he may present whether clerk he will :* howbeit the maker of the said sum saith, by the rigour of the law, the bishop in such case may present a stranger, because the patrons agree not. And in the same chapter *patronus*, the 15th article, it is said that he must be pre-ferred that hath the most merits, and hath the most part of the patrons : and if the number be equal, that then it is to con-sider the merits of the patron : and if they be of like merit, then may the bishop command them to agree, and to pre-sent again : and if they cannot yet agree, then the liberty to present is given to the bishop to take which he will : and if he may not yet present without great trouble, then shall the bishop order the church in the best manner he can : and if he cannot order it, then shall he suspend the church, and take away the relicks, to the rebukes of the patrons : and if they will not be so ordered, then must he ask help of the tem-poralty. And in the 15th article of the said title *patronus*, it is asked, Whether it be expedient in such case, that the more part of the patrons agree, having respect to all the patrons, or that it suffice to have the more part in com-parison of the less part? as thus : There be four patrons to present one clerk : the first and second present one, the

10 W. 3, c. 32, it is enacted that if any person educated in the Christian religion, or professing the same, shall, by *writing, printing, teaching, or advised speaking, deny any one of the persons in the holy Trinity to be God,* or maintain that there are more Gods than one, he shall upon the first offence be rendered incapable to hold any office or place of trust, and for the second be rendered incapable of bringing any action, being guardian, executor, legatee, or purchaser of lands, and shall suffer three years' im-prisonment without bail. If, however, within four months after the first conviction, the delinquent will, in open court, publicly renounce his error, he is discharged for that once from all disabilities.

*2 Leon, 68; Hob. 317; post. 197.

third presenteth another, and the fourth another : he that is presented by two hath not the more part in comparison of all the patrons, for they be equal; but he hath the more part having respect to the other presentments. To this question it is answered, That either the presentment is made of them that be of the college, and there is requisite the more part, having respect to all the college; or else every man presenteth for himself as commonly do laymen that have the patronage of their patrimony, and then it sufficeth to have the more part in respect of the other parties. Doth not the law of England agree to these diversities?

Stud. No, verily.

Doct. What order then shall be taken in the law of England, if the patrons vary in their presentments?

Stud. After the laws of England, this order shall be taken : if they be joint-tenants or tenants in common of the patronage, and they vary in presentment, the ordinary is not bound to admit none of their clerks, neither the more part nor the less ; and if the six months pass, or they agree, then he may present by the lapse :* but he may not present within the six months, for if he do, they may agree, and bring a *quare impedit* against him, and remove his clerk, and so the ordinary shall be a disturber. And if the patrons have the patronage by descent as coparceners, then is the ordinary bound to admit the clerk of the eldest sister, for the eldest shall have the preferment in the law if she will;† and then at the next avoidance the next sister shall present;‡ and so by turn one sister after another, till all the sisters or their heirs have presented, and then the eldest sister shall begin again. And this is called a *Presenting by turn*, and it holdeth alway between coparceners of an advowson, except they agree to present together, or that they agree by composition to present in some other manner ;

---

* 1 Burn's Ecl. Law, 12; Watson's Com. Inc. 227.

† And this privilege shall descend to her issuse, nay her assignee shall have it, and so shall her husband, who is tenant by the courtesy. Co. Litt. 166, tho' Kell. 49, seems con.

‡ 2 Inst. 365.

and if they do so, the agreement must stand.* But this must be always except, that if at the first avoidance that shall be after the death of the common ancestor, the king · have the ward of the youngest daughter, that then the king by his prerogative shall have the presentment, and at the next avoidance the eldest sister, and so by turn.† And it is to understand, that if after the death of the common ancestor the church voideth, and the eldest sister presented together with another of the sisters, and the other sisters every one in their own name or together; that in that case the ordinary is not bound to receive none of their clerks, but may suffer the church to run into the lapse, as it is said before ;‡ for he shall not be bound to receive the clerk of the eldest sister, but where she presenteth in her own name. And in this case where the patrons vary in presentment,§ the church is not properly said *litigious*, so that the ordinary should be bound at his peril to direct a writ to enquire *de juro Patronatus;*‖ for that writ lieth where two present by several titles, but these patrons present all in one title, and therefore the ordinary may suffer it to pass, if he will, into the lapse.¶ And this manner of presentments must be observed in this realm in law and conscience.

---

* 3 Com. Digest, 196.

† Quare impedit, 31 Ed. 3; Br. Prerogative, pl. 21.

‡ Co. Litt. 183; Watson's Com. Inc., pl. 227.

§ 1 Burn's Ecl. Law, 19, 12.

‖ The doctrine which seems to be laid down here, viz., that when a church is properly litigious, the ordinary is bound, *ex officio*, at his peril to award a *jure patronatus*, accords with the year book of 34 H. 6, 11. But the better opinion is, that in such case the ordinary is not obliged to direct a writ to enquire of the right of patronage, unless at the request of the parties at variance. Godolphin Rep. 180; Wats. Com. Inc. 113. And therefore if no such request is made, and the church continues litigious, he may let six months pass, and then he will have a lawful title to collate by lapse. Wats. Com. Ino. 228. But if such demand is made, and the ordinary neglects to decree a process to enquire to whom the right belongs, he becomes a disturber. 3 Com. Digest, 203.

¶ Hob. 317.

CHAP. XXXI.—*How long time the patron shall have to present to a benefice.*

Doct. This question is asked in *summa angelica*, in the title *jus patronatus*, the 16th article; and there it is answered, That if the patron be a layman, that he shall have four months, and if he be a clerk he shall have six months.

Stud. And by the Common law he shall have six months whether he be a layman or a clerk. And I see no reason why a clerk should have more respite than a layman, but rather the contrary.*

Doct. From what time shall the six months be accompted?

Stud. That is in divers manners after the manner of the avoidance;† for if the church void by death, creation or cession, the six months shall be counted from the death of the incumbent, or from the creation or cession, whereof the patron shall be compelled to take notice at his peril: and if the voidance be by resignation or deprivation, then the six months shall begin when the patron hath knowledge given him by the bishop of the resignation or deprivation.

Doct. What if he have knowledge of the resignation or deprivation, and not by the bishop, but by some other? Shall not the six months begin then from the time of that knowledge?

Stud. I suppose that it shall not begin till he have knowledge given him by the bishop.‡

Doct. An union is also a cause of voidance; how shall the six months be reckoned there?

Stud. There can be no union made but the patrons must have knowledge, and it must be appointed who shall present after that union, that is to say, one of them or both, either jointly or by turn one after another, as the agreement is upon the union;§ and sith the patron is privy to the avoid-

---

* Finch Law, 90; Watson's Incumbent, 12.
† 2 B. C. 278; 4 Rep. 75.
‡ Br. Notice, pl. 25.
§ Stat. 37 H. 8, c. 21; 3 Nels. Abr. 480; 17 Car. 2, c. 3.

ance, and is not ignorant of it, the six months shall be accounted from the agreement. ·

Doct. I see well, by the reason that thou hast made in this chapter,* that ignorance sometime excuseth in the law of England; for in some of the said avoidances it shall excuse the patrons, as it appeareth by the reasons above, and in some it will not: wherefore I pray thee shew me somewhat where ignorance excuseth in the law of England, and where not, after thine opinion.

Stud. I will with good-will hereafter do as thou sayest, if thou put me in remembrance thereof. But I would yet move thee somewhat farther in such questions as I have moved thee before, concerning the diversities between the laws of England and other laws: for there be many more cases thereof that, as me seemeth, have right great need, for the good order of conscience of many persons, to be reformed, and to be brought into one opinion, both among spiritual and temporal. As it is in the case where doctors hold opinion, that the statute of layman, that restrains liberty to give lands to the church, should be void; and they say farther, that if it were prohibit by a statute that no gift should be made to foreigners, that yet a gift made to the church should be good; for they say that the inferior may not take away the authority of the superior: and this saying is directly against the statutes,† whereby it is prohibit that lands should not be given in *Mortmain*. And they say also that bequests and gifts to the church must be determined after the law canon, and not after the laws and statutes of laymen: and so they regard much to whom the gift is made, whether to the church, or to make causways, or to common persons, and bear more favour in gifts to the church than to the other. And the law of the realm beholdeth the thing that is given and intended, that if the thing that is given be of lands or goods, that the determination thereof of right belongeth in this realm to the king's laws, whether it be to

---

* Ante, 77, 148; post. 253.

† Statutes 9 H. 3, c. 36; 7 Ed. 1; 13 Ed. 1, c. 32; 34 Ed. 1; 15 R. 2, c. 5; 29 H. 8, c. 10.

spiritual men or temporal, to the church or to other; and so is great division in this behalf, when one preferreth his opinion, and another his, and one this jurisdiction, and another that; and that, as it is to fear, more of singularity than of charity. Wherefore it seemeth that they that have the greatest charge over the people, specially to the health of their souls, are most bound in conscience before other to look to this matter, and to do that in them is, in all charity to have it reformed, not beholding the temporal jurisdiction or spiritual jurisdiction, but the common wealth and quietness of the people : and that undoubtedly would shortly follow, if this division were put away, which I suppose verily will not be, but that all men within the realm, both spiritual and temporal, be ordered and ruled by one law in all things temporal. Notwithstanding, forasmuch as the purpose of this writing is not to treat of this matter, therefore I will no farther speak thereof at this time.

Doct. Then I pray thee proceed to another question, that thou sayest thy mind is to do.

Stud. I will with good-will.

CHAP. XXXII.—*If a man be excommenged, whether he may in any case be assoiled without making satisfaction.*

In the sum called *summa rosella*, in the title *absolutio quarta*, the second article, it is said, that he that is excommunicate for a wrong, if he be able to make satisfaction, ought not to be assoiled, but he do satisfy; and that they offend that do assoil him, but yet nevertheless he is assoiled; and if he be not able to make amends, that he must yet be assoiled, taking sufficient gage to satisfy if he be able hereafter, or else that he make an oath to satisfy, if he be able. And these sayings in many things hold not in the laws of England.

Doct. I pray thee shew wherein the law of the realm varieth therefrom.

Stud. If a man be excommunicate in the spiritual court for debt, trespass, or such other things as belong to the

king's crown, and to his royal dignity, there he ought to be
assoiled without making any satisfaction, for the spiritual
court exceedeth their power in that they held plea in those
cases, and the party, if he will, may thereupon have a
Præmunire facias,* as well against the party that sued him
as against the judge,† and therefore in this case they ought
in conscience to make absolution without any satisfaction,
for they not only offended the party, in calling him to
answer before them*of such things as belong to the law of
the realm, but also the king; for he, by reason of such
suits, may leese great advantages by reason of the writs
originals, judicials, fines, amerciaments, and such other
things as might grow to him, if suits had been taken in his
courts according to his laws.   And according to this 'saying
it appeareth in divers statutes, that if a man lay violent
hands upon a clerk, and beat him, that for the beating
amends shall be made in the king's court;‡ and for the
laying of violent hands upon the clerk, amends shall be
made in the Court-christian.§   And therefore if the judge
in the Court-christian would award the party to yield
damages for the beating, he did against the statute.‖   But
admit that a man be excommenged for a thing that the
spiritual court may award the party to make satisfaction of,
as for the not inclosing of the church-yard, or for not ap-
parelling of the church conveniently;¶ then I think the
party must make restitution, or lay a sufficient caution, if

---

* 3 Inst. 122.

† And a wrongful excommunication by a spiritual judge, may likewise
be punished by an action upon the 'case, or an indictment at the suit of
the king. 2 Inst. 623.

‡ See the stat. Articuli Cler., 9 Ed. 2, c. 3.

§ Mr. Justice Blackstone says, that a person guilty of beating a clergyman, is subject to *three* kinds of prosecution, all·of which may be pursued for one and the same offence, viz., an indictment for breach of the
king's peace by such assault and battery; a civil action for the special
damage sustained by the party injured, and a suit in the Ecclesiastical.
Court. 4 B. C. 218.

‖ 2 Burn's Ecl. Law, 48.

¶ 1 Mod. 194; 1 Vent. 367; Gibs. 1063; 2 Burn's Eccl. Law, 227, 228.

he be able, or he be assoiled; but if the party offer sufficient
amends, and have his absolution, and the judge will not
make him his letters of absolution, if the excommengement
be of record in the king's court, then the king may write
unto the spiritual judge, commanding him that he make the
party his letters of absolution, upon pain of contempt:* and
if the said excommunication be not of record in the king's
court, then the party may in such case have his action
against the judge spiritual, for that he would not make him
his letters of absolution.† But if he be not able to make
satisfaction, and therefore the judge spiritual will not assoil
him, what the king's laws may do in this case I am somewhat in doubt, and will not much speak of it at this time;
but, as I suppose, he may as well have his action in that
case for the not assoiling him, as where he is assoiled, and
that the judge will not make him his letters of absolution.
And I suppose the same law-to-be, where a man is accursed
for a thing that the judge hath no power to accurse him in,
as for debt, trespass, or such other.‡

Doct. There he may have other remedies, as a *Præmunire facias*, or such other: and therefore I suppose the
other action lieth not for him.

Stud. The judge and the party may be dead, and then
no *Præmunire* lieth; and though they were alive, and were
condemned in *Præmunire*, yet that should not avoid the
excommengement: and there I think the action lieth,
specially if he be thereby delayed of actions that he might
have in the king's court if the said excommengement had
not been.

CHAP. XXXIII.—*Whether a prelate may refuse a legacy.*

It is moved in the said sum named *rosella*, in the title
alienatio 20, the 11th article, whether a prelate may refuse
a legacy? Wherein divers opinions be recited there,

---

* See post., c. 36.
† 2 Inst. 623.
‡ Ante, 180.

which, as methinketh, had need after the laws of the realm
to be more plainly declared.

Doct. I pray thee shew me what the law of the realm
will therein.

Stud. I think that every prelate and sovereign that may
only sue and be sued in his own name, as abbots, priors,
and such other, may refuse any legacy that is made to the
house :* for the legacy is not perfect till he to whom it is
made assent to take it : for else, if he might not refuse it, he
might be compelled to have lands, whereby he might in
some case have great loss. But that if he intend to refuse,
he must, as soon as his title by the legacy falleth, relinquish
to take the profits of the thing bequeathed ; for if one take
the profits thereof, he shall not after refuse the legacy ; but
yet his successor may, if he will, refuse the taking of the
profits, to save the house from yielding damages, or from
arrearages of rents, if any such be. And like law is of a
remainder as is in legacy. For though in the case of a remainder; and also of a devise, as most men say, the freehold is cast upon him by the law, when the remainder or
devise falleth : yet it is in his liberty to refuse the taking of
the profits, and to refuse the remainder, if he will, as he
might do of a gift of lands or goods.† For if a gift be made
to a man that refuseth to take it, the gift is void :‡ and if it
be made to a man that is absent, the gift taketh no effect in
him till he assent,§ no more than if a man disseise one to
another man's use, he to whose use the desseisin is made,
hath nothing in the land, ne is no disseisor, till he agree.‖
And to such disseisins and gifts an abbot or prior may disagree, as well as another man. But after some men, a
bishop, of a devise or remainder that is made to the bishop
and to the dean and chapter, nor a dean and chapter of a

---

* Ante, 31.

† Br. Done, pl. 7.

‡ Ib., pl. 30.

§ But the better law is, that the property vests in him till he disagrees.
Wood's Conv. 118; 1 Salk. 301.

‖ Co. Litt. 180; Bro., tit. Disseisin, 12.

devise or remainder made to them, ne yet the master of a college, of such a devisè or remainder made to him and to his
brethren, may not disagree without the chapter or brethren :
for the bishop of such land as he hath with the dean· and
chapter, ne the dean nor master of such land as they have
with the chapter and brethren, may not answer without the
chapter and brethren :* and therefore some say, that if the
dean or master will refuse or disclaim in fhe lands that they
have by the devise or remainder, that disclaimer without the
chapter or brethren is void.   And therefore it is holden in
the law, that if a bishop be vouched to warrant, and the
tenant bindeth him to the warranty by reason of a lease
made to him by the bishop, and by the dean and the chapter, yielding a rent, that in that case the bishop may not
disclaim in the reversion without the assent of the dean and
chapter :† but yet if a reversion were granted to a dean and
a chapter, and the dean refuse, the grant is void.   And so
it appeareth that the dean may refuse to take a gift or grant
of lands or goods, or of a reversion made to him and to
the chapter ;‡ and yet he may not disagree to a remainder
or devise.   And the diversity is, because the remainder and
devise be cast upon him without any assent, whereupon·
neither the dean nor the chapter by themselves may in no·
wise disagree without the assent of the other : but a gift or
grant is not good to them without they both assent.   And
in such gifts, as I suppose, an infant may disagree as well
as one of full age : but if a woman covert disagree to a gift,
and the husband agree, that gift is good.§

Doct. What if the lands in that case of a man and his·
wife be charged with damages, or be charged with more
rent than the land is worth, and the husband die ; shall the·
wife be charged to the damages or to the rent ?

Stud. I think nay, if the wife refuse the occupation of
the ground after her husband's death.   And I think the same·

* Co. Litt. 103.
† Br. Disclaimer, pl. 7 ; 40 Ed. 3, 27.
‡ Watson's Clergyman's Law, 377 ; Co. Litt. 263, 264.
§ Br. Done, pl. 4.

law to be, if a lease be made to the husband and the wife, yielding a greater rent than the land is worth, that the wife after the husband's death may refuse the lease, to save her from-the payment of the rent: and so may the successor of an abbot.*

Doct. And if the husband in that case out-live the wife, and then make his executors and die, whether may his executors in like wise refuse the lease?

Stud. If they have goods sufficient of their testator to pay the rent, I think they may not refuse it: but if they have not goods sufficient of their testator to pay the rent to the end of the term, I think, if they relinquish the occupation, they may by special pleading discharge themselves of the rent and the lease; and if they do not, they may lightly charge themselves of their own goods.† And if a lease be made for term of life, the remainder to an abbot for term of life of John at Stile, reserving a greater rent than the land is worth, and after the tenant for term of life dieth; the abbot may refuse the remainder, for the cause before rehearsed:‡ and in case that the abbot assent to the remainder, whereby he is charged to the rent during the time that he is abbot, and after he dieth or is deposed, living the said John at Stile, in that case his successor may discharge himself, by refusing the occupation of the land as is aforesaid. But I think that if such a remainder were made to a dean, and to the chapter, and the dean agree without the assent of the chapter, that in that case the dean and the chapter may afterwards disagree to the remainder, and that the act of the dean without the assent of the chapter shall not charge the chapter in that behalf. And thus it appeareth, though the meaning of the said chapter and article in the said sum be, that a prelate may not disagree unto a legacy for hurting of the house, yet he may after the laws

---

. *4 Danv. Abr. 714; Br. Abr., pl. 30; 43 Ass. 23.

† 1 Vent. 271; Salk. 297; 1 Mod. 185, 186.

‡ Br. Abbe. 30; 37 Ass. 17; Br. Waiver de Choses, pl. 20; post. 209; ante, 32.

of the realm disagree thereto where it should hurt his house. And if in a *Præcipe quod reddat* there be but one tenant, be he spiritual or temporal, and he refuse by way of disclaimer, in such case where he may disclaim by the law ;* there the land shall vest in the demandant: and if there be two tenants, then it shall·vest in his fellow, if he will take the whole tenancy upon him, or else it shall vest in the demandant. But if an abbot or layman refuse the taking of the profits, and shew a special cause why it should hurt him, if he do assent, and be thereby discharged, as is said before ; in whom the land shall then vest it is more doubt, whereof I will no farther speak at this time. And thus it appeareth by divers of the cases that be put in this chapter, that he that is ignorant in the law of the realm shall lack the true judgment of conscience in many cases. For in many of these cases what may be done therein by the law, must also be observed in conscience, etc.

CHAP. XXXIV.—*Whether a gift·made under a condition be void, if the sovereign only break the condition.*

In *summa rosella*, in the title *alienatio*, the 12th article, is asked this question, Whether a gift made under a certain form may be voided or revoked, because the prelate or sovereign only did break the form? And it is there answered, That it may not, for that the deed of the prelate only sought not to hurt the church : and if those words (*under a manner*) be understood of a gift upon condition, as they seem to be, then the said solution holdeth not in this realm neither in the law nor conscience.

· *Doct.* What is then the law of England if a man infeoff an abbot by deed indented, upon condition that if the abbot pay not to the feoffor a certain sum of money at such a day, that then it shall be lawful to the feoffor to re-enter, and at that day the abbot faileth of his payment; may the feoffor lawfully re-enter, and put out the abbot?

---

* Co. Litt. 362.

Stud. Yes, verily, for he has no right to the land but by
the gift of the feoffor, and his gift was conditional;* and
therefore if the condition be broken, it is lawful by the law
of England for the feoffor to re-enter and to take his land
again, and to hold as in his first estate : by which re-entry
after the laws of the realm, he disproveth the first livery of
seisin, and all the mesne acts done between the first feoffment and the re-entry.† And it forceth little in the law, in
whom the default be that the condition was not performed,
whether in the abbot, or in his covent, or in both, or in any
other person whatsoever he be, except it be in the feoffor
himself. And it is great diversity between a clear gift
made to an abbot without condition, and where it is made
with condition : for when it is made without condition, the
act of the abbot only shall not by the Common law disherit
the house, but it be in very few cases. But yet upon divers
statutes the sufferance of the abbot only may disherit the
house, as by his cesser, or by levying a cross upon a house
against the statute thereof made, in which case the house
thereby shall leese the land : and some say that by the
Common law upon his disclaimer in avowry a writ of right
of disclaimer lieth. But if the gift be upon condition, it
standeth neither with law nor conscience that the abbot
should have any more perfect or sure estate than was given
unto him : and therefore as the said estate was made to the
house upon condition, so that estate may be avoided for not
performing of the condition. And I think verily, that this
I have said is to be holden in this realm both in the law and
conscience, and that the decrees of the church to the contrary bind not in this case. But if the lands be given to an
abbot, and to his covent, to the intent to find a lamp, or to
give certain alms to poor men ; though the intent be not in
these cases fulfilled, yet the feoffor nor his heir may not
re-enter ; for he reserved no re-entry by express words : ne
in the words, when he said, *to the intent to find a lamp*, or

* Shep. Touch. 114.
† 4 Rep. 120; Plow. 186.

to give alms, etc., is implied no re-entry :* he the feoffor nor his heirs shall have no remedy in such cases, unless it be within the case of the statute of Westminster the second,† that giveth the *Cessavit de Cantaria.*‡

CHAP. XXXV.—*Whether a covenant made upon a gift to the church, that it shall not be aliened, be good.*

In the said sum, called *summa rosella*, the said title *alienatio*, the 13th article, is asked this question, Whether a covenant made upon a gift to the church, that it shall not be aliened, be good? And the same question is moved again in the said *summa* called *rosella*, in the title *conditio*, the first article, and in *summa angelica*, in the title *donatio prima*, the fifty-first and fifty-second articles. And the intent of the question the reis, Whether notwithstanding that the condition be good to some alienations, whether that yet it be good to restrain alienations for the redemption of them that be in captivity under the infidels, or for the greater advantage of the house? And though the better opinion be there, that the condition may not be broken for redemption of them that be in captivity; yet it is in manner a whole opinion that it may be sold for the greater advantage to the house; for it is said there, that it may not be taken but that the intent of the giver was so; and therefore they call the condition that prohibiteth it to be sold *conditio turpis*, that is to say, a vile condition; wherefore they regard it not. But verily, as I take it, if a condition may restrain any manner of alienations, then it shall as well restrain alienations for the two causes before rehearsed, as for any other causes; and though methinketh that the condition is good, and after

---

* Wood's Inst. 140; Co. Litt. 204; 1 Roll. Abr. 407; Reg. 238; 2 Inst. 460; F. N. B. 481, 483; 3 Black. Com. 232.

† 13 Ed. 1, c. 41.

‡ N. B. Since the suppression of religious houses, the laws relating to abbots and priors, which make so conspicuous a figure in our old books, are become quite abolished. See ante, 32. Consequently the matter of which this chapter is composed cannot now come into use.

14

the law of the realm, that upon gifts to the church alienation is restrained; yet I shall touch one reason that is made
to the contrary, that is this : There is a clear ground in the
law,* that if a feoffment be made to a common person in fee,
upon condition that the feoffee shall not alien to no man ;† that
condition is void, because it is contrary to the estate of a fee-
simple, to bind him that hath the estate that he should not alien
if he list.‡ And some say that an abbot that hath lands to him
and to his successors, hath as high and as perfect a fee-simple
as hath a layman that hath land to him and to his heirs ; and
therefore they say, that it is as well against the law of the
realm to prohibit that the abbot shall not alien, as it is to
prohibit a layman thereof.   And though it be therein true as
they say, as to the highness of the estate, yet methinketh
there is a great diversity between the cases concerning
their alienations.   For when lands be given in fee-simple
to a common person, the intent of the law is that the feoffee
shall have power to alien, and if he do alien, it is not
against the intent of the law, ne yet against the intent of
the feoffor; but when lands be given to an abbot and to his
successors, the intent of the law is, and also of the giver,
(as it is to presume) that it should remain in the house for
ever; and therefore it is called *Mortmain*, that is to say, *a
dead hand*,§ as who saith, that it shall abide there alway
as a thing dead to the house.   And therefore, as I suppose,
the law will suffer that condition to be good, that is made
to restrain that such *Mortmain* should not be aliened ;‖ and
that yet it may prohibit the same condition to be made upon
a feoffment made in fee-simple to a man and to his heirs :¶
for that is the most high, the most free, and the most pure

---

* 2 C. B. 157.
† Ante, 86, 63.
‡ Co. Litt. 8, 94.
§ If the reader wishes to be further acquainted with the doctrine of *Mort-
main*, and the several statutes made for restraining it, he may consult Doc-
tor Burn's Eccl. Law, title *Mortmain*, and the 2d vol. B. C. 268, where the
subject is discussed in a masterly manner.
‖ Co. Litt. 223 ; Wood's Conv. 277.
¶ Litt., sec. 11.

o

-estate that is in the law.   But the law suffereth such a condition to be made upon a gift in tail,* because the statute
prohibiteth that no alienation should be made thereof.†
And then, as the law suffereth such a condition upon a
gift in *Mortmain*, that is to say, that he shall not be
aliened, to be good; so it judgeth the condition also according to the words : that is to say, if the condition be general,
that they shall not alien to no man, as this case is, that it
shall be taken generally according to the words, and it shall
not be taken that the intent of the giver was otherwise than
he expressed in his gift: though percase if he were alive
himself, and the question were asked him, whether he
would be contented it should be aliened for the said two
causes or not, he would say yea; but when he is dead no
man hath authority to interpret his gift otherwise than the
law suffereth, nor otherwise than the words of the gift be.
And if the condition be special, that is to say, that the land
shall not be aliened to such a man or such a man, then the
condition shall be taken according to the words, and then
they may be aliened as for that condition to any other but
to them to whom it is expressly prohibited that the land
should not be aliened to.‡   And if the lands in that case be
aliened to one that is not excepted in the condition, then he
may alien the land to him that is first excepted without
breaking of the condition; for conditions be taken strictly
in the law, and.without equity.§   And thus methinketh,
that because the said condition is general, and restraineth
all alienations, that it may not be aliened neither by the
law of the realm, ne yet by conscience, no more for the
said two causes, than it may for any other cause.   And this

* Shep. Touch. 126.
† This must be understood of an alienation, by which the estate is discontinued tortiously, as a feoffment in fee, or a fine at Common law, for
't is clear that tenant in tail, notwithstanding the condition, may alien by
a fine according to the statute 4 H. 7, or by Common recovery.   1 Burr.
84; Co. Litt. 224; ante, 86.
‡ Litt., sec. 361; Wood's Conv. 276.
§ Co. Litt. 205.

case must of necessity be judged after the rules and grounds
of the law of the realm, and after no other law, as me
seemeth.

CHAP. XXXVI.—*If the patron present not within six
months, who shall present?*

In the same sum called *summa rosella*, in the title *bene-
ficium, in principio*, it is asked, if the patron present not
within six months, who shall present, and within what time
the presentment must be made? And it is answered there,.
that if the patron present not within six months, that the
chapter shall have six months to present; and if the chapter present not within six months, that then the bishop shall
have other six months; and if he be negligent, then the metropolitan shall have other six months; and if he present not,.
then the presentment is devolute to the patriarch; and if
the metropolitan have no superior under the pope, then the
presentment is devolute to the pope. And so, as it is said
there, the archbishop shall supply the negligence of the
bishop, if he be not exempt;* and if he be exempt, the presentment immediately shall fall from the bishop to the pope.
And, as I suppose, these diversities hold not in the laws of
the realm.

Doct. Then, I pray thee, shew me who shall present by
the laws of the realm, if the patron do not present within
six months.

Stud. Then for default of the patron the bishop shall
present, unless the king be patron; and if the bishop present not within six months, then the metropolitan shall present, whether the bishop be exempt or not:† and if the
metropolitan present not within the time limited by the law,
then there be divers opinions who shall present, for some
say the pope shall present, as it is said before, and some
say the king shall present.‡

---

* Ante, 188.
† God. 242.
‡ Watson's Com. Inc., c. 12, pp. 114, 115, 116.

Doct. What reason make they that say the king should present in that case?

Stud. This is their reason; they say that the king is patron paramount of all the benefices within the realm.* And they say farther, that the king and his progenitors, kings of England, without time of mind, have had authority to determine the right of patronages in this realm in their own courts, and are bound to see their subjects have right in that behalf within the realm, and that in that case from him lieth no appeal. And then they say, that if the pope in this case should present, that then the king should not only leese his patronage paramount, but also that he should not sometime be able to do right to his subjects.

Doct. In what case were that?

Stud. It is in this case : The law of the realm is, that if a benefice fall void, then the patron shall present within six months; and if he do not, that then the ordinary shall present :† but yet the law is farther in this case, that if the patron present before the ordinary put in his clerk, that then the patron of right shall enjoy his presentment; and so it is though the time should fall after to the metropolitan, or to the pope.‡ And if the presentment should fall to the pope, then though the advowson abode still void, so that the patron might of right present, yet the patron should not know to whom he should present, unless he should go to the pope, and so he should fail of right within the realm. And if percase he went to the pope, and presented an able clerk unto him, and yet his clerk were refused, and another put in at the collation of the pope, or at the presentment of a stranger; yet the patron could have no remedy for the wrong within thé realm, for the incumbent might abide still out of the realm. And therefore the law will suffer no title in this case to fall to the pope.§ And they say, that for a

* 1 Burn's Eccl. 126; Hob. 143.
† Hob. 154; Kelw. 50.
‡ 2 Inst 273; 2 B. C. 277; Br. Qua. Imp., pl. 131; Hutt. 24; Hob. 152; Moor, 900.
§ 30 Ass. 19; Fitzh. Excom., pl. 10; Roll. Abr. 883.

like reason it is, that the law of the realm will not allow an
excommengement that is certified into the king's court under the pope's bulls :* for if the party offered sufficient
amends, and yet could not obtain his letters of absolution,
the king should not know to whom to write for the letters
of absolution, and the party could not have right; and that
the law will in no wise suffer.

Doct. The patron in that case may present to the ordinary,
as long as the church is void; and.if the ordinary accept
him not, the patron may have his remedy against him
within this realm. But if the pope will put in an incumbent
before the patron present, it is reason that he have the presentment, as me seemeth, before the king.

Stud. When the ordinary hath surcessed his time,† he
hath lost his power as to the presentment, specially if the
collation be devolute to the pope.‡ And also when the
presentment is in the metropolitan, he shall put in the clerk
himself,' and not the ordinary. And so there is no default
in the ordinary, though he present not the clerk of the
patron, if his time be past; and so there lieth no remedy
against him for the patron.

Doct. Though the incumbent abide still out of the realm,
yet may a *Quare Impedit* lie against him within the realm :
and if the incumbent make default upon the distress, and
appear not to shew his title, then the patron shall have a
writ to the bishop according to the statute, and so is not
without remedy.

Stud. But in this case it cannot be summoned, attached,
nor distrained, within the realm.

Doct. He may be summoned by the church, as the tenant may in a writ of right of advowson.§

Stud. There the advowson is in demand, and here the

---

* Nor will it allow any bulls to be obtained from Rome, or to be used or
put in use by any person on pain of a præmunire, or high treason. See
the several statutes on this head in 3 Bac. Abr., title Præmunire.
† Ante, 212.
‡ 2 Roll. Abr. 368.
§ 11 H. 6, 3, b.

presentment is only in debate;* and so he cannot be summoned by the church here, no more than if it were in a writ of annuity, and there the common return is, *quod Clericus est beneficiatus, non habens Laicum feod, ubi potest summoneri.* And though he might be summoned in the church, yet he might neither be attached nor distrained there; and so the patron should be without remedy.†

Doct. And if he were without remedy, he should yet be in as good case as he should be if the king should present: for if the title should be given to the king, the patron had lost his presentment clearly for the time, though the church abide still void. For I have heard say, that in such presentments no time after the law of the realm runneth to the king.

Stud. That is true, but there the presentment should be taken from him by right, and by the law, and here it should be taken from him against the law, and there as the law could not help him; and that the law will not suffer.‡

Doct. Yet methinketh alway that the title of the lapse in such case is given by the law of the church, and not by the temporal law: and therefore it forceth but little what the temporal law will in it, as me seemeth.

Stud. In such countries where the pope hath power to determine the right of temporal things, I think it is as thou sayest; but in this realm it is not so. And the right of presentment is a temporal thing, and a temporal inheritance;§ and therefore I think it belongeth to the king's law to determine, and also to make laws who shall present after six months, as well as before, so that the title of examination of ability or non-ability be not thereby taken from the ordinary.‖ And in like wise it is of avoidance of benefices, that is to say, then it shall be judged by the king's laws

---

* F. N. B. 74; 2 H. 6, 3, b; 2 Inst. 4.
† 3 Burn's Ecc. Law, 188.
‡ Post. 216; Watson's Com. Inc. 16.
§ 2 Inst. 273; ante, 189.
‖ Ante, 188.

when a benefice shall be said void,* and when not, and
not by the law of the church :† as when a parson is made a
bishop,‡ or accepteth another benefice without a licence, or
resigneth, or is deprived; in these cases the common law
saith, that the benefices is void, and so they should be,
though a law were made by the church to the contrary.§
And so if the pope should have any title in this case to present, it should be by the law of the realm. And I have
not seen ne heard that the law of the realm hath given any
title to the pope to determine any temporal thing that may
be lawfully determined by the king's court.

Doct. It seemeth by that reason that thou hast made now,
that thou preferrest the king's authority in presentments before the pope's; and that methinketh should not stand with
the law of God, sith the pope is the vicar-general under God.

Stud. That I have said proveth not that for the highest
preferment in presentments ·he is to have authority to examine the ability of the parson that is presented, for if the
presentee be able, it sufficeth to the discharge of the ordinary by whomsoever he be presented, and that authority is
not denied by the law of the realm to belong· alway to the
spiritual jurisdiction.‖ But my meaning is, that as to the
right of presentments, and to determine who ought to present, and who not, and at what time, and when the church
shall be judged to be void, and when not, belong to the
king and to his laws: or else it were a thing in vain for him
to hold plea of advowsons, or to determine the right of
patronage in his own courts, and not to have authority to
determine the right thereof, and those claims seem not to
be against the law of God.¶ And so me seemeth in this
case the presentment is given the king.

Doct. And if the king should have right to present, then

---

* Post. 218.
† Pal. 344; Hob. 158.
‡ Without a commendam. Watson's Clergyman's Law, 206; Hob. 143.
§ 3 Comyn's Digest, 207; Watson's Com. Inc. 5, 8, 18, 19, 27.
‖ Watson's Clergyman's Law, 212; Burn's Ecc. Law, 137.
¶ Ante, 210.

might the church happen to continue void for ever; for as
we have said before, no time runneth to the king in such
presentment.

Stud. If any such case happen, if the king present not,
then may the ordinary set in a deputy to serve the cure, as
he may do when negligence is in other patrons that may
present, and do not;* and also it cannot be thought that
the king, which hath the rule and governance over the people, not only of their bodies, but also of their souls, will
hurt his conscience, and suffer a benefice continually to
stand without a curate, no more than he doth in advowsons
that be of his own presentment.

CHAP. XXXVII.—*Whether the presentment and collation
of all benefices and dignities, voiding at Rome, belongeth only to the pope.*

In the same sum called *summa rosella*, in the title *bene-
ficium primum*, in the 13th article, it is said, that benefices,
dignities and parsonages voiding in the court of Rome may
not be given but by the pope; and likewise of the pope's
servants, and of other that come and go from the court, if
they die in places nigh to the court within two days journey,
all these belong to the pope: but if the pope present not
within a month, then after the month they to whom it belongeth to present, may present by themselves only, or by
their vicar-general, if they be in far parts. And these sayings hold not in the laws of the realm.

Doct. What is the cause that they hold not in this realm
as well as in all other realms?

Stud. One cause is this: The king in this realm, according to the ancient right of his crown, of all his advowsons
that be of his patronage ought to present, and in like wise
other patrons of benefices of their presentment; and the
pleas of the right of presentments of benefices within this
realm belong to the king and his crown.† And these titles

* Watson's Clergyman's Law, 120; 2 B. C. 277.
† Ante, 215.

cannot be taken from the king and his subjects but by their assent; and the law that is made therein to put away the title bindeth nòt in this realm. And over that before the statute of 25 Ed. 3, there was a great inconvenience and mischief by reason of divers provisions and reservations that the pope made to the benefices in this realm, contrary to the old right of the king, and other patrons in this realm, as well to the archbishopricks, bishopricks, deanries and abbies, as to other dignities and benefices of the church. And many times aliens thereby had benefices within the realm that understood not the English tongue, so that they could not counsel ne comfort the people when need required; and by that occasion great riches was conveyed out of the realm. Wherefore, to avoid such inconveniences, it was ordained by the said statute, that all patrons, as well spiritual as temporal, should have the presentments freely : and in case the collation or provision were made by the pope in disturbance of any spiritual person, that then for that time the king should have the presentment; and if it were in disturbance of any lay patron, that then if the patron presented not within the half-year after such voidance, nor the bishop of the place witĥin a month after the half-year, that then the king should have also the presentment, and that the king should have the profits of the benefices so occupied by provision, except abbies and priories, and other houses that have college and covent, and there the college and covent, to have the profits. And because the statute is general, and excepteth no such benefices as shall void in the court of Rome, òr in such other place as before appeareth, therefore they be taken to be within the provision of the said statute, as well as the benefices that void within the realm : and all provisors and executors of the said collations and provisions, and all their attornies, notaries and maintainers, shall be out of the protection of the king, and shall have like punishment as they should have for executing of benefices voiding within the realm.*

---

* See likewise stat. 38 Ed. 3, st. 2; 12 R. 2, c. 15; 13 R. 2, st. 2; 7 R. 2, c. 12, and 16 R. 2, c. 5.

Doct. But I cannot see how the said statute may stand with conscience, that so far restrained the pope of his liberty, which as me seemeth, he ought in this case of right to have.

Stud. Because (as I suppose) that patrons ought of right to have their presentments under such manner as they claim them in this realm, as I have said before, and as in the 26th chapter of this book appeareth more at large. Also forasmuch as it appeareth evidently, that great inconvenience followed upon the said provisions, and that the said statute was made to avoid the same, which sith that time hath been suffered by the pope, and hath been alway used in this realm without resistance, it seemeth that the said statute should therefore stand with good conscience.

CHAP. XXXVIII.—*If a house by chance fall upon a horse that is borrowed, who shall bear the loss?*

In the said sum called *summa rosella*, the said title *casus fortuitus*, in the beginning, is put this case :* If a man lend another a horse, which is called there a *depositum*, and a house by chance falleth upon the horse, whether in that case he shall answer for the horse? And it is answered there, that if the house were like to fall, that then it cannot be taken as a chance, but as the default of him that had the horse delivered to him : but if the house were strong, and of likelihood, and by common presumption, in no danger of falling, but that it fell by a sudden tempest, or such other casualty, that then it shall be taken as a chance, and he that had the keeping of the horse shall be discharged. And though this diversity agreeth with the laws of the realm, yet for the more plainer declaration thereof, and for the more like cases and chances that may happen to goods, that a man hath in his keeping that be not his own, I shall add a little more thereto that shall be somewhat necessary, as methinketh, to the ordering of conscience. First, a man

* See William Jones, Essay on Bailments, 68.

may have of another by way of loan or borrowing money, corn, wine, and such other things, where the same thing cannot be delivered if it be occupied, but another thing of like nature and like value must be delivered for it; and such things he that they be lent to, may by force of the loan use as his own, and therefore if they perish, it is at his jeopardy; and this is most properly-called a loan.   Also a man may lend to another a horse, an ox, a cart, or such other things as may be delivered again, and they by force of that loan may be used and occupied reasonably in such manner as they were borrowed for, or as it was agreed at the time of the loan that they should be occupied : and if such things be occupied otherwise than according to the intent of the loan, and in that occupation they perish, in what wise soever they perish, so it be not in default of the owner, he that borrowed them shall be charged therewith in law and conscience :* and if he that borrow them occupy them in such manner as they were lent for, and in that occupation they perish in default of him that they were lent to, then he shall answer for them : and if they perish not through his default, then he that owneth them shall bear the loss.   Also if a man have goods to keep to a certain day, for a certain recompence for the keeping, he shall stand charged or not charged after as default or no default shall be in him, as before appeareth : and so it is if he have nothing for the keeping.   But if he have for the keeping, and make a promise at the time of the delivery, to redeliver them safe at his peril, then he shall be charged with all chances that may fall. But if he make that promise, and have nothing for keeping, I think he is bound to no such casualties, but that be wilful and his own default, for that is a nude or a naked promise, whereupon, as I suppose, no action lieth.†   Also if a man find goods of another, if they be after hurt or lost by wilful negligence, he shall be charged to the owner : but if they

----

* 2 B. C. 454; Lord Raym. 915.

† Hargrave's edition of Coke upon Littleton, 89, 90; Lord Raym. 909; 12 Mod. 487; Sir William Jones on Bailment, 45; Ow. 141; 1 Leon, 224; 1 Cro. 219.

be lost by other casualty, as if they be laid in a house tha*
by chance is burned, or if he deliver them to another to
keep, that runneth away with them, I think he is discharged.
And these diversities hold most commonly upon pledges, or
where a man hireth goods of his neighbour to a certain day
for certain money.* And many other diversities be in the
law of the realm, what shall be to the jeopardy of the one,
and what of the other, which I will not speak of at this
time. And by this it may appear, that it is commonly
holden in the laws of England, if a common carrier go by
the ways that be dangerous for robbing, or drive by night,
or in other inconvenient time, and be robbed;† or if he
overcharge a horse whereby he falleth into the water, or
otherwise, so that the stuff is hurt or impaired; that he
shall stand charged for his misdemeanor: and if he would
percase refuse to carry it, unless promise were made unto
him that he shall not be charged for no misdemeanor that
should be in him, the promise were void, for it were against
reason and against good manners, and so it is in all other
cases like. And all these diversities be granted by
secondary conclusions derived upon the law of reason,
without any statute made in that behalf. And peradventure
laws, and the conclusions therein, be the more plain, and
the more open. For if any statute were made therein, I
think verily more doubts and questions would arise upon
the statute, than doth now when they be only argued and
judged after the Common law.

CHAP. XXXIX.—*If a priest have won much goods by
saying of mass, whether he may give those goods, or
make a will of them.*

In the said sum called *summa rosella*, in the title *clericus
quartus*, the 3d article, is asked this question: If a priest
have won much goods by saying of mass,‡ whether he

---

* Sir William Jones on Bailment, 78.
† Noy's Max. 92.
‡ See the Statutes 23 Eliz., c. 1, s. 4, 9, 10, 11, and 11 and 12 W., c. 4, s.
3, 5, and 3 J., c. 5, s. 1, against saying and hearing mass.

may give those goods, or make a will of them? Whereto it
is. answered there, that he may give them, or make a will
of them, specially when a man bequeaths money for to have
masses said for him.* And the like law is of such things
as a clerk winneth by the reason of an office : for it is said
there, that such things come to him by reason of his own
person. Which sayings I think accord with the law of the
realm. But forasmuch as the said article, and in divers
other places of the said chapter, and in divers other chapters
of the said sum, is put great diversity between such goods as
a clerk hath by reason of his church, and such goods as he
hath by reason of his person ; and that he must dispose such
goods as he hath by reason of his church in such manner
as is appointed by the law of the church, so that he may
not dispose them so liberally as he may the goods that come
by reason of his own person : therefore I shall a little touch
what spiritual men may do with their goods after the law
of the realm.

First, A bishop, of such goods as he hath with the dean
and chapter, he may neither make gift nor bequest ;† but
of such goods as he hath of his own by reason of his church,
or of the gift of his ancestors, or of any other, or of his
patrimony, he may both make gifts and bequests lawfully.
And an abbot of the goods of his church may make a gift,
and that gift is good as to the law : but what it is in conscience, that is after the cause and intent and quality of the
gift. For if it be so much that it notably hurteth the house
or the covent, or if he give away the books or the chalices,
or such other things as belong to the service of God, he
offendeth in conscience ;‡ and yet he is not punishable in
the law, ne yet by *subpœna*, after some men, ne in none
otherwise but by the law of the church, as a waster of the
goods of his monastery. But nevertheless I will not fully

---

* Such a bequest as this would now be superstitious and void. Duke's
Charitable Uses, 106.

† Swin. on Wills, 107; Shep. Touch. 452; Perk., sec. 497; 1 Roll. Abr.
608.

‡ Ante, 32.

DIALOGUE II.—CHAP. 39.   223

hold that opinion, as to that that belongeth necessarily to
the service of God, whether any remedy lie against him or
not, but remit it to the judgment of other.*   And of a dean
and chapter, and a master and brethren, of goods that they
have to themselves, and also of goods that they have with
the chapter and brethren the same diversity holdeth, as appeareth before of a bishòp and the dean and chapter ; except
that in the case of a master and brethren the goods shall be
ordered as shall be assigned by the foundation.   And moreover, of a parson of a church, vicar, or chantry priest, or
such other, all such goods as they have, as well such as
they have by reason of the parsonage, vicarage, or chaun-
try, as that they have by reason of their own person, they
may lawfully give and bequeath where they will after the
Common law : and if they dispose part among the parishioners, and part to the building of churches, or give part to
the ordinary, or to poor men, or in such other manner, as
it is appointed by the law of the church, they offend not
therein, unless they think themselves bounden thereto by
duty, and by authority of the law of the church, not regarding the king's laws :† for if they do so, it seemeth they resist
the ordinance of God, which hath given power to princes
to make laws.   But there, as the pope hath sovereignty in
temporal things as he hath in spiritual things, there some
say that the goods of priests must in conscience be disposed
as is contained in the said sum.   But that holdeth not in
this realm ; for the goods of spiritual men be temporal in
what manner soever they come to them, and must be
ordered after the temporal law, as the goods of the temporal men must be.   Howbeit, if there were a statute
made in this case of like effect in many points as the law
of the church is, I think it were a right good and a profitable statute.

---

* 1 Roll. Abr. 608; Wood's Conv. 795; Swinburne on Wills, 107.
† Duke's Charitable Uses, 108, 109.

CHAP. XL.—*Who shall succeed a clerk that dieth intestate?*

In the said sum, called *rosella*, in the chapter *clericus quartus*, the 7th article, is asked this question, Who shall succeed to a clerk that dieth intestate? And it is answered, That in goods gotten by reason of the church, the church shall succeed;* but in other goods his kinsmen shall succeed after the order of the law, and if there be no kinsman, then the church shall succeed. And it is said farther, That goods gotten by a canon secular by reason of his church or prebend shall not go to his successor in the prebend, but to the chapter.† But where one that is beneficed is not of the congregation, but he hath a benefice clearly separate, as if he be a parson of a parish-church, or is a president, or an archdeacon not beneficed by the chapter, then the goods gotten by reason of his benefice shall go to his successor, and not to the chapter. And none of these sayings hold place in the laws of England.

Doct. What is then the law, if a parson of a church or a vicar in the country die intestate, or if a canon secular be also a parson, and have goods by reason thereof, and also by a prebend that he hath in a cathedral church, and he die intestate, who shall have his goods?

Stud. At the Common law the ordinary in all these cases may administer the goods, and after he must commit administration to the next faithful friends of him that is dead intestate that will desire it, as he is bound to do where laymen that have goods die intestate.‡ And if no man desire to have administration, then the ordinary may administer,§ and see the debts payed: and he must beware that

* Ante, 222.
† Swinb. 107.
‡ Swinb. 107; vide the Statutes 31 Ed. 3, c. 11, and 21 H. 8, c. 5; B. C. 2 vol. 511.
§ It is usual for the ordinary in case none of the friends or creditors of the deceased will administer to his effects, to commit administration to

he pay the debts in such order as is appointed in the Common law : for if he pay debts upon simple contracts before an obligation, he shall be compelled to pay the debt upon the obligation of his own goods, if there be not goods sufficent of him that died intestate.* And though it be suffered in such case that the ordinary may pay pound and poundlike, that is, to apportion the goods among the debtors after his discretion, yet by the rigour of the Common law he might be charged to him that can first have his judgment against him.† And furthemore, by that is said before in the last chapter it appeareth, that if a bishop that hath goods of his bishoprick or of his patrimony, or a master of a college, or a dean, of goods that they have of their own only to themselves, die intestate, that the ordinary shall commit administration thereof, as before appeareth :‡ and if they make executors, then the executors shall have the ministration thereof. But the heirs nor the kinsman, by that reason only that they be heirs or of kin to him that is deceased, shall have no meddling with his goods,§ except it be by custom of some countries, where the heirs shall have heir looms, or where the children (the debts and legacies‖ paid)

such persons of discretion as he approves of, or to grant him letters *ad colligendum bona defuncti.* Wood's Conv. 147.

* Office of Exec. 216; ante, 132; Noy's Max. 104.
† Ante, 130.
‡ Ante, 224.
§ Ante, 130; Co. Litt. 18, 185.
‖ The term *legacies* in this place appears to be improper, as the customs of London, principality of Wales, and the province of York, to which it is presumed a reference is here made, cannot take place but where a freeman or an inhabitant dies without making any disposition of his effects, and if so he can't give any legacies.

In London the children are intitled to their reasonable part (if not barred by advancement or will) after the debts, customary funeral expences, and the widow's chamber are deducted, 4 Burn's Eccl. Law, 376; and in the province of York, and principality of Wales (after the funeral expences and necessary charges are paid). Ib. 392. For the nature and quantum of this reasonable part within these three distinct places, see 1 P. Will. 341; 4 Burn's Eccl. Law, 392, 393, 412; and see further the several statutes relating to this subject, viz., 4 and 5 W. & M., c. 2, explained by 2 and 3 Ann.,

15

shall have a reasonable part of the goods, after the custom of the country.*

CHAP. XLI.—*If a man be outlawed of felony, or be attainted for murther or felony, or that is an Ascismus, may be slain by every stranger.*

Doct. It appeareth in the said sum, called *summa angelica*, in the 21st chapter, in the title of *Ascismus*, the second paragraph, that he is an *Ascismus* that will slay men for money at the instance of every man that will move him to it; and such a man may lawfully be slain not only by the judge, but by every private person. But it is said there in the fourth paragraph, that he must first be judged by the law as an *Ascismus*, ere he may be slain, or his goods seised. And it is said farther there in the second paragraph, that also in conscience such an *Ascismus* may be slain, if it be done through a zeal of justice, and else not. Is not the law of the realm likewise of men outlawed, abjured, or judged for felony?

Stud. In the law of the realm, there is no such law, that a man shall be judged as an *Ascismus:* ne if a man be in full purpose, for a certain sum of money that he hath received, to slay a man, yet it is no felony ne murther in the law till he hath done the act: for intent of felony nor murther is not punishable by the Common law of the realm,† though it be deadly sin before God;‡ but in treason, or in

---

c. 5, for the province of York; 7 and 8 W. 3, c. 38, for Wales, and 11 Geo. 4, c. 18, for London.
    ᶜ 4 Burn's Ecl. Law, 247.
    † But by the law as it stood in very ancient times, a bare intention to commit felony, was held so criminal that it was punishable as felony itself, when it missed its effect, through chance or accident. 1 Haw. P. C., cap. 25, p. 65; for voluntas reputabatur pro facto, 3 Inst. 161. And though it seems to be settled that at this day felony shall not be laid to the charge of an offender where in fact none is committed, yet the party may be severely fined for such an intent on. 1 Haw. P. C., cap. 25, p. 65. And by a modern statute, viz., 7 Geo. 2, 21, an assault with an *intent* to rob is felony, but the offender may chuse transportation.
    ‡ 1 H. P. C. 109; 3 Inst. 5, 6, 12; 5 Mod. 207, 208; Savil. 31, pl. 73.

some other particular cases, by statute* that intent may be punished. And though a man in such case kill a man for money, yet he shall not be attainted that he is an *Ascismus;* for, as it is said before, there is no such term of *Ascismus* in the law of the realm : but he shall in such case be arraigned upon the murther, and if he confess it, or plead that he is not guilty, and is found guilty by twelve men, he shall have judgment of life, and of member, and shall forfeit his lands and goods. And like law is of an appeal brought of the murther ; if he stand dumb, and will not answer to the murther, he shall be attainted of the murther, and shall forfeit life, lands and goods.† But if he be arraigned of the murther upon an indictment at the king's suit, and thereupon standeth dumb, and will not answer ; there he shall not be attainted of the murther, but he shall have Paine fort and dure, that is to say, he shall be pressed to death,‡ and he shall there forfeit his goods and not his lands. But in none of these cases, that is to say, though a man be outlawed for murther or felony, or be abjured, or that he be otherwise attainted ; yet it is not lawful for any man to murther him, or slay him, ne to put him in execution, but by authority of the king's laws. Insomuch that if a man be adjudged to have Paine fort and dure, and the officer beheadeth him, or on the contrary wise putteth him

---

* See stat. 25 Ed. 3 ; stat. 5, c. 2, par. 1.

† 4 B. C. 194 ; Co. Litt. 41 ; 1 Kelying, 37 ; 2 Inst. 178 ; Bro. Corone, pl. 43 ; Bro. Appeal, 40 ; 2 Hale's P..C. 317—contra, 21 Ed. 3, 18 ; Bro. Pain, pl. 8 ; 2 Haw. P. C. 329 ; Bacon's Use of the Law, 39 ; 2 Haw. P. C. 331, cap. 30, s. 19 ; 1 Hale's P. C. 497.

‡ But now by the statute 12 Geo. 3, c. 30, if any person being arraigned on any indictment of appeal of felony, or on any indictment for piracy, shall upon such arraignment stand mute, or will not answer directly to the felony or piracy, he shall be convicted of the offence, and the court shall thereupon award judgment and execution in the same manner as if he had been convicted by verdict or confession, and such judgment shall have all the same consequences as a conviction by verdict or confession. The reader will observe, that the crimes of treason and petit larceny are not mentioned in this act, and the reason is because in these offences, standing mute was equal to conviction before the statute, and the prisoner was not sentenced to the peine forte et dure. 2 Haw. P. C., c. 30, secs. 9, 10.

to paine forte and dure, where he should behead him he offendeth the law. And if an officer which hath authority to
put a man to death, may not put him to death but accord--
ing to the judgment, then methinketh it should follow that,
more stronger a stranger may not put such a man to death
of his own authority without commandment of the law.* But
if the judgment be that he shall be hanged in chains, and
the officer hangeth him in other things, and not in chains,
I suppose he is not guilty of his death. But some say he
shall there make a fine to the king, because he hath not
followed the words of the judgment.

Also, if a man that is no officer would arrest a man that
is outlawed, abjured, or attainted of murther or felony, as is
aforesaid, and he disobeyeth the arrest, and by reason of
the disobedience he is slain ;† I suppose the other shall not
be impeached for his death ; for it is lawful unto every man
to take such persons, and to bring them forth that they may.
be ordered according to the law. But if a *Capias* be directed unto the sheriff to take a man in an action of debt
or trespass, there no man may take the man, but he have
authority from the sheriff: and if any man attempt of his-
own authority to take him, and he resisteth, and in the re-
sisting is slain, he that would have taken him is guilty of
his death.

Chap. XLII.—*Whether a man shall be bounden by the*
act or offence of his servant or officer.

In the said sum called *summa angelica*, in the title *dominus,*
4th paragraph, is asked this question, Whether a man shall
be charged for his household? And it is said there, that
he shall, when the household offendeth in an office or min--
istry that the master is the chief officer of, and he hath the
work and the profit of the household: for it shall be his
default that he would chuse such servants, for he ought to-

*Finch Law, 31; 3 Inst. 54; 1 Hal. P. C. 501.
†4 B. C. 315.

appoint honest persons.* But is said there, that it is to be understood civilly, and not criminally, whereby, as it is said there, he that is a governour is bound for the offence of his officers; and that the same is to be holden of a captain, that he shall be bound for the offence of his squires, and an host for his guest, and such other. Nevertheless it is said there, that certain doctors, there rehearsed, said thereto, that if the office be an open or publick office, as an office of power, or other like, it sufficeth to bring forth him that offended : but it is otherwise if it be not a publick office, but an host or a taverner, or other like. But if the household offend not in the office, the lord is not bound as to the law, but in conscience he is bound if he were in default by not correcting them ; for he is bound to correct them both by word and example, and if he find any incorrigible, he is bound to put him away, except that he hath presumptions, that if he do so, he will be the worse, and then he may do that he thinketh best, and he is excused, and else not; for to such persons it is said *Error qui non resistitur approbatur*, that is to say, an error that is not resisted is approved. And though divers of the sayings before rehearsed agree with the law of the realm, yet all do not so ; and also they that do are to be observed by authority of the law of the realm, and not by the authority alleged in the said paragraph. And therefore I intend to treat somewhat where the master shall be charged by his servant or deputy, or by them that be under him in any office, and where not; and then I intend to touch some other things, where the master after the laws of the realm shall be charged by the act of his servant in other cases not concerning offices, and where not.

First, If a man be committed to ward upon arrearages of accompt, and the keeper of the prison suffereth him to go at large, then an action of debt shall lie against him. And if he be not sufficient, then it lieth against him that committed the keeping of the prison unto him ;† and that

* Post. 270.
† 2 Inst. 382; Cow. Rep. 405.

is by reason of the statute of Westminister 2, cap. 11.
Also if bailiffs of franchises that have return of writs make
a false return, the party shall have averment against it, as
well of too little issues as of other things, as well as he shall
have against the sheriff; but all the punishment shall be
only upon the bailiff, and not upon the lord of.the franchise :
and that doth appear by the statute made in the first year
of Edw. III., the fifth chapter.* But if an under-sheriff
make a return whereupon the sheriff shall be amerced, there
the high-sheriff shall be .amerced, for the return is made
expressly in his name.† But if it be a false return whereupon an action of disceit lieth, in that case it may be
brought against the under-sheriff. And see thereof the
statute that is called *statutum de male returnantibus brevia.*

Also, if the king's butler make deputies, he shall answer
for his deputies as for himself;‡ as appeareth in the statute.
made in the twenty-first year of king Edw. III. *De prodi-
tionibus,* the twenty-first chapter.

Also in the statute that is called *statutum scaccarii* it is
enacted, among other things, That no officer of the exchequer shall put any clerk under him, but such as he will
answer for. And forasmuch as the statute is general, it
seemeth that he shall answer as well for an untruth in any
such clerk as for an oversight.§

Also in the fourteenth year of king Edw. III., c. 9, it is
enacted, That all gaols shall be adjoined again to the
shires, and that the sheriff shall have the keeping of them,
and that the sheriff shall make such under-gardeins for the
which they will answer.‖ And nevertheless I suppose
that if there be an escape by default of the gaoler, that the
king may charge the gaoler, if he will.¶ But it is no doubt

---

* Dalton's Sheriff, 462, 177; 27 H. 8, c. 24, s. 9; Viner's Abr., title Return, 191.
† 3 Buls. 78; 1 Buls. 73; Dalt. Sher. 456.
‡ Obsolete.
§ Stat. 51 H. 3, stat. 5; 4 Inst. 107.
‖ Vent. 401; Skinn. 41.
¶ 2 H. P. C. 135, c. 19.

but he may charge the sheriff, by reason of this statute, if he will. But if it be a wilful escape in the gaoler, which is felony in him, the sheriff shall not be bound to answer to the felony, ne none other but the gaoler himself, and they that assented to him.*

Also, if a man have a sheriffwick, constableship, or bailiwick in fee, whereby he hath the keeping of prisoners, if he let any to replevin that be not replevishable, and thereof be attaint, he shall leese the office, etc.† And if it be an under-sheriff, constable, or bailiff, that hath the keeping of the prison, that doth it without knowledge of the lord, he shall have imprisonment by three years, and after shall be ransomed at the king's will; as appeareth in the statute of West. 1, the 15th chapter. And so it appeareth, that in this case, he that is lord of the prison is not bound to answer for the offence of them that have the rule of the prison under him, but that they shall have the punishment themselves for their misdemeanor. Also there is a statute made in the 27th year of king Edw. III., the 19th chapter, that is called the statute of the staple, whereby it is ordained, That no merchant, ne none other man, shall not leese their goods for the trespass, or forfeit of their servants; unless it be by commandment of his master, or that he offend in the office that his master hath put him in, or else that the master shall be bound to answer for the deed of his servant by the law-merchant, as in some places it is used.

Also it is enacted in the 14th year of king Edw. III., the 10th chapter, That wapentakers and hundreds that be severed from the counties shall be adjoined again unto them, and that if the sheriff hold them in his own hands, that he shall put in them such bailiffs that have lands sufficient, and those for which he will answer;‡ and that if he let them to ferm, that they be let to the ancient ferm: but after it is prohibited by the statute of the 23d year of king Hen.

---

* 2 Haw. P. C. 134; Salk. 272; 2 Inst. 592; post. 234.
† 2 Inst. 190, 191; 1 Comyn's Digest, 473.
‡ 3 Inst. 92; 4 Co. 34; Stat. 19 H. 7, c. 10.

VI., the 10th chapter, that no sheriff shall let his bailiwicks nor wapentakes to ferm. And when they be once in the sheriff's own hands, and the sheriff put in bailiffs, they be but as under-bailiffs to the king, and the sheriff the high-bailiff, and they in manner the sheriff's servants, and put in only by him; and therefore by the said statute of king Edw. III. he shall answer for them, if they offend in their office. But if the sheriff let them to ferm, then though the sheriff offend the statute in that doing, yet whether he shall be charged for their misdemeanor in the office or not, is a great doubt to some men; for they say that this statute is only to be understood where the bailiwicks be in the sheriff's hands, but here they be not·so, ne the bailiffs be not his servants, but his fermers; and therefore they say', that if the sheriff shall be charged for them, it is by the Common law, and not by the statute aforesaid. Also in the second year of king Henry VI., the 10th chapter, it is enacted, That officers by patent in every court of the king, that by virtue of their office have power to make clerks in the said courts, shall be charged and sworn to make such clerks under them for whom they will answer.* Also the hospitallers and templars be prohibit they shall hold no plea that belongs to the king's courts, upon pain to yield damages to the party grieved, and to make ransom to the king : that the superiors shall answer for their obediencers, as for their own deed. West. 2, c. 43.† Also the serjeant of the catery shall satisfy all the debs, damages, and executions that shall be recovered against any that is purveyor or achator under him, that offend against the statute of 36th of Edw. III., or against the statute of 24th of Hen. VI., in case the purveyor or achator be not sufficient, etc. And the party plaintiff shall have a *Scire facias* against the said serjeant in this case to have execution, as appeareth in the 24th year of king Henry VI., the first chapter.‡

---

* 4 Inst. 114, 115.
† 2 Inst. 465, 466; see stat. 32 H. 8, c. 24.
‡ Repealed by stat. 12 Car. 2, c. 24, and vide 13 and 14 Car. 2, cap. 20.

Also, if a man be sent to prison upon a statute-merchant
by the mayor before whom the recognizance was taken, and
the gaoler will not receive him, he shall answer for the debt,
if he have wherewith; and if not, then he shall answer
that committed the gaol to him, as appeareth in the statute
called the *Statute-merchant.* *

And if outragious toll be taken in the town-merchant,†
if it be the king's town let to farm, the king shall take the
franchise of the market into his hands ;‡ and if it be done
by the lord of the town the king shall do in like wise : and
if it be done by the bailiff, unknowing to the lord, he shall
yield again as much as he hath taken, and shall have imprisonment of forty days. And so it appeareth that the
lord in this case shall not answer for his bailiff. West. 1,
c. 3. And in all the cases before rehearsed, where the superior is charged by the default of him that is under him,
he in whose default his superior is so charged, is bound in
conscience to restore him that is so charged through his default: except the case before rehearsed of the hospitallers,
for all that the obediencer hath is the superior's if he will
take it.§ And therefore what recompence shall be made by
the obediencer in that case, is at the will of the superior.
And now I intend to show thee some particular cases, where
the master after the laws of the realm shall be charged by
the act of his servant, bailiff, or deputy, and where not;
and so for to make an end of this chapter.

First, For trespass of battery, or wrongful entry into
lands or tenements, ne yet for felony or murther, the master shall not be charged for his servant, unless he did it by
his commandment.‖

Also, if a servant borrow money in his master's name, the
master shall not be charged with it unless it come to his use,

---

* 13 Ed. 1, stat. 3.
† 2 Inst. 219, 220.
‡ That is, till it be redeemed by the owner. 2 Inst. 221. For the market
is not absolutely forfeited, but only the toll. Pal. 82.
§ Ante, 231.
‖ 2 Roll. Rep. 27; 2 Mod. 244; 1 B. C. 430.

and that by his assent. And the same law is, if a servant make a contract in his master's name, the contract shall not bind his master, unless it were by his master's commandment, or that it came to the master's use by his assent.* But if a man sends his servant to a fair or market to buy for him certain things, though he command him not to buy them of no man in certain, and the servant doth according, the master shall be charged : but if the servant in that case buy them in his own name, not speaking of his master, the master shall not be charged, unless the things bought come to his use.

Also, if a man send his servant to the market with a thing which he knoweth to be defective, to be sold to a certain man, and he selleth it to him, there an action lieth against the master :† but if the master biddeth him not to sell it to any person in certain, but generally to whom he can, and he selleth it according, there lieth no action of deceit against the master.‡

Also, if the servant keep the master's fire negligently, whereby his master's house is burnt,§ and his neighbour's also, there an action lieth against the master.|| But if the servant bear fire negligently in the street, and thereby the house of another is burned, there lieth no action against the master.¶

Also, if a man desire to lodge with one that is no common hostler, and one that is servant to him that he lodgeth with robbeth his chamber, his master shall not be charged for

---

* Bridgeman's Rep. 128.
† 1 Roll. Abr. 95 ; Poph. 143.
‡ Bridgeman's Rep. 128.
§ Noy's Maxims, c. 44 ; 1 B. C. 431.
|| The law is now altered in this respect by stat. 6 Ann , c. 8, sec. 3, which enacts that no action shall be maintained against any in whose house or chamber a fire shall accidentally begin ; but if such fire happens through negligence of any servant, such servant shall forfeit 100*l*, or in default of payment, be sent to the house of correction for eighteen months, to be kept to hard labour.
¶ 1 Black. Com. 419.

the robbing; but if he had been a common hostler he should have been charged.

Also, if a man be gardein of a prison wherein is a man that is condemned in a certain sum of money;* and another that is in prison for felony, and a servant of the gardein that hath the rule of the prison under him, wilfully letteth them both escape; in this case the gardein shall answer for the debt, and shall pay a fine for the escape of the other, as for a negligent escape, and the servant only shall be put to answer to the felony for the wilful escape.†

Also, if a man make another his general receiver, and that receiver receiveth money of a creditor of his master, and maketh him acquittance, and after payeth not his master; yet that payment dischargeth the creditor :‡ but if the creditor hath taken an acquittance of him without paying him his money, that acquittance only were no bar to the master, unless he made him receiver by writing, and gave him authority to make acquittances, and then the authority must be shewed. And if the creditor in such case, by agreement between the receiver and him, deliver to the receiver an horse, or another thing in recompence of the debt, that delivery dischargeth not the creditor, unless it be delivered over unto the master, and he agree to it.§ For the receiver hath no such power to make no such commutation, but his master give him special commandment thereto.

Also, if a servant shew a creditor of his master, that his master sent him for his money, and he payeth it unto him; that payment dischargeth him not, if the master did not send him for it indeed, except that it came after unto the use of the master by his assent.

Also, if a man make a bailiff of a manor, and after the lord of whom the manor is holden grant the seigniory to another, and the bailiff after payeth the rent to the grantee; that payment of the rent countervaileth no attornment.

---

* Noy's Max. 43.
† Ante, 230.
‡ Cases in Law and Equity, 110.
§ 2 Salk. 442; 11 Mod. 71.

though it were by fine, ne shall not bind his master, till he attorn himself: but if the lord of whom the land is holden dies seised of the seigniory, and the bailiff payeth the rent to the heir of the lord, that is a good seisin to the heir, though the bailiff had no commandment of his master to pay it : for it belongeth to his office to pay rent-service, but not rent-charge, as some men say.*

Also an encroachment by the bailiff shall not bind the master in avowry, if he had no commandment of the master to pay it. Also, if there be lord, mesne and tenant, and the tenant holdeth of the mesne as of his manor of D., the mesne maketh a bailiff, and after the tenant maketh a feoffment, the feoffee tendeth notice to the bailiff, and he accepteth is rent with arrearages ;† this notice shall not bind the lord, ne compel him to alter his avowry : for the office of a bailiff stretcheth not thereto, but he must have therein a special commandment of his master. Also, if a servant ride upon his master's horse to do an errand for his master, into a town that hath authority to make attachments of goods upon plaints of debt, etc., and there, upon a plaint of debt made against the servant, the master's horse is attached by the officers, thinking that the horse were his own, and, because the servant appeareth not, the officers seise the horse as forfeit ; in this case the lord shall have an action of trespass against the officers, and this attachment for the debt of his servant shall not bind him, etc. But that an host or keeper of a tavern shall be charged for their guests, unless it be done by their assent and commandment, I do not remember that I have read it in the laws of England.

Chap. XLIII.— *Whether a villain or a bondman may give away his goods.*

Doct. It appeareth in the said sum called *summa angelica*, in the title *donatio prima*, the 9th paragraph, that a bondman, or a religious man, a monk, ne such other that hath

* 1 Roll. Abr. 125.
† 1 Danv. Abr. 686; 12 Mod. 354.

nothing in proper, may not give, but it be by licence of their
superior :* but that saying is not, as it is said there, to be
understood of religious persons that have lawful ministration of goods; for if they give with a cause reasonable, it
is good, but without cause they may not.

Also, if they by the licence of the prelate, with the counsel of the more part of the covent, abide at school or go on
pilgrimage, they may give as other honest scholars and pilgrims be reasonably wont to do ; and they may also give
alms where there is great need, if they have no time to ask
licence.

Also, if they see one in extreme necessity, they may give
alms though their superiors prohibit them, for then all
things be in common by the law of God.† And therefore
they be bound for to do it, as appeareth in the aforesaid sum
called *summa angelica*, in the title *Eleemosyna*, the 6th
paragraph, Doth not the law of England agree with these
diversities?

Stud. Forasmuch as the question is only made, Whether
a villain or bondman may give away his goods or not?
And it seemeth that after the aforesaid sum in the title
which thou hast before rehearsed, that he, ne none other
that hath no property, may not give ; whereby it appeareth
that the said sum taketh it, that a bondman should have no
property in his goods, and that therefore his gift should be
void : I shall somewhat touch what property and what authority a villain hath in his goods after the law of the realm,
and what authority the lord hath over them. And I will
leave the diversities that thou hast remembered before of
religious persons to them that list to treat farther therein
hereafter.

First, If a villain have goods, either by his own proper
buying and selling, or otherwise by the gift of other men,
he hath as perfect a property,‡ and also as whole interest

* Ante, 32, 208.
† Ante, 16.
‡ Litt., sec. 177; Perk., sec. 29.

in them, and may as lawfully give them away, as any freeman may. But if the lord seise them before his gift, then
they be the lord's, and the interest of the villain the reinis
determined.*

Also, if the lord seise part of the goods of his villain in
the name of all the goods that the villain hath or shall hereafter have, that seisure is good for all the goods that he had
at the time of the seisure.† But if goods come to the villain after the seisure, he may lawfully give them away, notwithstanding the said seisure.‡

Also, if the lord claim all the goods of the villain, and
seiseth part of them : that seisure is void, and the gift of the
villain is good, notwithstanding the seisure.

Also, if a man be bound to a villain in an obligation in a
certain sum of money, and the lord seiseth the obligation ;
then the obligation is his, but yet he can take no action
thereupon, but in the name of the villain ;§ and therefore
if the villain release the debt, the lord is barred by that release.

Also, if a woman be a nief, and she marrieth a freeman,
the goods immediately by the marriage be the husband's,
and the lord shall come too late to make any seisure.‖
And if the husband in that case maketh his wife his executrix, and dieth, and the wife taketh the same goods again
as executrix to her husband ;¶ yet it shall not be lawful for
the lord to take them from her, though she be a nief, as she
was before the marriage.

Also, if goods be given to a man to the use of a villain,
and the lord seiseth those goods, the seisure, after some
men, is good by the statute made in the 19th year of king
Hen. VII.,** whereby it is enacted, That the lord shall enter

---

* Ante, 29, 154.
† Co. Litt. 118.
‡ Ib.
§ Co. Litt. 117.
‖ Litt., sec. 202.
¶ Co. Litt. 118.
** The statute of Hen. is now repealed.

into lands whereof other persons be seised to the use of his villain ; and they say that the same statute shall be understood by equity of goods in use, as well as of lands in use.

Also, if a villain be made a priest, yet nevertheless the lord may seise his goods and lands, as he might do before ; and until the seisure, he may alien them, and give them away, and as he might before he was a priest. And in this case the lord may order him, so that he shall do him such service as belongeth to a priest to do before any other ; but he may not put him to no labour, nor other business but that is honest and lawful for a priest to do.

Also, if a villain enter into religion, in his year of proof he may dispose his goods as he might have done before he took the habit upon him.*

Also, in like wise the lord may seise his goods as he might have done before :† but if he after make executors, and be professed, and the executors take the goods to the performance of the will ; then the lord may not seise the goods though the executors have them to the performance of the will of him that is his villain ; nor in that case the lord may not seise his body, ne put him to no manner of labour, but must suffer him to abide in his religion under the obedience of his superior, as other religious persons do that be not bondmen. And the lord hath no remedy in that case for the loss of his bondman, but only to take an action of trepass against him that received him into religion without his license, and thereupon to recover damages as shall be assessed by twelve men.‡ Many other cases there be concerning the gift of the goods of a villain, whereof I shall speak no more at this time ; for this that I have said sufficeth to shew, that the knowledge of the king's law is right expedient to the good order of conscience concerning such goods.

---

* Litt., sec. 202.
† Co. Litt. 118; Br. Villeinage, pl. 14, 73.
‡ Ante, 155.

CHAP. XLIV.—*If a clerk be promoted to the title of his patrimony, and after selleth his patrimony, and after falleth to poverty, whether shall he have his title therein or not?*

In the said sum called *rosella*, in the title *Clericus quartus*, the 24th article, it is asked, If a clerk be promoted to the title of his patrimony, whether he may alien it at his pleasure;* and whether in that alienation the solemnity needeth to be kept, that is to be kept in alienations of things of the church? And it is answered there, that it may not be aliened no more than the goods of a spiritual benefice, if it be accepted for a title, and expressly assigned unto him, so that it should go as into a thing of the church, except he have after another benefice whereof he may live. But if it be secretly assigned to his title, some agree it may be aliened. And in this case, by the laws of the realm, it may be lawfully aliéned, whether it be secretly or openly assigned to the title; for the ordinary, ne yet the party himself, after the old custom of the realm, have no authority to bind any inheritance by authority of the spiritual law; and therefore the land, after it is assigned and accepted to be his title, standeth in the self-same case to be bought, sold, charged, or put in execution, as it did before. And therefore it is somewhat to be marvelled, that ordinaries will admit such land for a title, to the intent that he that is promoted should not fall into extreme poverty, or go openly a begging, without knowing how the Common law will serve therein : for of mere right all inheritances within this realm ought to be ordered by the king's laws, and inheritance cannot be bound in this realm but by fine, or some other matter of record, or by feoffment, or such other, or, at least by a bargain that changeth an use.† And over that to assign a state for term of life to him that hath a fee-simple

---

* Cowel's Inter., title Patrimony; Statutes 1 Eliz., c. 12; 13 Eliz., c. 10; 32 H. 8, c. 28; 14 Eliz., c. 11; ante, 32; 18 Eliz., c. 11; 43 Eliz. 29.

† Ante, 23.

before, is void in the laws of England, without it be by such a matter that it work by way of conclusion or estoppel :* and in this case is no such matter of conclusion ; and therefore all that is done in such case in assigning of the said title is void. Also there is no interest that a man hath in any manor, lands or tenements for term of life, for term of years, or otherwise, but that he by the law of the realm may put away his right therein if he will. And then when this man alieneth his land generally, it were against the law of the realm that any interest of such a title should remain in him against his own sale : and there is no diversity, whether the assignment of the title were open or secret, and so the title is void to all intents. And in like wise, if a house of religion, or any other spiritual man that hath granted a title after the custom used in such titles, sell all the lands and goods that they have, that sale in the laws of England is good as against the title, and the buyer shall never be put to answer to the title.† Also some say, that upon the common titles that be made daily in such case, that if he fall to poverty that hath the title, he is without remedy ; for they be so made, that at the Common law there is no remedy for them ; and if he take a suit in the spiritual court, many men say that a *Prohibition* or a *Præmunire* lieth. And therefore it were good for ordinaries in such case to counsel with them that be learned in the law of the realm, to have such a form devised for making of such titles, that if need be, would serve them that they be made unto ; or else let them be promoted without any title, and to trust in God, that if they serve him as they ought to do, he will provide for them to have sufficient for them to live upon. And besides these cases that I have remembered before, there be many other cases put in the said sums for well-ordering of conscience, that, as methinketh, are not to be observed in this realm, neither in law nor conscience.

* 2 B. C. 295.
† Ante, 208.

Doct. Dost thou then think that there was default in
them that drew the said sums, and put therein such cases,
and such solutions, that as thou thinkest, hurt conscience,
rather than to give any light to it, specially in this realm?

Stud. I think no default in them, but I think that they
were right well and charitably occupied, to take so great
pain and labour as they did therein, for the wealth of the
people, and clearing of their conscience; for they have
thereby given a right great light in conscience to all
countries where the law civil and the law canon be used to
temporal things. But as for the laws of this realm they
know them not, ne they were not bound to know them:
and if they had known them, it would little have holpen
them for the countries that they most specially made their
treatises for. And in this country also they be right necessary and much profitable to all men, for such doubts as
rise in conscience in divers other manners not concerning
the laws of the realm. And I marvel greatly, that none
of them that in this realm are most bounden to do that in
them is to keep the people in a right judgment, and in a
clearness of conscience, have done no more in time passed
to have the law of the realm known than they have done:
for though ignorance may sometimes excuse, yet the knowledge of the truth, and the true judgment, is much better:*
and sometime though ignorance excuseth in part, it excuseth
not in all; and therefore methinketh they did very well if
they would yet be callers on to have that point reformed as
shortly as they could. And now because thou hast now
satisfied my mind in many of these questions that I have
made, I purpose for this time to make an end.

Doct. I pray thee yet shew me, or that thou make an
end, more of these cases, that after thine opinion be set in
divers books of learning of conscience, that, as thou
thinkest, for lack of knowledge of the law of the realm, do
rather blind conscience, than give a light unto it: for if
it be so, then surely, as thou hast said, it would be reformed.

* Post. 248.

For I think verily, the laws of the realm in many cases must in this realm be observed as well in conscience, as in the judicial courts of the realm.

Stud. I will with good-will shew to thee shortly some · other questions that be made in the said sum, to give thee another occasion to see therein the opinions of the said sums, and to see farther thereupon how the opinions and the laws of the realm do agree together. And yet besides these questions that I intend to shew unto thee, there be many other questions of the said sums that had as great need to be more plainly declared according to the laws of the realm, as those that I shall shew thee hereafter, or as I have spoken of before. But to the cases that I shall speak of hereafter I will shew thee nothing of my conceit in them, but shall leave it to others that will of charity take some farther pain hereafter in that behalf.

CHAP. XLV.—*Divers questions taken by the student out of the sums called summa rosella and summa angelica, which he thinketh necessary to be looked upon, and to be seen how they stand and agree with the law of the realm.*

The first question is this, Whether a custom may break a law positive? *summa rosella, titulo consuetudo,* parag. 13.*

The second is, If a man attainted or banished be restored by the prince, whether shall that restitution stretch to the goods? *summa rosella,* in the title *damnatus in principio.*†

· *Item,* If a man that is outlawed of felony, abjured, or attainted of murder or felony, or he that is an *ascismus,* may be slain by strangers? And see the like matter thereto, *summa angelica,* in the title *ascismus,* parag. 11.‡

This question is somewhat answered to in a new addition, as appeareth before in the 14th chapter.

Item, Whether the master shall be bound by the act or

---

* 3 Cro. 347; Doug. 102; ante, 79.
† 3 Mod. 101.
‡ Ante, 227.

offence of his servant or officer? *summa angelica*, in the title
dominus, parag. 4.*

This question is answered to in an addition, as appeareth
before in the 14th chapter.

Item, Whether a villain may give away his goods.
Summa angelica, in the title *donatio prima*, parag. 9.†

This question is answered to in an addition, as appeareth
before in the 43rd chapter.

Item, Whether an abbot may give, *etc.*, *summa angelica*,
in the title *donatio* 1, parag. 10 and 11.‡

Item, Whether a woman-covert may give away any
goods? And it is answered, *summa angelica*, in the title .
donatio 1, par. 11, that she may not, without she have
goods beside her dowry, but only in alms.§

Item, If a man do treason, whether the gift of goods after,
before attainder, be good? *summa angelica*, in the title
donatio 1, par. 12. And it seemeth there may, and look.
summa angelica, in the title *alienatio*, par. 24.‖

Item, If a man wittingly make a contract between two
kinsfolk, or other that may not lawfully marry together,
whether he hath forfeit his goods? *Summa angelica*, in the
title *donatio* 1, par. 14.

Item, Whether the father may give to the son? *summa
angelica*, in the title *donatio prima*, par. 19, and *summa
rosella*, in the title *donatio* 2, par. 42.

Item, Whether a man may give above five hundred
shillings, *absq; inquisitione? Summa angelica*, in the title
donatio 1 par. 20.

Item, Whether a gift shall be avoided by an ingratitude?
Summa rosella, in the title *donatio* 1, par. 17 and 29.
And there it is said, that the gift is void by the law of
nature; and look *summa angelica*, in the title *donatio prima*,
par. 42 and 45.

---

* Ante, 236.
† Ib.; Litt., sec. 177.
‡ Ante, 32.
§ Swin. 80, 81, 95.
‖ 2 Hawk. P. C. 454; Stat. 13 Eliz., c. 5; Skin. 357.

Item, Whether the gift between the husband and the wife may be good? And it is said yea, when the husband giveth it *causa remuncrationis*. *Summa rosella*, in the title *donatio* 1, par. 32. 2 Ves. 669.*

Item, If a man make a will, and enter into religion,† whether he may after revoke the will? And it is said, that friars minors may not, and others may. *Summa rosella*, in the title *donatio* 1, par. 35, *in fine*.

Item, If a man give another a town, with all the rights that he hath in the same, whether the patronage, etc., and the tithes pass? *Summa rosella*, in the title *ecclesia* 1, par. 56.

Item, Whether all that is bought with the money of the church be the church's? *Summa rosella*, in the title *ecclesia* 1, par. 7, and it seems to be so.

Item, If a gift made to a monastery may be avoided by that the giver hath children after the gift? *Summa rosella*, in the title *donatio* 1, par. 43.‡

Item, If a man buy any thing under the half price, whether he be bound by the law to restore it? *Summa rosella*, in the title *emptio et venditio*, par. 6.§

Item, Whether a common thief, *vel communis depopulator agrorum* may abjure? *Summa rosella*, in the title *emunitas* 2, *in principio*. *Et habetur ibi in fine, quod licet leges excipiant plures personas, tamen per jus canonicum legibus derogatum est*.‖

Item, Whether a man shall take the church for great and enormous offences that is not murther nor felony. *Summa rosella*, in the title *emunitas* 2, par. 3 and 11.¶

Item, If a man take one in the highway, and draw him out, and there beateth him, whether he shall have the pun-

---

* Co. Litt. 3, 112; 4 Co. 29; Bro. Custom, 56; 1 P. Wms. 441.

† Since the reformation the disabilities attending entering into religion are taken away. 1 Salk. 162.

‡ 2 B. C. 502; Gilb. on Wills, 99.

§ Wood's Civil Law, 231.

‖ Vide stat. 21 Jac. 1, c. 28.

¶ 4 B. C. 327.

ishment that is ordained for them that strike one in the highway? *Summa rosella*, in the title *emunitas* 2, par 6.

Item, Whether he that taketh the church, may, after the
offence, be adjudged to death? *Summa rosella*, in the title
emunitas 2, par. 8.*

Item, Whether the bishop's palace be sanctuary? *Summa
rosella*, in the title *emunitas* 2, par. 24.†

Item, Whether the dignity of the bishop or priesthood
discharge bondage? *Summa rosella*, in the title *episcopus*,
in principio.

Item, Whether a clerk is bound to pay any impositions
or tallages for his patrimony, or otherwise? *Summa rosella*, in the title *excommunicatio* 1, *divisione oct.*, par. 4,
5, and 6, *and divisione nona*, par. 1.‡

Item, If it were ordained by statute, that if a man sell,
etc., he shall give to the king two-pence, whether a clerk
be bound to give it, if he sell of his prebend? *Summa rosella*, in the title *Excommunicatio* 1, *divisione nona*,
par. 3.§

Item, If it be ordained by statute, that there shall not be
laid upon a dead person but such a certain cloth, or thus
many tapers or candles;‖ whether the statute be good?
And it is left for a question. *Summa rosella*, in the title
Excommunicatio 1, *divisione* 18, par. 8, *in fine*.

Item, If a man make a lease of a mill for term of years,
and it is agreed that the lessee shall grind the lessor toll-free
during the term,¶ after the lessor is made an earl or a duke,
and hath greater household than before; whether the lessee
be bound there, etc.? *Summa rosella*, in the title *Familia*,
par. 5.

Item, If a master will not pay his servant's wages that
hath served him faithfully, whether that servant may take

---

* 4 B. C. 327.
† 21 Jac. 1, c. 28.
‡ Dalt. Just. 254, cap. 73; 3 Keb. 255.
§ Post 307.
‖ Ib.
¶ Vin. Abr., title Trespass, 532.

secretly as much goods of his master, etc., and if he do, whether he be bound to restitution? *Summa rosella*, in the title *Familia*, par. 6, it seems he is.

Item, If things immoveable of the church may not be given?* *Summa rosella*, in the title *Feodum*, par. 1. And see there is *principio* what *Feodum* is.

Item, Whether the sons bastards and the sons lawfully begotten shall inherit together?† *Summa rosella*, in the title *Filius*, par. 1.

Item, Whether father·and mother may succeed to their bastards?‡ *Summa rosella*, in the title *Filius*, par. 4.

Item, Whether the father may leave any of his goods to his bastards? *Summa rosella*, in the title *Filius*, par. 5. And *Summa rosella*, in the title *Societas*, par. 23, it seems he may.

Item, Whether the offence of the father shall hurt the son in temporal things?§ *Summa rosella*, in the title *Filius*.

Item, If a man give all his lands and goods to his children, whether a bastard shall have any part?|| *Summa rosella*, in the title *Filius*, par. 22.

Item, To whom treasure found belongeth?¶ *Summa rosella*, in the title *Furtum*, par. 11.

Item, If a deer, or other wild beast, that is so sore hurt that he may be taken, cometh into another man's ground, whether it be his that owneth the ground, or his that strake him?** *Summa rosella*, in the title *Furtum*, par. 13.

Item, Whether theft be in a little thing as well as in a great thing?†† *Summa rosella*, in the title *Furtum*, par. 18.

Item, What pain a thief shall have?‡‡ *Summa rosella*, in the title *Furtum*, par. 22.

---

* Swin. on Wills, 106.
† Ante, 33.
‡ 1 B. C. 459.
§ Post. 261.
|| Ante, 180; 1 Comyn's Digest, 583.
¶ 1 B. C. 295, 296.
**2 B. C. 392.
†† 4 B. C., cap. 16.
‡‡ Ib.

Item, If the goods of dead men go to the heirs, and that of damned men?* *s. De terris. Summa rosella*, in the title *Hæreditas*, par. 1.

Item, Whether a man shall be said guilty of murder by commandment, counsel, or assent?† *Summa rosella*, in the title *Homicidium* 2, *per totum*. And like matter in *Homicidium* 4, *in principio*, and in divers other cases.

Item, A man maketh a privy contract with a woman, and after hath a child by her, and after marrieth another woman, and hath a child, she not knowing the first contract; which of the children shall be his heir? *Summa rosella*, in the title *Illegitimus*, par. 4, it seems the latter shall.

Item, Whether the pope may legitimate one to temporal things, and to succeed? *Summa rosella*, in the title *Illegitimus:* it seems he may not as the law now stands.

Item, If goods be found that were left of the owner as forsaken, who hath right to them?‡ *Summa rosella*, in the title *Inventa*, par. 2. And look *Summa rosella*, in the title *Furtum*, par. 17.

And thus I make an end of these questions: and because you desirest me in the 13th chapter to shew thee somewhat where ignorance excuseth in the law of the realm, and where not, I will answer somewhat to thy question, and so commit thee to God.

CHAP. XLVI.—*Where ignorance of the law excuseth in the laws of England, and where not.*

Ignorance of the law (though it be invincible) doth not excuse as to the law but in few cases;§ for every man is bound at his peril to take knowledge what the law of the realm is, as well the law made by statute as the common law: but ignorance of the deed, which may be called the

---

* Ante, 130, 225.
† 4 B. C. 36, 37.
‡ Post. 267.
§ Douglas Rep. 471; ante, 76; ante, 150; post. 250.

ignorance of the truth of the deed, may excuse in many cases.

Doct. I put the case that a statute penal be made, and it is enacted, that the statute shall be proclaimed by such a day in every shire, and it is not proclaimed before the day, and after the day a man offends against the statute; shall he run in the penalty?

Stud. I think yea, if there be no farther words in the statute to help him; that is to say, that if the proclamation be not made, that no man shall be bound by the statute. And the cause is this: there is no statute made in this realm but by the assent of the lords spiritual and temporal, and of all the commons;* that is to say, by the knights of the shire, citizens and burgesses, that be chosen by assent of the commons, which in the parliament represent the estate of the whole commons: and every statute there made is of as strong effect in the law, as if all the commons were there present personally at the making thereof. And like as there needed no proclamation, if all were there present in their own person; so the law presumed there needeth no proclamation when it is made by their authority: and then when it is enacted, That it shall be proclaimed, etc., that is but of the favour of the makers of the statute, and not of necesssity; and it cannot therefore be taken, that their intent was that it should be void if it were not proclaimed. Nevertheless some be of opinion, that if a man before the day appointed for the proclamation offend the statute, that he should not in that case be punished; for they say that the intent of the makers of the statute shall be taken to be, that none should be punished before the day; which is a doubt to some other. But admit it to be as they say, that he shall be excused, yet he is not excused by the ignorance of the law, but because the intent of the makers excuseth him.

Doct. It is enacted in the 7th year of Rich. II., cap. 6,†

---

* 4 Inst. 25.
† Repealed by stat. 1 Jac. 1, c. 25, and 21 Jac. 1, c. 28.

That every sheriff shall proclaim the statute of Winchester three times every year in every market town, to the intent the offenders shall not be excused by ignorance, and it seemeth by these words, That if no proclamation be made, that the offender may be excused by ignorance.

Stud. Some take the intent of that statute to be, that the people by that proclamation should have knowledge of the statute of Winchester, to the intent that the forfeiture therein may be taken as well in conscience as in law; and some take the statute to be of such effect as thou speakest of, that is to say, that no forfeiture should grow upon the statute of Winchester against them that were ignorant, but proclamation were made according to the said statute of Richard. And if it be so taken, the statute of Winchester is of small effect against most part of the people; for certain it is that the said proclamation is not made: but admit it to be as they say, then they that be ignorant be excused by the said particular estatute specially made in that case, and not by the general rules of the law: and sometimes, in divers statutes penal,* they that be ignorant be excused by the same statute, as it is upon the statute of Rich. II., the 13th year, the 2d statute, and the last chapter, where it is enacted, That if any person take a benefice by provision, that he shall be banished the realm, and forfeit all his goods, and that if he be in the realm, he avoid within six weeks after he hath accepted it, and that none shall receive him that is so banished after the said six weeks, upon like forfeiture if he have knowledge: and so he that hath no knowledge is excused by the express words of the statute. And in like wise he that offendeth against Magna Charta is not excommenged, but he have knowledge that it is prohibit that he doth. For they be only excommenged by the sentence called *Sententia lata super chartus*, that do it willingly, or that do it by ignorance, and correct not themselves within fifteen days after they have warning. And sometime they that be ignorant of the statute be excused from the penalty of the statute, because

† Ante, 187, 218.

it shall be taken that the intent of the makers of the statute was, that none should be bound but they that have knowledge : but that any man shall be discharged in the law by ignorance of the law, only for that he is ignorant, I know few cases, except it might be applied to infants that be in their infancy, and within years of discretion ;* for if ignorance of the law should excuse in the law, many offenders would pretend ignorance.†

Doct. Shall an infant that hath discretion, and knoweth good from evil, be punished by a penal statute that he is ignorant in?

Stud. If the statute be, that for the offence he should have corporal pain, I think he shall be excused, and have no corporal pain ;‡ but I suppose that that is not for the ignorance ; for though he knew the statute, and willingly offended, yet I think he shall have no corporal pain as where he pleads joint-tenancy by deed that is found against him, or if he plead a record in assise, and faileth of it at his day : but that is because the law presumeth, that it was not the intent of the makers of the statute that he should have that punishment.§   But if he be of years of discretion to know good from evil, whether he shall then forfeit the penalty of a penal statute, it is more doubt : for it is commonly holden, that if an infant had not been excepted in the statute of forejudgment, that the forejudgment should have bound him, and so shall his cesser, and his levying of a cross against the statute‖ or if he be gardein of a prison, and suffer a prisoner to escape, he shall pay the debt, because the statutes be general :¶ and if he ·should by the* statutes be bound within age, like reason will that he may by a statute penal leese his goods.

Doct. If an infant do a. murther or felony at such years

* Ante, 77, 249.
† Ante, 248.
‡ 1 Hale's P. C. 21; Plow. 364.
§ 1 Hale's H. P. C. 20.
‖ Obsolete.
¶ 2 Inst. 382.

.as he hath discretion to know the law, shall not he have the punishment of the law, as one of full age?

Stud. I think yea ;* but that is by an old maxim of the law for eschewing of murders and felonies : and so it is of a trespass.† But these cases run not upon the ground of ignorance, but with what acts infants shall be punishable or not punishable for the tenderness of their age, though they be not ignorant.

Doct. Be not yet knights and noblemen, that are bound most properly to set their study to acts of chivalry, for de- ·fence of the realm, and husbandmen, that must use tillage .and husbandry for the sustenance of the commonalty, and that may not by reason of their labour put themselves to know the law, discharged by ignorance of the law?

Stud. No verily : for sith all were makers of the statute, the law presumeth that all have knowledge of that that they make, as it is said before ; and as they be bound at their peril to take knowledge of the statute that they make, so be all them that come after them.‡ And as for knights and other nobles of the realm, me seemeth that they should be bound to take knowledge of the law, as well as any other within the realm, except them that give themselves to the study and exercise of the law, and except spiritual judges, that in many cases be bound to take knowledge of the law of the realm, as it is said before in Chap. 25.§ For though they be bound to acts of chivalry for defence of the realm, yet they be bound also to acts of justice, and that (it seemeth) more than other be, by reason of their great pos- sessions and authority, and for the well-ordering of the ten-

---

* The age of discretion at which infants are generally supposed to know good from evil, and consequently to be capable of committing crimes, is 14. Co. Litt. 247; 1 H. H. P. C. 25. But if an infant under fourteen, and .above seven years of age, commits a criminal offence; and upon his in- dictment there are circumstances in his case to induce the jury to believe that he was *capax doli* at the time the crime was perpetrated, he may be -convicted and punished, for *malitia supplet ætatum.* 4 B. C. 23.

† 12 Mod. 332.
‡ Ante, 31.
§ Ante, 18, 183.

ants, servants and neighbours, that many times have need
of their help; and also that they be oft called to be of the
king's council, and to the general councils of the realm,
where their counsel is right expedient and necessary for the
commonwealth. And therefore if the noblemen of this
realm would see their children brought up in such manner,
that they should have learning and knowledge more than
they have commonly used to have in time past, specially of
the grounds and principles of the law of the realm, wherein
they be inherit, (though they had not the high cunning of
the whole body of the law, but after such manner as Mr.
Fortescue in his book that he entituleth the book, *De laud-
ibus legum Angliæ,** advertiseth the prince to have knowledge of the laws of the realm) I suppose it would be a
great help hereafter to the ministration of justice of this
realm, a great surety for himself, and a right great gladness to all the people. For certain it is, the more part of
the people would more gladly hear that their rulers and
governors intended to order them with wisdom and justice,
than with power and great retinues. But ignorance of the
deed many times excuseth in the laws of England :† and I
shall shortly touch some cases thereof, to shew where it
shall excuse, and where it shall not excuse; and then the
reader may add to it after his pleasure, and as he shall
think to be convenient.

CHAP. XLVII.—*Certain cases and grounds where ignorance of the deed excuseth in the laws of England,
and where not.*

If a man buy a horse in open market of him that in right
had no property to him, not knowing but that he hath right,
he hath good title and right to the horse,‡ and the ignorance
shall excuse him. But if he had bought him out of the open

---

* Cap. 4.
† Post., cap. 47.
‡ Provided the directions laid down in the statutes, 2 P. & M., c. 7, and
31 Eliz., c. 12, are followed; for which *vide* the statutes, and 2 Inst. 719,
with 2 B. C. 451.

market, or if he had known that the seller had no right, the buying in open market had not excused him. Also if a man retain another man's servant, not knowing that he is retained with him, the ignorance excuseth him both of the offence that was at the common law against the maxim that prohibited such retaining of another man's servant, and also against the statute 35 Edw. III., whereby it is prohibit, upon pain of imprisonment, that none shall retain no servant that departeth within his term, without licence or reasonable cause : for it hath been alway taken, that the intent of the makers of the said statute was, that they that were ignorant of the first retainor should not run in any penalty of the statute.* And the same law is of him that retaineth one that is ward to another, not knowing that he is his ward. And if homage be due, and the tenant after that the homage is due maketh a feoffment, and after the lord, not knowing of the feoffment distraineth for the homage ;† in that case that ignorance shall excuse him of his damages in a replevin, though he cannot avow for the homage. But if he had known of the feoffment, he should have yielded damages for the wrongful taking. Also if a man be bound in an obligation that he shall repair the houses of him that he is bound to by such a certain time, as oft as need shall require, and after the houses have need to be repaired, but he that is bound knoweth it not ; that ignorance shall not excuse, for he hath bound himself to it, and so he must take knowledge at his peril.‡ But if the condition had been, that he should repair such houses as he to whom he was

---

bound should assign, and after he assigneth certain houses to be repaired, but he that is bound hath no knowledge of that assignment: that ignorance shall excuse him in the law, for he hath not bound himself to no reparation in certain, but to such as the party will assign, and if he assign none, he is bound to none;*. and therefore sith he that should make the assignment is privy to the deed, he is bound to give notice of his own assignment: but if the assignment had been appointed to a stranger, then the obligor must have taken knowledge of the assignment at his peril.† Also, if a man buy lands whereunto another hath title, which the buyer knoweth nòt, that ignorance excuseth not him in the law, no more than it doth of goods.‡ Also, if a servant come with his master's horse to a town that by custom may attach goods for debt, and upon a plaint against the servant an officer of the town,§ by information of the party, attached the master's horse, thinking that it were the servant's horse, that ignorance excuseth him not; for when a man will do an act, as to enter into lands, seise goods, take a distress, or such other, he must by the law at his peril see that that he doth be lawfully done, as in the case before rehearsed. And in like wise, if a sheriff by a replevin deliver other beasts than were distrained, though that the party that distrained shew him they were the same beasts, yet an action of trespass lieth against him, and ignorance shall not excuse him:‖ for he shall be compelled by the law, as all officers commonly be, to execute the king's writ at his peril according to the tenor of it, and to see that the act that he doth be lawfully done. But otherwise it is after some men, if upon summons in a *præcipe quod reddat*, the sheriff by information of the demandant summoneth the tenant in another man's land,

---

* 12 Mod. 44.
† March, 156.
‡ Ante, 149.
§ Ante, 236; Br. Trespass, pl. 99.
‖ Br. Office and Officer, pl. 10; Br. Notice, pl. 23.

thinking it for the tenant's-land;* there they say he shall
he excused : for in that case he doth not seise the land, ne
take possession in the land, but only doth summon the tenant upon the land ; and the writ commandeth him not that
he shall summon the tenant upon his own land, but generally that he shall summon him, and nameth not in what
land ; and then by an old maxim in the law it is taken, that
he shall summon him upon the land in demand : and therefore though he mistake the land, and be ignorant of it, yet
if the demandant inform him that that is the land that he
demandeth, that sufficeth to the sheriff as to his entry for
the summoning, as they say, though it be not the tenant's
land.   And here I make an end of these questions for this
time.

Doct. I pray thee yet or we depart take a little more
pain in my desire.   ;

Stud. What is that?

Doct. That thou wouldst shew me thy mind in divers
cases of the law of the realm, which (as me seemeth) stand
not so clearly with conscience as they should do.   And
therefore I would gladly hear thy conceit therein, how they
may stand with conscience.

Stud. Put the cases, and I shall with good-will say as I
think to them.

CHAP. XLVIII.—*The first question of the doctor, How
the law of England may be said reasonable, that prohibiteth them that be arraigned upon an indictment of
felony or murder, to have counsel.*

Stud. Methinketh that the law in that point is very good
and indifferent, taking the law therein as it is.

Doct. Why? what is the law in this point?

Stud. The law is as thou sayest, that he shall have no
counsel ;† but then the law is farther, that in all things that

† 10 H. C. 12, b; 11 H. C. 4; 18 E. 3, 52, b; 25 E. 3, 39, b.
  * Though this is the standing law of the land, yet the judges seldom refuse a prisoner indicted for felony the privilege of having a counsel to

pertain to the order of pleading, the judges shall so instruct
him and order him, that he shall run into no jeopardy by
his mispleading.* As if he will plead that he never knew
the man that was slain, or that he never had a pennyworth ·
of the goods that is supposed that he should steal : in these
cases the judges are bound in conscience to inform him that
he must take the general issue, and plead that he is *not
guilty :*† for though they be set to be indifferent between the
king and the party, as to the party and to the principal
matter, as they be in all other matters ; yet they be in this
case to see that the party take no hurt in form of pleading
in such matters as he shall shew to be the truth of the matter.‡ And that it is a great favour of the law. For in appeal, though the justices of favour will most commonly help
forth the party, and sometimes his counsel also, in the form
of pleading, as they do also many times in common pleas ;
yet they might in those cases, if they would, bid the party
and his counsel plead at their peril. But they may not do
so with conscience upon indictments, as me seemeth : for
it were a great unreasonableness in the law, if it should
prohibit him that standeth in jeopardy of his life, that he
should have no counsel, and to drive him to plead after the
strait rules and formalities of the law that he knoweth not.

Doct. But what if he be known for a common offender,
or that the judges know by examination, or by an evident
presumption, that he is guilty, and he asketh sanctuary, or
pleadeth misnomer, or hath some record to plead, that he
cannot plead after the form; may not the judges in these
cases bid him plead at his peril?

---

stand by him, and instruct him with respect to matters of fact, and in cases
of high treason or misprision of treason, the prisoner is enabled by stat.
7 W. 3, c. 3, to have two counsel to be named by him, and assigned by the
court or judge, and this indulgence by stat. 20 Geo. 2, c. 30, is (with great
reason) extended to parliamentary impeachments for high treason. 4 B. C.·
350; Foster's Crown Law, 232.

* 3 Inst. 137.
† 2 Haw. P. C. 399.
‡ 2 Buls. 147; 3 Inst. 137.

17

Stud. I suppose they may not: for though he be a common offender, or that he be guilty, yet he ought to have that the law giveth him, and that he shall have the effect of his pleas, and of his matters entered after the form of the law. And also sometime a man by examination, and by witness, may appear guilty that is not; and in like wise there may be a vehement suspicion that he is guilty, and yet he is not guilty: and therefore for such suspicion or vehement presumptions methinketh a man may not with conscience be put from that he ought to have by the law, ne yet although the judges knew it of their own knowledge. But if it were in appeal, I suppose that the judges might do therein as they should think best to be done in conscience;[*] for there is no law that bindeth them to instruct him, (but as they do commonly to the parties of favour in all other cases) but they may, if they will, bid him plead at his peril, by advice of his counsel; and if the appellee be poor, and have no counsel, the court must assign him counsel, if he ask it, as they must do in all other pleas: and that methinketh that are bound to do in conscience, though the appellee were never so great an offender, and though the judges knew never so certainly that he were guilty, for the law bindeth them to do it. And so methinketh that there is great diversity between an indictee and an appellee. And the reason why the law prohibiteth not counsel in appeal, as it doth in an indictment, I suppose is this: There is no appeal brought, but that of common presumption the appellant hath great malice against the appellee;[†] as when the appeal is brought by the wife of the death of her husband, or by the son of the death of his father, or that an appeal of robbery is brought for stealing of goods. And therefore if the judges should in those cases shew themselves to instruct the appellees, the appellants would grutch and think them partial: and therefore as well for the indemnity of the court, as of the appellee, in case that he be

---

* Br. Corone, pl. 54; 3 Inst. 29; 2 Haw, P. C. 400; Finch Law, 386.
† Haw. P. C. 401; Dy. 296; Finch Law, 386.

not guilty, the law suffereth the appellee to have counsel.. But when that a man is indicted at the king's suit, the king intendeth nothing but justice with favour, and that is to the rest and quietness of his faithful subjects, and to pull away misdoers among them charitably : and therefore he will be contented that his justices shall help forth the offenders according to the truth as far as reason and justice may suffer. And as the king will be contented therein, it is to presume that the counsel will be contented ; and so there is no danger thereby, neither to the court, ne to the party. And as I suppose for this reason it began that they should have no counsel upon indictments, and that hath so long continued, that it is now grown into a custom, and into a maxim of the law, that they shall none have.*

Doct. But if the judges knew of their own knowledge that the indictee was guilty, and then he pleadeth misnomer, or a record that he was *auterfoits* arraigned, and acquit of the same murther or felony, and the judges of their own knowledge know that the plea is untrue, may they not then bid him plead at his peril?

Stud. I think yes ; but if they know of their own knowledge that he were guilty of the murther or felony, but that the plea was untrue they knew not but by conjecture or information, I think they might not then bid him plead at his peril.

CHAP. XLIX.—*The second question of the doctor, Whether warranty of the younger brother that is taken as heir, because it is not known but that the eldest brother is dead, be in conscience a bar unto the eldest brother, as it is in law?*

Doct. A man seised of lands in fee hath issue two sons, the eldest son goeth beyond the sea, and because a common voice is that he is dead, the younger brother is taken for heir, the father dieth, the younger brother entereth as heir,

___
* 3 Cro. 147; Hutt. 133; ante, 255.

and alieneth the land with a warranty, and dieth without
any heir of his body, and after the eldest brother cometh
again, and claimeth the land as heir to his father; whether
shall he be barred by that warranty in conscience, as he is.
in the law?

Stud. It is a maxim in the law, that the eldest brother
shall in that case be barred;* and that maxim is taken to
be of as strong effect in the law, as if it were ordained by
statute to be a bar.   And it is as old a law that such a warranty shall bar the heir, as it is that the inheritance of the
father shall only descend to the eldest son.   And sith the
law so is, why then should not conscience follow the law,
as well as it doth in that point, that the eldest son shall have·
the land?

Doct. For there appeareth no reasonable cause whereupon the maxim ought to have a lawful beginning: for
what reason is it that the warranty of an ancestor that hath
no right to land should bar him that hath right?   And if it
were ordained by statute, that one man should have another man's land, and no cause is expressed why he should·
have it; in that case, though he might hold the land by
force of that statute, yet he could not hold it in conscience,
without there was a cause why he should have it.   And
these cases be not like, as me seemeth, to the forfeiture of
goods by an outlawry: for it will agree for this time, that
that forfeiture standeth with conscience, because it is ordained for ministration of justice: but I cannot perceive
any such case here; and therefore methinketh that this
case is like to the maxim that was at the Common law of
wreck of the sea, that is to say, that if a man's goods had·
been wrecked upon the sea, that the goods should have
been immediately forfeited to the king.†   And it is holden
by all doctors, that that law is against conscience, except in
certain cases that were too long to rehearse now.   And it
was ordained by the statute of West. 1,‡ that if a dog or

---

* Litt., sec. 707; Shep. Touch. 189.
† 2 Inst. 167; Molloy, 237; Finch Law, 137; Ld. Raym. 474; post. 265.
‡ Cap. 4.

cat come alive to the land, that the owner, if he prove the goods within a year and a day to be his, shall have them; whereby the said law of wrecks of the sea is made more sufferable than it was before. And some think in this case that this warranty is no bar in conscience, though it be a bar in the law.

Stud. I pray thee keep that case of wreck of the sea in thy remembrance, and put it hereafter as one of thy questions, and thereupon shew me farther thy mind therein, and I shall with good-will shew thee my mind. And as to this case that we be in now, methinketh the maxim whereby the warranty shall be a bar is good and reasonable : for it seemeth not against reason that a man shall be bound, as to temporal things, by the act of his ancestor to whom he is heir :* for like as by the law it is ordained, that he shall have advantage by the same ancestor, and have all his lands by descent, if he have any right; so it seemeth that it is not unreasonable, though the law, for the privity of blood that is between them, suffer them to have a disadvantage by the same ancestor.† But if the maxim were, that if any of his ancestors, though he were not heir to him, made such a warranty, that it should be a bar; I think that maxim were against conscience, for in that case there were no ground nor consideration to prove how the said maxim should have a lawful beginning, wherefore it were to be taken as a maxim against the law of reason. But methinketh it is otherwise in this case, for the reason that I have made before.

Doct. If the father bind him and his heirs to the payment of a debt, and die ;‡ in that case the son shall not be bound to pay the debt, unless he have assets by descent from his father. And so I would agree, that if this man have assets by descent from the ancestor that made the warranty, that he should have been barred : but else me-

* Ante, 247.
† Ante, 114.
‡ 2 B. C. 340; Strange, 665; P. Wms. Rep. 777.

thinketh it should stand hardly with conscience that it should be a bar.*

Stud. In that case of the obligation the law is as thou sayest: and the cause is, for that the maxim of the law in that case is none other, but that he shall be charged if he have assets by descent: but if the maxim had been general, that the heir should be bound in that case without any assets, or if it were ordained by statute that it should be so, I think that both the maxim and the statute should well stand with conscience. And like law is, where a man is vouched as heir, he may enter as he that hath nothing by descent: but where he claimeth the land in his own right, there the warranty of his ancestor shall be a bar to him, though he have no assets from the same ancestor: and though it be said in Ezekiel, cap. 18, "*That the son shall not bear the wickedness of the father*," that is understood spiritually. But as to temporal goods, the opinion of the doctors is, that the son sometime may bear the offence of his father.†

Doct. Now that I have heard. thy mind in this case, I will take advisement therein till a better leisure, and will now proceed to another question.

Stud. I pray thee do as thou sayest, and I shall with good-will make answer thereto as well as I can.

CHAP. L.—*The third question of the doctor, If a man prosecute a collateral warranty, to extinct a right that he knoweth another man hath to land, whether it be a bar in conscience, as it is in law, or not?*

Doct. A man is disseised of certain land, the disseisor selleth the land, etc., the alienee knowing of the disseisin, obtaineth a release with a warranty of an ancestor collateral to the disseisee, that knoweth also the right of the disseisee;‡ that ancestor collateral dieth, after whose death the warranty descendeth upon the disseisee: whether may

---

* Bac. El. 27.
† Ante, 247, 260.
‡ Shep. Touch. 188; ante, 91.

the alienee in that case hold the land in conscience as he
may by the law?

Stud. Sith the warranty is descended upon him, whereby
he is barred in the law, methinketh that he shall also be
barred in conscience;* and that this case is like to the case
in the next chapter before, wherein I have said that (as
methinketh) it is a bar in conscience.

Doct. Though it might be taken for a bar in conscience
in that case, yet methinketh in this case it cannot. For in
that case the younger brother entered as heir, knowing
none other but that he was heir of right, and after, when
he sold the land, the buyer knew not but that he that sold
it had good right to sell it, and so he was ignorant of the
title of the eldest brother; and that ignorance came by the
default and absence of himself that was the eldest brother;
but in this case as well the buyer, as he that made the collateral warranty, knew the right of the disseisee, and did
that they could to extinct the right, and so they did as they
would not should have been done to them: and so it seemeth that he that hath the land may not with conscience
keep it.

Stud. Though it be as thou sayest that all they offended
in obtaining of the said collateral warranty; yet such offence is not to be considered in the law, but it be in very
special cases: for if such alledgings should be accepted in
the law, releases, and other writings, should be of small
effect, and upon every light surmise all writings might
come in trial, whether they were made with conscience or
not. Therefore to avoid that inconvenience, the law will
drive the party to answer only whether it be his deed or
not, and not whether the deed were made with conscience or
against conscience: and though the party may be at a mischief thereby; yet the law will rather suffer the mischief
than the said inconvenience. And like law is, if a woman-
covert for dread of her husband by compulsion of him levy
a fine, yet the woman after her husband's death shall not

* 2 Inst. 335; ante, 260.

be admitted to shew that matter in avoiding of the fine, for
the inconvenience that might follow thereupon.* And
after the opinion of many men, there is no remedy in these
cases in the chancery. For they say that where the Common law, in cases concerning inheritance, putteth the party
upon any averment for eschewing of an inconvenience that
might follow of it among the people, that if the same inconvenience should follow in the Chancery, if the same
matter would be pleaded there, that no *subpœna* should lie
in such cases : and so it is in the cases before rehearsed ;
for as much vexation, delay, costs and expences might
grow to the party, if he should be put to answer to such
averments in the Chancery, as if he were put to answer for
them at the Common law : and therefore they think that no
subpœna lieth in the said cases, ne in other like unto them.
Nevertheless I do not take it that their opinion is, that he
that bought the land in this case may with good conscience
hold the land, because he shall not be compelled by no law
to restore it ; but that he is in conscience and by the law of
reason bound to restore it, or otherwise to recompence the
party, so as he shall be contented. And I suppose verily
it is so, if he will keep his soul out of peril and danger.
And after some men, to these cases may be resembled the
case of a fine with non-claim, that is remembered before in
the 24th chapter of this book,* where a man knowing
another to have right to certain land, causeth fine to be
levied thereof with proclaimation, and the other suffereth
five years to pass without claim ; in that case he hath no
remedy neither by Common law, nor by *subpœna*, and that
yet he that levied the fine is bound to restore the land in
conscience. And methinketh I could right well agree,
that it should be so in this case, and that specially, because
the party himself knoweth perfectly that the said collateral
warranty was obtained by covin and against conscience.

---

* 2 Inst. 515; Coke Reading, 7.
† Ante, 62, 110, 143.

CHAP. LI.—*The fourth question of the doctor is of the wreck of the sea.*

Doct. I pray thee let me now hear thy mind how the law of England concerning goods that be wrecked upon the sea may stand with conscience, for I am in great doubt of it.

Stud. I pray thee let me first hear thine opinion, what thou thinkest therein.

Doct. The statute of West. 1, that speaketh of wrecks is; That if any man, dog, or cat, come alive unto the land out of a ship, or barge, that it shall not be judged for wreck :* so that if the party to whom the goods belong come within a year and a day, and prove them to be his, that he shall have them ;† or else that they shall remain to the king. And methinketh that the said statute standeth not with conscience ; for there is no lawful cause why the party ought to forfeit his goods, ne the king or lords ought to have them, for there is no cause of forfeiture in the party, but rather a cause of sorrow or heaviness ; and so the law seemeth to add sorrow upon sorrow.‡ And therefore doctors hold commonly that he that hath such goods is bound to restitution, and that no custom may help ; for they say it is against the commandment of God, Levit. 19, where it is commanded, that a *man shall love his neighbour as himself,* and that they say he doth not that taketh away his neighbour's goods. But they agree, that if any man have cost and labour for the saving of such goods wrecked, specially for such goods as would perish if they lay still in the water, as sugar, paper, salt, meal, and such others, that he ought to be allowed for his costs and labour, but he must restore the goods, except he could not save them without putting his life in jeopardy for them ; and then if he put his life in such

* Ante, 261.
† 2 Inst. 166, 167.
‡ Vide the statutes 2 Ed. 3, c. 13; 12 Ann., stat. 2, c. 18, confirmed by 4 Geo. 1, c. 12, and 26 Geo. 2, c. 19, which have introduced many humane regulations if possible to prevent wrecks at all.

jeopardy, and the owner by common presumption had had no way to have saved them, then it is most commonly holden that he may keep the goods in conscience. But of other goods that would not só lightly perish, but that the owner might of common presumption save them himself, or that might be saved without any peril of life, the takers of them be bound to restitution to the owner, whether he come within the year, or after the year.

. And methinketh this case is somewhat like to a case that I shall put. If there were a law and custom in this realm, or if it were ordained by statute, that if any alien came through the realm in pilgrimage, and died, that all his goods should be forfeit; that law should be against conscience, for there is no cause reasonable why the said goods should be forfeit: and no more methinketh there is of wreck.

Stud. There be divers cases where a man shall leese his goods, and no default in him: as where beasts stray away from a man, and they be taken up, and proclaimed, and the owner hath not heard of them within the year and the day, though he made sufficient diligence to have heard of them; yet the goods be forfeited, and no default in him. And so it is where a man killeth another with the sword of John at Stile, the sword shall be forfeit as a *deodand*, and yet no default is in the owner.* And so methinketh it may be in this case; and that sith the Common law, before the said statute, was, that the goods wrecked upon the sea shall be forfeit to the king, that they be also forfeited now after the statute, except they be saved by following the statute;† for the law must needs reduce the properties of all goods to some man; and when the goods be wrecked, it seemeth the property is in no man: but admit that the property remain still in the owner, then if the owner, percase, would never claim, then it should not be known who ought to have them, and so might they be destroyed, and no profit come

---

* 1 B. C. 301.
† 2 Inst. 166, 167.

of them : wherefore methinketh it reasonable that the law shall appoint who ought to have them, and that hath the law appointed to the king, as sovereign and head over the people.

Doct. In the cases that thou hast put before of the stray and *deodand* there be considerations why they be forfeit, but it is not so here :* and methinketh that in this case, it were not unreasonable that the law would suffer any man that would take them, to take and keep them to the use of the owner, saving his reasonable expences ; and this methinketh were more reasonable law, than to pull the property out of the owner without cause.   But if a man in the sea cast his goods out of the ship as forsaken, there doctors hold that every man may take them lawfully that will ;† but otherwise it is (as they say) if he throw them out for fear that they should overcharge the ship.

Stud. There is no such law in this realm of goods forsaken : for though a man waive the possession of his goods, and saith he forsaketh them, yet by the law of the realm the property remaineth still in him, and he may seise them after when he will.‡   And if any man in the mean time put the goods in sâfeguard to the use of the owner, I think he doth lawfully, and that he shall be allowed for his reasonable expences in that behalf, as he shall be of goods found ; but he shall have no property in them, no more than in goods found.   And I would agree, that if a man prescribe, that if he find any goods within his manor, that he should have them as his own, that that prescription were void :§ for there is no consideration how the prescription might have a lawful beginning, but in this case methinketh there is.

Doct. What is that?

Stud. It is this : The king, of the old custom of the realm, as the lord of the narrow sea, is bound, as it is said,

* Ante, 110.
† 2 B. C. 9; 1 B. C. 292.
‡ Ante, 248.
§ Br. Prescription, pl. 93.

to scour the sea of the pirates and petit robbers of the sea :*
and so' it is read of the noble king Saint Edgar that he
would twice in the year scour the sea of such pirates : but
I mean not thereby that the king is bound to conduct his
merchants upon the sea against all outward enemies, but
that he is bound only to put away such pirates and petit
robbers. And because that cannot be done without great
charge, it is not unreasonable if he have such goods as be
wrecked upon the sea toward the charge.

Doct. Upon that reason I will take a respite till another
time.

CHAP. LII.—*The fifth question of the doctor, Whether it
stand with conscience to prohibit a jury of meat and
drink till they be agreed.*

If one of the twelve men of an inquest know the very
truth of his own knowledge, and instructeth his fellows
thereof, and they will in no wise give credence to him, and
thereupon, because meat and drink is prohibited them, he
is driven to that point, that either he must assent to them,
and give their verdict against his own knowledge and
against his own conscience, or die for lack of meat: how
may the law then stand with conscience, that will drive an
innocent to that extremity, to be either forsworn, or to be
famished and die for want of meat?

Stud. I take not the law of the realm to be, that the jury
after they be sworn may not eat nor drink till they be agreed
of the verdict :† but truth it is, there is a maxim and an old
custom in the law, that they shall not eat nor drink after
they be sworn, till they have given their verdict, without
the assent and license of the justices. And that is ordained
by the law for eschewing of divers inconveniences that
might follow thereupon, and that specially if they should
eat or drink at the costs of the parties; and therefore if

* Kitchen on Courts, 46.
† 1 Vent. 125; 3 B. C. 375, 376; Trials per Pais, 199, 200.

they do contrary, it may be laid in an arrest of the judgment: but with the assent of the justices they may both eat and drink.* As if any of the jurors fall sick before they be agreed of their verdict, so sore that he may not commune of the verdict, then by the assent of the justices he may have meat and drink, and also such other things as be necessary for him :† and his fellows also at their own costs, or at the indifferent costs of the parties, if they so agree, or by the assent of the justices, may both eat and drink.‡ And therefore if the case happen that thou now speakest of, and that the jury can in no wise agree in their verdict, and that appeareth to the justices by examination, the justices may in that case suffer them to have both meat and drink for a time, to see whether they will agree : and if they will in no wise agree, I think that the justices may set such order in the matter as shall seem to them by their discretion to stand with reason and conscience, by awarding of a new inquest,§ and by setting fine upon them that they shall find in default, or otherwise as they shall think best by their discretion ; like as they may do if one of the jury die before verdict, or if any other like casualties fall in that behalf.‖ But what the justices ought to do in that case that thou hast put, in their discretion, I will not treat of at this time.

CHAP. LIII.—*The sixth question of the doctor, Whether the colours that be given at the Common law in assises, actions of trespass, and divers other actions, stand with conscience, because they be most commonly feigned, and be not true.*

Doct. I pray thee let me hear thy mind to what intent such colours be given, and sith they be commonly untrue, how they may stand with conscience?

---

* 2 Haw. P. C. 146.
† Br. Verdict, pl. 102.
‡ Br. Jurors, pl. 51.
§ Noy, 49; 3 Buls. 173; Vaug. 152.
‖ Vin Abr., title Trial, 466.

Stud. The cause why such colours be given is this: There is a maxim and a ground of the law of England, that if the defendant or tenant in any action plead a plea that amounteth to the general issue, that he shall be compelled to take the general issue;* and if he will not, he shall be condemned for lack of answer;† and the general issue in *assise* is, that he that is named the disseisor hath done no wrong, nor no disseisin : and in a writ of *Entry* in the nature of assise the general issue is, that he disseised him not ; and in an action of *trespass*, that he is not guilty.‡ And so every action hath his general issue assigned by the law : and the tenant must of necessity either take the general issue, or plead some plea in abatement of the writ, to the jurisdiction to the party, or else some bar, or some matter by way of conclusion. And therefore if John at Stile infeoff H. Hart of land, and a stranger bringeth an assise against the said H. Hart for the land, whose title he knoweth not ; in this case, if he should be compelled to plead to the point of the assise, that is to say, that he hath done no wrong, ne no disseisin, the matter should be put to the mouths of twelve laymen, which be not learned in the law ;§ and therefore better it is that the law be so ordered, that it be put in the determination of the judges, than of laymen. And if the said H. Hart, in the case before rehearsed, would plead in bar of the assise, that John at Stile was seised, and infeoffed him, by force whereof he entered, and asked judgment if that assise should lie against him ; that plea were not good, for it amounteth but to the general issue, and therefore he shall be compelled to take the general issue, or else the assise shall be awarded against him for lack of answer.|| And therefore to the intent the matter may be shewed and pleaded before the judges, rather than before

---

* Co. Litt. 303; 3 Mod. 166; Booth on Real Actions, 214.
† 3 B. C. 305.
‡ Co. Litt. 226; Cro. Eliz. 257; Skin. 280; 10 Co. 91; Booth, 214.
§ Vaugh. Rep. 150; Finch Law, 399; 11 Rep. 10; 9 Rep. 12, 13; Finch Law, 381, 382; Co. Litt. 226.
|| Co. Litt. 303; 3 Mod. 166.

the jury, the tenants use to give the plaintiff a colour, that is
to say, a colour of action, whereby it shall appear that it were
hurtful to the tenant to put that matter that he pleadeth to the
judgment of twelve men : and the most common colour that
is used in this case is this : When he hath pleaded that such
a man infeoffed him, as before appeareth, it is used that he
shall plead farther, and say that the plaintiff claiming by a
colour of a deed of feoffment made by the said feoffor before the feoffment made to him, where no right passed by
the deed, entered, upon whom he entered, and asked judgment if the assise lie against him.* In this case, because it
appeareth to be a doubt to unlearned men, whether the land
passed by the deed without livery or not; therefore the law
suffereth the tenant to have that special matter to bring the
matter to the determination of the judges.† And in such
case the judges may not put the tenant, from the plea, for
they knew not as judges but that it is true ; and so if any default be, it is in the tenant, and not in the court. And
though the truth be, that there were no such deed of feoffment made to the plaintiff as the tenant pleadeth ; yet methinketh there is no default in the tenant, for he doth it to a
good intent, as before appeareth.

  Doct. If the tenant know that the feoffor made no such
deed of feoffment to the plaintiff, then there is a default in
the tenant to plead it, for he wittingly saith against the truth ;
and it is holden by all doctors, that every lie is an offence,
more or less ; for if it be of malice, and to the hurt of his
neighbour, then it is called *mendacium perniciosum*, and
that is deadly sin ; and if it be in sport, and to the hurt of
no man, nor of custom used, ne of pleasure that he hath in
lying, then it is venial sin, and it is called in Latin *mendacium jocosum:* and if it be to the profit of his neighbour,
and to the hurt of no man, then it is also venial sin, and it
is called in Latin *mendacium officiosum;* and thought it be

* 3 B. C. 309.
† 10 Rep. 89, 90; Finch Law, 382.

the least of those three, yet it is a venial sin, and would be eschewed.

Stud. Though the midwives of Egypt lied when they had reserved the male-children of the Hebrews, saying to the king Pharaoh, that the Hebrews had women that were cunning in the same craft, which ere they came had reserved the children alive, where indeed they themselves of pity, and of dread of God reserved them ; yet Saint Hierome expounded the text following, which saith, that our Lord therefore gave them houses, that is to be understood that he gave them spiritual houses, and that they had therefore eternal reward : and if they sinned by that lie, although it were but venial, yet I cannot see how they should have therefore eternal reward. And also if a man intending to slay another, ask me where that man is ; is it not better for me to lie, and say I cannot tell where he is, though I know it, than to shew where he is, whereupon murther should follow?

Doct. The deed that the midwives of Egypt did in saving the children was meritorious, and deserved reward everlasting, if they believed in God, and did good deeds beside, as it is to suppose they did, when they for the love of God refused the death of the innocents : and then, though they made a lie after, which was but venial sin, that could not take from them their reward, for a venial sin doth not utterly extinct charity, but letteth the fervour thereof : and therefore it may well stand with the words of Saint Hierome, that they had for their good deed eternal houses, and yet the lie that they made to be a venial sin. But nevertheless, if such a lie that is of itself but venial, be affirmed with an oath, it is always mortal, if he know it to be false that he sweareth. And to the other question, it is not like to this question that we have in hand, as me seemeth : for sometime a man for the eschewing of the greater evil may do a less evil, and then the less is no offence in him ; and so it is in the case that thou hast put, wherein because it is less offence to say he woteth not where he is, though he know where he is, than it is to shew where he is, where-

upon murther should follow, it is therefore no sin to say he
woteth not where he is : for every man is bound to love his
neighbour, and if he shew in this case where he is, knowing his death should follow thereupon, it seemeth that he
loved him not, ne that he did not to him as he would be
done to. But in the case that we be in here, there is no
such sin eschewed : for though the party pleadeth the general issue, the jury might find the truth in every thing ; and
therefore in that he saith that the plaintiff, claiming it by
the colour of a deed of feoffment, where nought passed,
entered, etc., knowing that there was no such feoffment, it
was a lie in him, and a venial sin, as methinketh. And
every man is bound to suffer a deadly sin in his neighbour,
rather than a venial sin in himself.

Stud. Though the jury upon a general issue may find
the truth, as thou sayest, yet it is much more dangerous to
the jury to inquire of many points, than to inquire only of
one point.* And forasmuch as our Lord hath given a·
commandment to every man upon his neighbour ; therefore
every man is bound to foresee as much as in him is, that
by him no occasion of offence come to his neighbour.
And for the same cause the law hath ordained divers
maxims and principles, whereby issue in the king's court
may be joined upon one point in certain, as nigh as may be,
and not generally, lest offence might follow thereupon
against God, and a hurt also unto the jury. Wherefore it
seemeth that he loveth not his neighbour as himself, ne
that he doth not as he would be done to, that offereth such
danger to his neighbour, where he may well and conveniently keep it from him, if he will follow the order of the
law ; and it seemeth that he putteth himself wilfully in
jeopardy that doth it, as it is written, Eccles. 3, *Qui amat
periculum in illo peribit*, that is to say, he that loveth
peril shall perish in it, and he that putteth his neighbour in
peril to offend, putteth himself in the same, and so should

---

* 9 Rep. 12.

18

he do, me seemeth, that would wilfully take the general
issue, where he might conveniently have the special matter.
And furthermore, it is no offence in princes and rulers to
suffer contracts, and buying and selling in markets and
fairs, though both perjury and deceit should follow thereupon ; because such contracts be necessary for the commonwealth : so it seemeth likewise, that there is no default in
the party that pleadeth such a special matter, to avoid from
his neighbour the danger of perjury, ne yet in the court,
though they induce him to it, as they do sometime for the
intent before rehearsed.   And in like wise some will say,
that if rulers of cities and commonalties sometime for the
punishment of felons, murtherers, and such other offenders,
will (to the intent they would have them confess the truth)
say to them that be suspected, that they be informed of
such certain defaults or misdemeanors in the offenders, and
that they do to the intent to have them confess the truth,
that though they were not so informed, that yet it is no
offence to say they were so informed, because they do it
for the commonwealth : for if offenders were suffered to go
unpunished, the commonwealth would eftsoons decay and
utterly perish.

Doct. I will take advisement upon thy reason in this
matter till another season, and I will now ask thee another
question somewhat like unto this : I pray thee let me hear
thy mind therein.

Stud, Let me hear thy question, and I shall with good-
will say as I think therein.

CHAP. LIV.—*The seventh question of the doctor, concerning the pleadings in assise, whereby the tenants use
sometime to plead in such manner that they shall confess
no ouster.*

Doct. It is commonly used, as I have heard say, that
when a tenant in assise pleadeth that a stranger was seised
and enfeoffed him, and giveth the plaintiff a colour in such

manner as before appeareth in the 52d chapter,* that the tenant many times, when he hath pleaded thus, and the plaintiff claimed by a colour of a deed of feoffment made by the said stranger, where nought passed by the deed entered; and that then they use to say farther, upon whom A. B. entered, upon whom the tenant entered; where indeed the said A. B. never entered, ne haply there was no such man; how can this pleading be excused of an untruth? And what reasonable cause can be why such a pleading should be suffered against the truth?

Stud. The cause why that manner of pleading is suffered is this : if the tenant by his pleading confessed an immediate entry upon the plaintiff, or an immediate putting out of the plaintiff, which in French is called an *Ouster;* then if the title were after found for the plaintiff, the tenant by his confession were attainted of the disseisin. And because it may be, that though the plaintiff have good title to the land, that yet the tenant is no disseisor, therefore the tenants use many times to plead in such manner as thou hast said before, to save themselves from confessing of an ouster : and so if there be any default it is not in the court, ne in the law, for they know not the truth therein till it be tried. And methinketh also that there is in this case right little default or none in the tenant, nor in his counsel, specially if the counsel know that the tenant is no disseisor. But as to that point, I pray thee, that as thou hast taken a respite to be advised, or that thou shew thy full mind in the question of a colour given in assise, whereof mention is made in the said 48th chapter, that I likewise may have a like respite in this case till another time, to be advised, and then I shall with good-will shew thee my full mind therein.

Doct. I am content it be as thou sayest. But I pray thee that I may yet add another question to the two questions before rehearsed of colours in assise, and feel thy mind therein, because that soundeth much to the same effect that the other do, (that is to say) to prove that there be

---

* Ante, 271.

divers things suffered in the law to be pleaded that be
against the truth : and I pray thee let me hereafter know
thy mind in all three questions, and thou shalt then with a
good-will know mine.

Stud. I pray thee shew me the case that thou speakest of.

Doct. If a man steal a horse secretly in the night, it is
used that thereupon he shall be indicted at the king's suit,
and it is used that in that indictment it shall be supposed
that he such a day and place with force and arms, (that is
to say) with staves, swords, and knives, etc., feloniously
stole the horse against the king's peace ; and that form must
be kept in every indictment, though the felon had neither
sword nor other weapon with him, but that he came secretly
without weapon :* how can it therefore be excused, but there
is an untruth ?

Stud. It is not alledged in the indictment by matter in
deed that he had such weapon, for the form of an indictment is this :

*Inquiratur pro Domino Rege, si A, tali die et anno apud
talem locum vi et armis, videlicet Gladiis, etc., talem equum
talis hominis cepit, etc.*

And then the twelve men be only charged with the effect
of the bill, that is to say, whether he be guilty of the felony
or not, and not whether he be guilty under such manner
and form as the bill specifieth or not ;† and so when they
say *Billa vera*, they say true, as they take the effect of
the bill to be. And therefore if there were false Latin in
the bill of indictment, and the jury saith *Billa vera*, yet
their verdict is true : for their verdict stretcheth not to the
truth or falshood of the Latin, but to the felony, ne to the

---

* But by statute 37 H. 8, c. 8, it is enacted, that these words, *vi et armis,*
viz., *baculis, cultellis arcubus, et sagittis,* or such like, shall not of necessity
be put in any indictment, nor shall the parties indicted of any offence have
any advantage by writ of error, plea, or otherwise, to avoid any such indictment for the want of these or the like words, but that the same lacking
of the said words shall be as good in law as indictments having them. And.
see 2 Hawk. P. C. 241, 242, and the authorities cited in the margin.

† 4 B. C. 301.

form of the words, but to the effect of the matter; and that is to enquire whether there were any such felony done by the person or not.* And though the bill vary from the day, from the year, and also from the place where the felony was done in, so it vary not from the shire that the felony was done in, and the jury saith *Billa vera*, they have given a true verdict;† for they are bound by their oath to give their verdict according to the effect of the bill, and not according to the form of the bill. And so is he that maketh a vow bound likewise to that that by the law is the effect of his avow, and not only to the words of his avow. And if a man avow never to eat white meat, yet in time of extreme necessity he may eat white meat, rather than die, and not break his avow, though he affirmed it with an oath : for by the effect of his avow extreme necessity was excepted, . though it were not expressly excepted in the words of the avow. And so likewise, though the words of the bill be, to enquire whether such a man such a day and year, and in such a place, did such a felony ; yet the effect of the bill is, to enquire whether he did the felony within the shire or no : and therefore the justices before whom such indictments be taken most commonly inform the jury, that they are bound to regard the effect of the bill, and not the form. And therefore there is no untruth in this case, neither in him that made the bill, ne yet in the jury, as me seemeth.

Doct. But if the party that owned the horse bring an action of trespass; and declareth that the defendant took the horse with force and arms, where he took him without force and arms ; how may the plaintiff there be excused of an untruth.

Stud. And if the plaintiff surmise an untruth, what is that to the court, or to the law? For they must believe the plaintiff, till that that he saith be denied by the defendant; and yet as this case is, there is no untruth in the plaintiff, to say he took the horse with force and arms, though he came

---

* 2 H. P. C. 237.
†4 B. C. 302.

never so secretly, and without weapon : for every trespass
is in the law done with force and arms ;* so that if he be
attainted, and found guilty of the trespass, he is attainted of
the force and arms : and sith the law judgeth every trespass
to be done with force, therefore the plaintiff saith truly that
he took him with force, as the law meaneth to be force.
For though he took the horse as a felon, yet upon the felo-
nious taking the owner may take an action of trespass if he
will ;† for every felony is a trespass and more.‡   And so I
have shewed thee some part of my mind, to prove that in
those cases there is no untruth, neither in the parties,
neither in the jury, nor in the law.   Nevertheless, at a better leisure I will shew thee my mind more fully therein with
good-will, as thou hast promised me to do in the case of
colours of the assise, and of the ouster, that be before rehearsed.

CHAP. LV.—*The eighth question of the doctor, Whether
the statute of forty-five of Edward the third, of Sylva
cædua, stand with conscience.*

Doct.. In the 45th year of the reign of Edw. III.§ it was
enacted, That a prohibition should lie where a man is im-
pleaded in the court-christian for dismes of wood of the age
of twenty years or above, by the name of *Sylva cædua*,‖
how may that statute stand with conscience, that is so directly against the liberty of the church, and that is made
of such things as the parliament had no authority to make
any law of?

---

* This is not true, for the law does not consider every trespass to be done
with force.   For instance, that species of injury which may be properly de-
nominated a trespass, and which subjects the wrong-doer to what we call
an action upon the case, is not accompanied with force.   5 Bac. Abr.,
title Trespass.

† Or it seems that he may have an action of trover, after the offender is
prosecuted.   4 Black. Com. 356; 1 Hale P. C. 546.

‡ Style, 346.

§ Cap. 3.

‖ Ante, 93.

Stud. It appeareth in the said statute,* that it is enacted, That a prohibition should lie in that case as it had used to do before that time; and if the prohibition lay by a prescription before the statute, why is not then the statute good as a confirmation of that prescription?

Doct. If there were such a prescription before the statute, that prescription was void; for it prohibiteth the payment of tithes of trees of the age of twenty years or above; and paying of tithes is grounded as well upon the law of God, as upon the law of reason; and against those laws lieth no prescription, as it is holden most commonly by all men.

Stud. That there was such a prescription before the said statute, and that if a man before the said statute had been sued in the spiritual court for tithes of wood of the age of twenty years or above, the prohibition lay, appeareth in the said statute, and it can not be thought that a statute that is made by authority of the whole realm, as well of the king, and of the lords spiritual and temporal, as of all the commons, will recite a thing against the truth. And furthermore, I cannot see how it can be grounded by the law of God, or by the law of reason, that the tenth part should be paid for tithe, and no other portion but that: but I think that it be grounded upon the law of reason, that a man should give a reasonable portion of his goods temporal to them that minister to him things spiritual; for every man is bound to honour God of his proper substance; and the giving of such portion hath not been only used among faithful people, but also among unfaithful, as it appeareth, Genesis 47, where corn was given to the priests in Egypt of common barns. And Saint Paul in his epistles affirmeth the same in many places; as in his first epistle to the Corinthians, cap. 9, where he saith, " He that worketh in the church shall eat of that that belongeth to the church :" and in his epistle to the Galatians, chap. 6, he saith, " Let him that is instructed in spiritual things, depart of his goods to

---

* 2 Inst. 643.

him that instructeth him." And Saint Luke, chap. 10, saith, "That the workman is worthy to have his hire." All which sayings may right conveniently be taken and applied to this purpose, that spiritual men, which minister to the people spiritual things, ought for their ministration to have a competent living of them that they minister unto. But that the tenth part should be assigned for such a portion, and neither more nor less, I cannot perceive that that should be grounded by the law of reason, nor immediately by the law of God. For before the law written there was no certain portion assigned for the spiritual ministers, neither the tenth part, nor the twelfth part, unto the time of Jacob : for it appeareth, Genesis 28, that Jacob avowed to pay dismes, which was among the Jews for the tenth part, if our Lord prospered him in his journey ; and if the tenth part had been his duty before that avow, it had been in vain to have avowed it, and so it had if it had been grounded by the law of reason. And as to that is spoken in the evangelists, and in the new law, of tithes it belongeth rather to the giving of tithes in the time of the old law, than of the new law ; as it appeareth, Matth. 23, and Luke 11, where our Lord speaketh to the Pharisees, saying, "Wo to you Pharisees, that tithe-mints, rue, and herbs, and forget the judgment and the charity of God ; these it behoveth you to do, and the other not to omit :" that is to say, it behoveth you to do justice and charity of God, and not to omit paying of tithes, though. it be of small things, as of mints, rue, herbs, and such other. And also that the Pharisee saith, Luke 17, "I pay my tythes for all that I have," it is to be referred to the old law, not to the time of the new law ; therefore, as I take it, the paying of tithes, or of a certain portion to spiritual men for their spiritual ministration to the people, have been grounded in divers manners. First, before the law written, a certain portion sufficient for the spiritual ministers was due to them by the law of nature, which, after them that be learned in the law of the realm, is called the law of reason ; and that portion is due by all laws. And in the law written, the Jews were bound to give the tenth part to their priests, as well by the said avow of Jacob, as by the law of God in the Old Testament, called the Judicials. And in the new law the paying of the tenth part is by a law that is made by the church. And the reason wherefore the tenth part was ordained by the church to be payed for the tithe was this : There is no cause why the people of the new law ought to pay less to the ministers of the new law, than the people of the Old Testament gave to the ministers of the Old Testament : for the people of the new law be bound to greater things than the people of the old law were, as it appeareth, Matth. 5, where it is said, "Unless your good works abound above the works of the Scribes and Pharisees, ye may not enter into the kingdom of heaven." And the sacrifice of the old law was not so honourable as the sacrifice of the new law is : for the sacrifice of the old law was only the figure, and the sacrifice of the new law is the thing that is figured; that was the shadow, this is the truth. And therefore the church upon that reasonable consideration ordained, that the tenth part should be paid for the sustenance of the ministers in the new law, as it was for the sustenance of the ministers in the old law ; and so that law with a cause may be increased or diminished to more portion or to less, as shall be necessary for them.

Doct. It appeareth, Gen. 14, that Abraham gave to Melchisedec dismes, and that is taken to be the tenth part ; and that was long before the law written : and therefore it is to suppose, that he did that by the law of God.

Stud. It appeareth not by any scripture that he did that by the commandment of God, ne by any revelation. And therefore it is rather to suppose that he did part of duty, and part of his own free will : for in that he gave the dismes as a reasonable portion for the sustenance of Melchisedec and his ministers, he did it by the commandment of the law of reason, as before appeareth ; but that he gave the tenth part, that was of his free-will, and because he thought it sufficient and reasonable : but if he had thought the twelfth part, or the thirteenth part had sufficed, he might have

given it, and that with good conscience. And so I suppose
that in the new law, the giving of the tenth part is by the
law of the church, and not by the law of God; unless it be
taken that the law of the church is the law of God, as it is
sometime taken to be, but not appropriately or immediately;
for that is taken appropriately to be the law of God, that is
contained in scripture, that is to say, in the Old Testament
and in the New.

Doct. It is somewhat dangerous to say that tithes be
grounded only upon the law of the church: for some men,
as it is said, say that men's law bindeth not in conscience,
and so they might happen to make a boldness thereby to
deny their tithes.

Stud. I trust there be none of that opinion; and if there
be, it is great pity: and nevertheless they be compelled in
that case by the law of the church to pay their tithes, as
well as they should be if paying of tithes were grounded
merely upon the law of God.

Doct. I think well it be as thou sayest, and therefore I
hold me contented therein. But I pray thee shew me thy
mind in this question: if a whole country prescribe to pay
no tithes for corn or hay, nor such other, whether thou
think that that prescription is good?

Stud. That question dependeth much upon that that is
said before: for if paying of the tenth part be by the law
of reason, or by the law of God, then the prescription is
void; but if it be by the law of man, then it is a good prescription, so that the ministers have a sufficient portion beside.

Doct. John Gerson, which was a doctor of divinity, in a
treatise that he named *Regulæ morales*, saith, that dismes
be paid to priests by the law of God.

Stud. The words that he speaketh there of the matter be
these, *Solutio decimarum sacerdotibus est de jure divino,
quatenus inde sustententur; sed quod tam hanc vel illam
assignare, aut in alios redditus commutare, positivi juris
existit:* that is thus much to say, The paying of dismes to
priests is of the law of God, that they may thereby be sus-

tained; but to assign this portion or that, or to change it to other rents, that is by the law positive. And if it should be taken that by that word *decimarum* which in English is called dismes or tithes, that he meant the 10th part, and that that 10th part should be paid for tithe by the law of God, then is the sentence that followeth after against that saying; for as it appeareth above, the next saith afterward thus; but to assign this portion or that, or to change it into other rents, belongeth to the law positive, that is to.the law of man; and if the tenth part were assigned by God, then may not a less part be assigned by the law of man, for that should be contrary to the law of God, and so it should be void. And methinketh that it is not so likely that so famous a clerk would speak any sentence contrary to the law of God or contrary to that he had spoken before. And to prove he meant not by the term *decimæ*, that dismes should always be taken for the tenth part, it appeareth in the fourth part of his works, in the 32d title *Literæ*, where he saith thus, *Non vocatur portio curatis debita propterea decimæ, eo quod semper sit decima pars, imo est interdum vicesima out tricesima:* that is to say, the portion due to curates is not therefore called dismes, for that it is alway the tenth part, for sometime it is the 20th or the 30th part. And so it appeareth that by this word *decimarum* he meant in the text before rehearsed a certain portion, and not precisely the tenth part: and that the portion should be paid to priests by the law of God, to sustain them with, taking as it seemeth the law of reason in that saying for the law of God, as it may one way be well and conveniently taken, because the law of reason is given to every reasonable creature by God : and then it followeth pursuantly, that it belongeth to the law of man to assign this portion, or that which necessity shall require for their sustenance. And then his saying agreeth well to that that is said before, that is to say, that a certain portion is due for priests, for their spiritual ministration, by the law of reason. And then it would follow thereupon, that if it were ordained for a law, that all paying of tithes should from henceforth cease, and that every curate should

have assigned to him such certain portion of land, rent, or
annuity, as should be sufficient for him, and for such ministers as should be necessary to be under him, according to the number of the people there, or that every
parishioner or householder should give a certain sum of
money to that use; I suppose the law were good. And
that was the meaning of John Gerson as it seemeth, in his
words before rehearsed, where he saith. But to change
tithes into other rents, is by the law positive, that is to say,
by the law of man. And some think that if a whole country prescribe to be quit of both tithes of corn and grass, so
that the spiritual ministers have a sufficient portion beside to
live upon, that is a good prescription, and that they should
not offend that in such countries paid no tithes;* for it were
hard to say that all the men of Italy, or of the East parts
be damned, because they pay no tithes, but a certain portion ·
after the custom. Therefore certain it is to pay such a certain portion, as well they as all other be bound, if the
church ask it, any custom notwithstanding. But· if the
church ask it not, it seemeth that by that not asking the
church remitteth it; and an example thereof we may take
of the Apostle Paul, that though he might have taken his
necessary living of them that he preached to, yet he took it
not, and nevertheless they that gave it him not, did not offend, because he did not ask it. But if one man in a town
would prescribe to be discharged of tithes of corn and
grass, methinketh the prescription is not good, unless he
can prove that he recompenseth it in another thing :† for it
seemeth not reasonable that he should pay less for his tithes
than his neighbours do, seeing that the spiritual ministers
are bound to take as much diligence for him, as they be
for any other of that parish :‡ wherefore it might stand with
reason that he should be compelled to pay his tithes as his
neighbours do, unless he can prove that he payeth in recompence thereof more than the tenth part in another thing.

---

* 3 Burn's Ecl. Law, 400; 2 Inst. 645; Br. Dismes, 14.
† 3 Burn's Ecl. Law, 397.
‡ Br. Prescription, pl. 93.

Nevertheless, I leave the matter to the judgment of others. And then for a farther proof, though the said prescription of not paying tithes for trees of twenty years and above were not good, yet that that of corn and grass should be good some make this reason; they say that there is no tithe but it is either a predial tithe, or a personal tithe, or a mixt tithe. And they say that if a tithe should be paid of trees when they be sold, that the tithe were not a predial tithe;* for the predial tithe of trees is of such trees as bring forth fruits and increase yearly, as apple-trees, nut-trees, pear-trees, and such other, whereof the predial tithe is the apples, nuts, pears, and such other fruits as come of them yearly;† and when the fruits be tithed, if the owner after sell the trees, there is no tithe due thereby, for two tithes may not be paid of one thing.‡ And of those tithes, that is to say, of predial tithes, was the commandment given in the old law to the Jews, as appeareth Levit. 27, where it is said, *Omnes decimæ terræ, sive de pomis arborum, sive de frugibus, Domini sunt, et illi sanctificantur;* that is to say, all tithes of the earth, either of apples, of trees, or of grains, be our Lord's, and to him they be sanctified: and though the said law speaketh only of apples, yet it is understood of all manner of fruits. And because it saith that all the tithes of the earth be our Lord's, therefore calves, lambs, and such other must also be tithed: and they be called by some men predial tithes, that is to say, tithes that come of the ground; howbeit they call them only *predials mediate;*§ and they be the same tithes that in this writing be called mixt tithes: and the other tithes, that is to say, tithes of apples and corn, and such other, be called *predials immediate,* for they come immediately of the ground, and so do not mixt tithes, as evidently appeareth.‖

---

* 3 Burn's Ecl. Law, 374.
† 1 Roll. 635; 2 Inst. 649.
‡ 2 Inst. 621, 652.
§ Wats., c. 49.
‖ 2 Inst. 649.

Doct. But what thinkest thou shall be the predial tithe
·of ashes, elms, sallows, alders, and such other trees as
bear no fruits whereof any profit cometh? Why shall not
the tenth part of the self thing be the tithe thereof, if they
be cut down, as well as it is of corn and. grass?

Stud. For I think that there is to that intent great diversity between corn, grass, and trees; and that for divers
considerations, whereof one is this, The property of corn
and grass is not to grow over one year, and if it do, it will
perish and come to nought, and so the cutting down of it is
the perfection and preservation thereof, and the special
·cause that any increase followeth of the same;* and therefore the tenth part of the increase shall be paid as a
predial tithe, and there no deduction shall be made for the
charges of it: and so it is of sheep and beasts, that must be
taken and killed in time, for else they may perish and come
to nought: but when trees be felled, that felling is not the
perfection of the trees, ne it causeth not them to increase,
but to decay; for most commonly the trees would be better,
if they might grow still. And therefore upon that that is
the cause of the decay and destruction of them, it seems
there can no predial tithe arise. And some men say, that
this was the cause why our Lord in the said chapter of
Levit. 27, gave no commandment to tithe the trees, but the
fruits of the trees only.

Doct. It appeareth in Paralip. 31, that the Jews at the
time of the king Ezechias offered in the temple all things
that the ground brought forth; and that was trees as well
as corn and grass.

Stud. It appeareth not that they did that by the commandment of God, and therefore it is like that they did it
for their own devotion, and of a favour that they had above
their duty to the repairing of the temple, which the king
Ezechias had then commanded to be repaired: and so that
text proveth nothing that tithe should be paid for trees.
And therefore they say farther, that truth it is, that if a man

---

* Ante, 280.

to the intent he would pay no tithe, would wilfully suffer his corn and grass to stand still, and to perish, he should offend conscience thereby : but though he suffer his trees to stand still continually without felling, because he thinketh the tithe would be asked if he felled them (so that he do it not of an evil will to the curate), he offendeth not in conscience, ne he is not bound to restitution therefore, as he should be if it were of corn and grass, as before appeareth.* And another diversity is this : In this case of tithe-wood, the tithe thereof would serve so little to that purpose that tithes be paid for, that it is not likely that they that made the law for payment of tithes intended that any tithe should be paid for trees or wood : for the spiritual ministers must of necessity spend daily and weekly, and therefore the tithes of trees or wood, that cometh so seldom, would serve so little to the purpose that it should be paid for, that it would not help them in their necessity : so that if they should be driven to trust thereto, though it might help him in whose time it should happen to fall, yet it should deceive them that trusted to it in the meantime, and also should leave the parish without any to minister to them.

Doct. I would well agree, that for trees that bear fruit there should no predial tithe be paid when they be sold, for the predial tithe of trees is the fruits that come of them, and so there cannot be two predials of one thing, as thou hast said.† But of other trees that bear no fruit, methinketh that a predial tithe should be paid when they be sold. And so it appeareth that there ought to be by the constitution provincial made by the reverend father in God, Robert Winchelsey, late archbishop of Canterbury, where it is said and declared, that *Sylva cædua* is of every kind of trees that have being, in that they should be cut, or that be able to be cut :‡ whereof we will, saith he, that the possessor of the said wood be compelled by the censures of the

---

* Ante, 284.
† 3 Burn's Eccl. Law, 375; ante, 285.
‡ 2 Inst. 642; see Stat. 45 Ed. 3, c. 3.

church to pay to the parish-church, or mother-church, the tithe, as a real or predial tithe. And so by virtue of that constitution provincial a predial tithe must be paid of such trees as have no fruit: for I would agree, that the said constitution provincial stretched not to trees that bear fruit, although the words be general to all trees, (as before appeareth.)

Stud. I take not the reason why a predial tithe should not be paid for trees that bear fruit, to be because two predial tithes cannot be paid for one thing: for when the tithe is paid of lambs, yet shall tithe be paid of wool of the same sheep; for it is paid for another increase: and so it may be said that the fruit of a tree is one increase, and the felling another.* But I take the cause to be, for the two causes before rehearsed; and also forasmuch as the felling is not properly an increase of trees, but a destruction of the trees, as it is said before. And farther, I would hear thy mind upon the said constitution provincial, which will, that tithe should be paid for trees by the possessors of the wood; that if the possessor fell the wood for C*l.*, and give the buyer a certain time to fell it in, what tithe shall the possessor pay as long as the wood standeth?

Doct. I think none, for the predial tithe cometh not till the wood be felled: and a personal tithe he cannot pay, no more than if a man pluck down his house and selleth it, or if he sell all his land: in which cases I agree well he shall pay no tithe, neither personal nor predial.

Stud. And then I put case that the buyer selleth the wood again as it is standing upon the ground to another for CC*l.*, what tithe shall be paid then?

Doct. Then the first buyer shall pay tithe of the surplusage that he taketh over the C*l.* that he paid as a personal tithe.

Stud. And then if the second buyer after that cut it

---

* 2 Inst. 652; 1 Roll. Abr. 640; Bunb. 10, 314; 1 Roll. Abr. 642; Bunb. 90; 3 Burn's Ecl. Law, 452.

down, and sell it when it is cut down for less than he paid,
what tithe shall then be paid?

Doct. Then shall he that selleth them pay the tithe for
the trees as a predial tithe.

Stud. I cannot see how that can be : for he neither hath
the trees that the predial tithe should be paid for, if any
ought to be paid; nor he is not possessor of the ground
where the trees grow. And therefore if any predial tithe
should be paid, it should be paid either by the first possessor by reason of the words of the said constitution provincial,
which be, that the tithe shall be paid by the possessor of
the wood : or by the last buyer, because he hath the trees
that should be tithed ; and by the first possessor the tithes
cannot be paid as a predial ; for he cut them not down, ne
they were not cut down upon his bargain ; and by the last
buyer it cannot be paid, neither as a predial tithe, for the
said constitution saith, that the possessor of the woods
should be compelled to pay it. And therefore I suppose
that the truth is, that in that case no tithe shall be paid : for
as to the last seller, he shall pay no personal tithe, for he
gained nothing, as it appeareth before ; and no predial tithe
shall be paid, for it should be against the said prescription ;
and also the cutting down is the destruction of trees, and
not their preservation, as is said before.

Doct. Then takest thou the said constitution to be of
small effect, as it seemeth.

Stud. I take it to be of this effect : That of wood above
twenty years it bindeth not, because it is contrary to the
Common law, and to the said prescription, that standeth
good in the Common law, but of wood under twenty years,
whereof tithe hath been accustomed to be paid, the constitution is not against the said prescription, because paying
of tithe under twenty years is not prohibited, but suffered
by the said statute.* Howbeit some say, that by the very
rigour of the Common law tithes should not be paid for

---

* Ante, 278, 279.

19

wood under thirty years, no more than for above twenty
years, and that prohibition in that case lieth by the Common law : nevertheless, because it hath been suffered to the
contrary, and that in many places tithes hath been paid
thereof, I pass it over : but where tithe hath not been paid
of wood under twenty years, I think none ought to be paid
at this day in law or conscience. But admit that the said
constitution taketh effect for payment of the wood under
twenty years as of a predial tithe, yet I cannot see how the
tithe thereof should be paid by the possessor of the wood,
if he sell them, but that it should be paid rather by him that
hath the trees : for the constitution is, that the tithe shall be
paid as a real or predial tithe, and that is their part of the
same trees, as it is of corn. And if a man buy corn upon
the ground, the buyer shall pay the tithe, and not the
seller :* and so it would seem to be here. And what the
constitution meant, to decree the contrary in tithe wood, I
cannot tell, unless the meaning were to induce the owners
to pay tithes of great trees when they fell them to their own
use ; which methinketh should be very hard to stand with
reason, though the said statute had never been made, as I
have said before. And furthermore, I would here (under
correction) move one thing, and that is this, That, as it
seemeth, that they that were at the making of the said constitution, and knew the said prescription, did not follow the
direct order of charity therein so perfectly as they might
have done : for when they made the said constitution provincial directly against the said prescription, they set law
against custom, and power against power, and in a manner.
the spiritualty against the temporalty, whereby they might
well know that great variance and suit would follow. And
, therefore if they had clearly seen that the said prescription
had been against conscience, they should first have moved
the king and his council, and the nobles of the realm, to
have assented to the reformation of that prescription, and
not to make a law as it were by authority and power against

---

* Noy, 150, con. Cro. Jac. 362 ; Brownl. 34.

the prescription, and then to threat the people, and make them believe that they were all accursed that kept the said prescription, or that maintained it.   And it seemeth to stand hardly with conscience to report so many to stand accursed for following of the said statute, and of the said prescription as there do, and yet to do no more than hath been done to bring them out of it.

Doct. Methinketh that it is not convenient that laymen should argue the laws and the decrees or constitutions of the church :* and therefore it were better for them to give credence to spiritual rulers that have cure of their souls, than to trust to their own opinions : and if they would do so, then such matters would much the more rather cease than they will do by such reasonings.

Stud. In that that belongeth to the articles of the faith, I think the people be bound to believe the church, for the church gathereth together in the Holy Ghost cannot err in such things as belongeth to the catholick faith ; but where the church maketh any laws whereby the goods or possessions of the people may be bound, or by this occasion or that may be taken from them, there the people may lawfully reason whether the laws bind them or not ; for in such laws the church may err and be deceived, and deceive other, either for singularity, or for covertise, or some other cause.   And for that consideration it pertaineth most to them that be learned in the law of the realm to know such laws of the church as treat of the ordering of lands or goods, and to see whether they may stand with the laws of the realm or not.   And therefore it is necessary for them to know the laws of the church that treat of dismes, of executors, of testaments, of legacies, bastardy, matrimony, and divers other, wherein they be bound to know when the law of the church must be followed, and when the law of the realm :† whereof because it is not our purpose to treat, I leave to speak any more at this time, and will resort again

---

* 2 Comyn's Digest, title Canons, 1, 2
† Ante, 16.

to speak of tithes; wherein some men say that of tin, coal, and lead, no tithe should be paid when they be sold by the owner of the ground, because it is part of the inheritance, and it is more rather a destruction of the inheritance than any increase.* And therefore they say, that if a man take a tinwork, and give the lord the tenth dish, according to the custom, that the lord shall pay no tithe of that tenth dish, neither predial nor personal: but if the other that taketh the work, have gains and advantage by the work, it seemeth that it were not against reason that he should pay a personal tithe of his gains, the charge deducted.†

Doct. I pray thee shew me first what thou takest for a personal tithe, and upon what ground personal tithes be paid, as thou thinkest, so that one of us mistake not another therein.

Stud. I will with good-will. And therefore thou shalt understand that, as I take it, personal tithes be not paid for any increase of the ground, but for such profit as cometh by the labour or industry of the person, as by buying and selling, and such other;‡ and such personal tithes, as I take it, must be ordered after the custom, and the church hath not used to levy those tithes of compulsion, but by conscience of the parties. Nevertheless Raymond saith, that it is good to pay personal tithes, or with the assent of the parson to distribute them to poor men, or else to pay a certain portion for the whole. But as Innocent saith, where the custom is that they should be paid, the people be bound to pay them as well as predials, the expences deduct. Howbeit in the church of England they use to sue for such personal tithes as well as for predials;§ and that is by reason of the constitution provincial that was made by Robert Winchelsey, by the which it was ordained, that personal tithes should be paid of crafts and merchandise, and of the

---

* But by custom tithes of any of these may be payable. 2 Inst. 651; 1 Roll. Abr. 646.
† Lind. 195; post. 293.
‡ 3 Burn's Ecl. 375.
§ Lind. 195.

lucre of buying and selling, and in like wise of carpenters, smiths, weavers, masons, and all other that work for hire, that they shall pay tithes of their hire,* except they will give any certain thing to the use or the light of the church, if it so please the parson. And in another place the said archbishop saith, that of the pawnage of woods and such other things, etc., and of fishings, trees, bees, doves, and of divers other things there remembered, and of crafts, and of buying and selling, and of the profits of divers other things there recited, every man should help satisfy competently in the church, to the which they be bound to give it of right;† no expences by the giving of the said tithes deducted or withholden, but only for the payment of tithes of crafts, and of buying and selling. And by reason of the said constitutions provincial, sometimes suits be taken in the spiritual court for personal tithes; and therefore many men do marvel because deductions many times must be referred to the conscience of the parties. And they marvel also why a law should be made in this realm for paying of personal tithes, more than there is in other countries. And ·here I would gladly move thee farther in one thing concerning such personal tithes, to know thy mind therein, and that is, If a man give to another a horse, and he selleth that horse for a certain sum, shall he pay any tithe of that sum?

Doct. What thinkest thou therein?

Stud. I think that he shall pay no tithe : for there, as I take it, the profit cometh not to him by his own industry, but by the gift of another ;‡ and, as I take it, personal tithes be not paid for every profit or advantage that cometh newly to a man, except it come by his own industry or labour, and so it doth not here. And also if he should pay

---

* N. B. By the statute of 2 and 3 Ed. 6, c. 13, the rigour of the Canon Law as to personal tithes is much softened, and it may be observed that they are now scarce any where paid in England, unless for mills or fish. caught at sea. Wood, b. 2, c. 22; 1 Roll. Abr. 641, pl. 1; 2 P. Wms. Rep. 463.

† Cro. Car. 339; 1 Lev. 179; Sid. 271; 3 Burn's Ecl. Law, 471, 472, 473. ‡ 1 Roll. Abr. 656, N. pl. ; post. 297; 2 Inst. 649.

tithe of that he sold the horse for, he should pay tithe for the very whole value of the thing: and, as I take it, the personal tithes for buying and selling shall never be paid for the value of the thing, but for the clear gains of the thing. And therefore I take the cases before rehearsed, where a man selleth his land, or pulleth down a house and selleth the stuff, that he should there pay no tithe, that it is there to be understood, that he that hath land or house by gift, or by descent: for if a man buy land, or buy timber and stuff of a house, and sell it for gain, I suppose that he should pay a personal tithe for that gain. And this case is not like to a fee or annuity granted for counsel, where the whole fee shall be tithed for the charges deducted, or some certain sum for it by agreement: for there the whole fee cometh for his counsel, which is by his own industry; but in the other case it is not so. And the same reason as for the personal tithe might be made of trees, when they descend or be given to any man, and he selleth them to another, that he shall pay no personal tithe.

Doct. Methinketh that if the horse amend in his keeping, and then he sell the horse, that then the tithe shall be paid of that that the horse hath increased in value after the gift: and so it may be of trees, that he shall pay tithe of that that the trees may be amended after the gift or descent.

Stud. Then the tithe must be the tenth part of the increase, the expences deducted: and then of trees the charges must also be deducted, for it is then a personal tithe; and there is no tree that is so much worth as it hath hurt the ground by the growing: therefore there can no personal tithe be paid by the owner of the ground when he selleth them, though they have increased in his time. Nevertheless I will speak no farther of that matter at this time, but will shew thee, that if tin, lead, coal, or trees be sold, that a mixt tithe cannot grow thereby. For a mixt tithe is properly of calves, lambs, pigs, and such other that come part of the ground that they be fed of, and part of the keeping, industry and oversight of the owners, as it

is said before.* But tin, lead, and coal are part of the
ground, and of the freehold, and trees grow of themselves,
and be also annexed to the freehold, and will grow of themselves. And also the mixt tithe must be paid yearly at
certain times appointed by the law, or by custom of the
country : but it may happen that tin, lead, coal, and trees
shall not be felled or taken in many years, and so it seemeth it cannot be any mixt tithe. And these be some of the
reasons, which they that would maintain that statute and
prescription to be good, make to prove their intent, as they
think.

Doct. What think they, if a man sell the lops of his
wood, whether any tithe ought there to be paid?

Stud. They think all one law of the trees and of the
lops.†

Doct. And if he use to sell the lops once in fifteen or
sixteen years, what hold they then?

Stud. That all is one.

Doct. And what is the reason why tithe ought not to be
paid there as well as for wood under twenty years?

Stud. For they say that the lops are to be taken of the
same condition as the trees be, what time soever they be
felled; and that no custom will serve in that case against
the statute, no more than it should do of great trees.‡

Doct. And what hold they of the bark of the tree?

Stud. Therein I have not heard of their opinion, but it
seemeth to be one law with the lops.

Doct. I perceive well by that thou hast said before, that
thy mind is, that if a whole country prescribe to be quit of
tithes of trees, corn, and grass, or of any other tithes, that
that prescription is good, so that the spiritual ministers
have sufficient beside to live upon.§   Dost thou mean so?

* Wats., c. 49: 2 Inst. 648; 1 Roll. Abr. 635.'
† See the great case of Walton and Lady Mary Tryon, Dec. 15, 1751,
mentioned by Dr. Burn in his Ecl. Law, 3 vol., p. 440, which finally settles
this point.
‡ 11 Rep. 48; 1 Cro. 478; Br. Dismes, pl. 14.
§ 3 Burn's Ecl. Law, 400; ante, 284.

Stud. Yea verily.

Doct. And then I would know thy mind, if any man contrary to that prescription were sued in the spiritual court for corn and grass, or any other tithes, whether a prohibition should lie in that case, as it did after thy mind before the said statute, where a man was sued in the spiritual court for tithe wood.

Stud. I think nay.

Doct. And why not there, as well as it did where a man was sued for the tithe wood?

Stud. For, as I take it, there is great diversity between the cases, and that for this cause : There is a maxim in the law of England, that if any suit be taken in the spiritual court whereby any goods or land , might be recovered, which after the grounds of the law of the realm ought not to be sued there, though percase the king's court shall hold no plea thereof, that yet a prohibition should lie :* and after when it had continued long that no tithes were paid of wood, because of the said prohibition, and that after by process of time some curates began to ask tithe of wood, contrary to the law, and contrary to the said prescription, so that variance began to arise between curates and their parishioners in that behalf; then for appeasing the said variance the said statute was made, and that, as it seemeth more at the calling on of the spiritualty than of the temporalty : for the statute doth not expressly grant that the prohibition in that case of tithe wood should lie so largely as some say it lay by the law ; howbeit it doth not restrain the Common law therein, as it appeareth evidently by the words of the statute.‡ And so after some men, it appeareth before the statute, and also after the statute, (as I have touched before) that the spiritual court ought not in that case to have made any process for tithe wood : and therefore if they did, a prohibition lay by the Common law. And like law as if the spiritual court make process upon such legacy

---

* Ante, 181.

† Ante, 279, 290.

as by the law of the realm is void.   As if a man bequeath
to one another man's horse, and the spiritual court thereupon maketh process to execute that legacy, there a. prohibition lieth : for it appeareth evidently in the libel, if all
the truth appeareth in the libel, that in the law of the realm
the legacy is void to all intents ; and that he to whom the
legacy is made shall neither have the horse nor the value
of the horse.   And in like wise if a man sell his land for one
hundred pounds, and he is sued after in the spiritual court for
tithe of the said hundred pounds, there a prohibition shall
lie ;* for it appeareth in that case openly in the libel, that
no tithe ought to be paid, and that the spiritual law ought not
in that case to make any process whereby the goods of
him that sold the land might be taken from him against the
law of the realm.   And upon this ground it is, that if a man
were sued† in the spiritual court now sith the statute‡ for
a *Mortuary*,§ that a prohibition should lie, for it appeareth in
the libel, that sith the statute there ought no snit to be taken
for mortuaries ;‖ and the same law is, if any suit were taken
in the spiritual court for a new duty, that is of late taken in
some places upon leases of parsonages and vicarages, which
is called a *Dimission noble*, for it appeareth evidently in the
libel, if any be made thereupon, that no such process ought
by the law of the realm to be made in that behalf.   But in
the case of tithe corn or grass, or such other things, wherein
thou hast desired to know my mind, there appeareth nothing
in the libel, but that the suit thereof of right appertaineth
to the spiritual law ;¶ and so for any thing that appeareth
the party may be holpen in the spiritual court by the pre-

---

* Ante, 284.
† Post. 303, 305.
‡ 21 H. 8, c. 6.
§ See post. 304, of what in general a mortuary consisted before the act
of Henry.
‖ But a man may be sued in the spiritual court for the money given by
the statute, for it is recoverable there as an ecclesiastical right, just as a
mortuary was before the statute.   12 Mod. 416, Johnson *v.* Rysons.   The
money may be sued for as a mortuary, as it has now obtained that name.
¶ 2 Burn's Eccl. Law, 481, 482.

scription. And if the case were so put, that in the spiritual court they would not allow the said prescription, yet I think no prohibition shall lie. For though the spiritual judges in a spiritual matter deny the parties of justice, yet the king's laws cannot reform that, but must remit it to their conscience. But if there were some remedy provided in that case, it were well done; for some men say, that in the spiritual court they will admit no plea against tithes. And also if a composition were made by assent of the patron, and also of the ordinary, between a parson and one of his parishioners, that the parson and his successors should have for a certain ground so many quarters of corn for his tithe yearly, and after, contrary to the composition, the parson in the spiritual court asketh the tithes as they fall;* that in this case no prohibition should lie; ne yet though the case were farther put, that the composition were pleaded in the court, and were disallowed; but all resteth in the conscience of the judge spiritual, (as is said before.)† Howbeit, because some be of opinion that a prohibition should lie in this last case, therefore I will refer it to the judgment of other; but in the case of prescription, before rehearsed, I take it for the clearer case, that no prohibition should lie, as I have said before. And I beseech our Lord, that this matter and such other like thereto, may be so charitably looked upon, that there be not hereafter such divisions, ne such diversities of opinions therein, as has been in time past, whereby hath followed great costs and charges to many persons in this realm; and that hath moved me to speak so far in this chapter, and in divers other chapters in this present book, as I have done : not intending thereby to give occasion to any person to withhold his tithes that of right ought to be paid, ne to alter the portion therein before accustomed; but that (as methinketh) they ought to be claimed by the same title as they ought to be paid, and by none other ; and that it may also somewhat appear that the

* 2 Black. Com. 28, 29.
† See 2 Inst. 610.

said statute of 45 Edw. III.* was well and lawfully made, and upon a good reasonable consideration, and that the said prescription is good also ; so that no man was in any danger of excommunication for the making of the said statute, nor yet is not for the observing thereof, ne yet of the said prescription, as it is noted by some persons that there should be.   And thus I commit thee unto our Lord, who ever have both thee and me in his blessed keeping everlastingly. Amen.

---

* 2 Inst. 642.

ADDITIONS

TO THE

SECOND DIALOGUE

OF THE

DOCTOR AND STUDENT

CONTAINING

THIRTEEN CHAPTERS

ON THE

POWER AND JURISDICTION OF THE PARLIAMENT, Etc.

(301)

ADDITIONS

TO THE

SECOND DIALOGUE

OF

DOCTOR AND STUDENT, ETC.

CHAP. I.—*What the parliament may do concerning the spirituality and the spiritual jurisdiction, and what not.*

Doct. I pray thee let me know thy mind in this question, Whether laymen (as thee thinketh) have power to make any laws of mortuaries?

Stud. There was a law made of mortuaries in the parliament holden in the 21 Hen. VIII., c. 6,* by the assent of the king, and of all the lords spiritual and temporal of the realm, and of all the commons ;† and I hold it not best to reason, or to make arguments, whether they had authority to do that they did or not. For I suppose, that no man would think that they would do anything that they had not power to do.

Doct. I mean not only of mortuaries, that that statute meaneth of, but I mean of such things as be brought to

---

* This statute, which limits the sums which shall be taken for mortuaries, now stands in full force, except as to the seventh clause, which is repealed by 12 Ann., st. 2, c. 6, and 28 Geo. 2, c. 6.

† Ante, 297.

burials of dead persons;* whereof some concern the service of God, or the relief of the soul, and some the worldly
countenance : as in some places, the church claimeth to have
the taper that standeth in the middle of the hearse over the
heart of the corpse, and some claim to have all the tapers;
some also claim to have one of the torches that is about the
hearse, and some to have all the torches. And if the body
be brought in a chariot, or with coat armour, or such other,
then they claim all the horses and chariot, and the apparel,
or part thereof; and the coat armours or other like, as se-
queses to the body. And these rights and duties be called
in some places mortuaries :† and of these I mean most principally in this question. I pray thee let me know what
thou thinkest therein.

Stud. I pray thee let me first know what is thy opinion
in this question.

Doct. I think that of such of the said mortuaries as the
church hath right in, in such manner as is before rehearsed
by prescription or otherwise, and of such things as be ordained at such burials to the service of God, or to the relief of the soul, that the parliament hath no power to prohibit them ; as to prohibit that the church should have no
such mortuaries, or that there should not be bidden to the
burial so many priests, or that there shall not be above so
many tapers or torches ; or that there shall not be given
above such a certain sum in alms : I suppose that the parliament hath no power to these things, for they be annexed
to the right spiritual whereof the temporal jurisdiction hath
no power : for the inferior may not judge upon the superior.
But to make a law, that there shall not be given above so
many black gowns, or that there shall not be any herald of
arms there, but he that is buried were of such a degree ; or
that no black cloths shall be hanged in the streets from the
house where he died to the church, as is used in many

* Wats. Com. Inc. 1053, cap. 23; 3 Burn's Eccl. Law, 500, 501.
† But they are all entirely abolished by the statute of H. 8, and subse-
quent statutes relating to mortuaries.

cities and good towns, or to prohibit such other things as
be but wordly pomps, and be rather consolations to the
friends that be alive than any relief to the soul that is de--
parted, wherefore the church favoureth them not.   I think
the parliament hath good authority to make a law ; I pray
thee let me know thy mind what thou thinkest in these
diversities.

Stud. Verily I think that in all the cases before rehearsed,
the parliament with a cause, hath good authority to make
laws ; as if it were ordained by the parliament, that at such
burials the church should neither have torch nor taper,
horse nor chariot, nor none other thing like, but that they
should always pertain to the executors to the use of the
testator : it were a good statute, and ought to be observed,
as well by spiritual men as by temporal ; and this I take to
be the reason why, for all goods, though they be in the
hands of spiritual men, be temporal concerning the body,
and nourishing the body, as they do to temporal men.
And John Gerson holdeth the same opinion, as it appeareth
in his treatise of the Spiritual Life of the Soul, the second
lesson, and the third corollary, whereof mention is made
more at large in the first dialogue in English, chap.
3.* And all temporal things the king and his progenitors, as in the right of the crown, have in this realm
alway ordered and judged by his laws : and therefore I
suppose that the parliament may enact, that there shall not
be laid upon a deceased person but such a cloth, or thus
many tapers or candles set up about him.† And here I
would say farther in one thing, and that is this, that no
prescription had by the authority of the spiritual law,‡ may
give no right within this realm to those mortuaries that we

---

* Ante, 215.
† Ante, 247.
‡ The ecclesiastical law allows of different times in creating customs or
prescriptions. Sometimes thirty, Godolphin's Orphan's Legacy, 62; sometimes forty, 1 P. Wms. 667; Str. 422; and sometimes fifty years, Str. 83,
make a prescription.

20

speak of now, nor to the said mortuaries that be put alway
by the said statute, nor yet to any pension or annuity ;* but
if any right shall be won therein by prescription, it must be
by a prescription had after the course of the law of the
realm ;† and the least prescription thereof is this, that is to
say, that no man's mind may remember the contrary
thereof whereof the prescription is made. And if this be
true, then have many mortuaries been claimed, and taken
in time past, without title, whereby the takers have been
bounded to restitution. And that is true that I have said
of such prescriptions of mortuaries and pensions, methinketh it may appear thus : If there were a law made by the
church, that at every burial the curate should have all the
tapers and torches that were about the corpse, I suppose
that it is clear, that that law bound not in this realm there
as no prescription was thereof before. And if a law made
by the church should not in this case bind, how should
then a prescription, grounded only upon the laws of the
church, bind? I cannot see how : but if it were in a
country where the church hath sovereignty in temporal
things, it were a greater doubt. And in this case many
say, that a prohibition ought of right to be granted to prohibit the spiritual judges, that they shall not give sentence
against the prescription of the king's law, whereby any
temporal goods may be bound, as well as that they shall
not hold plea of that that belongeth to the king's law, but
such a prohibition is not in use.‡ But if it were enacted,
that a prohibition should hereafter lay in that case, I suppose that it were a right good and a reasonable statute.
And also whether such a prescription, after the law of the
church, give title for tithes, is after some men the greater
question : but I will no farther speak thereof at this time.
And as to the coat armour, shield and sword and such other
things as be sometime set up at the burial of noble men,

§ 2 Inst. 491.
† Ante, 27; Co. Litt. 114.
‡ Ante, 181.

some men say that they belong not to the church, but to the executors;* and that they ought to remain there to the honour of the body, and to the memorial of the soul, as long as they will endure. For there was never gift thereof made to the curate, whereby any property might grow unto him. And a case much like to their sayings is in the 9 Edward IV.,† where an action of trespass was brought for taking away such a coat armour, etc. And there some were of opinion, that the action lay well, howbeit the case is not judged; but whatsoever the law be therein, I think it be no great doubt, but that if a statute be made that they should belong to the executors, that the interest of the curate, whatsoever he had thereto before by prescription, constitution, or otherways, were determined; and so methinketh that the parliament may as directly make a law concerning such mortuaries as it may do of any other temporal goods within the realm; and then as to the number of priests and clerks, that should be bidden to such burials, I think that the parliament may well, upon a certain pain, prohibit, that none shall call to such a burial above a certain number of priests and clerks to be assigned by the parliament after the degree of him that is buried; and especially to prohibit, that none shall give any money, or other reward, to any above that number, though they come uncalled. For such statutes be for ordering of temporal things, and to force that the king's subjects should not be charged but as the parliament should think expedient for the wealth of the realm, and therefore they are to be observed in law and conscience. And thus I have shewed the part of my conceit, what methinketh concerning the said mortuaries. ➤

Doct. I thank thee for the pain thou hast taken therein: and since thou hast somewhat touched what the parliament may do in these mortuaries, which concerneth somewhat the spirituality, I pray thee that thou wouldest shew me somewhat more of thy mind, what the parliament

---

* 1 Burn's Ecc. Law, 343; 3 Inst. 110.
† 3 Inst. 202.

may do in other things concerning the spirituality; for I think it were good and necessary to be known for the good ordei of conscience of many persons, and the appeasing of many and great diversities of opinion in this realm.

Stud. To treat of this matter at length, it would ask a great time; but I shall with good-will briefly touch some articles thereof, and haply thou shalt by them know the better what the parliament may do concerning the spiritual jurisdiction in other cases like. But I pray thee take me not, that my meaning is, that I would that such statutes should be made as I shall speak of; for I do it not to that intent, but only to shew the power of the parliament what they may do if they list to execute their power.

CHAP. II.—*What the parliament may do concerning the spirituality and the spiritual jurisdiction, and what not.*

Stud. I suppose it may be enacted by the parliament, that no lands, nor other inheritance, shall hereafter be given into mortmain by licence, nor without licence, but that all feoff-ments, fines, leases, and recoveries by covin, or by assent of the parties hereafter made, or had for mortmain, shall be void and that the house shall take no interest by it;* but that it shall remain still with the feoffors or givers, or to such other use as the parliament shall appoint. For like as the parliament may ordain, that all feoffments and fines, made to any manner of person, shall be void, and that every man shall stand still seised of his land without making of any alteration of posession thereof to any other, more stronger it may ordain, that no alteration of possession shall be made into mortmain. And that a statute may be made that there shall be no alteration of possession, made of lands to no man, it may appear by the words of John Gerson, in his treatise of Contracts, the 6th considera-tion, where he says thus: "Contracts be not therefore precisely to be said unlawful and void, because they may ·

---

* Ante, 200, 210.

be redeemed by the law made for such redemption. For he sayeth, ' That they that would say so, would condemn the high maker of laws, that is God himself:' which in the judicial law given by Moses to the Jews (as the text is open) Levit. xxv, willeth, ' That he that selleth his inheritance may redeem it: and if he redeem it not, yet it should return again in the year of Jubilee:' for it is there said to the Jews thus : 'All the region of your possession · shall be sold under the condition of redemption.' And though that law bindeth not now christian people, yet a like law thereto might be made by christian princes, which then by that new institution ought to be observed and kept, as divers of the said judicials have been in many countries." Thus far be the words of John Gerson. And methinketh, that if a law might be made, that if a man sell his land, that he may nevertheless redeem it within certain years, whether the buyer will or no, though no such condition were spoken of at the making of the bargain : that like reason is that a law may be made, that there shall be no sales, but that every man shall continually stand still seised of his lands, as I have said before. And I suppose verily that such a statute should be good and profitable, as well · for them that have such lands in mortmain as for many other. And Basdus de Perusio saith, that such a statute · should be good to prohibit that no lands should come into mortmain, but not to prohibit that no goods should come into mortmain. And methinketh his saying is good and reasonable.

CHAP. III.— *What the parliament may do concerning the spirituality, and what not.*

Stud. I think also that the king by parliament may break all appropriations that be made against any statute, or against the good order of the people, or against the commonwealth ; and the cause is this : there can be no church appropriated, but that the patronage of the advowson thereof must be given before the appropriation to the

abbot, or prior, or other, to whom the propriation shall be
made, and to their successors, for if it be given but for term
of life, the appropriation cannot stand in effect but for term
of life.*   And because the advowson is a temporal inheritance, therefore it is under the power of the parliament to
order it as it seeth cause, and to bring it again to be
presentable as it was first : and in likewise if a man bring a
writ of right of advowson against him that hath such an
advowson appropried to his house, and recovereth the
advowson, the appropriation is dissolved : for the appropriation can no longer continue than they have the patronage.   And the parliament may leave the advowson to the
house, as an advowson presentable if they see cause ; or
they may give it to the first giver, or otherwise dispose it,
as the matter requireth.   And under such manner all the
vicarages that were unyed, annexed, or appropried from
the first year of king Richard II., unto the parliament holden
in the fourth year of king Henry IV., were disapproved.†
And by the same statute of Henry IVth it is enacted, That
all vicarages appropriated after the statute made in the
fifteenth year of king Richard against the form of the
statute, shall be disappropried, except the vicarage of Had-
dénham in the diocese of Ely, as in the said statute appeareth.   But yet I suppose, that the parliament may not
make an appropriation without spiritual assent; ne I mean
not that it were good that all appropriation should be
broken ; but I have spoken this to show what authority the
parliament hath if they would execute it; and if there be
a reasonable consideration why it is done, then the disap-
propriation holdeth as well in conscience as in the law.
And good it is, that the authority of parliament be known
in this behalf to the intent that it may cause them the rather
to observe such statutes as be already made of such appropriations, and to dispose some part of the fruits thereof
among the poor parishioners, according to the statute of the

* Ante, 189.
† Plow. 495.

15 Rich. II. made in that point. And it were asked them, why they have not observed the said statute, they have none other excuse, but either to say that they knew not the statute, or else that the statute had no power to bind them to it. And I suppose verily that neither of those sayings can be any reasonable excuse unto them in that behalf.*

Chap. IV.—*Concerning the power of the parliament as against the spirituality.*

Stud. All the sanctuaries in England,† as well in churches as other,‡ and also where a man shall have his clergy, and where not, be under the power and authority of the parliament.

Doct. I suppose that it is by the spiritual authority that a man shall be defended by a sanctuary, or have his clergy.

Stud. Nay verily, but by the old customs and maxims of the law of the realm; and therefore the king's justices shall judge where a man shall have sanctuary or his clergy, and where not. And if the ordinary will not come to receive them that be clerks, the king's justices may set a fine upon him. And also the king's pardon shall discharge one, both of the sanctuary, and out of the bishop's prison; and so it appeareth that the bishops have the keeping of such as be admitted to their clergy by authority of the king's laws, and not by their own authority.§ And though the title of sanctuary, and the liberty where a man shall have his clergy, be under the power of the parliament, yet the parliament hath not broken nor extended his whole power on them, to put them generally away.

Doct. Might the parliament break a sanctuary that is granted by the pope?

Stud. The pope by himself may make no sanctuary in

---

* For further information relating to appropriations, see 1 Burn's Ecc. Law, title Appropriation.

† Ante, 93, 240.

‡ Sanctuary is now abolished by stat. 21 Jac. 1, c. 28.

§ See stat. 18 Eliz., c. 7, and 4 B. C. 362.

this realm : but if the king and the pope together do it, the
old custom of the realm serveth, as most men say, that it
is good. But yet if the king after that grant, by authority
of his parliament avoid his own grant, then remaineth but
only the, pope's grant; and that sufficeth not to make a
sanctuary, as I have said before : but the parliament without the pope may make a sanctuary, with such penalties as
they shall think convenient to set upon the breakers thereof.
But if the pope do after confirm that sanctuary, and grant
that no man under the pain of the censures of the church
do break it, it is the stronger, howbeit the sanctuary taketh
his full strength in that case as to the law by the parliament.

CHAP. V.—*Concerning the power of the parliament
against the spirituality.*

Stud. I suppose also, that the parliament may assign of
the·trees and grass in church-yards either to the parson, to
the vicar,* or to the parish if they see cause : for though it
be hallowed ground, yet the freehold thereof, the trees and
herbs are things temporal, as they were before the hallowing ; and that the parliament hath power to order them (as
is said before) it appeareth by a statute that is called *Ne
rector prosternat arbores in cœmeterio,* 35 Edw., stat. 2,
that is to say, the statute against persons, that they shall
not cut down trees in the church-yards. In which statute
it is recited, that the soil of the church-yard (which in the
laws of England is called the freehold) belongeth to the
church : and then the statute goeth farther, and prohibiteth

---

* As the law now stands, if there is a rector only, or a vicar only of the
church, the trees and grass belong to him; but if there is both rector and
vicar in the same church, it is doubtful to which of them they belong.
Linwood seems to think the rector has the property in them, unless they
are otherwise assigned in the endowment of the vicarage. Lind. 267.
But this is mere conjecture. In short, there appears to be no direct authority one way or the other. In Bellamy's case, in the spiritual court,
where the vicar sued the parson impropriate for cutting down trees, the
point to which of the two the trees did belong was indeed considered; but
the case at last went off upon another ground, so that the right was not
determined. 2 Roll. Abr. 337.

all persons, that they shall not fell them, but it be for necessary reparations of the chancel,* but that they shall let
them stand still to defend the church from the great tem-
pestuous winds and weather. And then it seemeth, that
like as the parliament hath authority to prohibit persons,
that they shall not fell the trees in the church-yard when
they would, that it hath authority as well to take the whole
property of the trees from them if they see cause, and that
they may give them to the parish, if there be reasonable
consideration to move them to it. And yet nevertheless
the judges for a church-yard will most commonly put the
court out of jurisdiction, and remit it to the spiritual law, to
determine to whom it belongeth of right; but I take that to
be by a custom, and a favor of the law, and not of a mere
right, as of the law of God. And therefore if the parliament would ordain, that the right of church-yards, and of
all things in them, should be tried in the king's courts, I
think the statute might well do it. But, as I have said
before, the parliament will not extend their power to many
things, that they might do if they would (I think), and
especially in these matters they will not. And surely as
well the parliament as the king's courts, of the king's bench
and common pleas, and all the common law (as I suppose)
have been and be as favourable to the spiritual jurisdiction,
as well in such church-yards, tithes, offerings, and such
other, as any law hath been; insomuch that in the king's
bench and common pleas they will suffer no issue to be
joined, especially betwixt person and person, whereby the
right of tithes might be tried; howbeit that in the exchequer

---

* It seems that the rector or vicar may cut them down to repair the
parsonage or vicarage house, or the pews belonging to either. He may
likewise take botes for repairing the barns and outhouses belonging to the
house. And Lindwood says, if the nave of the church wants repairing,
the rector or vicar will do well not to be difficult in granting leave to cut
down a tree or two for that use. Lind. 267. But if the trees are cut
down for any other purposes, the persons cutting them down may be restrained by injunction. 2 Atk. 217. May be indicted upon the statute 35
Ed. 1; 11 Co. 49. May be sued in an action of trespass at common law.
2 Roll. Abr. 337. Or be proceeded against in the spiritual court.

some time they have done otherwise. And for a farther proof, that the parliament may order. a church-yard, and trees and grass,. as is aforesaid, some make this reason; they say it is enacted by the statute 15 of Rich. II., ch. 5, that lands that be made church-yards, and be hallowed and made burials without licence of the king and chief lords, shall be in case of mortmain : and they say, that of that it followeth, that if the king or lord enter, for that the church-yard was made against the statute, that the hallowing thereby is annulled, for else (they say) the statute should be void. And if the statute have power to annul the hallowing, made against the statute, they say more stronger it may order the trees and grass that be growing upon it, because they be temporal, as is said before. And in that case if the lord enter by reason of the statute, and the person putteth him out, and the lord bring assise, and the person pleadeth, that it is a church-yard, and demand judgment, if the court will hold plea thereof, and then the lord sheweth how he entered by force of the said statute, and pleadeth in certain; that is a good plea to give the court jurisdiction. And thus I suppose verily that the parliament may order the trees and grass in a church-yard, as I have said, and yet the ground to remain still hallowed, as it did before.

CHAP. VI.—*Concerning the power of the parliament against the spirituality.*

Stud. I suppose also, that it may be enacted by authority of parliament, that if a spiritual man suffer his houses to decay and die : that his successor shall have remedy in the king's court, against his executors, and that it may be prohibited, that no suit of dilapidation should be hereafter taken in the spiritual court, for it is brought to have amends for the waste and decay done in houses by his predecessor, which is all temporal, and belongeth to the king's courts, as wastes and trespass do. And howbeit, that no action lieth for the successor in such case for the waste at the common law :* yet that is not sufficient to prove, that an action may lie therefore at the spiritual laws : for if a person of a church make a lease for term of years, and the lessee doth waste, in that case the person shall have no remedy at the common law, and yet he shall not therefore have any remedy at the spiritual law.† And also in divers statutes it appeareth, that if a man have judgment in the spiritual law to do penance, as is enjoined him, that the judges spiritual may not turn that penance into money, unless the party will freely ask it ;‡ lest they might by that means give judgment of temporal things. And if they may not turn penance into money, but by the free will of the party ; then more stronger, they may not hold plea in this matter, where none other thing is in variance but waste of houses, and where are demanded damages, as was in the prohibition of waste at the common law : and therefore some men say, that a *præmunire facias*, or a *prohibition* lieth in this case, at this day, if the grounds of the law were thoroughly looked upon ;§ howbeit, because of the custom so long used and suffered to the contrary, peradventure it were not good to alter the law therein without parliament; but they think verily that the parliament may well alter it ; and to enforce their reason they say, that since the court christian may not by the law award damages for beating of a clerk, but only put

---

* Actions have been and may be brought upon the custom of the realm in the king's court for dilapidations. 3 Lev. 268; Cart. 244.

† Ante, 101.

‡ In the days of popery the ecclesiastics for a little advantage were used to enjoin pecuniary penances, and to demand them as their just dues. Whereupon the statute of *articuli cleri*, 9 Ed. 2, st. 1, c. 2, was made, which entirely prohibited this practice; but further provided, that if prelates enjoined corporal penance, and the party to be punished would upon his own accord redeem such penance for money, it should be allowed. By virtue therefore of this provision, money may be taken as a commutation for corporal penance, and if it is not paid, a suit may be instituted for it in the spiritual court. 4 B. C. 217.

§ It is most clear, that a prohibition will not lie, as the ecclesiastical court has undoubted cognizance of dilapidations, and may decree satisfaction to be made for them out of the ecclesiastical or patrimonial goods of the person suffering such dilapidations. Lind. 250; Gibson, 753; 3 B. C. 92.

him to penance for laying violent hands upon the clerk, that more stronger they may not in this case award damages for the waste, that is nothing else but a temporal offence.*

CHAP. VII.—*Concerning the authority of the parliament and the spirituality.*

Stud. If it were ordained by statute, that no priest should wear any cloth made out of the realm, nor above such a price, upon a certain pain, or that chaplains shall not take above so much for their salary, I suppose that these statutes were good, because they concern the ordering of temporal things; but ·to appoint the fashion of their garments, or their tonsure, it is more doubt whether the parliament may set pain upon it or not.

Doct. It hath not been seen, that any penal statutes have been made by parliament concerning apparel of the clergy in this realm, for that hath always been ordered by the con-vocation.† And also it appeareth in the statute made in the _36_ Edw. III., c. 8,‡ that when default was found by the commons for excessive wages of chaplains, that the parlia-ment did not order the wages, but the king and his lords, at the petition of the commons, moved the archbishop of Canterbury thereof; and thereupon he and other bishops afterward informed the parliament, that they had set the wages in certain, and that no chaplain˙ should take more than they had appointed, upon a pain by them limited; and if any spiritual men gave more, etc., they to forfeit the double to certain uses by the convocation appointed. And that no chaplain should remove ˙from one diocese to another without letters of the ordinary, from whose diocese they re-moved. And it was then ordained by the parliament, that no temporal man should give more wages than the bishops

---

* 2 Inst. 492; ante, 303.

† The principal canons which respect the habit of clergymen are a con-stitution of Archbishop Stratford, in the year 1343, in the reign of king Edward the Third, and the 74th canon of the canons in the year 1603.

‡ Post. 317; repealed.

had assigned, upon pain to forfeit as much to the king, as in the said statute appeareth. And also the statute willeth farther, that he that findeth him grieved against that ordinance, shall have his remedy in the chancery; but it appeareth not, that there should be any remedy thereupon at the common law.

Stud. The virtue of spiritual men, and the favour of the realm to them, and their wisdom, policy, and high authority be and have been great in this realm, whereby many things have been forborne, that might lawfully have been done, as I suppose. And in the statute made in the 3 Hen. V. wages of chaplains were set in certain by the parliament: and truth it is, that by the said statute of 36 Edw. III.,* ch. 9, it is enacted, That whosoever findeth him grieved against the said ordinance, made of the said wages, shall have remedy in the chancery, as thou sayest; and therefore it followeth thereupon, that if chaplains may by authority of the parliament be lawfully put to answer in the chancery before the chancellor, which sitteth there only by the king's authority, that they may as well upon a reasonable cause be put to answer by authority of the parliament after the process of the common law.·

Doct. By *subpœna*, which is the process used in chancery, the person shall not be arrested, but be only warned to appear.† And it is directly against the canons, that a priest should be arrested, and peradventure at the making of the said statute, the parliament had respect thereto, and thought it reasonable, that they should rather be put to answer in chancery, where their bodies should not be arrested, than at the common law, where they might be arrested.‡

Stud. Though the person shall not be arrested by a *subpœna*, yet if he appear not in the end he shall be proclaimed rebel, and then thereupon his body shall be arrested.§ And.

---

* These statutes are repealed by 21 Jac, c. 28.
† 3 B. C. 443.
‡ See Statutes 50 Ed. 3, c. 5, and 1 R. 2, c. 15.
§ 3 B. C. 444.

also if the party will not perform the judgment given upon
the *subpœna*, there is none other execution in the Chancery,
but to commit him to prison till he have performed it ;* and
therefore (as it seemeth) the parliament regarded not that
point. Wherefore I suppose rather, that the statute was
made as to that article upon this consideration, that because
upon a decree made by the convocation,† there lieth no
action at the Common law, but at the Spiritual law, and
because this matter concerned giving of wages, which were
things temporal, it was thought reasonable that the offenders
against the decree made in the convocation, should be put
to answer in the Chancery, which is the king's court : bul
it might as well have been enacted, that they should have
been put to answer at the Common law as in the Chancery,
if the parliament would, as I suppose. But to that point,
that thou hast spoken of before, that it is against the canons
of the church, that a priest should in any cases be arrested.‡
The Common law pretendeth, that the king, as in the right
of his crown, and by his Common laws, hath that authority,
and so it is daily put in execution. And if the Common
law be so already, then there needeth no statute to be made
of it. Nevertheless, because our intent now at this time is
to speak only, what the parliament may do concerning the
spirituality, and what not, therefore I will no farther speak
of that matter but only this, that if there be offence in them,
that execute the Common law therein, that it is a great
marvel, that spiritual men have done no more to reform it,
than they have done; and if there be no offence therein,
then were it good, that it were so openly known, that all
scrupulosity of conscience might be avoided. For as it
standeth now, there resteth in some persons, that execute
the law therein, a doubt in conscience ; and by reason of
that doubt they offend, that should not offend, if the matter were plainly declared. For then would they either

---

* 1 Harr. Chan. Prac. 316.
† Dav. 70.
‡ Ante, 317.

clearly cease, or else proceed according to the law with good authority.

CHAP. VIII.—*Concerning the authority of the parliament and the spirituality.*

Stud. If there were a schism in the papacy, who were right wise pope, the king in his parliament, as the high sovereign over the people, which hath not only charge on the bodies, but also on the souls of his subjects, hath power for the quietness and surety of his realm to ordain and determine, who shall be in this realm holden for right wise pope, and may command, that no man spiritual nor temporal shall name any other to be pope, but him that is so authorised in the parliament; nor sue to any other as pope, but only to him. And a statute of like effect was made in the 2 Rich. II., ch. 7,* where pope Urban was adjudged in the parliament to be lawfully chosen pope. And the parliament, for appeasing divisions that might rise in the realm by such a schism in the papacy, may set a remedy; why then may not the king and his parliament in like wise, as well to the strength of the faith, and to the health of the souls of many of his subjects, as to save his realm from being noted of heresy, search the cause of such division as is now in the realm by diversities of sects and opinions; and to know also by whom, and by what occasion the noise hath arisen, that there should be so many heresies in this realm as are noted to be : and whether there be such heresies or not, and not to put any to answer thereupon after the process of the law; but charitably to examine the truth therein, and thereupon by their wisdoms to devise some charitable way for unity and peace. And great reward shall they have of God, that put their hands to avoid the great danger that is like to fall to many souls, as well of men spiritual as temporal, if this division continue long. And as far as I have heard, all the articles that be misliked in this behalf, sowneither against the

---

* Post. 320; obsolete.

worldly honour, worldly power, or worldly riches of
spiritual men ; but to express the articles I hold it not most
expedient. And verily if. it be true that some have
reported, many of them be so far against the truth, that I
suppose no christian man will hold them, believing them to
be true : but that they do it for some other consideration.
And though they do not well in that doing, how good
soever the consideration be, for no evil is to be done that
good should follow ; yet they do not so evil, as if they held
'them, believing them also to be true ; nor it will not be so
hard to remove them from it, as it would be, if they did
believe them indeed. For if it be so, that they believe
them not, then the cause removed, it is to think, that they
would be lightly reformed : and therefore if it were ordained
for a law, that every curate at the death of every of their
parishioners, should say for their souls in audience *Placebo*
and *Dirige*, and mass, without taking any thing therefore :*
and that they should also at a certain time, there to be
assigned by parliament, as it were once in a month, or as
shall be thought convenient, do in likewise, and pray
especially for the souls of their parishioners, and for all
christian souls, and for the king and the whole realm :†
and religious houses to do after the same manner, I suppose, that in short time there would be but few, that would
say, there were no purgatory. And in likewise if it were
ordered so by the pope, that there might be certain general
pardons of full remission in divers parts of the realm, which
the people might have for saying certain orisons and
prayers, without paying any money for it, it is not unlike,
but in short time there would be very few, that would find
any default at pardons :‡ for verily it is a great comfort to

* Ante, 221.
† Ante, 31, 208.
‡ In the dark ages of ignorance and superstition, the Pope had great
power in the management of affairs both civil and ecclesiastical here in
England. The title he assumed, and which was thought to belong to him,
was that of vicar general under God. His decrees were considered as just,
and his opinions infallible. In short, he was looked up to as one that had

all christian people to remember, that our Lord loved his
people so much that he would to their relief and comfort,
leave behind him so great a treasure, as is the power to
grant pardons : which, as I suppose, next unto the treasure
of his precious body in the sacrament of the altar,* may be
accounted among the greatest.   And therefore he laboured
greatly to his own hurt, and to the great heaviness of all
other also, that would endure himself to prove, that there
was no power left by God.   And I suppose verily that if
such free pardons were granted (as I have spoken of
before) and that then other pardons were afterward granted,
to have the aid of the people for some charitable cause, as
to resist the Turk, or such other, that the people would as
diligently receive those pardons to be partakers of the good
deed, as they would be, if there were no such free pardons
granted before.   And I think verily, that if the king's
grace, and his parliament, look not upon these matters, it
will be hard to tell who shall be able to do it.   And under
this manner Naitanus, king of Picts, took great labour and
diligence for the appeasing of the division and variance,
that was amongst his subjects (as well spiritual as temporal) for the due time of keeping the Easter.   For some
men in that variance kept Easter, when other kept Palm

---

a right to do and say just what he pleased.   Of this power the Pope did not
fail to make a handle. He turned it entirely to his own pecuniary advantage,
and the benefit of-the holy see; so that it is scarcely to be believed what
large sums of money were drained annually out of this kingdom in the
purchase of bulls, indulgences, etc. However, this trade was too shock-
ing to be endured in any state but that of absolute ignorance and blind devotion. Accordingly, when letters began to flourish, and the minds of
Englishmen were by degrees enlightened by learning and the sciences,
they soon perceived that the tyranny and encroachments of papal Rome
were horrid in the extreme. They therefore began to oppose them : and
oppose them they did, with such firmness and success, aided, no doubt, by
the hand of providence, that in the happy and pious reign of Elizabeth the
reformation was effected, an æra which gave a fatal blow to the papal
power both as to religion and government within this realm.

* See stat. 30 Car. 2, cap. 1, which requires a declaration against the
doctrine of transubstantiation.

21

Sunday; and that was seen some time in one house.* In
which schism many great clerks and holy men were of
several opinions, insomuch that the blessed man Saint
Aidan, which was a holy bishop, erred long in the due
time of keeping of Easter, and had many followers, and
yet was he no heretic. For that that he did therein, he did
with meekness, and as he thought stood according to the
truth : and therefore there was but little offence in him.
For appeasing of this schism,† the said king Naitanus sent
messengers to Saint Colfrid, then being abbott of the monasteries of Saint Peter and Paul, that be upon the rivers of
Tyne and Tweed, and whereas venerable Bede was
brought up, to be instructed in the due time of keeping
Easter, and of the tonsure of clerks, which was then also
in variance, whereupon the said holy man Colfrid wrote a
letter unto the said king Naitanus, declaring unto him, by
many authorities of scripture, the very due time of keeping
Easter, and shewed his mind also in the said tonsures : and
when the said letter was read before the king and his lords,
and that the tenure thereof was plainly interpretate and declared unto him, he rose up from among his lords, and
kneeled down upon his knees, and thanked Almighty God,
that had sent him such a gift out of the country of England.
And it is not to think, that he did this, intending to give
sentence therein by his own authority, for that belonged
not to him, but he did it to know the truth, and that he
might thereupon shew his favour to the better part. And
if the king's grace would in this case endeavour himself to
know the truth of the cause of this division, I suppose that
he shall in some article shew his favour to the one part,
and in some other article to the other part. Also when the
heresy of Enticetis‡ rose at Constantinople, which erred in
the Trinity, the blessed man Saint Theodore, then arch-

---

* Vide the statute 24 Geo. 2, c. 23, s. 3, which points out the time when
the feast of Easter shall be celebrated, in conformity to a decree of the
council of Nice.
  † Ante, 32.
  ‡ Ante, 195.

bishop of Canterbury, to the intent he would keep the church of England from that error, gathered all the clergy together, and examined them diligently what they thought concerning the articles of the heresy : and when he found them all stedfast in the catholick faith, he wrote a letter of their belief; and for instruction of them that should come after, sent it to Rome ; and the effect of his letter was this : "We believe and constantly confess after holy fathers, to be verily and truly, the Father, the Son, and the Holy Ghost, a Trinity in Unity, and a Unity consubstantial in Trinity, that is, one God in three persons consubstantial of equal glory and honour." And among other things that he wrote, which pertained to the faith, he said afterward : "We also accept the holy and universal sine synodals of holy fathers : and we accept and glorify our Lord Jesu Christ as they glorified him, nothing adding or diminishing ; and we glorify God the Father without beginning, and his only Son gotten of the Father before the worlds, and the Holy Ghost proceeding of the Father and the Son, so as they cannot be spoken as they, that we have remembered, the holy apostles and prophets and doctors have preached and taught. And methinketh, that these examples should somewhat encourage them, that now may do good in this evil and perilous time, to follow somewhat after, and every man after his degree is, to do the best that he can therein to help it, not regarding worldly honour, worldly riches, nor singular profit : but only the honour of God, and the love of their neighbours, and health of their souls. And if they do so, undoubtedly the work shall prosper well in their hands. And let no man, that may do good in this matter, suffer it to over pass as though it pertained not to him : for Almighty God hath given a commandment to every man upon his neighbour. And to encourage them-selves yet the more unto it, let them remember the words, that be spoken in the first book of the Revelations of Saint Bridget, the 58th chapter, where our Lord Jesu, among

* Ante, 195.

other things, said to our lady thus : " I would (said he) if it were possible, suffer for every man such a pain as I once suffered for all men upon the cross, so that they might come to the inheritance promised." Happy be they then, that help souls to that inheritance, that our Lord desired so much to have them come unto. And sometime it hath been brought about by fair means, that could not be done by rigour and compulsion. And if my lords and masters spiritual will needily forthwith their streight corrections and punishments, without finding some provision, that the minds of the people may somewhat be eased, in such things as they have misliked and grudged at in times past ; it is to fear that there will not follow so good fruit of it as there would do, if they would do it ; and that they would shew themselves evidently to do nothing but only of a zeal and love unto the people. And it is a doubt to some men, whether some of the things that the people mislike and find default at; be occasions active or passive to the people to offend : but whether they be the one or the other, charity would (as it seemeth) that some diligence should be put to amove them, though percase they were not evil but indifferent, or peradventure good of themself.

CHAP. IX.—*Concerning the authority of the parliament and the spirituality.*

Stud. If it were enacted by the parliament, that if a man call another a thief or a murderer, that an action should lie thereupon at the Common law, and that no suit should lie thereupon at the Spiritual law ;* I think it were a good statute, for the matters whereupon the words rise are only to be determined by the Common law.† And so it is if a man

---

* 1 Roll. Abr. 74; Cro. Jac. 214.

† But calling a man whoremaster, 2 Salk 692; a cuckold, 3 Cro. 110; a cuckoldy knave, Cro. Car. 399; or calling a woman a whore, 2 Salk. 696; Goulsb. 172; Ld. Raym. 1136 (except in London and Southwark); a jilt, a strumpet, Str. 823; or a bawd, is only suable in the spiritual court. So likewise the defaming of a clergyman in any point relating to the discharge of his office, is properly triable in the spiritual court, as to call him an adulterer or an heretic. 1 Cro. 502, 94.

call another villain, an action lieth thereon at Common law if he be free,* and not at the Spiritual law; because the right of the villainage may not be tried but at the Common law; and most men say, that if there be an indictment of felony at the Common law, that then there lieth no suit thereof in the Spiritual law, so that there needeth no statute to be make in that point.

Doct. If a statute were made, that an action should lie at the Common law of such words as a man hath any loss or worldly hindrance by, though they have before time been used to be sued only in the spiritual court, thinkest thou the statute were good?

Stud. I think the statute were good; and most commonly upon such words some worldly loss or hindrance one way or other doth follow; but I think that in those cases the parliament may not prohibit, but that they that list may also take their suits at the Spiritual law, if they will, so that the Spiritual law make no recompence to the party.† Also of all annuities, whether they have beginning by prescription, composition real or otherwise, I suppose it may be enacted, that the suit shall be taken only in the king's court, and not in the spiritual court, for nothing is to be recovered in such suits but money, which is temporal in whose hands soever it come, spiritual to temporal.‡

CHAP. X.—*Concerning the authority of the parliament as to the spirituality.*

Stud. If it were enacted, that no religous person should

---

* Since villainage is taken away, it should seem that no action can lie for calling another villain.

† The Ecclesiastical Court, as we have seen before, cannot in any case award damages. Ante, 316, and see Wats., c. 30. For defamatory words, penance is enjoined at the discretion of the ordinary. 2 Burn's Ecl. Law, 124.

‡ When a parson sues in the Spiritual court for a pension or an annuity, claimed by prescription, it is the safest way for him to libel generally as in the common case of a pension, and not to lay a prescription, for if he goes upon a prescription, and the prescriptive right comes in question, a prohibition will issue. Strange, 879, Dr. Gouche *v.* The Bishop of London.

receive into the habit of their religion any child under a
certain age to be appointed by the parliament, and that after
this entry he should not be removed from the place that he
was received in within a year after upon a certain pain,
without assent of his friends; I think it were a good statute; for that statute should not prohibit entry into religion.
For if it did so, I suppose it were not to be observed : but
it ordereth the manner of entry into religion for such infants
which is right expedient for the commonwealth; and a statute of like effect is made for the four orders of friars in the
4 Hen. IV.,* where the four provincials of the said four
orders were sworn, by laying their hands upon their breasts
in open parliament, to observe the said statute. And upon
the same grounds some say, that if it were enacted, that no
man upon a certain pain should affie the daughter in her
farther's house, without assent of the father, it were a good
statute ; and yet a statute hath no authority to prohibit, nor
to confirm no right of matrimony; but as the church prohibiteth it, or confirmeth it. And therefore if it were prohibited, that no lord's son should affie an husbandman's
daughter, or such other, and if he did, the affiance to be
void, I think that statute were void. But if the statute were,
that no lord's son, upon a pain, should make affiance with
any woman, that is a stranger born, without the king's
licence, I think that statute were good : for it prohibiteth
not matrimony, but setteth an order after what manner it
shall be made, and that under such form as may haply be
necessary for the surety of the realm. And of a like effect
thereto is the law, that the king's widow shall not marry
without the king's licence, and that she shall be sworn
thereto in the Chancery when she is endowed. And like
law is also, that the lord shall have the marriage, or the
value of the marriage or sometimes the double value of the
marriage of his ward by knight's service.† And also if a
man marry a bond women without licence, the lord by the

---

* Ante, 32, 208.
† Ante, 26.

Common law shall have an action of trespass against him that marrieth her. And all these laws be good, for merely they prohibit not marriage, no more should a statute do for entry into religion : as me seemeth. For it prohibiteth not entry into religion ;* but it prohibiteth that none should be received into the habit before his years of discretion, and that after his entry he shall be ordered in such manner, that if he will after be professed it shall rise of his own free will, and of a love to serve God, and not by any sinister means, nor coloured persuasions.

Also, as I suppose, the parliament may well enact, that every man that hath the profit of any offering, by recourse of pilgrims, shall, upon a certain pain, not only set up certain tables to instruct the people under what manner they shall worship the saints, but also to cause certain sermons to be made there yearly to instruct the people, how they shall worship them, so that through ignorance and disordering of themself, they do not rather displease the saints than please them. ·

It may also prohibit, that no miracle shall be noised upon so light occasions as they have been in some places in time past. And they shall not, upon a certain pain, be set up as miracles nor be noised, nor reported as miracles by no man, till they be proved for miracles, under such manner as by the parliament shall be appointed. And it is not unlike, but that many persons grudge more at the abuse of pilgrimages than at the self-pilgrimages. And in likewise of divers other articles, if the truth were groundly searched. And under this manner it hath been already enacted by parliament, to the strength of the faith, that no man shall presume to preach without licence of the diocesan, except certain persons excepted in the statute, as appeareth in the second year of king Hen. IV.† And under this manner the parliament may ordain many good laws for strength of the faith, and for the good order of all the people, as

* Ante, 245.
† Repealed by 25 Ed. 3, c. 14; 1 H. 6, c. 12; 1 Eliz., c. 1; 29 Car. 2, c. 9.

well spiritual as temporal, though it judge not upon the
right of things that be mere spiritual. And all these diversities, and many other more than I can rehearse now,
they that be learned in the laws of the realm be especially
bounden to know, that they may instruct the parliament
when need shall require, what they may lawfully do concerning the spiritual jurisdiction, and what not. And therefore spiritual men are bound charitably to hear their opinions therein, and what they think be immediately grounded
upon the law of God, or upon the law of reason, and what
not. For commonly the parliament hath over those laws
no direct power, but to strengthen them, and to make them
to be more surely kept it hath good power. And if spiritual men, and temporal men, would charitably lay their
heads together, and fully determine what the parliament
may do, as well concerning the spiritual jurisdiction as the
temporal, taking these additions as little titleings, whereby
they by their wisdom may call to their remembrance greater
things, so that hereafter it shall not stand in the case as it
doth now, that when the parliament hath made a law concerning the spirituality, that spiritual men shall not say,
it bindeth not in conscience, as many have done in time
past, and yet do to this day : I think verily that there
would nothing do more good to appease such variances,
schisms, and divisions as be now abroad in the realm. And
then also would all men, as well spiritual as temporal, rather
take heed to themself, to see that they did nothing to give
occasion to the parliament to extend his power upon them
or their possessions, than to resist or deny the authority of
the parliament.   .

CHAP. XI.—*Concerning the authority of the parliament
and the spirituality.*

Doct. Whether may the parliament prohibit, that no
ordinary upon a certain pain shall admit none to the order
of priesthood, except he be sufficiently learned?

Stud. I am in doubt in this question, and the thing that

causeth me to doubt therein is this, if it were enacted, as thou sayest, and after an action were brought upon the penalty, and the ordinary would plead, that he that was made priest was sufficiently learned; and thereupon an issue were joined, that issue should be tried by twelve men, and as it seemeth, it were not reasonable, that twelve men, which commonly be unlearned, should try whether a man were sufficiently learned to be a priest, for they have no knowledge therein. And therefore if any such penalty should be set by parliament, it seemeth that it must be farther enacted, that if the issue were joined (as is said before) that then it should be tried by spiritual men, or temporal men that be sufficiently learned thereto, or by both.

Doct. But thinkest thou then, that the parliament may ordain, that spiritual men shall be compelled to pass upon inquests? It seemeth, that were against the law of God, and against the perfection of their order, and to break them from the devotion of contemplation, that is requisite to them. For Saint Paul saith in his second espistle to Timothy, the second chapter: "*Nemo militans Deo, implicat se negotiis secularibus;* that is to say, "Let no man that hast set himself to serve God, intryke himself in secular business." Which words be specially spoken of priests. And therefore it seemeth, he should do against the saying of Saint Paul, that would compel priests to go upon inquests.

Stud. Verily there is a writ in the Register* (which is a book of the law of England) that no sheriff shall impanel any priests upon any inquest, and that writ may every priest have, that will sue for it. And I think right well, that that writ is grounded upon the law of the realm: taking in that point his effect upon the law of God.† And therefore I think, that the parliament may not enact, that priests should go universally upon inquests; but to enact, that in this special case, which is not mere temporal, but to enquire of

---

* Reg. 179.
† Lamb. Just. 369; Trials per Pais, 86.

the sufficiency of learning, and that to a good and necessary purpose, I suppose the parliament may assign them to it without breaking the liberty of the church. And so they be many times upon a writ to enquire *de jure patronatus,* where priests and laymen shall be joined together to enquire of the right of the patronage.* And methinketh, they might do in like case here, either by themself, or to be joined with laymen.†

Doct. There they be called by the authority of the ordinary, and here they should be called by the temporal authority.

Stud. Whether they be called by spiritual authority, or by temporal authority, their business is all one. For as great let is it to devotion and contemplation, when they be called thereto by the bishop, as when they be called thereto by the king. And though, as thou sayest, the bishops shall command to appear in that case, yet it is by the king's law, that he shall do so : which law the convocation may not alter nor change, but the parliament might change it with a cause : for it pertaineth to the ordering of temporal inheritance, that is to say, to the ordering the patronage, and of presentments of advowsons, which be temporal.

Doct. I can in no wise see how it may stand with the law of God, that the parliament should compel spiritual men to go upon inquest. And therefore if such a statute should be made, the inquest must be taken all of temporal men, that have sufficient learning thereto : and yet I regard not this point so much in this question, as I do that the matter of itself is so mere spiritual, that the parliament hath no power to set any pain upon it. For as it seemeth, if it might do that, it might as well set a pain upon the tonsures of clerks, or upon the order of the service, or what use they should keep, and that I suppose thou thinkest it may not, and methinketh it may no more do it in this case.

---

* So they may be joined with laymen in mandates for inquisitions to be made of dilapidations of houses or other things belonging to ecclesiastical benefices. Lind. 254.

† Vin. Abr., title Presentation:

Stud. I think well it be as thou sayest in those cases ꞉ but in this case, that is so necessary for the good order of the king's subjects, and for the commonwealth, methinketh they may, for if curates have virtue and cunning, commonly the people be virtuous, and virtue is the most chief and principal branch of the commonwealth. And therefore for increase thereof, methinketh that the parliament may well set a pain, although there were no spiritual law made in that point before, as well as it may of infants, that be received into the habit of religion, whereof mention is made before in the tenth addition. But in this case, since the spiritual law is already, that none shall be made priests, but they that be sufficiently lettered, methinketh that the parliament may much more the rather do it.* And therefore, if the people would not assent to keep an holiday, that were ordained by the church, I suppose that the parliament if they thought it reasonable to be kept, might set a pain upon all them that would not obey unto it. And that it might do likewise upon all other laws, that be made by the church for the good order of the people, though it might not percase make a new law in the self points, for that should not be a breaking of the liberty of the church, but rather an affirmance of it.

Doct. I feel thy conceit well; howbeit I cannot fully as yet, assent unto it: and therefore I pray thee give me a sparing therein, and at a better leisure, I shall with goodwill shew thee farther of my mind therein. And now I will ask thee another question.

CHAP. XII.—*Concerning the authority of the parliament and the spirituality.*

Doct. It was asked of me but late, if certain waste ground, whereof was never any profit taken, and that lay within no parish, but in some forest, or that is newly won from the sea, were brought into arable land, whether the parliament

---

* Ante, 189.

might appoint, who should have the tithe thereof; and he that asked me the question thought it might. I pray thee shew me thy conceit, what thou thinkest therein?

Stud. I think that if the freehold be in the king, that he may assign the tithes thereof to whom he will: and if the freehold be in a common person, that he may do likewise.* But then I think, that if that common person do not assign the tithes so, as it may stand conveniently to the maintenance of the service of God, that the parliament may do it, and order the tithes to the increase of God's service, as they shall think convenient.

Doct. I cannot see how the parliament, nor yet the party should have authority to meddle with tithes, that be spiritual, and pertain alway to the spiritual jurisdiction. And therefore I suppose, that in this case the archbishop, as sovereign head over the spirituality, should in this case have the ordering of the tithes, as things spiritual to whom none other hath right: and neither the king nor no common person.

Stud. Though tithes be spiritual, yet the assignment of the tithes to other is a temporal act, which the parliament with a cause may order, as it may do all temporal things within the realm: and that the king, or any other, that hath the freehold of such waste grounds as be in no parish, may assign the tithes thereof to whom they will, it may appear thus: Before parishes were divided,† and before that it was ordained by the law of the church,‡ that every

---

* 1 Roll. Abr. 657; 2 Inst. 647

† For the æra of the division of parishes, see 1 B. C. 111; 3 Burn's Ecl. Law, p. 59; 2 Wils. 182.

‡ It is probable the author alludes here to the council of Lateran, Anno Domini 1179, Anno 25 H. 2, which has often been mistaken by many of our ancient authors to be the time when this law was made. The fact is, that tithes were not assigned to any spiritual person or church in particular before the year 1200, which is twenty-one years after the council of Lateran was held. In the year 1200, Pope Innocent the Third wrote a decretal epistle dated at Lateran; the purport of which was, that for the time to come the tithes of all parishes should be paid to the persons having *curam animarum* in the respective parishes. This epistle was thought very reasonable and just, and accordingly was well received, and became

man should pay his tithes to his own church ;* every man
might have paid his tithes to what church he would, and
might one year have given it to one church, and another
year to another ;† or have granted them to one church for
ever if he would. And like as every man, before the said
severing of parishes, might have given his tithes to what
church he would, because he was bound to no church in
certain : so may they do now, that have lands that lie in no
parish ; for they be at liberty to assign them to what church
they will, as all men were before the said law made, that
tithes should be paid to the proper church. And if the
archbishop should have right to them, because no man can
of right claim them, then before the said law made, arch-
bishops had right to all the tithes, within their provinces :
for no man had right to any tithes, but by the assignment
of the owners. And therefore if the freehold, in this case
that thou hast put, be in the king, then he shall assign the
tithes where he will : and in like wise of other of his subjects, as I have said before.

Doct. Thou speakest in this case as thou were learned
in the Spiritual law, for these matters pertain thereto,‡ and
not to the laws of the realm.

Stud. I speak therein according to the old law and custom of the realm, which yet continueth in such places, as
be out of any parish, as it did before parishes were limited,
and before the said law was made, that tithes should be paid
to their proper churches : and that there is such a custom,
partly it appeareth in a case, that is in the laws of England,

---

in process of time part of the law of the land. It was this decretal then
which ordained that every man should pay tithes to his own church ; and
the circumstance of its being dated at Lateran appears to be the foundation of the mistake I have mentioned above. See 2 Inst. 641.

° Post. 335.

† In this opinion Lord Coke, Hobart, and many other respectable law-
yers concur with our author; but Dr. Prideaux differs from him. See
Prid. 302.

‡ By the canon law, all tithes arising in an extra-parochial place belong
to the bishop of the diocese in which the place lies. 2 Inst. 647.

which happened long time since the said law was made,
that tithes should be paid to their proper churches.

Doct. I pray thee shew me what case that is.

Stud. In the twenty-second year of king Edward the
third, in the book of Assise it appeare'h, that the king
granted the tithes of certain asserts, that were newly taken
out of the forest of Rock, to a provost, and he thereupon
brought a *Scire facias* against divers, that took the said
tithes, returnable into the Chancery; and there exception
was taken, that the suit pertained to the spiritual court, and
not to the Chancery : and it was answered again, that that
was to be understood, where the suit was taken against
them that ought to pay the tithes, and not where it was
brought against them, that were wrongful takers of the
tithes. And thereupon the defendants were put to answer,
and pleaded to an issue, which was sent down into the
King's Bench to be tried according to the law, and there
the defendants made default : whereupon the plaintiffs
prayed execution. And in this case Thorpe said, "That
the old law hath been alway, that the king in such case
should assign the tithes where he would." And that saying I take to be understood, where the freehold is in the
king, as I have said before. And though the said case be
not judged, yet it appeareth thereby, that the king made
assignment of tithes, which was admitted to be good, so
that the parliament shall not need to meddle therein, unless
it be his pleasure to assign them by authority of his parliament : as he may do, if he will, to make his letters patents
to be of the mcre higher record than they should be without the parliament.

Doct. Truth it is, that the king and other owners and
possessioners of land sometime paid their tithes to what
church they would ;* but when it was ordained by the
church, that tithe should be paid to their own church, then
the people were bounden by that ordinance to pay them according, and so they did ; and therefore if there were a law

* Ante, 333.

made now by the church of such particular tithes, as yet remain still out of any parish, that they should be paid to the parish next adjoining, or to the ordinary, or to the metropolitan, or in such other manner as the church should think reasonable; methinketh it were a good law, and ought to be obeyed as well of the particular tithes, as it was first of all tithes generally. And if the church may make a law therein, then methinketh the parliament should have no power to make any law therein.

Stud. When the church had ordained, that the tithes of every man should be paid to their own church, and the people received that law, and paid their tithes according: then by that assent the law was confirmed: and if the church would not have made that law, I think the parliament might: for it was for the rest and quietness of all the people: and then none might have refused that law so made by parliament: but to the law made by the church some did not obey, but paid their tithes to other churches as they did before. And those churches unto this day have good right to those tithes, as portions belonging to their churches, though the ground lie not within their parish;* and so hath the king and the owners and possessors of such waste grounds,† that be out of all parishes at this day, good right to assign the tithes thereof, where they will.‡ For as to those grounds they never received any law to the contrary: and so I think it bindeth them not in that behalf. And no more should any new law do, that were made by the church of such tithes, nor pull the liberty from them to assign them where they will, without their assent. And where thou sayest, that if the church may make a law of a thing, that then the parliament hath no power to make any law therein, I think that ground holdeth not; for if the

* 2 Black. Com. 29.

† Ante, 331.

‡ See now the stat. 2 and 3 Ed. 6, c. 13, by which it appears that the tithes of cattle depasturing in a waste or common extra-parochial, or if the parish is unknown, are to be given to the parson of the parish where the owner dwells. 2 Inst. 651.

church would grant a dismes to be paid to the king, it were well granted : but if they would not, the parliament may. And in like wise though the church hath made a law, that curates should be resident upon their benefices ;* yet the parliament also hath made a law, that they shall be so,† and both laws stand in good strength and effect, as I suppose. And in like wise it is of the statute of usury,‡ which was made in the tenth year of king Henry the Seventh.

CHAP. XIII.—*Concerning the power of the parliament and the spirituality.*

Doct. Whether may the parliament prohibit, that none ordinary, nor none other, that hath power to visit, shall not take any money or pension of the houses or places, that they visit, at their visitation.

Stud. I think the parliament hath good power to do it. For the money that they receive, though it be given by occasion of a spiritual thing, is temporal, and is under the power of the parliament, as all temporal lands and goods be. And if there be a cause reasonable why they should make that prohibition, then it bindeth as well in conscience as it doth in the law : and an example is thereof by probate of testaments. For though the probate be a thing spiritual, yet the parliament hath of late, as it might lawfully do, set a pain, that none shall pay for the probate above a certain sum limited by the statute.§ And also by the statute that is called in Latin *Statutum de Caroli de asportatis religiosorum*, it is enacted, That no house of religion of beyond the sea, should from thenceforth, under colour of visitation,

---

* Vide Athon, 36, and Gibs. 827, on this head.

† See statute 21 H. 8, c. 13, commonly called the statute of non-residence, explained by 25 H. 8, c. 16; 28 H. 8, c. 13, and 33 H. 8, c. 28. It likewise appears to be the intention of the Common law, that a parson should be resident upon his cure as it has provided a writ for his discharge, in case he is chosen to any civil office. 2 Inst. 625.

‡ Abolished, but vide statutes 37 H. 8, c. 9; 13 Eliz., c. 8; 21 Jac. 1, c. 17; 12 Car. 2, c. 13, and 12 Ann., stat. 2, c. 16.

§ The author, I apprehend, here means the statute 21 H. 8, c. 5, an act upon which Dr. Gibson has the following observation, viz., that the fees

or other colour, set any tallage or imposition upon any house of religion, that is subject unto it in England, upon the pain to forfeit all that it hath under the king's power. And the statute will further, That nevertheless the said abbots and priors aliens shall not cease of their visitation within this realm : so that they bear no money nor goods from the houses in England.* And methinketh, that like as the parliament had then power to prohibit, that the abbots and priors aliens should not under colour of visitation or otherwise, set any tallage or imposition upon any house of religion to them subject in England, that the parliament may now as well prohibit, that none under colour of visitation, or otherwise, shall take of any house of religion or church, that they shall visit, any sum of money, or other thing, whatsoever it be. For methinketh, that the reason in the one case, and in the other, is all one.

Doct. It seemeth nay. For at the making of that statute the parliament intended principally to provide, that no goods should be conveyed out of the realm by any religious persons, which they did sometime under colour of visitation : but in this case it needeth not to provide any remedy in that behalf, as it is evident of itself. For there be no goods conveyed out of this realm by reason of such visitations.

Stud. Though the principal intent of the said parliament was to provide, that no goods should be conveyed out of the realm by religious persons :† yet as for a special surety that it should be so, they thought it necessary to prohibit, that the head houses of beyond the sea should not by colour of their visitation in England do it. For they thought that

given by it, are become much too small by the great alteration of the value of money, and the price of things, and, therefore, the rule now is the known and established custom of every place, provided it is reasonable. Gibs. 487. The statute therefore is not at all to be depended upon. But if the reader wishes to know the fees and expences in obtaining the probate of a will, particularly in the prerogative court, he may find them set down in a table by Mr. Lovelass in his Law of Intestacy and Wills, 192.

* Ante, 32, 208; 2 Inst. 583; 587.

† 2 Inst. 583.

22

that was a ready way to bring the money into their hands,
that they might after carry it with them into their country:
and since the parliament had then authority to prohibit, that
the said visitors should not, by colour of their visitations,
gather any tallage or imposition set upon them, that they
visited in England: why might not the parliament now
likewise prohibit, that the visitors, at their visitations, should
gather no such tallage or imposition, as hath been set in
time past upon such houses and churches as they do visit.
For certain it is, that at the beginning of visitations no such
impositions nor pensions were paid : but that they have been
brought up since that time, either at the motion of them that
were visited, to the intent that they might thereby have the
more favour of their visitors, or else by power or compulsion of the visitors, or for their singular lucre, or haply by
both ways. But what way soever it began : if it should
hereafter come to the point, that the visitors at their visitations, by reason of the said impositions or pensions, should
be inclined to any singular affection, and so to forbear the
good reformations, that they ought to look to in the monas-
tries and churches that they visit, whereby evil-doers should
take boldness to continue in evil,* and well-doers be dis-
couraged from their virtuous exercises in the service of God,
I suppose verily, that they that by good authority, and with
a charitable intent, would take the said impositions and pensions from the said visitors, should deserve thereby right
great thank, and reward of God. But I trust, there should
be no such cause to move them to it. And now I intend
thus to make an end of the authority of the parliament for
this time, and will ask of thee but one short question concerning the matter that we treated of in the first addition,
and so commit thee to our Lord.

Doct. What is that?

Stud. It is this : If a curate since the statute of mortuaries, thinking the said statute to be against the liberty of the
church, persuadeth his parishioners to believe, that all they

* Ante, 208.

that keep the statute, stand in the censures of the church, and thereby induceth many of them, specially at the point of death, to recompence him as much as their mortuaries by estimation would have amounted to : whether hath he good right to that, that is given under that manner?

Doct. If it be as thou sayeth, that the statute standeth with conscience, then hath he no right thereto in conscience. For he cometh to it by an unjust means, and grandeth himself for the having of it, upon an untruth : and so the giver is deceived in his gift, and therefore it bindeth not in conscience, though it bind in the law. And I suppose, that though the curate say, as he thinketh therein, that yet it sufficeth not, but that he is bound to restitution, for ignorance, as methinketh, cannot excuse the restitution, though peradventure it may excuse him, that it shall not be in him any deadly sin.

Stud. I think it be as thou sayest, and as it is in this point, it is in divers other articles, upon the said jurisdictions. Wherefore methinketh it would be more plainly declared in many things what belongeth to the one jurisdiction, and what to the other, than it 'is yet, as I have said before, and that hath caused me to treat farther this matter now at this time, than I thought to have done.

Doct. I think it be as thou sayest : but if I might be so bold, I would desire to know thy mind in one thing and no more, and that is this : Of what effect the statute is, that was made the 2 Hen. V., ch. 1, whereby it is enacted, That ordinaries shall have power by the king's commission to inquire of the hospitals of his foundation and of their governance, and to certify the king in his Chancery thereof.* And of hospitals of others foundation they have power to enquire, and do correction after the law of holy church.

Stud. At a leisure I will gladly shew thee my mind therein, but for this time I pray thee hold me excused, for I will no more speak of that matter as now. And thus God of peace and love be alway with us.   Amen.

---

* That is where there are no visitors appointed. See statute 14 Eliz., c. 5, and 2 Burn's Ecl. Law, 289.

TWO PIECES

CONCERNING

SUITS IN CHANCERY

BY SUBPŒNA.

I. A Replication of a Serjeant at the Laws of England, to certain Points alledged by a Student of the said Laws of England,
in a Dialogue in English between a Doctor of Divinity and the
said Student.

II. A little Treatise concerning Writs of SUBPŒNA.

[These pieces are printed from a manuscript in the Cottonian library at the
British Museum. See Cott. MSS. Cleopatra, A. 15. The title at the
beginning of the manuscript is, "A Treatise concerning Sutes in the
Chauncery by *Subpœna;*" to which is added the following notice :
"Founde amongste the bookes of Sir Edward Saunders, late chiefe
"justice of England, and after chiefe baron of the exchequer, and
"noted by his hande writinge to be entitled on the outsyde, *The*
"*Dialogue betweene a Serjaunte at the lawe and Christopher Seinte*
"*Jerman;* and on the inside, *The Answer of this Treatise by*
"*Christopher Seinte Jerman.*"
Both of the pieces were clearly written in the reign of Henry the 8th, soon
after the first edition of the DOCTOR and STUDENT, which I take to have
been first printed by John Rastell in 1523. See Ames' Histor. Account
of Printing, 145.]

(341)

TWO PIECES

CONCERNING

SUITS IN CHANCERY

BY

SUBPŒNA.

PART I.

Here followeth a replication of the serjeant at the laws of England, to certain points alledged by a student of the said laws of England, in a dialogue, in English, between a doctor of divinity and the said student.

A serjeant of the law of England hearing the communication and dialogue between a doctor of divinity, and a student in the laws of England, saith to the doctor in this wise :

Mr. Doctor, after my mind you have right well declared divers laws, that is to say, the law eternal, the law of reason, the law of God, and the law of man. And you, Mr. Student, have right well shewed, how the law of England is grounded upon the law of reason, and have shewed your mind therein right well, against which I intend not to reply. But mine intent is, Mr. Student, to reply against your opinion in one point in a case demanded of you by Mr. Doctor, which is this.* If a man be bound in a single ob-

---

* See Doct. and Stud., dial. 1, ch. 12.—EDITOR.

.(343)

ligation to pay a certain sum of money at a day to the obligee, and the obligor payeth the money at the day and
taketh none acquittance neither the obligation wherein he
is bound; and notwithstanding this he that hath the obligation bringeth an action of debt upon the said obligation
against the obligor; you have said, that in this case the
obligor hath no remedy by the common law at [of] the
realm, and you have shewed the cause why right well, as
it appeareth by your declaration, the which I need not to
rehearse. But you say further in this case, that the defendant may be helped by a subpoena in the king's chancery; and to that I intend to reply. Notwithstanding I
shall first of all move you, that in this case after my mind
the defendant may have remedy at the common law. For
after this payment, if the defendant bring an action of debt
against the obligee and declare upon a prompt, if the obligee will plead that he received the said money for the
contentation [satisfaction] of his obligation, this plea
pleaded in court of record shall discharge the obligor of
the said obligation; and if the obligee will wage his law,
then the obligor is without remedy; and yet he is at no
greater mischief than he should be, if he had lent him the
money without writing, in which case, if the defendant
wage his law, the plaintiff hath no remedy at the common
law, nor yet in the chancery against his wager of law. I
think that in this case the obligee cannot wage his law and
discharge his conscience. For when a man is bound in a
single obligation, there is a condition implied in the law,
that this obligation cannot be discharged but by matter in
writing, or by matter of record. Then if the obligee would
wage his law, thinking that it is a satisfaction of his obligation, that is not so; for the obligation cannot be discharged
but by matter in writing or by matter of record, and so he
cannot wage his law and discharge his conscience after my
mind: but either he must plead in court of record that he
receiveth it in satisfaction of his obligation, and then the
obligor shall be discharged; or else he must repay the
money again, or else he cannot discharge his conscience.

Now to that you say, that this obligor may be helped by a
subpœna in the king's chancery. As to that I say, after my
mind, that it standeth neither with the law of reason, neither
with the law of God, nor yet with the common weal of
the realm, that this man should be helped by a subpœna
in the chancery. First it is not reasonable, that for a
particular man's cause, which hath hurt himself by his own
negligence and by his own folly, that the good common
law of the realm (which is this, that the matter in writing
with or without condition cannot be answered but by matter
in writing or by matter of record) should be made void or
be set at nought by the suit of any particular person made
in the chancery or any other place. But if reformation be
had in this case in the said chancery by a subpœna, it must
needs follow, that this good common law must be made as
void and set at nought. For by a subpœna the plaintiff is
prohibited to sue [at] the common law, and is compelled
to make answer in the chancery, where the obligor shall be
admitted to plead a payment of the debt contained in a
single obligation without writing, which is clean contrary
to the common law; so that if that be admitted for law, the
common law that is contrary to this must needs be no law.
For these two laws, one being contrary to the other, cannot
stand together, but one of them must be as void. Wherefore it must needs follow, that if this law be maintained in
the chancery by a subpœna, the common law, which is
contrary to that, must needs be as void and of none effect.
I marvel much what authority the chancellor hath to make
such a writ in the king's name, and how he dare presume
to make such a writ to let [hinder] the king's subjects to
sue his laws, the which the king himself cannot do righteously; for he is sworn the contrary, and it is said, *hoc possumus quod de jure possumus.* Also the king's judges of
this realm, that be appointed to minister his laws of his
realm be sworn to minister his laws of the realm indifferently
to the king's subjects; and so is not the chancellor. Also
the serjeants at the law be sworn to see the queen's subjects
to be justified by the laws of this realm, determinable by

the king's judges, and not by my lord chancellor. Yet
this notwithstanding, if the king's subjects, upon a surmised
bill put into the chancery, shall be prohibited by a subpœna
to sue according to the laws of the realm, and be compelled
to make answer before my lord chancellor, then shall the
law of the realm be set as void and taken as a thing of none
effect, and the king's subjects shall be ordered by the
discretion of the chancellor and by no law, contrary to all
good reason and all good policy. And so me seemeth,
that such a suit by a subpœna is not only against the law
of the realm, but also against the law of reason. Also me
seemeth, that it is not conformable to the law of God. For
the law of God is not contrary in itself, that is to say, one
in one place, and contrary in another place, if it be well
perceived and understood, as you can tell, Mr. Doctor; but
this law is one in one court, and contrary in another court.
And so me seemeth, that it is not only against the law of the
realm, and against the law of reason, but also against the
law of God. Also me seemeth, that this suit by a subpœna
is against the common weal of the realm. For the common weal of every realm is to have a good law, so that the
subjects of the realm may be justified by the same; and the
more plain and open that the law is, and the more
knowledge and understanding that the subject hath of the
law, the better it is for the common weal of the realm; and
the more uncertain that the law is in any realm, the less and
the worse is it for the common weal of the realm. But if the
subjects of any realm shall be compelled to leave the law
of the realm, and to be ordered by the discretion of one man,
what thing ·may be more unknown or more uncertain?*
But if this manner of suit by a subpœna be maintained, as you,
Mr. Student, would have it, in what uncertainty shall the
king's subjects stand, when they shall be put from the law
of the realm, and be compelled to be ordered by the discretion and conscience of one man! And, namely, forasmuch

---

* Bonum est secundum literas et leges, et non secundum proprium men-
tem judicare. Aristot. in Polit.

as conscience is a thing of great uncertainty, for some men think that if they tread upon two straws that lie across, that they offend in conscience; and some man thinketh that if he lack money and another hath too much, that he may take part of his with conscience; and so divers men, divers conscience; for every man knoweth not what conscience is so well as you, Mr. Doctor. So me seemeth, that if the king's subjects be constrained to be ordered by the discretion and conscience of one man, they should [woud] be put to a great uncertainty, which is against the common weal of a realm. And so me seemeth, it is not only against the common law, but also against the law of reason, against the law of God, and against the common weal of this realm.

Stud. How is it then, that the chancellors of England have used this?

Serj. Verily I think for lack of knowledge of the goodness of the laws of the realm; for most commonly the chancellors of England have been spiritual men, that have had but superficial knowledge in the laws of the realm; and when such a bill hath been made unto them, that such a man should have great wrong to be compelled to pay two times for one thing, the chancellor, not knowing the goodness of the common law, neither the inconvenience that might ensue by the said writ of subpœna, hath temerously directed a subpœna to the plaintiff in the king's name, commanding him to cease his suit that he hath before the king's justices, and to make answer before him in the chancery; and he regarding no law, but trusting to his own writ and wisdom, giveth judgment as it pleaseth himself, and thinketh that his judgment being in such authority, is far better and more reasonable than judgments that be given by the king's justices according to the common law of the realm. In my conceit in this case I may liken my lord chancellor, which is not learned in the laws of the realm, to him that stands in the Vale of White-horse, far from the horse and holdeth the horse, and the horse seemeth and appeareth to him a goodly horse, and well proportioned in every point, and that if he come near to the place where the horse is, he can perceive no horse, nor proportion of any horse. Even so it fareth by my lord chancellor that is not learned in the laws of the realm; for when such a bill is put unto him, it appeareth to him to be a matter of great conscience and requireth reformation; and the matter in the bill appeareth so to him, because he is far from the understanding and the knowledge of the law of the realm, and the goodness thereof; but if he draw near to the knowledge and understanding of the Common law of the realm, so that he may come to the perfect knowledge and goodness of it, he shall well perceive that the matter contained in the bill put to him in the chancery, is no matter to be reformed there, and namely in such wise as is used. Moreover, Mr. Student, I marvel much that you say that men that have wrong may be helped in many cases by a subpœna, insomuch as you have in your *Natura Brevium* several writs and [of] divers natures for the reformation of every wrong that is done and committed contrary to the laws of the realm; and among all your writs that you have in your *Natura Brevium*, you have none there called a subpœna, neither yet the nature of him [it] declared there, as you have of all the writs specified in the said book. Wherefore me seemeth it standeth not with your study, neither yet with your learning of the laws of the realm, that any man that is wronged should have his remedy by a subpœna. If a subpœna had been a writ ordained by the law of the realm to reform a wrong, as other writs in the said book be, he [it] should have been set in the book of *Natura Brevium*, and the nature of him [it] declared there, and for the reformation of that [what] wrong it layeth, as it is in the writs contained in the said book; and forasmuch as it is not so, it is a writ abused, in my mind, contrary to the common law of the realm, and contrary to reason and all good conscience, and yet is coloured by the pretence of conscience. But it fareth by that, as it doth by other vices, *quia vitia aliquando mentiuntur se esse virtutes;* for vice at some time will untruly count itself to be virtue, as pride at some time will shew himself [itself] to be meek, and pretend much humility to have his [its] pretended purpose. And so this writ of subpœna is colour of conscience to have that [what] he [it] ought not to have by the law of the realm, nor by the law of reason, nor yet by the law of God as I think, and by all [all by] pretence of conscience. Mr. Student, you speak much of conscience, and you move a question whether conscience shall be ruled after the law, or that the law shall be left for conscience. Methinketh that the law ought not to be left for conscience in no case; for the law commandeth all that is good for the commonwealth to be done, and prohibiteth all things that are evil and against the common weal. Wherefore if you observe and keep the law, as in doing all thing that is for the common weal, and eschew all things that is evil, and against the common weal, you shall not need to study so much upon conscience, for the law of the realm is a sufficient rule to order you and your conscience what you shall do in every thing, and what you shall not do. If you therefore follow the law truly, you cannot do amiss, nor offend your conscience; for it is said, *quod implere legem est esse perfecte virtuosum*, to fulfil the law is to be perfectly virtuous.

Stud. That is to be understood by [of] the law of God.

Serj. It is also to be understood by [of] the law of man; for the law of man is made principally to cause the people [to keep] the law of God; and some seemeth, that if you follow the law of the realm truly, you shall not need to leave the law of conscience.——Moreover you speak much of conscience, and put many cases concerning conscience; and though law will, yet whether it will stand with conscience. For me to reply and make answer to every one of your cases, it were too tedious, and is not mine intent. But mine intent is to move you to apply your study principally to have the very and true knowledge of the laws of the realm, and that had and known to practice the same truly without any craft or subtle invention; and then you shall not need to speak so much of conscience. But I perceive by your practice, that you leave the common law of the realm, and you presume much upon your own mind, and think that your conceit is far better than the common law; and thereupon you make a bill of your conceit, and put it into the chancery, saying, that it is grounded upon conscience; and so you bring your conceit in argument in the chancery, and leave the common law as it were a thing of no goodness, nor of no reputation; in the which practice methinketh you much abuse yourself. And though my mind be not to reply against every of your cases, yet my mind is to reply against your saying, in your answer made to a question demanded of you by Mr. Doctor in the latter end of the 21st chapter, in your second dialogue. And the question is this, to know how uses began, and why so much land hath been put in use? To the which question you make answer in the 22d chapter then next following, saying, that uses were reserved upon a secondary conclusion of the law of reason, as you have declared in the same chapter. I say, under correction and reformation of my lords and masters the judges of the law of this realm, that they began of an untrue and crafty invention to put the king and his subjects from that which they ought to have of right by the good, true, common law of the realm: as the king's highness from his escheats, his wards, and his primer seisins, and from other things that now come not to my mind; and his subjects from their escheats and wards, women from their dowers, and the husbands of such women that be inheritors from their tenures by the curtesy of England, the which they ought to have by the laws of the realm; and those that have good right and title to any land to recover it by action after the course of the common law be put from their actions, and if they bring their actions to cause such delays that they shall never have recovery. And though some of these inconveniences be helped by divers statutes, as you have said, yet there rest many and great inconveniences, more that I can rehearse at this time, that be not remedied; and in special [especially] one, and that is this. By such uses the good common law of the realm, to the which the king's subjects be inherit, is subverted, and made as void, so that

none of the said subjects can be and stand in any surety of
any possession. For if he claim and prove his title by a
deed of feoffment, the other party will say he was but a
feoffee of trust; and if he claim by a fine or by a recovery,
he will say like wise that he was of trust; so that neither
deed, nor fine, nor yet recovery, which make men's titles
by the common law, maketh or enforceth any man's title
at this day; and all because of this false and crafty invention of uses as I think. To prove that it began upon an
untruth and false purpose, it appeareth by that, that he,
which maketh such a feoffment, saith and doth one thing
and thinketh another thing clean contrary. For he sayeth
by his word and by his deed, and writing, and livery and
seisin, that the feoffee shall have the land to him and to his
heirs: and his mind and intent is, that he shall not have it,
but he will have it himself. What a falseness is this to
speak and do one thing, and think another thing clean contrary to the same! Every man may perceive in my mind,
that of this can come no goodness, but craft and falsehood.
And so me seemeth, that these uses began by an untruth and
crafty invention, and are continued by an untruth and for a
deceit; and yet do you, that be students of the common
law of the realm, maintain this untrue and crafty invention
in the chancery by the colour of conscience, contrary to
the study and learning of the common law, and contrary to
reason, and also to the law of God. What reason is it,
that if I give you my land, with all the circumstances that
belong to a gift of land by the law, or levy a fine or suffer
a recovery against me, and yet I to have the disposition of
the land myself! So that it appeareth in my mind, that
these uses began by an untrue and crafty invention, and is
maintained in the chancery by the colour of conscience, to
the subversion of the good common law of this realm,
against all reason, and contrary to the law of God, which
teacheth nothing but truth, not only to the express wrong
and hurt of the king's highness and of all his subjects, but
also as much as in them is to bring the king's highness to
the detestable offence of perjury, as it appeareth by a stat-

ute made the 20th year of King Edward the 3d,* wherein
is contained as here followeth :

" Edward, by the grace of God, etc., to the sheriffe of
Stafford, etc., greeting : For that, that by divers plaintes
made to us wee have knowlege, that the lawe of this lande,
the which we be bound by our oathe to maintaine, is not
well kepte, and the execution of it disturbed manie ways
by maintenaunce and procurement, as well in courte as in
countrie, wee, mooved greatlie in conscience of this matter, and for that cause desyring, as well for the pleasure of
God and ease and quietnes of our subjects, as for the savinge of our conscience, and for savinge and keepinge of our
oathe aforesaid, by the assente of the lords and other sage
wise men of our counsel, have ordeyned and comaunded ex-
presslie to all our justices, that they shall do egall [equal]
lawe and execution of right to all our subjects riche and poore
without having regard to any person, and not to cease to
do righte for any letters or comaundements that maye
come from us or from any other, or for any other cause
whatsoever it be ; and in case that any letters writs commaundements come to the justices or to their deputies, to
let [hinder] the law and righte after the usage of the realme
in disturbance of the lawe or of the execution of the same
or of right to the parties, the saide justices and other afore-
saide shall go forthe and holde their courtes and their process where their plees and busines be dependinge before
them, as though no soche letters writs or commaundements
weare come unto them, and they to certifie us and our counsell of soche commaundements, which be contrarie to the
lawes as is abovesaied.   And to the ende that our justices
shall do egall righte to all men in manner as is aforesaid,
without shewinge more favour to one than another, we have
caused our saide justices to sweare, that they shall not
take, from hencefoorthe as longe as they be in office, fee
or liverie of no man but of ourself, and that they shall not take
guifte ne reward themselves ne by other prively ne openlie

---

* Lord Coke denies this to be a statute.   See 3 Inst. 224, 146.—EDITOR.

of no man that shall have to do before them by any manner
of waie, excepte it be manger and boyer, and that of little
value; and that they shall give no counsell to greate nor to
small in case wher we be partie, or that toucheth us or may
touche us in any poincte, upon payne to be at our will both
bodie and lande and to do our pleasure in case that they do
the contrary. And for this cause we have encreased the
fees of our justices in soche a manner as it may reasonablye
suffice them."

So that you may perceive by this statute, that my lord
chancellor nor none other ought to send any writ or writing
to any justices to let [hinder] them to proceed according to the common law of the realm, the which law the
king is bound to see maintained, as it appeareth by the said
statute. And all is one mischief to send a writ, or a commandment to the party, that he shall not proceed to sue
[at] the common law, as it was before the making of the
said statute to send it to the justices; so that the sending of
such a writ or commandment can not be justified no more
in the one than in the other. Notwithstanding it is commonly used now, so that the common law of the realm is
taken for nothing, but all the law that now is used is to determine what is conscience, and which is no conscience,
and so the common law of the realm is now-a-days by you
that be students turned all into conscience, and so you make
my lord chancellor judge in every matter and bring the
laws of the realm in such an uncertainty, that no man can
be sure of any lands be it inheritance or purchase, but
every man's title shall be by this mean brought in question
into the chancery; and therefore it shall be tried whether it
be conscience or no conscience, and the law of the realm,
by which we ought to be justified, nothing regarded. And
so in conclusion after my conceit, if this be not reformed by
the great wisdom and policy of my lords and masters, the
judges of this realm, the law of this realm will be undone,
and all by the mean of these uses and the crafty and sub-
tile inventions that you that be students make upon the said
uses.

23

PART II.

HEREAFTER FOLLOWETH A LITTLE TREATISE CONCERN-
ING WRITS OF SUBPŒNA.

Whether a subpœna ought to lie in any case.

CHAPTER I.

It appeareth in the king's chancery in the time of so
many noble princes and kings of this realm, and in the
time of so many of their chancellors, whereof some have
been spiritual men, and some temporal men, that so many
have been put to answer upon writs of subpœna in the
chancery, that it is not to presume that the chancellors
have directed them temerously in the king's name without
authority, but rather by good authority, and by commandment of the king and his council, and by knowledge of all
the realm. For else it were rather to presume, that they
should long before this time have utterly been annulled and
put away; and because they have been suffered to continue
so long it is to suppose, that in some cases they may be
lawfully awarded. Also it appeareth in divers years of
terms, that many times when the chancellor hath been in
doubt in matters that have depended before the king in his
chancery upon subpœnas between party and party, that he
hath asked advice of the justices some times, whether a
subpœna lay in the case or not, and some times admitting
that the subpœna hath laid in the case, a doubt hath arisen
upon matter that the defendant hath pleaded in bar of the
subpœna; and many times the justices in such case determined that the subpœna hath laid, and some times have
reasoned to the doubt that hath risen betwixt the parties,
admitting the subpœna to lay, and so hath the defendant
done and all his counsel; and there be so many cases re-

ported thereof, that it needeth not to recite them here.
Also by the statute made in the 17th year of the king, R.
the 2d, it is enacted, that a man wrongfully vexed by a
subpœna shall recover his damages by advice of the chancellor. And in a statute made in the 15th year of the king,
H. the 6th, it is enacted, that no subpœna shall be granted
till surety be found to satisfy the party grieved of his damages, if the matter in the bill be not proved true. By
which statutes it appeareth, that in case that the defendant
be righteously vexed in the chancery, and be sued upon a
true cause, he shall recover no damages; and thereby appeareth that they that were of the parliament at the making
of the said statutes assented, that in some cases a man
might be righteously sued in the chancery, and that they
intended to set the diversity of the recovery of damages,
whether he was righteously sued and whether not. And
if it be said it is against the statute of the 2d and 20th of E.
3, and also against divers other statutes, which will, that
the justices shall not surcease to do right for the grand seal,
or privy seal, nor for none other commandment of the king,
it may be answered, the statutes are to be understood,
where such commandment is directed to the justices, that
they shall not therefore surcease to do justice; but a subpœna is alway directed to the party and not to the justices,
whether there be any suit hanging thereon in the court
or not, and then when the party by reason of the said
mination [commandment] surceaseth to call upon the justices for any more process, they cease also to give it him;
but if the mination [commandment] were delivered to the
justices, commanding them to cease, and notwithstanding
the party calleth for justice, there I think the justices are
bound by reason of the said statutes to proceed and to do
justice, the said mination [commandment] notwithstanding.
And me thinketh that all these things well considered, no
man ought to marvel, what authority the chancellor hath to
make such a writ of subpœna in the king's name; for the
old custom, not restrained by any statute, warranteth him
by reason of his office so to do, after certain grounds, and

under certain manner, as I shall partly touch hereafter in
this little treatise, to give other occasion to speak further
therein hereafter.

_____

*Here followeth one consideration, why it hath been thought
reasonable, that a subpœna should lie.*

CHAPTER II.

There is a ground in the common law, that a declaration
must be certain; especially that it must shew, who bringeth
the action, against whom it is brought, and what thing is
demanded; and most commonly it must shew also the day
and year when the cause of the action began. And because it happeneth many times, that some man that hath
right to evidences that be in another man's hand and that
neither be under lock nor seal, cannot shew the very certainty how many deeds there be, or if it be but one deed,
yet percase [because] he cannot tell the name of him that
made the deed, nor of him to whom it was made, nor peradventure the certainty of the land comprised therein, nor
all the town's names where it lieth, wherefore he is without
remedy by the course of the common law; there it hath
been thought reasonable in times past, that a subpœna should
lie for him that hath right, and rather to suffer him to have
right there, than to leave him without remedy in all places.
And this is one of the most common cases where a subpœna
hath been sued in times past. And here it is to be noted,
that it is not against the common law; though the party
have remedy in the chancery in the said case, though he
can have none by the common law. For the common law
doth not prohibit, but that there shall be remedy in the chancery in the said case, and other like; and if it did, it would
be hard to prove that prohibition were reasonable. Wherefore the reasonableness of the law doth suffer it, rather than
it would [should] break his rules and grounds, and to suffer the plaintiff to have an action, and could not declare nor
shew whereof he brought his action.

Another consideration why it should seem reasonable that a subpœna should be granted.

CHAPTER III.

There is a maxim in the law, that a rent, a common, annuity, and such other things as lie not in manual occupation, may not have commencement, nor be granted to none other, without writing. And thereupon it followeth that if a man for a certain sum of money sell another forty pounds of rent yearly to be percepted of [received from] his lands in D., etc., and the buyer, thinking that the bargain is sufficient, asketh none other, and after he demandeth the rent, and it is denied him, in this case he hath no remedy at the common law for lack of a deed; and therefore in as much as he that sold the rent hath *quid pro quo*, the buyer shall be helped by a subpœna. But if that grant had been made by his mere motion without any recompence; then he to whom the rent was granted should neither have had remedy by the common law nor by subpœna. But if he that made the sale of the rent had gone farther, and said, that he before a certain day would make a sufficient grant of the rent, and after refused to do it, there an action upon the case should lie against him at the common law ; but if he made no such promise at the making the contract, then he, that bought the rent, hath no remedy but by subpœna, as it is said before. And the same law, which is of a rent that had no being, but is sold as a rent newly to begin by the sale, is of a rent that had being before, and is sold without deed for a certain recompence, as is before rehearsed.

Another consideration why it hath been thought reasonable,
that a subpœna should be granted.

CHAPTER IV.

In the statute that is called *Quia emptores terrarum,* it
is enacted, among other things, that it shall be lawful for
every freeman to make a feoffment of his lands, or of part
of his lands, to whom he will, so that the feoffee hold always of the chief lord of the fee. By reason of which
statute, if a man since that statute, made a feoffment without deed, or by deed poll, reserving a rent, that reservation
is void as for any remedy that you shall have by the common law. And so it is if a man being seized of lands for
term of life, grant over his whole interest without deed, or
by deed poll, as is aforesaid, reserving a rent, that reservation is void in the law, as for having any remedy by the
common law; for there is a maxim by the law, that a reservation of rent shall not stand in effect, unless he that
maketh a reservation have a reversion in him; or else that
the land may be holden of him by that rent reserved, as it
might have been before the said statute of *Quia emptores*
terrarum; and, therefore, since it cannot be holden of him,
because of the said statute, and seeing also that he hath no
reversion in him, therefore for that reservation he shall have
no remedy in the courts of the common law, as in the king's
bench, the common pleas, and other courts of lower authority than they be. And the very reason why it is so, is,
because the maxims and customs of the law hath given no
remedy in that case; for though a man have right by the
law, yet some time he shall have no remedy by the law,
but it is as void as for any remedy he shall have at the
common law, as is aforesaid, but yet is good by the law of
reason. For reason will, that, forasmuch the intent of the
parties was that the rent should be paid, and that the feoffee
take the land to the same intent, and hath the profits of it,
he should pay the rent according to the agreement. And
if any man would say that this reservation is void to all in-

tents, because it is against the law; for if it be against the law, either it is void, or else the law is void: and therefore if a statute were made that all reservations of rents out of lands should be void, and then a man, contrary to the statute, would make such a reservation, that reservation were void in law and conscience, for it were directly against the statute: and that it should be so in likewise in this case: to that it may be answered, that though it be void in that case, yet it is not like in this case. For in this case there is no law that prohibiteth the reservations to be made, but if they be made the law judgeth them by the rules of the law of the realm, that there shall be no remedy for them by the common law, as it is said before; but taking the law of the realm to be grounded as well upon the law of reason and the law of God, as upon the said customs, maxims, and statutes, as it is indeed, for else it were a very gross law, and far insufficient, and also against reason in many things; then is the reservation good in the law of the realm. So generally taken upon all his grounds; howbeit that yet in that case there is no remedy for that that [which] is reserved in the king's courts of the common law, as is said before; but yet the law is not against it, but that remedy may be had therefore in the chancery.

Another consideration why it should seem reasonable, that a subpœna should be granted.

CHAPTER V.

There is a maxim in the laws of England, that if a man bring an action of debt upon an obligation the defendant shall not be received to plead *nihil debet*, that he oweth nothing, but that he shall be compelled to plead an acquittance or some other thing of as high nature in the law as the obligation is. And of that it followeth, that if a man that is bound in an obligation, pay that money and taketh an acquittance, and after leaseth [releaseth] the acquittance, and thereupon the obligor [obligee] bringeth an action of debt upon the obligation against the obligor; in this case the obligor has no remedy·to help himself at the common law, but shall be compelled. by the common law to pay the money again; and then, as it is said in a dialogue called the first Dialogue in English between a Doctor of Divinity and a Student, the 22d chap., he that hath no remedy but by a subpœna, which as is said there, he shall well have. And to that saying an exception is taken by a certain person in a treatise that he hath made in the name of a Serjeant at the law, where he assigned divers reasons and considerations why a subpœna ought not to lie in that case.

And one cause that he alledged is this. He saith, that the defendant in that case may have sufficient remedy by the common law, so that he needeth not to take a subpœna; and his reason is this. He saith, if the obligor after the payment will bring an action of debt against the obligor [obligee], supposing that he lent him the money, that then, if the obligee will plead that he receiveth the money for the contentation [satisfaction] of his obligation, this plea thus pleaded in court of record shall discharge the obligor of the said obligation.—And methinketh that his reason is not made according to the grounds and learning of the law; for in an action of debt upon a prompt, it is no plea to say, that he receiveth the money in contentation [satisfaction] of his obligation, or of another duty, or that there was no such a prompt, nor any other matter like that amounteth to the general issue; but he shall be compelled to take the general issue, or be condemned for lack of answer. And if he plead that special matter before rehearsed, and conclude over to the general issue, (that is to say,) " and so he oweth him nothing," then is the special matter waived, and all the effect of the plea resteth upon the general issue, which is clear with the obligee; for he receiveth the money as a contentation of his obligation, and not as a loan; and though the obligor, after the payment, lease [released] his acquittance, that cannot hurt the obligee, ·nor alter the nature of the payment that was made before. Wherefore whether he put him on the country, or wage his law, it is clear for him in law and conscience, and so methinketh that this reason maketh title [little] for that purpose.

The second reason that he maketh that a subpœna should not lie in this case is this. He saith, that it is not reasonable that for a particular man's cause, which hath hurt himself through his own negligence, and by his own folly, the good common law of the realm, that is this, that matter in writing without condition, may not be answered but by matter in writing, or by matter of record, should be made void, or be set at nought by the suit of any particular person in the chancery, or in any other place. And then he saith further, that if reformation should be had in the chancery in this case, it must needs follow that the common law must be void and set at nought; for these two laws, being, as he saith, one contrary to another, cannot stand together. —To this it may be answered, as methinketh, that though it be prohibited by the common law, that a man should not plead a payment against an obligation without writing, and that in the chancery he shall, that yet the law in the one court, and in the other, as to the right of the debt, is all one. For the judges of the common law know as judges by the grounds of the law, that the payment sufficiently dischargeth the debt in reason and conscience, as the chancery doth : but yet they may not by the maxims and customs of the law, admit the only payment for a sufficient plea before them, not for that they think it not sufficient in reason and conscience to discharge the debt, but that they may not break the grounds and principles of old time used in the courts where the action is taken. But the common law pretendeth not, that the maxim stretcheth to all courts, nor to the whole common law, but to certain courts according to the custom before time used. And therefore, at this day, if an action of debt be brought upon an obligation under the sum of 40s. in the county, hundred, or court baron, the defendant shall wage his law; and in London the defendant shall confess the deed, and pray that it may be enquired of the duty. And so it is oftentimes seen that several courts have several customs, and the law suffereth them all: as in the common pleas an outlawry shall be sometime reversed without a writ of error; and in the king's bench no outlawry shall be reversed without a writ of error; and also in the common pleas upon the first default in a *scire facias*, execution shall be awarded; and in the king's bench an *alias* shall be awarded. And why may then the said maxim hold in the king's bench and common pleas, and in some other courts of record as be holden after the common law, and yet not be holden in the chancery? And I would think further, that if it were enacted, that upon an obligation every man that would, might have a subpœna in the chancery, it were then no great doubt but that the defendant in such a sub-pœna, might plead a payment against the obligation, without offending the common law. And yet if an officer of the chancery after that statute sued another upon an obligation by the privilege of the chancery, in that suit the defendant should not plead a payment without writing. And if such diversity of pleading should be suffered in one court, it is little marvel then though it be suffered in several courts. And then it followeth furthermore thereupon, that if the defendant in that suit taken against him by the privilege of the chancery, as is said before, hath paid the money, and hath taken no acquittance, then he hath no remedy but upon a bill containing the matter, to desire, that the plaintiff may have an injunction to surcease in that suit there taken in the chancery, after the maxims of the common law, and to answer to his bill there after the law used upon writs of subpœna; and yet no contrariety be in it; for the common law claimeth not, that that maxim should secure in any other place but at the common law, and that only in courts of record, as is said before. And it seemeth a great reasonableness in the law, that it willeth the said maxim to stretch to no other courts, but to the courts of the common law. For if [it] did, it should seem to be far [very] unreasonable; for certain it is, that if the

money be paid, the debt in reason and conscience is discharged, though there were no acquittance made, and then
hat maxim should [would] universally put the party that
hath paid the money without acquittance from all remedy.
And therefore methinketh it should more commend the
common law that it suffereth remedy to be had in this case
in the chancery, than it should [would] do if it should
clearly prohibit it; and therefore they speak rather against
the common law, that would so have it, than with it. And
if any man would say, that if such remedy may be had in
this case in the chancery, as I have said before, that then
the said maxim is void, and serveth to no purpose; for upon
every obligation such surmise may be made though the
money be not paid, and so shall all plaintiffs be delayed by
such untrue surmises; to that it may be answered, that if
he that maketh the surmise cannot prove his bill, he shall
yield damages to the plaintiff, and the plaintiff shall also
proceed at the common law. And also it serveth to this
purpose, that it maketh them that be bound, the rather to take
acquittance, or the obligation in lieu of acquittance, whereby
shall follow the plainer reckoning, and the less variance
among the people; and if that maxim were not, many defendants would plead a payment, or that they owe nothing,
though it be untrue, that will not sue to have a subpœna,
and find surety to pay damages, if he cannot prove his bill
to be true, knowing it to be untrue. And thus methinketh,
that the said maxim is good and reasonable, and also
profitable to the commonwealth, though remedy may be
had in the chancery, as is aforesaid.

*Another consideration why it hath been used that a sub-
pœna should lie.*

CHAPTER VI.

It hath been used, that when feoffees have been seized to
the use of a man and his heirs, and that they have been required to make estate according to the use that they were
infeoffed to do it, that then he to whose use they be so seized,
should have a subpœna to cause them to make the re-feoff-
ment unto him. But if a feoffment be made to the use of
a [person in] tail, and it was agreed that the feoffees shall
stand still seized to the use of the tail [entail], without
making any estate thereof, then in that case there lieth no
subpœna against the feoffees to make estate. But if the
tenant-in tail in use, after the use made in tail, had granted
to the feoffees, that they should stand still seized without
making any estate to him or to the heirs of his body; in
that case if the tenant in tail die, his heirs may have a subpœna against the feoffees, if they refuse to execute the state
[estate] truly; for the tenant in tail had no power to bind
his heir, but that he might ask of the feoffees execution of
the tail [entail] if he likes. And this was wont to be the
most common case where a subpœna was sued till the statute of Richard was made. But yet since that statute,
though the feoffor may enter and make a feoffment, yet he
may have a subpœna to cause the feoffees to make him estate if he will. Also if feoffees of trust grant a rent charge,
the feoffor hath no· remedy to discharge that rent by the
rules of the common law, but by a subpœna. And as an
use is of lands, so there may be of goods and debts. And
there be so many diversities where a man shall be seized to
the use of another, and where not; and where a subpœna
lieth against them that be seized to the use of other to make ·
them estate, and to maintain actions to their use and where
not, that it would ask a special treatise to declare it; and
therefore I omit the articles for this time, and shall only

touch how use [uses] first began; wherein I will follow a
little treatise in English called the Second Dialogue between a Doctor of Divinity and a Student in the Laws
of England, where it is said, as in the 22d chapter thereof
appeareth, that uses were reserved by a secondary conclusion of the law of reason in such manner as in the said
22d chapter appeareth. Against which saying the same
person of whom mention is made before in the said treatise
taketh exception, and saith that they began, as he thinketh,
of an untrue and false purpose, which he saith appeareth
by that, that he which maketh such a feoffment saith and
doth one thing, and thinketh another clean contrary. For
he saith, that he saith by his word and by his deed and
writing and livery and seisin, that the feoffee shall have the
land to him and to his heirs; and yet his mind and his intent is, that he shall not have it, but that he will have it
himself. Then saith he further, what a falseness is this, to
speak and do one thing and to think another clean contrary
to the same! Every man may perceive, saith he, that
thereby may come no goodness but craft and falsehood;
and so he thinketh, that uses began by untrue and crafty
invention, and are continued by an untruth and for a deceit.
And at this reason somewhat I marvel. For methinketh
it is not grounded according to truth; for most commonly
when feoffments of trust be made, the feoffor maketh the
feoffees, or at least some of them, privy to his intent, for
commonly there is no feoffment of trust made by deed,
though it may be otherwise, but is seldom seen; and then
the feoffees or one of them must take livery of seisin, or
else make a letter of attorney to take it. What falsehood then is it, when the feoffees or part of them be made
privy thereto? And admit that none of them be made
privy, as some time it may be, as if a man make a lease
for a term of life the remainder to certain persons to his
use, and they know not of it, nor never gave any money
nor other recompence for it; what falseness is there, though
the lessor after the death of the tenant for term of life take
the profits? I see none. And therefore all the doubt is-

when such a feoffment of trust is made, whereby it appeareth by the words of the deed, and as the very truth is, that
the land is given to the feoffees as to the possessors, how
an use may be reserved by the law contrary to the word.
And yet doth the law suffer such a reservation of an use
upon such grounds as in the said dialogue is spoken; and
therefore if any default be it is in the law, for the party
sheweth commonly what his intent is to do if the law will
suffer it; and because the law doth suffer it, it taketh effect
accordingly; that is to say, that the feoffees shall have the
possession and another the use, which use many times is
appointed to be made by indentures of marriage or of bargains and sales, or to declare their wills, and that many
times by the advice of learned counsel nor of no craft nor
falsehood. But yet whether it were good to break all uses
or to let them stand, I will not treat of at this time; for it is
not the intent of this writing. And if they should be
broken, the cause to break them were not, because they
began of craft and falsehood, as in the same treatise is
said, but for unquietness and trouble that cometh by them,
and specially by uses in tail. And as to the mischief that
is alledged in the same treatise that cometh by them by
loss of escheats, and by avoiding tenancy by the curtesy
and in dower, and such other, methinketh it is little to be
regarded; for though it be certain, that where such titles
be once given by the law that it is against right and conscience to take them from them that they be so fallen unto,
yet to prevent their title therein, so that no title shall come
it is not against conscience, so it be not done of an evil will
to him that the title should fall to. And therefore if a man
that holdeth by knight's service being sick and like to die
married, his son being within age, because he would have
the half of his marriage himself to pay his debts, he doth
no wrong to the lord. And so it is in all the cases that be
spoken of in the said treatise where such titles be put away
by means of uses. And likewise if a man that hath no
heir general nor special selleth his land, or giveth it away,
to the intent that it should not escheat, he doth no wrong to

the lord. And these articles and the articles that are treated of in the 5th chapter, make me some time to conjecture, that the said treatise was not made by any serjeant at the law, as it is entitled to be, but of some other, that, as it seemeth, had a zeal to the law, though peradventure some of the motions that he maketh were rather to the discommendation of the law than to the commendation of it. For what praise were it to the law to prohibit all writs of subpœna, and yet no remedy to be therein at the common law? But if remedy were provided at the common law, it were the less force [consequence], if writs of subpœna were put away. But in some cases where subpœnas lie, it were very hard to provide any remedy to be at the common law, as in the case of the evidences whereof the party knoweth not the number, and whereof mention is made in the 2d chapter. And also in divers other cases, whereof I intend to touch briefly by certain cases and grounds, a man some time may have right to a thing in conscience, and where he has no means to come unto it at the common law, and yet there lieth no subpœna.

Hereafter follow divers cases and grounds, whereby it appeareth that a man may have right in conscience which he cannot come unto by the common law, and that yet he shall have no subpœna.

CHAPTER VII.

If lord and tenant be, and the tenant holdeth of the lord by knight's service and certain rent; the lord distraineth the tenant's beasts, and thereupon maketh avowry upon his supposing that he holdeth of him by fealty and certain rent, and so thereupon hath return; and after the tenant dieth, his heir being within age : in this case the lord is concluded as against the heir to say that his ancestor held of him by knight's service, and that is, by reason of the said avowry, whereby [it] appeareth of record that he himself averred the land was holden of him in socage; and yet the truth is, that the tenant holdeth of him by knight's service. And therefore if he bring a writ of intrusion *maritagio non satisfacto*, against the heir at lawful age, and the heir pleadeth the said record against him by way of conclusion, the lord is without remedy at the common law, and yet he shall have no remedy by subpœna in the chancery; for if he should, he would say directly against that which he affirmed before in the king's court of record; and therefore though he have right, the chancery will suffer him to be without remedy, as for any help that he shall have of the law, rather than to suffer such an open contradiction to remain of record in the king's courts, and rather than it will give him remedy against his own confession. But yet in this case the heir is bound in conscience to restore him the value of his marriage, and the profits of the land during the nonage; yet he is not compellable thereunto by no [any] law. And also against all other strangers that would take the wards [wardship] of the said heir, the lord may have good remedy by the common law; for none shall have advantage of that estoppel, but they that be party or privy to the said record.

Also if a man levy a fine with proclamation of land, that he knoweth another man hath right to, and he giveth him no notice thereof; after this five years pass without claim, whereby he that had the right is barred in the law; yet he that levied the fine is bound in conscience to restore him that had the right, for he wittingly deceived him, and did as he would not have been done unto. And yet though he be bound in conscience to restore him, [yet] there lieth no subpœna to compel him thereto; for there is no subpœna directly against a statute, nor directly against the maxims of the law; for if it should lie, then the law should be judged to be void, and that may not be done by no [any] court but by parliament. And therefore if a man procure a collateral warranty to extinct [extinguish] the right of another, and the warranty descendeth upon him that hath

right, whereby he is barred of the land in the law; though
he that procureth it be bound in conscience to restore him
that had right, yet he shall have no subpœna to compel
him thereto, for the cause before remembered [stated]; for
the law is, that he shall be barred, not only in this court or
that, but generally. And therefore if it were enacted, that
if an alien came through the realm as a pilgrim and died,
that all his goods should be forfeited, this statute were
against reason and not to be observed in conscience, and
yet there should lie no subpœna for the executors of the,
pilgrim; for if there should, then should the chancellor
give judgment directly against the statute, and that may
not be in no wise; but if the statute be not good, it must be
broken by parliament as it was made. And so it is of the
cases of the fine with proclamations, and of the collateral
warranty before remembered.

Also if the grand jury in attaint affirm a false verdict
given by the petty jury in assize, yet there lieth no subpœna
though the party hath right and hath no remedy at the
common law. And that for two causes.—Whereof one is,
when the common law hath gone as far for remedy as the
law suffereth, so that there can be then no further trial, if
then the party should have a subpœna, then the common law
would have no end, and thereupon would fall many inconveniencies. Wherefore the party shall rather be suffered to
be without remedy than the inconvenience should fall. But
in that case he that hath the land is bound in conscience to
restore, if he will save himself from deadly sin, though he
cannot be compelled thereto by no [any] law.—The other
cause is this. There is a statute made in the 4th year of king
Henry the fourth in the 22d* chapter, that judgments given in
the king's courts shall not be examined in the king's chancery, parliament, nor elsewhere, but by error or attaint. And
therefore if a subpœna should lie, it would be directly
against the statute.† And like law is, if the defendant in

* Chap. 23 in the printed statutes.—EDITOR.
† It has been long settled, that notwithstanding the 4th of Henry 4, our
24

an action of debt upon a contract wage his law untruly, whereby the plaintiff is barred; yet in that case he hath no remedy by subpœna, for the causes aforesaid.

Also if a man buy goods of another for a certain sum of money, and after maketh his executors and dieth, in that case there lieth no action at the common law against his executors : because their testator might have waged their law, and they may not; and therefore the law for eschewing of a great inconvenience and mischief that might follow to all executors, if such actions should be maintainable against them upon a bare surmise, and where their testator, if the action had been brought upon an untrue surmise, might have waged his law and they may not, will not suffer any action in that case to lie against them.* And then I have heard this taken for a ground, that when the common law putteth a man from his remedy, though he have right, for eschewing of an inconvenience that might follow upon it, and that then if the remedy should be had in the chancery, in the same case the same inconvenience should follow, as should have done at the common law, that there no subpœna shall lie. And that it should be so in this case to all executors is evident; and therefore no subpœna shall lie as me seemeth. And like law is, as I take it, upon an untrue presentment in a leet for such a thing as toucheth not freehold, that like as there is no remedy at the common law

---

courts of equity may relieve as well *after* as *before* judgment at law. However, in Lord Coke's time, and for some time after, it was a controverted point. Those who wish to trace this controversy through its several stages will be able to gratify their curiosity by consulting the following books, namely: Cro. Jam. 335, 343; 3 Bulstr. 115; 3 Inst. 122; 4 Inst. 85; Car. Rep. 144, 163; March, 83; Hardr. 23, 120; 1 Mod. 59; T. Raym. 227; Jurisd. of Chanc., vindicated at the end of vol. 1 of Rep. in Chanc., and Sir Rob. Atkyn's Enquiry into the Jurisd. of Chanc. 39.—EDITOR.

*But in latter times the judges have allowed actions of *assumpsit* in which wager of law is not allowed, for debts on simple contract, against the original debtor, and consequently against his executors; and since this deviation from the rigor of the law, as it was formerly understood, it has been determined, that though in debt on simple contract, an executor may abate the action, yet he is at liberty to plead to it, and will be justified for so doing. Vaugh. 100, and 1 Lev. 200.—EDITOR.

to traverse it, so there shall be none by subpœna; for the chief cause why the common law suffereth no traverse in this case, as I take it, is to eschew the great trouble that might ensue upon such traverses, considering the great multitude of such presentments in all sheriffs' tournes and leets within the realm; and as great trouble and suit would ensue if a subpœna should lie in this case as would do by traverses, and therefore no subpœna shall lie. And though some books assign another reason why there lieth no traverse against such presentments, that is to say, because the law presumeth such presentments, which be made by twelve men, in the same place where the offence is supposed to be, to be true, and will suffer the party to have no traverse to it, unless he put in his traverse to the presentment the same day, and that if he pass the day no traverse shall lie for him; and though this consideration may seem somewhat to prove that no traverse shall lie against such presentments, yet I think the most principal cause thereof is for eschewing of great suits and unquietness, that might follow among the people, if such traverse were suffered. And the law much provideth and foreseeth that no hurt shall grow unto a multitude, and for that consideration it is, that the law will suffer no man to enter upon a descent, and that by a sale in open market the property is altered from him that hath right; and divers other such laws be ordained to eschew mischiefs from a multitude.

Also if a woman covert induce her husband to sell her land, and she taketh the money and converteth it to her more profit than the land was, and after of her own free will maketh an affidavit that if her husband die, she shall never claim the land, but shall make such further surety [assurance] to the buyer as he shall devise, and thereupon she and her husband maketh him a feoffment; then the husband dieth, and she bringeth a *cui in vita* and recovereth the land; in this case the woman is bound in conscience to recompence the buyer the money [he paid], and all the charges that he hath sustained by that occasion, and yet he shall have no subpœna, nor other remedy to compel her to it. For the law presumeth, that what is done by the woman covert is done by the means of her husband, and against that presumption shall lie no suit against her. And yet in her own conscience she is bound to restitution.

Also if there be two joint tenants of goods, and the one taketh the whole profit to his own use, the other hath no remedy by subpœna nor otherwise; and yet he doth against conscience to take the whole profits, and as he would not be done unto; but for as much as they put confidence each in [the] other to occupy jointly together, therefore, though one of them break that confidence, yet the other shall have no remedy neither by subpœna nor otherwise, against his own agreement.

Hereafter followeth a short titling of divers cases wherein a subpœna lieth not; but the cause why it lieth not is not shewed, but is left to other that list to entreat further of the matter.

CHAPTER VIII.

If a man recover against a tenant for term of life or tenant in the tail by false verdict, and entereth by force of the same recovery, and after all the jurors die, so that he that lost the land is clearly without remedy at the common law, yet he shall have no subpœna.

Also if a man without title recover land by a default in a *præcipe quod-reddat*, and enter and taketh the profits, and after he against whom the recovery was had bringeth a writ of right and recovereth the land without damages as he should do by the law; in this case, though he that first recovereth be bound in conscience to restore the damages for the time he had the land, yet the other shall have no subpœna against him to recover them.

Also if a man purchase an advowson, and after suffereth an usurpation before any presentation, and the six months pass: so that he hath no remedy by the common law to have a writ of right, yet no subpœna lieth for him.

Also if the tenant for term of life had at the common law ·done waste, there had lain no subpœna against him, nor yet doth.

Also if a man make a lease for a term of life, and the tenant for term of life doth waste, and after surrendereth his estate to him in reversion, and he in the reversion was ignorant that the taking of the said surrender should extinct [extinguish] his action, yet no subpœna lieth in that case.

Also if a man offend [upon] a penal statute by ignorance ·of the law or of the deed, and thereupon is sued and condemned in the law, yet thereupon lieth no subpœna for him.

Also if a man's servant through negligence of his master, though it be not by his commandment or assent, but for lack of correction, do offences and trespass to his neighbour, whereby the master is bound in conscience to make restitution if his servant be not able, yet there lieth no subpœna against the master to compel him to it.

Also if a man take land for term of life, and bindeth himself in an obligation that he shall leave the ground, in as good case [condition] as he found it, and after the woods thereof be destroyed by sudden tempest or strange enemies without any fault in him ; yet he shall be condemned at the common law by reason of his own bond, and he shall also be without remedy as for any subpœna he shall have in that behalf.

Also when tenants for term of life before the statute that giveth the *quod ei deforciat* have lost their lands by default, whereby they were without remedy at the common law, yet there lay no subpœna for them in the chancery.

Also if a man of his mere motion and without any recompence make a lease for a term of life, the remainder to the sheriff of such a shire and to his heirs, without naming his surname * or his proper name ; in this case like as the remainder is void in law, so it is in conscience, and no sub-

---

* That is, no name of purchase.

pœna lieth thereupon; and yet a feoffment to the use of the sheriff of Dale and his heirs without naming his surname or proper name, had been good before this parliament. Also if a man can prove by sufficient writing, that in the time of king Henry the 2d an annuity was granted to his ancestors, but by reason that they had no seisin since that time he is without remedy at the common law; so is he also without remedy by subpœna.

Hereafter followeth a short titling of divers things, which it will be right expedient for the chancellor of England to have in remembrance; lest haply if he advertise them not, he may charge himself in conscience some time with damages, some time with the whole thing that is in demand before him, though he cannot be compelled thereto because he is a judge of record.

Chapter IX.

First if the chancellor grant a subpœna and taketh no surety that the plaintiff shall satisfy the party grieved for his damages, if the matter in the bill be not found true, and after the matter is found against the plaintiff and he is not sufficient to yield damages to the defendant, I think, that in that case the chancellor is bound in conscience to yield damages himself; because he took no surety at the granting of the subpœna, as he should have done by reason of the statute made in the 15th year of king Henry the 6th, the 4th chapter, whereby it is enacted, that no subpœna shall be granted till surety be found for the truth.*

---

* In Mr. Ruffhead's edition of the statutes, it is observed, that chap. 4, of 15 H. 6, is not upon the roll; and therefore its being a statute seems questionable. However, Lord Coke concurs with the writer of this treatise in considering it as a statute; nor is it objected to by the learned observer on ancient statutes. 4 Inst. 84; Barr. on Ant. Stat., 4th ed. 403. Whether it is a statute or not, it has long been the practice in chancery to issue subpœnas without taking security, except in some special cases, as

But if he taketh such surety, that is sufficient discharge for him, though the sureties after [afterwards] decay, and be not able to yield the damages.

Also if a judgment be given in the king's court, and after that judgment the party, surmising that the judgment was given against conscience, prayeth a subpœna to have it examined in the chancery, and thereupon the chancellor compelleth the plaintiff to find surety according to the said statute that he shall yield damages to the party grieved if he cannot prove his bill true, and after it is found against the plaintiff; in this case if the plaintiff and his sureties, for that they be decayed surety taken, be not able to yield the damages, then the chancellor is charged in conscience to pay them. For though he have observed the law in taking the sureties, yet by the granting of the subpœna he hath done against the statute made in the 4th year of Henry the 4th, whereby it is enacted, that judgments given in the king his courts shall not be examined in the chancery, parliament, nor elsewhere, but that the parties and their heirs shall be in peace till the judgment be reversed by error or attaint if any be; and therefore if the party and his sureties be not sufficient to yield the damages, the chancellor, as many men say, is bound in conscience to do it.

Also if the chancellor, either from vehement conjectures or by other information, giveth sentence without proofs, then he putteth himself to this jeopardy, that if afterward it come to his knowledge in more credible manner than the first conjectures were of, that the conjecture were not true, then he is bound in conscience either to redress the sentence or to restore the party to all that he lost by that sentence. And therefore it is a most sure way, that either he give judgment by proofs, or else upon his own knowledge; as I suppose well he may if he know soothfastly [of a certainty] the truth of his own knowledge. And here I would

where the plaintiff resides, or is going, abroad, and the defendant on that ground applies to the court to have security given. Prac. Reg. in Cha. 340.—Editor.

put this diversity in this matter, that if the chancellor give judgment according to the proofs, though they be untrue, that it sufficeth for his discharge unless he know the contrary of his own knowledge. For he hath followed the order of the trial appointed by the law in that case, and that sufficeth to him. As it doth for the ordinary if he present the clerk of him that is found true patron by the *jure patronatus*, though he be not so indeed ; for he hath done that that the law would he should do for knowledge of the truth therein : but if he will not grant any writ to inquire *de jure patronatus*, but will present by other examinations and presumptions the clerk of him that he thinketh to be right patron, he bindeth himself to this jeopardy, that if another be right patron indeed, a *quare impedit* lieth against him. And so methinketh, that the chancellor likewise bindeth himself to yield damages if he give judgment upon conjectures, though he thinketh never so clearly in his conscience that they be true, unless they be true indeed. And yet some will say, that though they be true indeed, that yet he offendeth, because he hath set a certainty of his judgment in that thing that is uncertain, and that is not appointed in the law for him to follow for his warranty ; and they think he may not do so with conscience ; for it is said, *qui amat periculum peribit in illo*, he that will wilfully put himself in jeopardy to offend shall perish thereby. And though that text may also be reasonably expounded, to other jeopardies, yet it seemeth, that it may conveniently be applied to this purpose, that is to say, that he putteth himself in jeopardy to offend, that [who] giveth a judgment and is not certain of himself nor by the order of the law that his judgment is true. And so it is, if a man taketh another and sweareth precisely that such a thing is true, which he knoweth not but by conjecture. And I believe their saying rather to be true for this reason. For I have taken it always for a learning, that if a man have no sufficient proof of his title by witness in writing or otherwise, that he is without remedy in the chancery ; and if the chancellor might give judgment upon conjectures, that were not so, he might then judge as his conscience judgeth him to do after, [dictates to him, according] as he thought to be the most reasonable conjecture. And where some men have said, that the chancellor upon a subpœna is not bound to judge *secundum allegata et probata*, but according to the truth; as I take it, that is to be understood in this manner, [viz.] that, though proofs be brought into the chancery which prove sufficiently for one of the parties, that if the other party can sufficiently instruct the chancellor that he hath better matter than he pleaded first, and that is newly come to his knowledge, and prayeth that he may be admitted thereto, the chancellor may admit him to it as well after publishing of witnesses as before, if he will; but that is not to be used without a very special cause, for it is against the common form of the chancery. And also he may suffer the parties to change their demurrer, and that is a great favour; for they shall not be admitted thereto in none other court of the king. Also in the chancery a double plea, nor a departure from his plea, nor two pleas where the one goeth to the whole, shall not condemn him that pleadeth it; but the very truth in conscience is to be searched, and that truth cannot be searched by conjectures as me seemeth.

And some men say, that if the chancellor grant a subpœna upon a bill that appeareth evidently to belong to the common law and not to the chancery, and though he there taketh surety according to the said statute of Hen. 6, yet in that case he is bound nevertheless to yield damages to the defendant, though the bill be proved true; because he hath done against the law. And some men will say, that in that case an action lieth upon the statute of *Magna Charta* against the plaintiff. Howbeit I will not determinately speak therein, but will likewise remit it to others that will further treat thereof for the plainer declaration of that matter.

And I would therein take this diversity. If the matter in the bill were apparent and without doubt or argument that it belonged to the common law, that then it should

seem that the chancellor should be bound in conscience to
yield damages if the party be not sufficient, as it is said before.   But if the matter in the bill be doubtful, whether a
subpœna lie thereupon or no, and he taking the law to be
that a subpœna should lie in the case granteth forth a writ,
it were hard to say, that he should be bound in conscience
to yield damages, though it appeared afterward by reasoning of the judges or otherwise that no subpœna lay in the
case.   For they that be learned in the law may after most
common opinion be some time excused, though they give
counsel otherwise than the law is, so that they gave counsel
as they thought the law to be, and that they had taken sufficient time and study to learn the law, and that specially
in such cases as be very hard to come to the knowledge of
the law in.   And so it seemeth to be of the chancellor in
granting of writs of subpœna.

Also if the chancellor delay the parties, either in the
pleading, or in the bringing in of witness [evidence], or
after the publishing of witness [evidence], more than he
would be contented to be delayed himself if he were in like
case, either for favour to any of the parties, or to keep many
sureties before him, or for such other cause like [similar
cause], he is bound in conscience to restore the party so delayed, or haply [perhaps] both parties, of all their costs
and damages that they have sustained by reason of that
delay; for he hath done as he would not be done unto.
But if the matter be very doubtful, and he therefore re-
spiteth it, to be advised, or to have counsel of the justices,
or for that he may not attend it for other more necessary
causes as he thinketh, there he may be excused in conscience.   And so the intent and cause of the delay is the
very charge or discharge of conscience in this behalf as me
seemeth.

Hereafter followeth a titling of divers objections, which the maker of the aforesaid dialogue layeth against writs of subpœna, with answers to them.

CHAPTER X.

First he saith, that he marvelleth how the chancellor may make such a writ to let [hinder] the king's subjects to· sue his laws, the which the king himself cannot do righteously, for he is sworn to the contrary.—To that it may be answered, that the king's oath in that point is this, that he shall grant to hold the laws and customs of the realm ; and then if the laws and customs of the realm shall be understood as well the laws and customs used in the chancery as at the common law, as I suppose they be, and as I have somewhat touched before in the 5th chapter of this treatise that they be, then it is not against the king's oath, though the chancellor by means of a subpœna minister justice unto the subjects.

Another objection is this. He saith that the king's justices and his serjeants be sworn to minister justice unto the king's subjects, and that so is not the chancellor; whereby it should seem that his meaning is, that the chancellor should therefore be at liberty to break justice.—To that it may be answered, that though he be not bound to do· justice by his oath, yet he is bound thereto in conscience, and that more deeply than the judges be, for he must form· his judgments according to the law of God or to the law of reason, or to the laws of the realm made to determine the right of lands and goods, and that be not contrary to the said laws. And therefore if he err in his judgment, there is greater default in him than is in the judges if they err; for the law of God and the law of reason, and also the law of the realm, grounded upon those laws are much more evident and apparent to give judgment upon, than are the general grounds, maxims, and some customs of the realm ; for the chancellor shall not need to meddle with the estopple

of the law, nor with the general rules of the law, nor yet
with the form of writs nor form of pleading, wherein the
greatest difficulties of the law depend.   And peradventure
this may be the case why a writ of error doth not lie upon
a judgment given by the chancellor upon a subpœna; for
the law presumeth that no man contrary to so evident laws
will err in his judgment.   But if he do err indeed, he is as
highly bound to reform it or to make restitution as the
judges of the common law be, and more.

Another objection that he maketh is this.   In what uncertainty (saith he) shall the king's subjects stand, when
they shall be put from the law of the realm, and be compelled to be ordered by the discretion and conscience of one
man : and namely for as much as conscience is a thing of
great uncertainty, for some men (he saith) think, that if they
tread upon two straws that lie across that they offend in
conscience, and that some man thinketh that if he lack
money, and another hath too much, that he may take part
of his with conscience, and so divers men divers conscience;
for every man knoweth not what conscience is as well
(saith he) as Mr. Doctor.—And to that he may be answered,
that the said two consciences by him before remembered,
whereof the one is a scrupulous conscience and the other
an erroneous conscience, are not such a conscience as the
chancellor or any other are bound to follow.   But they are
errors in conscience ; and errors in conscience come seven
manner of ways, as is expressed in the said first dialogue,
the 15th chapter, which he that will keep himself in a
clean conscience must clearly abject and cast away.
But the conscience, which the chancellor is bound to follow, is that conscience, which is grounded upon the law
of God and the law of reason, and the law of the realm not
contrary to the said law of God and law of reason.   And
therefore to be ruled by such a conscience seemeth neither
to be against the law of God nor the law of reason, nor the
commonwealth of the realm, as in that said treatise it is
supposed to be.   And that the chancellor is bound to order
his conscience after the law of God and the law of reason

is evident of itself, and needeth no further proof. And that he is also bound sometime to order his conscience by the law of the realm and after none other law of man, it may appear thus. If a man, seized of lands in fee, maketh his will that another shall have it to him and his heirs, and after dieth seized; if it come afterwards in question in the chancery, whether this will be good, the chancellor is bound in conscience to judge it to be void in conscience, because it is void by the law.* And likewise if father and son be, the son purchaseth lands in fee, and dieth without any heirs of his body, the uncle by the law shall have the land as heir unto him and not his father; but if the father have afterward another son, then that son shall have the land from his uncle as next heir to his brother; and if this matter come after in variance in the chancery for evidence or otherwise, the chancellor is bound to order his conscience and to give his judgment accordingly as the law is. And therefore though no writ of error lie upon a judgment given by the chancellor upon a subpœna, yet it will appear upon the matter whether the judgment stand with conscience or not. For it is not to think, that whatsoever the chancellor at the time of his judgment thinketh to stand with conscience sufficiently dischargeth him in conscience; for if there be any error in his conscience and in his judgment by any of the causes contained in the said 15th chapter of the said first dialogue, or otherwise, he is bound to reform it. And that he is bound to more than any other judge; for other judges may some time give judgment against their own knowledge, and also against the truth, and yet

---

* It should be remembered here, that our author wrote before making of the statutes of 32 and 34 and 35 of Hen. 8, for which the power of devising land commenced. Indeed before those statutes there was an *indirect* mode of devising land through the *medium* of trusts. But it seems from our author's doctrine, that this evasion was only endured where the testator previously to his will had actually parted with the legal estate to a trustee; and consequently that the refinement of considering the heir as a trustee was not then established in our courts of equity. See the preamble to the statute of u es of 27 Hen. 8, and the clause in it in favour of prior wills, and also Dy. 143.—EDITOR.

no default to be in them, as it is in all trials, except death of man, where they may not give judgment against their own knowledge; but the chancellor shall never be bound to give judgment against his own knowledge, nor against that that appeareth evidently to stand against conscience, for no manner of trial. And though some men may be deceived through a scrupulous conscience, or an erroneous conscience, or in such other manner, yet it is not to presume, that the chancellor, who is always appointed to his office by the king as a man of singular wisdom and good conscience, will be deceived by such errors in conscience, having such straight rules to the order of his conscience as he shall have. And so methinketh it is not against the common weal of the realm, though such cases as writs of subpœna lie upon, be committed only to the judgment of the chancellor.

Also another objection that he layeth to the Student is this. He saith, that the law of the realm is a sufficient rule to order you and your conscience what you shall do in every thing, and what you shall not do. If you therefore follow the law truly, you cannot do amiss, nor offend your conscience, nor you shall not need to leave the law for conscience : by which saying it seemeth, that it is in vain in any case to sue by subpœna, as though a man should never have help by conscience where he could have none by law.—And to this saying it may be answered thus, that if he take the law of the realm as a law grounded upon the law of reason and the law of God, with the customs and maxims of the law ordained by the realm, I think well that (as he saith) the law of the realm will be a sufficient rule to order a man and his conscience what he shall do. But yet it will not always give him remedy, when he hath right, as appeareth in the 2d chapter and the 3d, and also the 7th chapter of this present book. And after this law it is that the judges reason when they sit with the chancellor in the chancery, and also when they sit upon arbitrements. And if he that made the same treatise take the law of the realm as a law grounded upon the maxims and customs and the

rules of the law, and according to the process, as is used
in the king's bench, common pleas, and such other courts
of record as be commonly taken for courts of the common
law, I suppose that he will not say, that the law of the
realm so taken is sufficient to order him and his conscience
in all things; and if he do, methinketh he erreth greatly
therein; and that may appear in divers cases, whereof some
be put in the same 7th chapter, and some shall hereafter
appear. If an infant of the age of 20 years sell his land
for £100, I suppose also he buyeth land with the same
money of greater value than his own land was : in this case
by the law he may enter again into his own land; yet the
other shall have no remedy against him by the law of the
realm for the said £100. I think that no man will say that
[the] infant may with conscience both retain the land and
the £100 also; and, yet the law will suffer him to do it if
he will. Also in all cases where a man hath right and is
estopped by some record or otherwise, so that he therefore
can have no remedy by the law to recover his right, yet may
not he that doth him wrong, retain that [which] he keepeth
wrongfully from him, with conscience : and yet if he will
the law will not prohibit him the contrary, and therefore he
must there of necessity be ruled after conscience if he will
be saved. Also if a man owe another an £100, and the
debtor by sudden loss on the sea, or by fire, or such other
casualties loseth all that he hath, in this case the debtee by
the law may recover his debt, and thereupon take a *capias
ad satisfaciendum* and lay the debtor in prison, there to remain till he hath paid the debt, without any help that he
shall have in the law. And yet I suppose that he that hath
made the said treatise will not say, that if the debtee know
perfectly that the debtor lost his goods by such casualty,
and not through his own fault, and that he hath nothing left
to pay him with, that he may in conscience keep him still
in prison; for if he do, I suppose verily, he snith as he
would not be done to. And therefore it is good always to
use the law, with a dread that he offend not his conscience,
in executing all that he may do by the general rules thereof,

as he may undoubtedly do, and yet the law in itself to be good, as it will appear in the 16th chapter of the said first dialogue.

Also another objection is this. He saith to the Student, that he marvelleth much, that the Student will say that men that have wrong, may be helped by a subpœna in many cases, in as much as he saith there are in *Natura Brevium* several writs and of divers natures for the reformation of every wrong, that is done or committed contrary to the laws of the realm ; and in all the *Natura Brevium*, as he saith, there is no writ called a subpœna, nor yet that the nature thereof is not there declared, as there is of all the writs specified in the said book : and so it seemeth that his meaning is, that because a subpœna is not in *Natura Brevium*, therefore there should be no such writ. And this should seem to be but a slender objection. For the said book is not taken of such authority, that all things that is in it is clear law, nor that it is not so perfect that all writs that pertain to the law should be contained therein. And therefore I suppose that it will be hard to find in *Natura Brevium*, where an action upon the case or a writ of forcible entry lie ; and so I suppose it will be of divers other actions upon statutes if it were thoroughly searched.

And so I think, that the said objections be but of small strength and of small effect to prove that a subpœna may not lie in some cases.

FINIS.

INDEX.

Abatement : If an action real be sued against any man that has nothing in the thing demanded, the writ shall abate, 32.

But not by alienation of the tenant hanging the writ, 32.

Nor by his being made a knight, 32.

Nor by a woman's taking a husband, *pendente lite*, 32.

But if demandant or plaintiff enters into the thing demanded, hanging the writ, it abates it, 33. See *Formedon*.

Abbots : Abolished, 32, 209.

Accessary : How accessaries shall be tried, 32.

Action : If John at Stile lets a chamber to Henry Hart, and it is agreed that said Henry should go to board with said John, and said Henry to pay for the chamber and boarding a certain sum, etc., this is properly called a concord, and an action lies, 174.

If a man says to another, heal such a poor man of his disease, or make an highway, and I will give thee thus much, an action lies, and there is no occasion for the promise to be in writing, 177.

But if two come to a shop, and one of them contracts for goods, and the seller does not care for trusting him, whereupon the other says, let him have them, and I will undertake he shall pay you. This is an agreement within the statute, and must be reduced into writing, in order to ground an action, 178.

If a man says to another, fast for me all the next Lent, and I will give thee 20*l.*, and he performeth it, an action lies, 178.

And likewise if a man says to another, marry my daughter, and I will give thee 20*l.*, an action lies, but the promise must be in writing, 178.

No action lies upon a decree made by convocation, 318. See *Nudum pactum* and *Promise*.

Administrator : Shall have goods and chattels, 21.

Must pay debts according to the common law, 225.

May be charged to him that can first get his judgment against him, 225.

Aiel : Writ of, fallen into disuse, 138.

Alien : How the sons of an alien shall inherit, 20.

Amerciament : For amerciament in a leet, the lord may distrain, 126.

But for amerciament in a court baron he can not distrain, unless by prescription, 126. See *Debt* and *Distress*.

Annuity : For an annuity a writ of annuity is the proper action, 87.

Is not assets, 88.

Is no freehold, 88.
Cannot be put in execution, 88.
Nor be entailed, 88.
Appropriation, 309, 310.
Attainder: Of the son the land shall escheat that the father hath, though
    he has other sons, 28.
Attaint; How far in use, 51.
Attornment: To tenant for life is attornment to him in reversion, 160. .
    Now almost rendered unnecessary by statute, 160. '
Bailiff: What acts of a bailiff of a manor are good, and what not, 235.
Bailment: How a man shall be charged upon bailment, or finding the
    goods of another, 220.
Bastard and Bastardy: Is he who is born before espousals, 20.
    Cannot inherit, 20.
    If a man is certified bastard by the ordinary, he is bound by that cer-
        tificate, because it is the highest trial of bastardy, 116.
    But if bastardy is laid in one that is a stranger to the writ, the bastardy
        shall be tried by twelve men, by which he in whom the bastardy is
        laid shall not be concluded, because he can not have an attaint, 116.
    Father may leave goods to his bastard, 247.
    If a man give all his lands and goods to his children, whether a bastard
        shall have any part, 247.
Benefice: Patron shall have six months to present to a benefice, 199.
    From what time the six months shall be accounted in case of death, cre-
        ation, cession, resignation, deprivation, or union, 199.
    There can be no union of a benefice but the patron must have knowl-
        edge, 199.
    A benefice is void when a parson is made a bishop without a com-
        mendam, 216.
    So if a parson accepts another benefice without a licence, 216.
    Or resigns, 216.
    Or is deprived, 216. See *Presentation.*
Benefit of Clergy: How it stood at common law, and how it stands at this
    day, 93.
Billa vera: The effect of, 276, 277.
Bishop: Bishop may examine the ability of the incumbent; and if he find
    him by examination not able to have cure of souls, he may then refuse
    him, and the patron must present another; and if he is able, then the
    bishop must admit and institute him, 189.
    Of what goods a bishop may make a gift or bequest, and of what not,
        222.
Borrower and Lender: If a house by chance fall upon a horse that is bor-
    rowed, who shall bear the loss, 219.
Bulls: No bulls can be brought from Rome, 214. See *Excommunication.*
    Capias ad satisfaciendum, where it lies, 30.'
Chancery: Cannot examine a judgment at law, 50.
    But if unfairly obtained, may prevent any advantage being taken of it, 51.

Chancellor Is made by delivering the great seal to him, and taking an oath to serve the king and his people faithfully in his office, 19.

Challenge Where a challenge may be taken on default of hundredors, 24. How many jurors may be challenged upon an indictment or appeal, 29.

Charitable Use: What disposition shall be good as a charitable use, 223.

Church, 245, 246.

Civil Law: In the civil law, if a man have another's goods with a title . three years, thinking he has right to them, it gives him a title, 68. What *cedere bonis* is, 84.

Clausum fregit: Where it lies, 30.

Clergyman: How a man may be punished for laying violent hands upon a clergyman, 202.
Is bound to contribute to parliamentary or parochial impositions, 246.
Ecclesiastical court can not award damages for beating a clergyman, 315.
Habits of, 316.
Can not be impannelled upon a jury, 329.
But may be joined with laymen upon a writ to enquire *de jure patronatus,* 330.
Or in mandates for inquisitions to be made of dilapidations, 330.

Condition: If a man enfeoffs another in fee, upon condition that he shall not alien, the condition is void, 65, 86, 210.
So if he devises in fee upon condition that the devisee shall not alien, 65.
No man shall take advantage of a condition but he who is party or privy, 159.
If a feoffment is made upon condition that the feoffee shall pay rent to a stranger, if the rent is not paid, the feoffor may re-enter by virtue of the words upon condition, 161.
If a condition is broken, it is lawful for the feoffor to re-enter, by which re-entry he disproves all mesne acts, 208.
If there is a condition upon a gift in tail that the donee shall not alien by feoffment in fee or fine at common law, the condition is good, 211.
So a condition that is made to restrain mortmain, is good, 211.
So a condition which restrains alienation to a particular man is good, 211.

Colour: Giving of colour, why it is, and to what purpose, 269.

Contract: To make a good contract, there must be *quod pro quo,* 178. See *Nudum pactum.*

Copyhold: Sprung from villainage, 155.
Custom is the life of a copyhold, 155.
Is held at the will of the lord, according to the custom of the manor, 156.
While the services are performed, copyholds have a sure estate, 156.

Cosenage: Writ of, fallen into disuse, 140.

Counsel: For prisoners on an indictment or appeal, 256.

Court Baron: Incident to every manor, 19.

County Court: Is in every shire, 18.

Court of King's Bench: Chief Justice of, is made by writ, 18.

Court of Piepowders: Incident to a fair and market, 19.

Court Spiritual: May hold plea of a temporal thing, but must judge after the temporal law, 186.

Cannot award damages, 202.

A suit will be there for calling another whoremaster, a cuckold, or a cuckoldy knave, or for calling a woman a whore (except in London and Southwark) a jilt, a strumpet, a bawd, 324.

So likewise for calling a clergyman an adulterer or an heretick, 324. See *Clergyman, Prohibition,* and *Mortuary,* and *Perjury.*

Curtesy by Tenant: A man shall be tenant by the curtesy of a fee simple, fee tail general or special, 21.

Must have a child by his wife, 21.

A man shall not be tenant by the curtesy of his wife's land, unless she has possession in deed, 143.

But he shall be tenant by the curtesy of a rent, though his wife die before the day of payment; and likewise of an advowson, though she die before the avoidance, 143.

Qu. Whether he shall not be tenant by the curtesy, notwithstanding the advowson becomes void during the coverture, and the wife dies after the six months past, and before any presentment by the husband, and the ordinary presents by lapse, 143. See *Waste, Presentation,* and *Trust.*

Custom: Against God's law is void, 15.

Cannot be changed or altered without the aid of parliament, 19.

Of borough English, what, 35.

Cannot break a positive law, 243.

Custom of London: By the custom of London, freemen by their testament inrolled may bequeath their lands to whom they will, except to mortmain; and if they are citizens, may bequeath them to mortmain, 35.

Damages: If tenant for term of life is disseised, and die, and the disseisor dieth, and his heir enters and takes the profits; and after the reversioner recovers the land against the heir, he can recover no damages, 139.

For breaking pound the distrainers shall recover treble damages if the beasts are impounded for rent, 192.

Debt: Lies against a gaoler for an escape, 229.

Lies for an amercement in a court leet, 126.

Deodand: Deodand is forfeited to the king, unless lords of franchises are intitled to it by grant, 110, 266.

Descent: By the laws of descent, the eldest son is only heir to his ancestor, 19.

And if no sons but daughters, then all the daughters are heirs, 19.

So if sisters and others kinswomen, 19.

Lands cannot ascend from son to father or mother, nor any other ancestor on the right line, 19.

How brothers shall inherit each other, 20.

How the inheritance shall be when the ancestor takes by descent or purchase, 20.

He that makes continual claim shall not be barred by a descent cast, 47.

Disagreement: A bishop of a devise or remainder that is made to him and the dean and chapter, may not disagree without the chapter, 204, 206.
Nor can a dean of a devise or remainder made to him and the chapter, 204.
Nor can the master of a college of a devise to him and his brethren disagree without the brethren, 205. See *Bishop.*
Disceit: It seems that if a counsellor gives counsel which he knows to be wrong, he is liable to answer in an action of deceit, 157.
Disclaimer: If the dean will disclaim in the lands that he has by devise or remainder, that disclaimer without the chapter is void, 205.
And if a master of a college will disclaim in the lands that he has by devise or remainder without the brethren, it is void, 205.
But the dean may refuse to take a gift or grant of lands or goods, or of a reversion made to him and the chapter, 205.
On a *præcipe quod reddat,* 207.
Desseisin: What title disseisor has, 32.
If a disseisin is made to another man's use, he to whose use the disseisin is made hath nothing in the land, nor the disseisor till he agree, 204.
Distress: May be for rent reserved upon a gift in tail, lease for life, years or at will, 23.
May be of the beasts of a stranger, 23.
Cannot be taken on an obligation or contract, 122.
May be taken for damage feasant, and if reasonable tender of amends is made by the owner before the beasts are impounded, and the distrainer accepts it, he is not bound to restore, 124.
A man may distrain for real service, suit of court fealty, and relief, 23, 125.
No distress can be taken for rent but by him who has the reversion, unless a distress is expressly reserved, 23, 125.
No distress can be for rent reserved on a lease for years, after the determination of the lease, unless the distress is made six months afterwards, and during the continuance of the landlord's title, and the possession of the tenant from whom the arrears are due, 126.
If a township is amerced, and the neighbours assess a sum certain upon every inhabitant, and agree, that if it is not paid by such a day, that certain persons shall distrain at such a day, the distress is lawful, 127.
If a man makes a gift in tail to another, reserving fealty and certain rent, and after he grants away the fealty, reserving the rent and reversion to himself, he may distrain for the rent, 127.
A distress may be for a rent seck, 127.
And if rent is assigned, to make a partition or assignment of dower legal, a distress may be taken for it, 127.
A man cannot distrain in the night but for damage feasant, 127.
No distress of cattle can be driven out of the hundred where it is taken, unless to a pound overt in the same county, within three miles distance, 191. See *Amerciament.*
Dower: Wife intitled to one-third of the husband's inheritance for her dower, 22, 82.

May be of a seisin in deed or law, 143.

Wife must be of the age of nine years at the death of her husband, 21.

By the common law, a woman was not intitled to damages in dower, 139.

But they are now given by the statute of *Merton*, 139.

Immediately after the death of her husband, the widow ought to have her dower if she ask it, 139.

She is intitled to costs, as well as damages, 139.

Can recover damages from the death of the husband only where the tenant cannot say that he is and hath been ready to yield dower, 141.

See *Trusts* and *Gavelkind.*

Easter: Feast of, when it shall be celebrated, 322.

Escheat: If there is no heir general or special, the land escheats to the lord, 19.

Estopple: Where it will bind, and where not, 55.

Exchequer: No officer of the exchequer shall put any clerk under him but such as he will answer for, 230.

Excommunication; Is no plea in a *qui tam,* 15.

He who is excommunicated for a wrong, if he is able to make satisfaction, ought not to be assoiled, unless he does satisfy, 201.

But if he is not able to make amends, he must be assoiled, if sufficient caution is taken to satisfy, 201.

A man cannot be excommunicated for debt or trespass, 201.

In what case the king may write to the spiritual judge, commanding him that he make the party his letters of absolution, upon pain of contempt, 202.

For a wrongful excommunication, *præmunire* lies, or the spiritual judge may be punished by an action upon the case or an indictment, 202.

Where the spiritual court ought to make absolution without any satisfaction, 202.

A man may be excommunicated for not inclosing the church yard, or not repairing the church, 202.

In what case an action will lie for refusing to make the party his letters of absolution, 203.

The law will not suffer an excommunication to be certified under the pope's bull, 214.

Executor: Intitled to goods and chattels real and personal, 21.

Not answerable for the trespass of his testator, 128.

Must pay funeral expenses before all other things, 129.

Has the whole disposition of the goods of the testator, 130.

Has authority to recover all debts due to the testator, 132.

Where debts are in equal degree, must pay him that can first obtain judgment, 131.

Has a power to delay actions by essoin, imparlance, or dilatory plea, 131.

Is guilty of a devastavit if he pays legacies before lawful debts, 132.

Cannot pay a debt upon an obligation whereof the day is yet to come before one that is past; but if he to whom the debt is owing forbear till after the day of the other obligation is past, then he may pay him without danger, 132.

May bear a lawful but not covenous favour to a creditor, 132.

Is now liable to pay debts upon simple contract, 135.

Should be careful how he pays legacies where his testator dies much indebted, without taking security to refund, or putting himself under the direction of a court of equity, 135.

Damages recovered in an action are but a chattel, and go to the executor, 137.

The coat armour, shield and sword, and such things as are set up at the burial of a nobleman, belong to the executor, 306.

Fair: By a contract made in a fair, the property is altered except in certain cases, 67.

Fealty: Cannot be severed from the reversion, 127.

Felony: To steal to the value of 12*d*, or above, is felony, 29.

Feoffment: A freehold cannot pass by feoffment without livery of seisin on the land, or in sight of it, 22.

A feoffment of two acres of land lying in two counties, and livery only of one in the name of both, the acre only passes of which the livery is made, 172.

But it had been otherwise if both acres had been in one county, 57.

And if the scite of a manor extends into two counties, and livery is only made of that part which lies in one county, yet the whole manor passes, 57.

By a feoffment of a manor, the advowsons pass as incidents, 57.

But in the case of the king they do pass, unless they are expressly named, 57.

By a feoffment to two men and a woman in fee, and the intermarriage of one of the men with the woman, and the alienation and death of the husband, the woman only intitled to one-third, 59.

But if the intermarriage had been before the first feoffment, then the woman, notwithstanding the alienation, would have been intitled to a moiety, 59.

If a man makes a deed of feoffment to another, and deliver the deed to him as his deed, he to whom the deed is delivered has no title before livery of seisin made to him, but he may occupy at the will of the feoffor, 172.

Now almost superseded by lease and release, 22.

Fee Simple: In the highest estate in law, 210.

Fees: For probate of a will, 337.

Fiere Facias: Where it lies, 30.

Fine: At common law a stranger had only one year after a fine levied to make their claim, 66.

Has now five years, 66.

An entry to avoid a fine must be an actual entry, 66.

If a feme covert for dread of her husband, or by compulsion of him, levy a fine, yet the woman after her husband's death shall not be admitted to avoid the fine, 263.

Forcible Entry : For forcible entry without title, a man may recover treble damages, and treble costs, 36.

Forfeiture : If a man is outlawed for felony, he forfeits real and personal estate to the lord, 28.

Goods stolen and seized for the king, or waived, are forfeited to the king, unless an appeal or indictment is sued, 110.

Of life, lands, and goods, for murder, 227. See *Outlawry*.

Formedon : If tenant in tail is disseised, and the disseisor dies seised, the heir may bring a formedon, 54.

No damages in a formedon, 54.

In formedon, if plaintiff does not make himself heir to him that was last seised, this may be pleaded in abatement, 121.

Now seldom brought, 54.

Frank Fees : Land which is frank fee is not pleadable in a court of ancient demesne, 106.

Freehold : How it will pass, 22.

Gaols : Gaols shall be adjoined to the shires, and the sheriff shall have the keeping of them, and must put in such under-guardians for which they will answer, 230.

Gavelkind : By the custom of gavelkind, all the brethren shall inherit together, 34, 56.

And if the father is hanged for felony, the sons shall inherit, but not if he is hanged for treason, 35.

In gavelkind the wife shall have half the husband's land, as her dower while she remains sole, 35.

And the husband half the inheritance of the wife, though he have no issue, 35.

By the custom, an infant of the age of fifteen may make a feoffment, 35.

Divers lands disgavelled in Kent, 56.

General Issue : In assise, what, 270.

In trespass, what, 270.

No plea can be pleaded which amounts to the general issue, 270.

Gift : If a gift is made to a man who refuseth to take it, the gift is void, 204.

And if it is made to a man who is absent, the property vests in him till he disagrees, 204.

Grants : If donor grants to donees in tail that they shall not be punishable in waste, it is void, 103.

Goods Derelict : If goods are found which were left by the owner as forsaken, who hath right to them, 267.

Heir : May have goods by custom, 225.

Who is, 19.

If the father bind him and his heirs to the payment of a debt, and die, in that case the son shall not be bound to pay the debt, unless he hath assets by descent from his father, 261.

Where a man is vouched as heir, he may enter, as he that hath nothing by descent, 262.

Heretick and Heresy: An heretick cannot make executors, 195.

May be punished by ecclesiastical censures, 195.

And if an heretick in maintenance of his errors sets up conventicles, and raises factions, he may be indicted, 195.

Denying the Trinity is an heresy which may be punished by the civil magistrate, 196.

Heriot: For heriot service, the lord may distrain or seize, 127.

But for heriot service he can only seize, 127.

Hospitals: Ordinaries to enquire of hospitals unless there are visitors appointed, 339.

Hundreds: To be adjoined to the counties, 231.

And if the sheriff holds them in his own hands, he must put in such bailiffs for which he will answer, 232.

Husband and Wife: Husband absolutely intitled to chattels personal of his wife by the intermarriage, 21.

And her chattels real, if he survives her, 21,

But if he gives them away, the interest of his wife is determined, 21.

If the wife disagree to a gift, and the husband agree, the gift is good, 205.

If lands in case of a husband and wife are charged with damages, or charged with more rent than the land is worth, and the husband dies, the wife shall not be saddled with the damages or rent, if she refuse the occupation of the ground after her husband's death, 205.

And if the husband outlive the wife, and make his executors, and die, the executors may refuse the lease if they have not goods sufficient to pay the rent, 206.

Whether the wife may give away goods, 244.

Whether a gift between husband and wife is good, 245.

Indictment: Wanting what words, good, 276.

Infant: Shall not be barred by a descent cast, 47.

The feoffment of an infant is not void, but voidable, 61.

The age of an infant, to give or sell his land, is twenty-one, 193.

But he may be charged for his meat, drink, or apparel, before that age, 193.

May act as executor at seventeen, 193.

Is not of age in the civil law till twenty-five, 193.

May disagree to a gift, 205.

Where he shall be excused of corporal pain, 251.

Is punishable for an escape, 251.

Is supposed to arrive at years of discretion at fourteen, 252.

But may be *capax doli* before, 252.

Insolent Debtors: Statutes relating to, 85.

Intent: In many cases is void, if it be not according to the rules of law, 159.

A man makes a feoffment by deed indented, by which it is agreed that the feoffee shall pay to A. B. and his heirs a certain rent at certain days; and if he pay not the rent, then it is agreed, that A. B. or his heirs shall enter. A. B. shall have his rent by the intent of the feoffor, but he cannot enter into the land, 165, 167, 170, 173.

In felony or murder, how punishable formerly and at this day, 226.

Is punishable in treason, 226.

Issues : If a man that has land for life is impanelled upon an inquest, and loseth issues, and dies, they may be levied upon him in reversion, 62.

Joint Tenants : If one joint tenant receives more than his share of the profits, the other may have an account against him, 53.

Jointure : Tenant in tail may suffer a recovery in order to make a jointure upon his wife, 83.

What alienation by the wife against the statute 11 H. 7, c. 20, of jointures is good, 89.

And if the husband forfeits issues, and dies, they shall be levied on the lands of the wife, 63.

Judges Spiritual : Are bound to take notice of the common law, 17, 182.

Judgment : Of death, where it must be precisely pursued, and where not, 227.

Jury : In civil cases must come from the body of the county, 23.

Cannot determine what is a maxim of law, 25.

Must not be of affinity to the parties, 23.

May eat, when, and at whose charge, 268.

When they may be fined, 269.

When a new inquest shall be awarded, 269.

Jus Gentium : Contracts are grounded upon the law that is called *jus gentium*, 61, 171.

King : His coronation oath, 18.

The king can disseise no man, and no man can disseise the king, 30.

The head in every parliament, 72.

The king, as lord of the narrow seas, is bound to scour the seas of pirates and robbers, 268. See *Presentment* and *Prerogative*.

Knight Service : Abolished, 26.

Larceny : To steal under the value of 12*d*. is only petit larceny, 29.

Laws : Are of four kinds, *Introd.* 2.

Eternal, what, 3.

Eternal are the fountain of all other, 3.

Eternal may be known three ways, 4.

Of reason and nature, what and what not, 4, 5.

Of God, what, and why so called, 7, 8.

Of man, what, and why so called, 10.

Common, what is said to be, 18.

Legacies : To be sued for in the spiritual court, 182.

Livery and Seisin : A term of years will pass without livery and seisin, 23.

Where a court of equity will supply it, 62.

Marlebridge : Statute of, a remedial law, as well as a penal one, 103.

Mass : Forbid to be said or heard, 221.

If a man gives money to have mass said for him, it is a superstitious bequest, 221.

Master and Servant: Master is chargeable by the act of his servant, and where not, 233, 243.

Shall not answer for the servant's beating of one, 233.

Shall answer for things bought by his servant, and where not, 234.

Shall answer for things sold by his servant, and where not, 234.

If a fire happens in a man's house through negligence of a servant, such servant shall forfeit 100*l.* or be sent to the house of correction, 234.

And if the servant bear fire negligently in the street, and the house of another is burnt, no action lies against the master, 234.

A man shall not be charged for his servant's robbing the chamber of a lodger, unless he is a common hostler, 234.

Master's goods are not attachable for his servant's debts, 236.

A man may have an action against another for retaining his servant after notice, 254.

Market Overt: Changes the property of things, where not, 254.

Maxims of Law: Neighbours are presumed to know the deeds of neighbours, 24.

Ignorance of the law excuses no man, except it is invincible, 77.

A common error maketh a right, 77.

The law compels none to impossibilities, 114.

He who takes the advantage must likewise take the disadvantage, 114.

A mischief should be suffered rather than an inconvenience, 116.

No time runneth against the king, 215.

Malice supplies the want of age, 252.

Metropolitan: If it come in variance, whether he that is presented be able or not, it shall be tried by the ordinary; but if he is party, by the metropolitan, 189.

Mort d'ancestor: Formerly in use, but cannot now be brought, 137, 138.

Mortmain: Statutes relating to, 200.

Mortuary: To be sued for in the spiritual court, 297.

Murder: If a man who is no officer would arrest a man who is outlawed, abjured, or attainted of murder or felony, and he disobeys the arrest, and by reason of the disobedience is slain, the other is not guilty of murder, 228.

But if a capias is directed to the sheriff to take a man in an action of debt or trespass, there no man may take him, but he who has authority from the sheriff; and if any man attempts, of his own authority, to take him, and he resisted, and in the resistance is slain, he that would have taken him is guilty of murder, 228.

Whether a man shall be said guilty of murder by commandment, counsel or assent, 248.

Mute: How a man was formerly punished for standing mute on an appeal and indictment, and how he is to be dealt with at this day, 227.

Night: Is after sun-set, and before sun-rising, 127.

Nudum pactum: If a man says to another man, I sell thee all my lands or goods, and nothing is assigned that the other shall give or pay, it is a nude contract, 175.

And where a man promises another to give him certain money such a
day, or to build an house, or to do him certain service, and nothing is
assigned for the money, for the building, or the service, these are nude
contracts, 175.

Also if a man promises another to keep him such certain goods safely
to such a time, and after he refuse to take them, there lieth no action
against him, 175.

But if he takes them, and they are lost through his negligent keeping,
there action lieth, 175.

Obligation ; An obligation cannot be avoided by a bare promise, 38.

If a man is bound in an obligation to repair the houses of him that he
is bound to, by such a certain time as oft as need shall require, and
after the houses have need to be repaired, but he who is bound knows
it not, that ignorance shall not excuse him, 254.

Ordinary : May commit administration of him that dies intestate, 224.

Where he may grant letters *ad colligendum bona defuncti*, 225.

Outlawry : What a man forfeits by outlawry in a personal action, 107.

The process in outlawry, 108.

Parish : Parishes, division of, 332.

Parliament : The highest court in the realm, 73.

Parson : Of what goods a parson may dispose, and what not, 222.

Penance : Money may be taken as a commutation for corporal penance;
and if it is not paid, a suit may be instituted for it in the ecclesiastical
court, 315.

For defamatory words, penance is enjoined at the discretion of the ordinary, 325.

Pension : If got by prescription, must be by a prescription time out of
mind, 306.

Pension claimed by prescription, how to be sued for, 325.

Perjury ; If a man wages his law untruly in an action of debt upon a contract in the king's court, he cannot be sued for the perjury in the ecclesiastical court, 181.

Pope : His power destroyed, 188, 217, 218, 248.

Pound Overt : A pound overt is every place where beasts may be put in
lawfully, not making the owner an offender for being there, 191.

If the owner of the beasts break the pound, the distrainer may have a
writ of pound breach, or an action upon the case, 192.

Prerogative : The king by his prerogative is lord paramount of all the
benefices within the realm, 213. See *Presentation.*

Prescription : No prescription in lands makes a right, 27.

But a prescription for rent and profits out of land does, 27.

A prescription is from the time no man's mind runneth to the contrary, 27.

If a man prescribe that if he find any goods within his manor that he
shall have them as his own, the prescription is void, 267.

Of a country *non decimando* is good, where not, 284.

A single man in a town cannot prescribe to be discharged of the tithes

of corn and grass, unless he can prove that he recompenseth it in an·
other way, 284.

The spiritual court allows of different times in creating a prescription,
305. See *Statute*.

Presentation : The right of presentation to a church is a temporal inheritance, 189, 215.

If there be joint tenants, or tenants in common of the patronage, and
they vary in presentment, the ordinary is not bound to admit any
of their clerks; and if six months pass, he may present by lapse, but
he may not present within six months, 197.

If there be coparceners, the ordinary is bound to admit the clerk of the
eldest sister, 197.

And if the eldest sister dies, her assignee may present, and so may her
husband, who is tenant by the curtesy, 197.

But at the next avoidance the next sister shall present, and so by turns
one sister after another, 197.

Parceners may agree to present by composition, 197.

What presentment the king shall have by his prerogative, 198.

Ordinary is not bound to admit the clerk of the eldest coparcener, but
where she presents in her own name, 198.

A church is not litigious but where two present by different titles, 198.

If the patron make default in presenting, the bishop shall present; and.
if the bishop present not within six months, then the metropolitan
shall present; and if he neglects to present, then it shall go to the
king, 212.

If the church falls to the bishop by lapse, yet if the patron present
before the bishop puts in his clerk, then the patron shall enjoy his
presentment, 212.

So likewise if it falls to the metropolitan, 213.

The right of presentation, and when a church shall be said to be void,
belongs to the king and his laws to determine, 216.

When the king presents not to a benefice the ordinary may put in a
deputy to serve the cure, 217.

Prohibition : Will lie where a man is sued in the spiritual court for tithe
of wood above twenty years' growth, 93, 278.

If an action is brought for breach of a promise in the spiritual court, a
prohibition will lie, 179.

If a man bequeath to one another man's horse, and the spiritual court
thereupon maketh process to execute that legacy, a prohibition lies,.
297.

And if a man sell his land for 100*l.* and he is sued afterwards in spiritual
court for tithes of said 100*l.* a prohibition lies, 297.

Where a prohibition will not lie, although the spiritual court will not
allow a prescription, 298.

Will not lie to the ecclesiastical court when the executor of a parson is
sued there for dilapidations, 315.

Promise : A man can have no action upon a nude or naked promise, 173.

If a promise is made to an university or a city, the party making.

the promise shall not be bound by it if he intended not to be bound, 176.

If I promise another 10*l.* for that he has builded me an house, no action lies, because the consideration is past, 179.

But if there had been a precedent request to build the house on the part of him who made the promise, the action would lie, although the consideration was executed, 179.

Purchaser : It seems that a purchaser for a valuable consideration will be relieved in chancery against latent incumbrances, 149.

Purveyance : Abolished, 232.

Quare impedit : If the incumbent is out of the realm, a *quare impedit* will lie against him, 214.

Reasonable Part : When children are intitled to their reasonable part within the city of London, province of York, and principality of Wales, 225.

Receiver : Where the acts of a receiver shall bind, and where not, 235.

Recoverors : May avow and justify, 75.

Recovery Common : The manner of suffering it, 68.

It is a bar to the tail, on account of the supposed recompense, 69.

Is good in conscience, 69.

The origin of, supposed to be in the reign of Edward the Fourth, 76.

Has been countenanced by the judges, 76.

If disseisor makes a gift in tail, and the disseisee releases his right to the donee, and a recovery is suffered against the donee, it is good, 81.

Cannot be suffered of an annuity, but may of rent, 88.

Release : Good, and where not, 27.

Religion : The disabilities attending entering into religion are taken away, 245.

Remainder : If a man makes a release to another for term of life, and after he confirms his estate for term of life to remain after his death to another and his heirs, the remainder is void, 159.

But if a lease is made to a man for term of another man's life, and after the lessor confirms the land to the lessee for term of his own life the remainder over in fee, the remainder is good, 160.

No grant can be made but to him that is party to the deed, except it be by way of remainder, 160.

Remitter : If land descends to him that has right to it before, he shall be remitted to his better title if he will, 32.

Rent : If land and rent come into one man's hand, the rent is extinct, 32, 153.

If rent is granted to a man in fee to perceive of two acres of land, and after the grantor enfeoffs the grantee of one of the acres, rent is extinct, 146.

Cannot be granted without deed, 148.

A rent charge may be apportioned by the act of the party, 148.

Rent service may be apportioned, 148.

Where part of the land descends to the grantee of a rent charge, there may be an apportionment, 151.

A man by the common law may have remedy for rent by distress or assise, 153.

Replevin: A man may have a replevin for taking a distress without cause, 123.

Where beasts are impounded the owner may sue a replevin; and if the issue is found against the distrainer, he shall yield damages, 192.

Rescue: If a distress is taken without cause, the owner may rescue it before it is impounded, 123.

Reservation: No reservation of a rent can be without deed; and if a gift in tail, or a lease for term of life is made, remainder over in fee, reserving a rent, the reservation is void, 126.

If *cestui que use* makes a lease for term of years, or for term of life, or a gift in tail, reserving a rent, the reservation is good, 127.

A reservation of the profits, or any part of the profits, as the grass, wood, etc., is void, 166.

Residence: Of clergyman is required by the canon common and statute law, 336.

Restitution: Where it shall be made, 125, 243, 245, 247.

Return: In a writ of annuity against a parson, the common return is *quod clericus est beneficiatus non habens laicum feodum ubi potest summoneri,* 215.

A bailiff of the lord of a franchise may be punished for a false return, 230.

Right of Action: Cannot be given or granted to any other but to the tenant of the ground, or him that has the reversion or remainder, 27.

Serjeant at Law: Is sworn to give counsel according to law, 119.

Sheriff: Where the sheriff shall be amerced for a bad return by the undersheriff, 230.

Where he shall be punished or amerced for the wilful escape of the gaoler, 230.

Cannot let his bailiwick or wapentakes to farm, 231.

But if he does, *Qr.* Whether he may be charged for the misdemeanour of his servants, 232.

If upon summons in a *præcipe quod reddat*, the sheriff, upon information of the demandant, summons the tenant in another man's land, the tenant shall be excused, 255.

Statute: Against God's law, is void, 15.

Is made by king, lords, and commons, 35.

A prescription prevails not against a statute, 79.

But a statute which is in the affirmative may be prescribed against, 79.

So may a statute in the negative, which is in affirmance of the common law, 79.

But a statute which is introductive of a new law cannot be prescribed against, 79.

Many times the intent of the letter shall be taken, and not the bare letter, 83.

But no intent can be taken against the express words of the statute, 83.

Statute de Donis: Said to be made from singularity and presumption, 72.

Statute Merchant : When ordained, 231.

Statute Staple : When ordained, 231.

Strays ; If they are proclaimed, are forfeited; if not claimed within a year and a day, 110, 266.

Tenant in tail after Possibility, etc. : Not punishable for waste by the law, 101.

But may be restrained in equity from committing wilful and malicious waste, 101.

Is in fact only tenant for life, 102.

If he aliens in fee by a forfeiture, 102.

If he makes default in a *præcipe,* the *donor* shall be received, 102.

If lands are given to a man and his wife, and the heirs of their two bodies, and one dies without heir, the survivor is tenant in tail after possibility, 104.

Theft : Of what theft may be committed, 247.

Tithes : Are not due of trees of twenty years' growth, 281.

Due by what law, 279, 280.

When they first began, and by whom they were first granted, 279.

Are of three sorts, prædial, mixt and personal, 285.

Prædial, what, 285, 287.

Mixt, what, 285.

Of trees and grass, their diversity, 286.

Tithe of lambs does not discharge the payment of wool, for it is another increase, 288.

Are payable by the buyer, not by the seller, 289.

Are not due of coal, or tin, except by custom, 292.

Personal tithes are now scarce, any where paid in England, unless for mills, or fish caught at sea, 293.

Are not due of gifts, though they be after sold, 293.

Are not due of lops of trees of twenty years' growth, 295.

Nor of the bark, 295.

In extra-parochial places belonging to the king, 333.

Before the division of parishes, it seems a man might have paid his tithes to what church he would, 333.

Traitor : May dispose of his goods after the treason committed, 244.

Transubstantiation : Declaration against, 321.

Treasure Trove : To whom it belongs, 248.

Trespass : Where a man may justify in trespass, 46.

A special action of trespass may be brought against a man for taking a distress without cause, 123.

If a sheriff by a replevin deliver other beasts than are distrained, an action of trespass lies against him, 255.

May be committed with force, or without, 278.

May be brought for stealing a horse, 277.

Is included in every felony, 278.

Trial : If a bond bears date at Madrid in Spain, or Bourdeaux in France, it may be tried here, 106.

Trover: May be brought for goods which are stolen after the offender is prosecuted, 278.

Trusts: Are exactly of the same nature as uses were at common law, 169.
Are governed nearly by the same rules and subject to every charge in equity which the legal ownership is subject to in law, 169.
Are not subject to dower, 169.
Nor to escheat, 169.
But husbands may be tenants by the curtesy of trusts, 169.

Uses: Origin of, 165.
Inconveniencies of, 167.
An use *in esse* may be given away without recompence, 171.
Cannot commence without livery of seisin, 172.
Or a recompence or bargain, 172.
Possession and use joined together in the feoffor, 58.

Villeinage: Abolished, 155.

Wager of Law: In what actions will lie, 28.
Out of use, but not out of force, 28.

Warranty: Where it bars, and where not, 92, 260, 262.

Waste: If a lease for years is made to an infant, and a stranger does waste, the infant must answer, 47.
So a *feme covert*, to whom a lease is made, is liable to be punished for waste, and committed by a stranger, if she agrees to the estate after her husband's death, 48.
How punishable in tenant for term of years for life in dower, or by the curtesy, 64, 71, 101, 111, 112.

Will: By the ancient law a man could not make a will of his lands, 58.
But might dispose of the use, 58.
The ancient law abolished, 59.
Words: An action will lie at common law for calling another man thief or murderer, 324.
But not for calling him villain, 325.

Wreck: What, 261, 265.

Writ of Right of Dismes: Where it will lie, 185.

www.ingramcontent.com/pod-product-compliance
Lightning Source LLC
Chambersburg PA
CBHW030505100426

42813CB00002B/339